FROMMER'S
EasyGuide
TO
COSTA RICA

By
Eliot Greenspan

Easy Guides are ✦ Quick To Read ✦ Light To Carry
✦ For Expert Advice ✦ In All Price Ranges

FrommerMedia LLC

Published by
FROMMER MEDIA LLC

Copyright © 2016 by Frommer Media LLC. All rights reserved. No part of this publication may be repro-
duced, stored in a retrieval system, or transmitted in any form or by any means, electronic, mechanical,
photocopying, recording, scanning or otherwise, except as permitted under Sections 107 or 108 of the
1976 United States Copyright Act, without the prior written permission of the Publisher. Requests to the
Publisher for permission should be addressed to customer_service@FrommerMedia.com.

Frommer's is a registered trademark of Arthur Frommer. Frommer Media LLC is not associated with any
product or vendor mentioned in this book.

ISBN 978-1-62887-172-2 (paper), 978-1-62887-173-9 (e-book)

Editorial Director: Pauline Frommer
Development Editor: Shelley Bance
Production Editor: Lynn Northrup
Cartographer: Roberta Stockwell
Photo Editor: Meghan Lamb
Indexer: Maro Riofrancos

For information on our other products or services, see www.frommers.com.

Frommer Media LLC also publishes its books in a variety of electronic formats. Some content that
appears in print may not be available in electronic formats.

Manufactured in the United States of America

5 4 3 2 1

FROMMER'S STAR RATINGS SYSTEM

Every hotel, restaurant and attraction listed in this guide has been ranked for quality and value. Here's
what the stars mean:

★   Recommended
★★   Highly Recommended
★★★ A must! Don't miss!

AN IMPORTANT NOTE

The world is a dynamic place. Hotels change ownership, restaurants hike their prices, museums
alter their opening hours, and buses and trains change their routings. And all of this can occur
in the several months after our authors have visited, inspected, and written about these hotels,
restaurants, museums and transportation services. Though we have made valiant efforts to keep
all our information fresh and up-to-date, some few changes can inevitably occur in the periods
before a revised edition of this guidebook is published. So please bear with us if a tiny number
of the details in this book have changed. Please also note that we have no responsibility or liability for any inaccuracy or errors or omissions, or for inconvenience, loss, damage, or expenses suffered by anyone as a result of assertions in this guide.

CONTENTS

ABOUT THE AUTHOR

Eliot Greenspan is a poet, journalist, musician, and travel writer who took his backpack and typewriter the length of Mesoamerica before settling in Costa Rica in 1992. Since then, he has worked steadily as a travel writer, food critic, freelance journalist, translator, and personal travel planner, while continuing his travels in the region. In addition to this book, he has authored *Frommer's Belize, Frommer's Cuba, Frommer's Ecuador, Frommer's Guatemala, Costa Rica For Dummies,* and *Costa Rica Day by Day.*

ABOUT THE FROMMER'S TRAVEL GUIDES

For most of the past 50 years, Frommer's has been the leading series of travel guides in North America, accounting for as many as 24% of all guidebooks sold. I think I know why.

Though we hope our books are entertaining, we nevertheless deal with travel in a serious fashion. Our guidebooks have never looked on such journeys as a mere recreation, but as a far more important human function, a time of learning and introspection, an essential part of a civilized life. We stress the culture, lifestyle, history, and beliefs of the destinations we cover, and urge our readers to seek out people and new ideas as the chief rewards of travel.

We have never shied from controversy. We have, from the beginning, encouraged our authors to be intensely judgmental, critical—both pro and con—in their comments, and wholly independent. Our only clients are our readers, and we have triggered the ire of countless prominent sorts, from a tourist newspaper we called "practically worthless" (it unsuccessfully sued us) to the many rip-offs we've condemned.

And because we believe that travel should be available to everyone regardless of their incomes, we have always been cost-conscious at every level of expenditure. Though we have broadened our recommendations beyond the budget category, we insist that every lodging we include be sensibly priced. We use every form of media to assist our readers, and are particularly proud of our feisty daily website, the award-winning Frommers.com.

I have high hopes for the future of Frommer's. May these guidebooks, in all the years ahead, continue to reflect the joy of travel and the freedom that travel represents. May they always pursue a cost-conscious path, so that people of all incomes can enjoy the rewards of travel. And may they create, for both the traveler and the persons among whom we travel, a community of friends, where all human beings live in harmony and peace.

Arthur Frommer

THE BEST OF COSTA RICA

Costa Rica is one of the hottest vacation and adventure-travel destinations in Latin America, and for good reason. The country is a place rich in natural wonders and biodiversity, where you can still find yourself far from the madding crowds. Costa Rica boasts a wealth of unsullied beaches that stretch for miles, jungle rivers for rafting and kayaking, and spectacular cloud forests and rainforests with ample opportunities for bird-watching and hiking. In addition to the country's trademark eco- and adventure-tourism offerings, you will find fetching resorts, spas, and some truly spectacular boutique hotels and lodges.

Having lived in Costa Rica for more than 22 years, I continue to explore and discover new spots and adventures—and my "best of" experiences keep coming. This chapter is meant to give you an overview of the highlights so that you can start planning your own adventure.

COSTA RICA'S best AUTHENTIC EXPERIENCES

- **Taking a Night Tour in a Tropical Forest:** Most Neotropical forest dwellers are nocturnal, so nighttime tours are led at most rainforest and cloud forest destinations throughout the country. Some of the better spots for night tours are **Monteverde** (p. 177), **Tortuguero** (p. 240), and the **Drake Bay** (p. 219).
- **Soaking in a Volcanic Hot Spring:** Costa Rica's volcanoes have blessed the country with a host of natural hot spring spots. From the opulent grandeur of **Tabacón Grand Spa Thermal Resort** (p. 163) to the more humble options around **Rincón de la Vieja** (p. 119), all have mineral-rich, naturally heated waters to soothe what ails you.
- **Spotting a Resplendent Quetzal:** The iridescent colors and long, flowing tail feathers of this bird are breathtaking. Revered by ancient Mesoamerican peoples throughout the region, this extremely endangered species can still be regularly sighted in the **Monteverde Cloud Forest Biological Reserve** (p. 185).

o **Meeting Monkeys:** Costa Rica's rainforests and cloud forests are home to four species of New World monkeys—howler, capuchin, squirrel, and spider. I can't guarantee you'll see one or more, but your odds are good if you visit the trails and reserves around **Monteverde** (p. 177), **Tortuguero** (p. 240), **Manuel Antonio** (p. 202), or the **Osa Peninsula** (p. 220).

o **Zipping Through the Treetops:** You'll find zip-line canopy tours all over Costa Rica. In most cases, after a bit of a hike, you strap on a harness and zip from treetop to treetop while dangling from a cable.

Zip-lining through the cloud forest of Monteverde.

o **Pouring on the Salsa Lizano:** Try some Salsa Lizano, a tangy, tamarind-based sauce, native to Costa Rica, that's used on everything from salad to rice and beans to grilled meats and poultry.

o **Touring a Coffee Plantation:** World renowned and highly coveted, freshly brewed Costa Rican coffee can be enjoyed at its source all across the country. Go deeper and learn how the bean is grown and processed. Coffee tours are offered around the Central Valley and outside Monteverde. See chapters 5 and 7.

COSTA RICA'S best PLACES TO SEE WILDLIFE

o **Santa Rosa National Park** (northeast of Liberia, in Guanacaste): One of the largest and last remaining stands of tropical dry forest in Costa Rica, Santa Rosa National Park is a great place for viewing all sorts of wildlife. The sparse foliage, especially during the dry season, makes wildlife observation that much easier for novice naturalists. See p. 125.

o **Monteverde Cloud Forest Biological Reserve** (in the mountains northwest of San José): There's something both eerie and majestic about walking around in the early-morning mist surrounded by bird calls, animal rustlings, and towering trees hung heavy in broad bromeliads, flowering orchids, and hanging moss and vines. The reserve has a well-maintained network of trails, and the community is truly involved in conservation. See p. 185.

o **Manuel Antonio** (near Quepos on the central Pacific coast): The reason this place is so renowned? Monkeys! Manuel Antonio is full of them, even the endangered squirrel monkeys. White-faced capuchin monkeys are quite common here, and have been known to rifle through backpacks in search of a snack. See chapter 8.

Squirrel monkey in Manuel Antonio National Park.

- **Osa Peninsula** (in southern Costa Rica): This is Costa Rica's most remote and biologically rich region. **Corcovado National Park,** the largest remaining patch of virgin lowland tropical rainforest in Central America, takes up much of the Osa Peninsula. Jaguars, crocodiles, and scarlet macaws all call this place home. See chapter 9.
- **Tortuguero Village & Jungle Canals** (on the Caribbean coast, north of Limón): Tortuguero has been called Costa Rica's Venice, but it actually has more in common with the South American Amazon. As you explore the narrow canals here, you'll see a wide variety of herons and other water birds, three types of monkeys, three-toed sloths, and caimans. If you come between June and October, you could be treated to the awe-inspiring spectacle of a green turtle nesting—the small stretch of Tortuguero beach is the last remaining major nesting site of this endangered animal. See "Exploring Tortuguero National Park" in chapter 10.

COSTA RICA'S best ECOLODGES & WILDERNESS RESORTS

Ecolodge options in Costa Rica range from tent camps with no electricity, cold-water showers, and communal, buffet-style meals to some of the most luxurious accommodations in the country.

- **Arenal Observatory Lodge** (near La Fortuna): Originally a research facility, this lodge now features comfy rooms with impressive views of Arenal Volcano. Excellent trails lead to nearby lava flows and a remote waterfall. Toucans frequent the trees near the lodge, and howler monkeys provide the wake-up calls. See p. 165.

o **Monteverde Lodge & Gardens** (Monteverde): One of the original ecolodges in Monteverde, this place has only improved over the years, with great guides, updated rooms, and lush gardens. The operation is run by the very dependable and experienced Costa Rica Expeditions. See p. 182.

Leatherback turtle heading to sea.

o **La Paloma Lodge** (Drake Bay): If your idea of the perfect nature lodge is one where your front porch provides prime-time viewing of flora and fauna, this place is for you. If you decide to leave the comfort of your porch, the Osa Peninsula's lowland rainforests are just outside your door. See p. 224.

o **Bosque del Cabo Rainforest Lodge** (Osa Peninsula): Large, unique, and cozy private cabins perched on the edge of a cliff overlooking the Pacific Ocean and surrounded by lush rainforest make this one of my favorite spots in the country. There's plenty to do and great guides here. See p. 231.

o **Lapa Ríos** (Osa Peninsula): This was one of Costa Rica's first luxury ecolodges to gain international acclaim, and it remains one of the best. The attention to detail, personalized service, and in-house guides and tour leaders are all top-notch. See p. 231.

o **Playa Nicuesa Rainforest Lodge** (Golfo Dulce): This lodge is by far the best option on the Golfo Dulce. Set in deep forest, the individual bungalows here are a perfect blend of rusticity and luxury, and the guides, service, and surrounding wildlife are all superb. See p. 237.

o **Tortuga Lodge** (Tortuguero): This is another of the excellent ecolodges run by Costa Rica Expeditions, and it features a beautiful riverfront restaurant and swimming pool. The canals of Tortuguero snake through its maze of lowland primary rainforest. The beaches here are major sea-turtle nesting sites. See p. 244.

o **Selva Bananito Lodge** (in the Talamanca Mountains south of Limón): This is one of the few lodges providing direct access to the southern Caribbean lowland rainforests. You can hike along a riverbed, ride horses through the rainforest, climb 30m (100 ft.) up a ceiba tree, or rappel down a jungle waterfall here. See p. 262.

COSTA RICA'S best HOTELS

o **Hotel Grano de Oro** (San José): San José boasts dozens of old homes that have been converted into hotels, but few provide the luxurious accommodations or professional service found at the Grano de Oro. All the guest rooms have attractive hardwood furniture, including antique armoires in some rooms. When it's time to relax, you can soak in a hot tub or have a drink in the rooftop lounge while taking in San José's commanding view. See p. 70.

o **Finca Rosa Blanca Coffee Plantation & Inn** (Heredia): If the cookie-cutter rooms of international resorts leave you cold, perhaps this unusual inn will be more your style. Square corners seem to have been prohibited here in favor of turrets and curving walls of glass, arched windows, and semicircular built-in couches. It's set into the lush hillside just 20 minutes from San José. See p. 73.

o **Hotel Capitán Suizo** (Tamarindo): With a perfect beachfront setting, spacious rooms, lush gardens and grounds, and a wonderful pool, this

Finca Rosa Blanca eco-boutique hotel.

is easily the best lodging in Tamarindo, and one of the best along the whole Gold Coast. Wild and rescued howler monkeys live in the tall trees here, and if you're not careful, your poolside snack could be stolen by a brazen magpie-jay or stealthy iguana. See p. 130.

o **Florblanca Resort** (Playa Santa Teresa): The individual villas at this intimate resort are some of the largest and most luxurious in the country. The service and food are outstanding, and the resort is spread over a lushly planted hillside on the quiet northern end of Playa Santa Teresa. See p. 155.

o **Hidden Canopy Treehouses** (Monteverde): The individual cabins here are set on high stilts and nestled into the surrounding cloud forest canopy. All abound in brightly varnished local hardwoods. There's a refined yet convivial vibe here, especially in the afternoon over tea or cocktails, when guests enjoy the main lodge's sunset view. See p. 181.

o **Arco Iris Lodge** (Monteverde): This small lodge is set on a sprawling piece of property, but is within easy walking distance of everything in Santa Elena. It's the best deal in the Monteverde area, to boot. The owners are extremely knowledgeable and helpful. See p. 183.

o **Arenas del Mar** (Manuel Antonio): With large and ample rooms, excellent service and amenities, a beautiful little spa, and the best beach access and location in Manuel Antonio, this hotel has a lot to offer. The whole resort is set amidst old-growth rainforest on a hilly piece of land abutting two distinct beaches. See p. 207.

o **Playa Negra Guesthouse** (Cahuita): Located just across a dirt road from a long, desolate section of Playa Negra, the individual Caribbean-style bungalows here are cozy and beautifully done. The grounds are a riot of tropical flowers and tall palm trees, and there's a refined ambience to the whole operation. See p. 252.

COSTA RICA'S best RESTAURANTS

o **Grano de Oro Restaurant** (San José): This elegant boutique hotel has an equally fine restaurant serving contemporary fusion dishes based on fresh local ingredients and decadent desserts. The open-air seating in the central courtyard is delightful, surrounded by potted palms and ornate stained-glass windows. See p. 77.

o **Abbocato** (Playa Panamá): The dynamic husband-and-wife team here serves up two nightly tasting menus executed with skill and creativity. This is "author cuisine" as it should be, adventurous and personal, appealing to a refined palate. See p. 106.

o **Ginger** (Playa Hermosa): Serving an eclectic mix of traditional and Pan Asian–influenced tapas, this sophisticated little joint is taking this part of Guanacaste by storm. A list of creative cocktails complements the inventive dishes. See p. 107.

o **Papaya** (Brasilito): Housed in a simple, unassuming roadside hotel, this lively little spot serves up a creative and tasty mix of dishes based on the region's freshest fish, seafood, and other local ingredients. Asian and Latin American influences serve as inspiration for the fusion fare served here. See p. 116.

o **Pangas Beach Club** (Tamarindo): This relaxed, casually elegant restaurant serves up fresh seafood and grilled meats in creative, contemporary preparations. Executive chef Jean-Luc Taulere combines his Catalan heritage with classical French training, fresh local ingredients, and a mix of local and far-flung world cuisine touches. See p. 132.

o **Lola's** (Playa Avellanas): With a perfect setting on the sand and excellent hearty fare, Lola's gets my vote for best casual beachfront restaurant in the country. Heavy wooden chairs and tables are handmade on-site and set under broad canvas umbrellas. The ocean-loving namesake mascot—a pet pig—adds to the restaurant's quirky charm. See p. 136.

o **Playa de los Artistas** (Montezuma): This place has an ideal blend of refined Mediterranean cuisine and beachside funkiness. There are only a few tables, so get here early. Fresh grilled seafood is served in oversize ceramic bowls and on large wooden slabs lined with banana leaves. See p. 151.

o **Café Caburé** (Monteverde): In addition to the eclectic world cuisine served here, these folks have a delicious, wide-ranging, and very tempting selection of homemade chocolate treats. I love the casual open-air seating, friendly attention, and broad and always tasty menu. See p. 184.

- **Graffiti Resto Café & Wine Bar** (Playa de Jacó): From the small sushi bar in one corner to the graffiti-painted walls, this place is full of whimsy and surprise. Pan Asian cuisine is blended with the chef's Alabama roots and New Orleans training. The nightly chalkboard specials are always worth checking out, but so are the longstanding regular menu staples. See p. 198.
- **Milagro** (Manuel Antonio): A casually elegant little place, Milagro has made a name for itself in the Manuel Antonio area. A humble coffee shop, breakfast joint, and lunch stop, things get kicked up a notch at night with a creative Nuevo Latino menu that takes full advantage of the freshest local ingredients available. See p. 210.
- **La Pecora Nera** (Puerto Viejo): You'll probably be as surprised as I was to find such fine Italian cuisine in a tiny surfer town on the remote Caribbean coast. The menu features a wide range of Northern Italian pastas and main dishes, as well as fresh fish infused with local flavors. Your best bet here is to allow yourself to be taken on a culinary roller-coaster ride with a mixed feast of the chef's nightly specials and suggestions. See p. 255.

COSTA RICA'S best FAMILY DESTINATIONS

- **La Paz Waterfall Gardens** (near Varablanca and the Poás Volcano): This multifaceted attraction features paths and suspended walkways set alongside a series of impressive jungle waterfalls. Kids will love the variety and vibrancy of the various things, from the hummingbird, wild cat, and reptile exhibits to the impressive power of the waterfalls. See p. 84.

- **Playa Hermosa:** The protected waters of this Pacific beach make it a family favorite. Just because its waters are calm, however, doesn't mean it's boring. Check in at **Aqua Sport** (p. 107), where you can rent sea kayaks, sailboards, paddleboats, beach umbrellas, and bicycles.

- **Playa Tamarindo:** This surf town has a bit of something for everyone. It's a great spot for kids to learn how to surf or boogie board, and a host of tours and activities will please the entire family. See chapter 6.

Windsurfing on Lake Arenal.

- **Arenal Volcano:** This adventure hot spot provides a nearly inexhaustible range of activities for families of all ages. From gentle safari floats to raging white-water rafting, and from flat easy hikes over hanging bridges to challenging scrambles over cooled-off lava flows, you're sure to find things that fit the interests, abilities, and activity levels of all family members. See chapter 7.

- **Monteverde:** This area not only boasts the country's most famous cloud forest, but also provides a wide variety of attractions and activities. After hiking through the reserve, you should be able to keep everyone happy and occupied riding horses, squirming at the serpentarium, or visiting the Monteverde Butterfly Garden, Frog Pond, Bat Jungle, and Orchid Garden. See "Monteverde" in chapter 7.

- **Playa de Jacó:** Jacó's streets are lined with souvenir shops, ice-cream stands, and inexpensive eateries. Activity choices range from surf lessons and bungee jumping to a small-boat cruise among the crocodiles on the Tárcoles River. See chapter 8.

- **Manuel Antonio:** Manuel Antonio has a bit of everything: miles of gorgeous beaches, tons of wildlife (with almost guaranteed monkey sightings),

Playa Montezuma.

and plenty of active-tour options. See "Manuel Antonio National Park" in chapter 8.

COSTA RICA'S best BEACHES

With more than 1,200km (745 miles) of shoreline on its Pacific and Caribbean coasts, Costa Rica offers beach-goers an embarrassment of riches.

- **Playa Nacascolo:** With silky-soft white sand, this is the best stretch of beach on the Papagayo Peninsula. The waters here are protected from ocean swells and are great for swimming. See "Exploring Playa Hermosa, Playa Panamá & Papagayo" in chapter 6.

- **Playa Avellanas:** Just south of Tamarindo, this long white-sand beach is a favorite haunt for surfers, locals, and those in the know. Playa Avellanas stretches on for miles, backed largely by protected mangrove forests. See p. 135.

- **The Beaches Around Playa Sámara:** Playa Sámara is nice enough, but venturing just slightly farther afield, you'll find two of the prettiest beaches along the entire Pacific coast. **Playa Carrillo** is a long crescent of palm-backed white sand located just south of Sámara, while **Playa Barrigona** is a hidden gem tucked down a rugged dirt road to the north. See "Playa Sámara" in chapter 6.

- **Playa Montezuma:** This tiny beach town at the southern tip of the Nicoya Peninsula retains a funky sense of individuality, with plenty of isolated spots to plop down your towel or mat. Nearby, you'll find two beautiful waterfalls, as well as the **Cabo Blanco** wildlife preserve. See p. 147.

- **Malpaís & Santa Teresa:** With just a smattering of luxury lodges, surf camps, and assorted hotels and hostels, this is the place to come if you're looking for miles of deserted beaches and great surf. See "Malpaís & Santa Teresa" in chapter 6.

- **Manuel Antonio:** Manuel Antonio National Park was the first beach destination to become popular in Costa Rica, and its beaches are still idyllic. The views from the hills approaching the park offer captivating views over thick primary rainforest to the Pacific Ocean, pocked with a series of offshore islands. This is also one of the few remaining habitats for the endangered squirrel monkey. See chapter 8.

- **Punta Uva & Manzanillo:** These beaches deliver true Caribbean splendor, with turquoise waters, coral reefs, and palm-lined stretches of nearly deserted white-sand beach. Tall coconut palms line the shore, providing shady respite, and the water is usually quite calm and good for swimming. See chapter 10.

COSTA RICA'S best ADVENTURE SPORT EXPERIENCES

- **Mountain Biking the Back Roads of Costa Rica:** The lack of infrastructure and paved roads here that most folks bemoan is a huge boon for mountain bikers. The country has endless back roads and trails to explore. The area around La Fortuna and Lake Arenal is my favorite destination for mountain biking. The views are stunning and the terrain is widely varied. See p. 170.
- **Rafting the Pacuare River** (near Turrialba): Arguably the best and most beautiful river for rafting in Costa Rica, the Pacuare winds through primary and secondary forests and features one breathtaking section that passes through a gorgeous steep gorge. For a real treat, take the 2-day Pacuare River trip, which includes an overnight at a lodge or tent camp on the side of the river. See p. 293.
- **Surfing & Four-Wheeling Guanacaste Province:** From Witch's Rock at Playa Naranjo near the Nicaraguan border to Playa Nosara, more than

Rafting the Pacuare River.

100km (60 miles) away, you'll find scores of world-class surf spots. In addition to the two mentioned, try a session at Playa Grande, Punta Langosta, and playas Negra, Avellanas, and Junquillal. Or find your own secret spot. See chapter 6.

o **Trying the Adventure Sport of Canyoning:** While every canyoning tour is unique, it usually involves hiking along and through the rivers and creeks of a steep mountain canyon, with periodic breaks to rappel down the face of a waterfall, jump off a rock into a jungle pool, or float down some small rapids. See chapters 6, 7, and 9.

o **Diving or Snorkeling Off Caño Island:** Located off the Osa Peninsula, this uninhabited island is believed to have been used as a ceremonial burial site by the pre-Columbian residents of the area. Today, the underwater rocks and coral formations here provide, arguably, the best scuba diving and snorkeling opportunities in the country—aside from the far offshore Isla del Coco. See chapter 9.

COSTA RICA'S best DAY HIKES & NATURE WALKS

o **Lankester Gardens:** If you want a really pleasant but not overly challenging day hike, consider a walk among the hundreds of distinct species of flora on display here. The trails meander from areas of well-tended open garden to shady natural forest, and the orchid collection is stellar. See p. 97.

o **Rincón de la Vieja National Park:** This park has trails through a variety of ecosystems. My favorite hike is down to the Blue Lake and Cangrejo Falls, where you'll find a pristine turquoise pool fed by a rushing jungle waterfall. The Las Pailas loop, with its bubbling mud pots and fumaroles, is ideal for those seeking a less strenuous hike. See p. 119.

o **Arenal National Park:** Arenal National Park has several excellent trails that visit a variety of ecosystems, including rainforest, secondary forest, savanna, and, my favorite, old lava flows. Most of them are on the relatively flat flanks of the volcano, so there's not too much climbing involved. See "Exploring Arenal Volcano & La Fortuna" in chapter 7.

o **Monteverde Cloud Forest Biological Reserve:** Take a guided tour in the morning to familiarize yourself with the cloud forest, and then spend the late morning or afternoon (your entrance ticket is good for the entire day) exploring the reserve on your own. Off the main thoroughfares, Monteverde reveals its rich mysteries with stunning regularity, even without a guide. See p. 185.

o **Corcovado National Park:** The park has a well-designed network of trails, ranger stations, and camping facilities. Most of the lodges in Drake Bay and Puerto Jiménez have day hikes through the park, but if you really want to experience it, you should hike in and stay at one or more of the campgrounds. See "Puerto Jiménez: Gateway to Corcovado National Park" in chapter 9.

o **Cahuita National Park:** Fronted by the Caribbean and a picture-perfect white-sand beach, the trails here are flat, well-maintained paths through thick lowland forest. Most of the way, they parallel the beach, so you can hike out on the trail and back along the beach, or vice versa. White-faced and howler monkeys are a common sight, as are brightly colored land crabs. See p. 256.

COSTA RICA ITINERARIES

Costa Rica is a compact yet immensely varied destination. On a trip to Costa Rica, you can visit rainforests, cloud forests, and active volcanoes, and walk along miles of uncrowded beaches on both the Pacific and Caribbean coasts. Adventure hounds will have their fill choosing from an exciting array of activities, and those looking for some rest and relaxation can grab a hammock and a good book. Costa Rica's relatively small size makes visiting several destinations during a single vacation both easy and enjoyable.

Costa Rica rightfully should be called "Costas Ricas" because it has two coasts: one on the Pacific Ocean and one on the Caribbean Sea. These two coasts are as different from each other as are the Atlantic and Pacific coasts of North America.

Costa Rica's **Pacific coast** is the most extensive, and is characterized by a rugged (although mostly accessible) coastline where forested mountains often meet the sea. It can be divided into four distinct regions—Guanacaste, the Nicoya Peninsula, the Central Coast, and the Southern Coast. With some spectacular stretches of coastline, most of the country's top beaches are here. This coast's climate varies from dry and sunny in the northwest to hot and humid in the rainforests of the south.

The **Caribbean coast** can be divided into two roughly equal stretches. The remote northeast coastline is a vast, flat plain laced with rivers and covered with rainforest; it is accessible only by boat or small plane. Farther south, along the stretch of coast accessible by car, are uncrowded beaches and even coral reefs.

Bordered by Nicaragua in the north and Panama in the southeast, Costa Rica is only slightly larger than Vermont and New Hampshire combined. Much of the country is mountainous, with three major ranges running northwest to southeast. Among these mountains are several volcanic peaks, some of which are still active. Between the mountain ranges are fertile valleys, the largest and most populated of which is the Central Valley. With the exception of the dry Guanacaste region, much of Costa Rica's coastal area is hot and humid and covered with dense rainforests.

Costa Rica Regions in Brief

See the map on p. 15 for a visual reference of the regions detailed below.

San José   San José is Costa Rica's capital and its primary business, cultural, and social center—it sits fairly close to the country's geographical center, in the heart of its Central Valley (see below). It's a sprawling, urban area, with a population of around 1 million. Its streets are narrow, in poor repair, poorly marked, and often laden with traffic. However, a few notable parks, like the Parque La Sabana and Parque del Este, do serve to lessen the urban blight. San José is home to the country's greatest collection of museums, fine restaurants, and stores, galleries, and shopping centers.

The Central Valley   The Central Valley is surrounded by rolling green hills and mountains that rise to heights between 900 and 1,200m (3,000–4,000 ft.) above sea level. The climate here is mild and spring-like year-round. It's Costa Rica's primary agricultural region, thanks to its rich, volcanic soil, with coffee farms making up the majority of landholdings. The country's earliest settlements were in this area, and today the Central Valley (which includes San José) is densely populated, crisscrossed by decent roads, and dotted with small towns. Surrounding the Central Valley are high mountains, among which are four volcanic peaks. Two of these, **Poás** and **Irazú,** are still active and have caused extensive damage during cycles of activity in the past 2 centuries. Many of the mountainous regions to the north and to the south of the capital of San José have been declared national parks (Tapantí, Juan Castro, and Braulio Carrillo) to protect their virgin rainforests against logging.

Guanacaste   The northwestern corner of the country near the Nicaraguan border is the site of many of Costa Rica's sunniest and most popular **beaches,** including **Playa del Coco, Playa Hermosa, Playa Flamingo, Playa Conchal, Tamarindo,** and the **Papagayo Peninsula.** Because many foreigners have chosen to build beach houses and retirement homes here, Guanacaste has experienced considerable development over the years. You won't find a glut of Cancún-style high-rise hotels, but condos, luxury resorts, and golf courses have sprung up. Still, you won't be towel-to-towel with thousands of strangers. On the contrary, you can still find long stretches of deserted sands. However, more and more travelers are using Liberia as their gateway to Costa Rica, bypassing San José and the central and southern parts of the country entirely.

With about 165cm (65 in.) of rain a year, this region is by far the driest in the country and has been likened to west Texas. Guanacaste province is named after the shady trees that still shelter the herds of cattle roaming the dusty savanna here. Guanacaste has semi-active volcanoes, several lakes, and one of the last remnants of tropical dry forest left in Central America. (Dry forest once stretched all the way from Costa Rica up to the Mexican state of Chiapas.)

The Nicoya Peninsula   Just south of Guanacaste lies the Nicoya Peninsula. Similar to Guanacaste in many ways, the Nicoya Peninsula is somewhat more inaccessible, and thus much less developed and crowded. However, this is already starting to change. The neighboring beaches of **Malpaís** and **Santa Teresa** are perhaps the fastest-growing hot spots anywhere along the Costa Rican coast.

As you head south from Guanacaste, the region, although similar in terms of geography, climate, and ecosystems, begins to get more humid and moist. The forests are taller and lusher than those found in Guanacaste. The Nicoya Peninsula itself juts out to form the Golfo de Nicoya (Nicoya Gulf), a large, protected body of water. **Puntarenas,** a small fishing city, is the main port found inside this gulf, and one of the main commercial ports in all of Costa Rica. Puntarenas is also the departure point for the regular ferries that connect the Nicoya Peninsula to San José and most of mainland Costa Rica.

The Northern Zone   This inland region lies to the north of San José and includes rainforests, cloud forests, hot springs, the country's two most active volcanoes (**Arenal** and

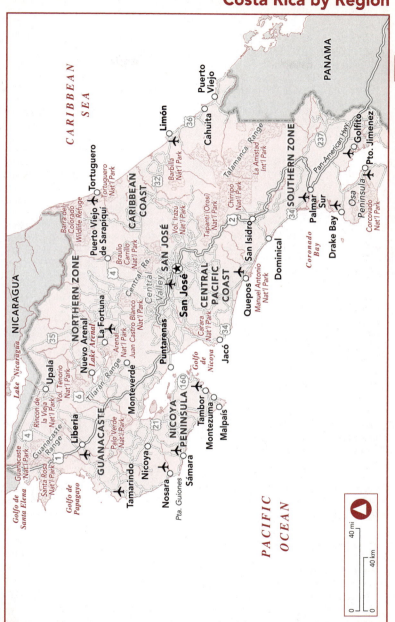

Rincón de la Vieja), **Braulio Carrillo National Park,** and numerous remote lodges. Because this is one of the few regions of Costa Rica without any beaches, it primarily attracts people interested in nature and active sports. **Lake Arenal** boasts some of the best windsurfing and kitesurfing in the world, as well as several good mountain-biking trails. The **Monteverde Cloud Forest,** perhaps Costa Rica's most internationally recognized attraction, is another top draw in this region.

The Central Pacific Coast Because it's the most easily accessible coastline in Costa Rica, the central Pacific coast has a vast variety of beach resorts and hotels. **Playa de Jacó,** a beach just an hour or so by car from San José, attracts sunbirds, charter groups, and a mad rush of Tico tourists every weekend. It is also very popular with surfers and has a distinct party vibe to it. **Manuel Antonio,** one of the most emblematic destinations in Costa Rica, is built up around a popular coastal national park, and caters to people looking to blend beach time and fabulous panoramic views with some wildlife-viewing and active adventures. This region is also home to the highest peak in Costa Rica—**Mount Chirripó**—a beautiful summit where frost is common.

The Southern Zone This hot, humid region is one of Costa Rica's most remote and undeveloped. It is characterized by dense rainforests, large national parks and protected areas, and rugged coastlines. Much of the area is uninhabited and protected in **Corcovado, Piedras Blancas,** and **La Amistad** national parks. A number of wonderful nature lodges are spread around the shores of the **Golfo Dulce** and along the **Osa Peninsula.** There's a lot of solitude to be found here, due in no small part to the fact that it's hard to get here and hard to get around. But if you like your ecotourism authentic and challenging, you'll find the southern zone to your liking.

The Caribbean Coast Most of the Caribbean coast is a wide, steamy lowland laced with rivers and blanketed with rainforests and banana plantations. The culture here is predominantly Afro-Caribbean, with many residents speaking an English or Caribbean patois. The northern section of this coast is accessible only by boat or small plane and is the site of **Tortuguero National Park,** which is known for its nesting sea turtles and riverboat trips. The towns of **Cahuita, Puerto Viejo,** and **Manzanillo,** on the southern half of the Caribbean coast, are increasingly popular destinations. The beautiful beaches and coastline here, as yet, have few large hotels. This area can be rainy, especially between December and April.

BLUEPRINTS FOR FABULOUS VACATIONS

The following itineraries were designed to help you make the most of your time in Costa Rica—feel free to follow them to the letter. But if that's too structured for you, you might also use one or more of them as an outline and then fill in blanks with other destinations and attractions that strike your fancy.

COSTA RICA HIGHLIGHTS IN 1 WEEK

The timing is tight, but this itinerary packs a lot into a typical, weeklong vacation. This route takes you to a trifecta of Costa Rica's primary tourist attractions: Arenal Volcano, Monteverde, and Manuel Antonio. You can explore and enjoy tropical nature, take in some beach time, and experience a few high-adrenaline adventures, to boot. If you have an extra day or two or three,

Streets of San José.

simply add on an extra night at any (or all) of the major destinations here, as all have plenty more to offer.

Day 1: Arrive & Settle into San José

If your flight gets in early enough and you have time, head downtown and tour the **Museos del Banco Central de Costa Rica (Gold Museum)** ★★ (p. 81) and the nearby **Museo de Jade Marco Fidel Tristán (Jade Museum)** ★★ (p. 80). But if you've enough time for only a little walk, stop at one of the roadside stands selling small bags of cut-up fruit. Depending on the season, you might find mango, pineapple, or papaya on offer. If you're lucky, they'll have *mamón chino,* an odd-looking, golf ball–size fruit you might also know as rambutan or litchi nut.

While downtown, try to stop by the **Teatro Nacional (National Theater)** ★★ (p. 90). If anything is playing that night, buy tickets for the show.

Day 2: Get Close to the Hot Stuff ★★

Rent a car and head to the Arenal National Park and **Arenal Volcano** ★★ area. After checking into your hotel, head to Arenal National Park, and hike the **Sendero Coladas (Lava Flow Trail)** ★★, which will take you onto and over a cooled-off lava flow. Spend the evening soaking in the natural hot springs at the **Tabacón Grand Spa Thermal Resort** ★★★ (p. 163), working out the kinks from the road and hike. (The volcano may be technically dormant right now, but the natural hot springs are still working just fine.) I recommend reserving a massage or spa treatment in advance.

Day 3: Adventures Around Arenal, Ending Up in Monteverde ★★

Spend the morning being adventurous around Arenal National Park. Your options range from white-water rafting to mountain biking to horseback riding and then hiking to the Río Fortuna Waterfall. My favorite is the **canyoning** adventure offered by **Desafío Expeditions** ★★ (p. 169). Allow at least 4 hours of daylight to drive around **Lake Arenal** to **Monteverde.**

Day 4: Monteverde Cloud Forest Biological Reserve ★★★

Wake up early and take a guided tour of the **Monteverde Cloud Forest Biological Reserve** ★★★ (p. 185). Spend the afternoon visiting several of the area's attractions, which might include the **Butterfly Garden** ★ (p. 189), the **Orchid Garden** ★★ (p. 189), the **Monteverde Serpentarium** ★ (p. 189), **Monteverde Theme Park** (p. 189), and the **Bat Jungle** ★★★ (p. 189).

Day 5: From the Treetops to the Coast ★★★

Use the morning to take one of the **zip-line canopy tours** here. I recommend **Selvatura Park** ★★ (p. 187), which has a wonderful canopy tour and hanging bridges, as well as other interesting exhibits. Be sure to schedule the tour early enough so that you can hit the road by noon for your drive to **Manuel Antonio National Park** ★★. En route, you'll want to stop at the bridge over the Tárcoles River to look at all the crocodiles gathered below.

Day 6: Manuel Antonio National Park ★★

In the morning, take a boat tour of the **Damas Island estuary** (p. 213), and then reward yourself with an afternoon lazing on one of the beautiful beaches inside **Manuel Antonio National Park** ★★ (p. 211). If you just can't lie still, hike the loop trail through the rainforest here and around **Punta Catedral (Cathedral Point)** ★★.

Day 7: Saying Adiós

Drive back to **San José** in time to drop off your rental car and connect with your departing flight home.

THE BEST OF UNDISCOVERED COSTA RICA

Despite Costa Rica's booming tourism industry, there are still plenty of places that are off the beaten track. And believe me, you'll be richly rewarded for venturing down the road less traveled. If you have only a week, you can end this itinerary in Montezuma. If you have more time, explore the lush and remote southern zone.

Day 1: Rincón de la Vieja National Park ★★

Not nearly as popular as the Arenal Volcano, the **Rincón de la Vieja volcano,** along with its namesake **national park** ★★ (p. 119), is an underexplored gem. The park features challenging and rewarding hikes, sulfur hot springs, volcanic mud deposits, and stunning jungle waterfalls. My favorite hike here is a vigorous 2-hour trek to **Blue Lake and La Cangrejo Waterfall** ★★ (p. 122), which leads to a beautiful forest waterfall emptying into a postcard-perfect turquoise lake. This is a great spot for a picnic lunch and a cool dip. If you have the time and energy afterward, finish up with the relatively short and gentle **Las Pailas Loop** ★, which showcases the volcanic fumaroles and mud pots here.

Waterfall at the Rincón de la Vieja National Park.

Day 2: Horses, High Wires & Hot Springs

You did plenty of hiking yesterday, so start this day off with something a little different. **Hacienda Guachipelín ★★** (p. 122) offers a range of adventure activities, including horseback riding, river tubing, two zip-line canopy tours, and a waterfall rappel canyoning tour (see p. 288 for more about canyoning), in addition to boasting a gorgeous set of natural hot mineral springs set alongside a jungle river.

Day 3: Going Deep Down Under

Sitting on top of a massive cave system, **Barra Honda National Park ★** (p. 141) is Costa Rica's top spot for spelunking. On a typical tour here, you'll descend into the depths of the **Terciopelo Cave** and visit the waterfalls and pools of **La Cascada.** After your visit here, drive to nearby **Playa Sámara,** about an hour away, and visit this lovely beachside trattoria for a meal:

Gusto Beach ★★

With tables set in the sand and palm trees strung with rope lighting, this place serves up excellent Italian fare, as well as fresh grilled fish and meats. See p. 139.

Day 4: Beautiful Beaches

The Nicoya Peninsula has many of the same charms and nearly as many miles of beach as Guanacaste, but fewer crowds. Although the beach at **Playa Sámara** is nice enough, I recommend heading to neighboring gems **Playa Barrigona ★★** (p. 140) and **Playa Carrillo ★★** (p. 140). While in the area, be sure to sign up for an ultralight flight with the folks at the **Flying Crocodile** (p. 140).

Days 5 & 6: Montezuma

Montezuma is a great place to mix more beach time with wildlife sightings and visits to some wonderful waterfalls. While you can certainly hike to the foot of the **Montezuma Waterfall ★★** (p. 152), I prefer visiting it as part of the **Waterfall Canopy Tour ★** (p. 152). I recommend taking a horseback tour to **El Chorro ★** falls (p. 152). If you time it right, you can take a horseback ride home along the beach at sunset.

While in Montezuma, visit **Cabo Blanco Absolute Nature Reserve ★★** (p. 153), the country's first officially protected area. The main trail inside this park, **Sendero Sueco,** leads to the gorgeous and almost always deserted **Playa Balsita.** A trip to Cabo Blanco Nature Reserve can be combined with a **kayaking and snorkeling tour** to the tiny cemetery isle located just off the village of **Cabuya.**

Playa de los Artistas ★★★

Fresh grilled fish and other Mediterranean fare are the specialty at my favorite restaurant in Montezuma. If you're limber, slide onto a tatami mat set around one of the low tables closest to the water. See p. 151.

Days 7, 8 & 9: The Osa Peninsula & Golfo Dulce

The area way down south on the Osa Peninsula and along the Golfo Dulce is Costa Rica's most remote (and in many ways most rewarding) region. Here you'll find tiny towns and villages bordering vast tracts of lowland tropical forest that cascade down to the sea. This area is home to **Corcovado National Park ★★★**, the **Piedras Blancas National Park ★★**, and a host of other private reserves and protected areas. It is Costa Rica's prime area for wildlife-viewing and ecotourism. There are three main gateways to this region, **Drake Bay, Puerto Jiménez,** and **Golfito.** All are reached by small commuter flights, and all offer access to some of the top nature lodges in the country. These remote lodges provide all meals and tours for their guests. See chapter 9 for more information.

THE BEST COSTA RICA ADVENTURES

Costa Rica is a major adventure-tourism destination. The following basic itinerary packs a lot of adventures into a single week; if you want to do some surfing, mountain biking, or kayaking, just schedule more time.

Day 1: Starting Out in San José

Arrive and get settled in **San José.** If your flight gets in early enough and you have time, head downtown and tour the **Museos del Banco Central de Costa Rica ★★** (p. 81), and the **Museo de Jade Marco Fidel Tristán (Jade Museum) ★★** (p. 80).

Days 2 & 3: Get Wet & Wild

Take a 2-day white-water rafting expedition on the **Pacuare River** with **Ríos Tropicales ★★** (p. 95). You'll spend the night at its remote riverside lodge. When you finish running the Pacuare, they'll transport you (as part of the trip package) to **La Fortuna ★★**. Settle into your hotel and head to the **Tabacón Grand Spa Thermal Resort ★★★** (p. 163) to have a soothing soak.

Day 4: Waterfalls Two Ways

Go canyoning with **Desafío Expeditions ★★** (p. 169) in the morning, and then hop on a horse or a mountain bike in the afternoon and be sure to stop at the **Río Fortuna waterfall ★★** (p. 170). Take the short, but quite steep, hike down to the base of the falls and take a chilly dip in one of the pools there. In the evening, check out the hot springs at **Eco Termales ★★** (p. 173).

Day 5: Getting There Is Part of the Fun & Adventure

Arrange a **taxi-to-boat-to-horse** transfer over to **Monteverde** with **Desafío Expeditions ★★** (p. 169). Take a zip-line **canopy tour** in the

Hiking through Monteverde Cloud Forest.

afternoon. I recommend **Selvatura Park** ★★, which is located near the **Santa Elena Cloud Forest Reserve.** Finally, if you've got the energy, take a **night tour** through either the Santa Elena or Monteverde Cloud Forest Reserve.

Day 6: Monteverde Cloud Forest Biological Reserve ★★★

Wake up early and take a daytime guided tour of the **Monteverde Cloud Forest Biological Reserve** ★★★, even if you did the night tour on Day 5. Be sure to pack a lunch. After the guided tour, spend the next few hours continuing to explore the trails through the cloud forest here. See if you can spot a **quetzal** on your own. Then transfer back to San José.

Day 7: Squeeze in a Soccer Game Before Departing

You may have an early flight home from **San José.** If you have a few hours to kill, take a **hike** or **jog** around Parque La Sabana or, better yet, try to join a **pickup soccer game** here.

COSTA RICA FOR FAMILIES

Costa Rica is a terrific destination for families. If you're traveling with very small children, you might want to consider a large resort with a children's program and babysitting services. But for slightly older kids and teens, particularly those with an adventurous streak, Costa Rica is a lot of fun.

Day 1: Arrive in Guanacaste

Fly directly into **Liberia.** From here, it's a 30- to 45-minute drive to any of the area's many beach resorts or boutique hotels, especially around the **Papagayo Peninsula.** I recommend either the **Four Seasons Resort Costa Rica ★★★** (p. 105) or the **Hotel Playa Hermosa Bosque del Mar ★★★** (p. 106). The former is a large-scale luxury resort with an excellent children's program and tons of activity and tour options; the latter is a lovely beachfront boutique hotel on a quiet and calm section of Playa Hermosa.

Day 2: Get Your Bearings & Enjoy the Beach

Get to know and enjoy the facilities and activities at your hotel or resort. Spend time on the beach or at the pool. Build some sand castles, or get involved in a pickup game of beach volleyball or soccer. In the afternoon, go on a **sail and snorkel cruise.** If you choose a large resort, check out the **children's program** and any scheduled **activities** or **tours** that particularly appeal to anyone in the family. Feel free to adapt the following days' suggestions accordingly.

Day 3: Rafting on the Corobicí River

The whole family will enjoy a **rafting tour** on the gentle Corobicí River. **Ríos Tropicales ★★** (p. 95) offers leisurely trips that are appropriate for all ages, except infants. In addition to the slow float and occasional mellow rapids, there'll be plenty of opportunities to watch birds and other wildlife along the way. If you're here between late September and late February, book a **turtle-nesting tour** (p. 133) at nearby **Playa Grande** for the evening. The whole family will be awestruck by the spectacle of a giant leatherback turtle digging a nest and laying its eggs.

Day 4: El Viejo Wetlands ★★

Located about an hour's drive from the Guanacaste beaches, **El Viejo Wildlife Refuge & Wetlands ★★** (p. 118) is a fabulous day-trip destination. Set on a massive old farmstead bordering Palo Verde National Park, this private reserve offers up some of Guanacaste's best wildlife-viewing, with boat trips on the Tempisque River and safari-style open Jeep tours through surrounding wetlands, as well as a host of other cultural and adventure tour options. Lunch is served in a beautiful, century-old farm building.

Day 5: Hacienda Guachipelín ★★

It's time to head for the hills, which are mostly volcanoes in this neck of the woods. Book a full-day Adventure Pass outing to **Hacienda Guachipelín ★★** (p. 122), near **Rincón de la Vieja National Park.** Older and more adventurous children can go river tubing, enjoy a **horseback ride,** or take one of the zip-line **canopy tours.** Younger children should get a kick out of visiting the working farm and cattle ranch, butterfly garden, and serpentarium here.

Day 6: Learn to Surf

Head to **Playa Tamarindo ★** (p. 127) for the day and arrange for the whole family to take **surf** or **boogie-board lessons.** You can arrange classes in advance and rent equipment with either **Kelly's Surf Shop ★** (p. 134) or **Witch's Rock Surf Camp ★** (p. 134). Be sure to rent your boards for a full day so you can practice after the lesson is over.

Day 7: Leaving Liberia

Use any spare time before your flight out of **Liberia** to buy last-minute souvenirs and gifts, or just laze on the beach or by the pool.

THE BEST OF SAN JOSÉ & THE CENTRAL VALLEY

While most tourists seek to almost immediately get out of San José for greener pastures, Costa Rica's vibrant capital and the surrounding Central Valley provide plenty to see and do. If you have even more days, take a whitewater rafting trip on the Pacuare River, tour a coffee farm, or head out to a beach on the Central Pacific coast.

Day 1: Getting to Know the City

Start your day on the **Plaza de la Cultura.** Visit the **Museos del Banco Central de Costa Rica ★★** (p. 81), and see if you can get tickets for a performance that night at the **Teatro Nacional ★★** (p. 90). From the Plaza de la Cultura, stroll Avenida Central to the **Museo Nacional de Costa Rica (National Museum) ★★** (p. 82).

Restaurante Nuestra Tierra ★

It's a bit of a tourist trap, sure, but this Costa Rican–themed restaurant is very conveniently located and serves up dependable local cuisine. Order a *casado* (blue plate special) for lunch. It will come served on a banana leaf spread over a large platter, delivered by a waiter or waitress in traditional rural garb from a bygone era. See p. 76.

After lunch, head over to nearby **Museo de Jade Marco Fidel Tristán (Jade Museum) ★★** (p. 80). As soon as you're finished taking in all this culture, some shopping at the open-air stalls at the **Plaza de la Democracia** (p. 89) is in order.

Café Mundo ★

Try dinner at this trendy local hangout, at Calle 15 and Avenida 9, 3 blocks east and 1 block north of the INS building. This bustling hotspot serves up a mix of bar food, local classics, and world cuisine in a rambling old converted home. See p. 76.

After dinner, head to the **Teatro Nacional** for the night's performance.

Day 2: Alajuela, Heredia & Environs

Rent a car for the next 2 days, and get an early start for the **Poás Volcano ★★** (p. 96), before the clouds sock in the main crater. After visiting the volcano, head to **La Paz Waterfall Gardens ★★** (p. 84). Take a walk on the waterfall trail, and also enjoy the immense butterfly garden and lively hummingbird garden. This is a good place to have lunch. On your way back to San José, you'll be making a loop through the hills of **Heredia,** with a stop at **INBio Park ★★** (p. 83). In addition to being a fascinating natural history museum, INBio Park has a wonderful collection of intriguing animal sculptures by Costa Rican artist José Sancho.

Day 3: Cartago & the Orosí Valley

Start off the day taking in the scenery from 3,400m (11,080 ft.), at the top of the **Irazú Volcano ★** (p. 96). After admiring the view and hiking the crater trail, head down into the country's first capital city, visiting **Las Ruinas** (p. 95) and the **Basílica de Nuestra Señora de los Ángeles ★★★** (p. 95), on your way out to the Orosí valley. As you drive the loop road around Lake Cachí, stop in **Ujarrás** (p. 97) to see the ruins of Costa Rica's oldest church and check out the sculptures at **La Casa del Soñador (House of the Dreamer) ★** (p. 97).

After Ujarrás, continue on to Orosí valley, stopping at **Lankester Gardens ★★** (p. 97), one of the top botanical gardens in the country. You'll want to spend at least 2 hours wandering around the gardens here. Upon returning to San José, you can return the rental car and rely on taxis in the city, as it's much easier and less stressful than dealing with downtown traffic.

Day 4: More City Sights & Shopping

Spend this day further exploring the capital. Start by heading out on Paseo Colón to the **Museo de Arte Costarricense (Costa Rican Art Museum) ★★** (p. 82). Be sure to spend some time in its continually growing open-air sculpture garden. After visiting the museum, take a stroll around the beautiful and expansive downtown **Parque La Sabana ★★** (p. 85). Intrepid travelers can also do some shopping at the **Mercado Central ★** (p. 89).

Grano de Oro Restaurant ★★★

For your final dinner, splurge a bit and head to this elegant restaurant, located inside the boutique hotel of the same name. Enjoy sophisticated contemporary fusion cuisine in a dimly lit courtyard setting. See p. 77.

After dinner, take a late-night turn on the dance floor at **Castro's ★** (p. 90) for some classic salsa and other Latin rhythms, or **Vértigo ★★** (p. 90) if you prefer something more contemporary and electronic.

COSTA RICA IN CONTEXT

*P*ura Vida! (Pure Life!) is Costa Rica's unofficial national slogan, and in many ways it defines the country. You'll hear it exclaimed, proclaimed, and simply stated by *Ticos* (slang for Costa Ricans) from all walks of life, from children to octogenarians. It can be used as a cheer after your favorite soccer team scores a goal, or as a descriptive response when someone asks you, *"¿Como estas?"* ("How are you?"). It is symbolic of the easygoing nature of this country's people, politics, and personality.

Costa Rica itself is a mostly rural country with vast areas of protected tropical forests. It is one of the biologically richest places on earth, with a wealth of flora and fauna that attracts and captivates biologists, photographers, ecotourists, and casual visitors alike.

COSTA RICA TODAY

Costa Rica has a population of a little more than 5 million, more than half of whom live in the urban Central Valley and surrounding hillsides. Some 94% of the population is of Spanish or otherwise European descent, and it is not at all unusual to see fair-skinned and blond Costa Ricans. This is largely because the indigenous population in place when the first Spaniards arrived was small and was quickly reduced to even more of a minority by wars and disease. Some indigenous populations still remain, primarily on reservations around the country; the principal tribes include the Bribri, Cabécar, Boruca, and Guayamí. In addition, on the Caribbean coast and in the big cities lives a substantial population of English-speaking black Creoles who came over from the Antilles in the late-19th and early-20th centuries to work on building the railroad and on the banana plantations.

In general, Costa Ricans are a friendly and outgoing people. While interacting with visitors, Ticos are very open and helpful. Time has relative meaning to Ticos. Although most tour companies and other establishments operate efficiently, don't expect punctuality, in general.

In a region historically plagued by internal strife and civil wars, Costa Ricans are proud of their peaceful history, political stability, and relatively high level of development. However, this can also translate into arrogance and prejudice toward immigrants from neighboring countries, particularly Nicaraguans, who make up a large percentage of the workforce on the banana and coffee plantations.

Roman Catholicism is the official religion of Costa Rica, although freedom to practice any religion is guaranteed by the country's constitution. More than 75% of the population identifies as Roman Catholic, while another 14% comprise a number of evangelical Christian congregations. There is a small but visible Jewish community, as well. By and large, a large section of Ticos are religiously observant, if not fervent, though it seems that just as many lead quite secular lives.

THE MAKING OF COSTA RICA

Early History

Little is known of Costa Rica's history before its colonization by Spanish settlers. The pre-Columbian Indians who made their home in this region of Central America never developed the large cities or advanced culture that flowered farther north in what would become Guatemala, Belize, and Mexico. There are no grand pyramids or large Mayan cities in Costa Rica. However, ancient artifacts indicating a strong sense of aesthetics have been unearthed from scattered excavations around the country. Ornate gold and jade jewelry, intricately carved grinding stones, and artistically painted terra-cotta objects point to a small but highly skilled population.

Spain Settles Costa Rica

In 1502, on his fourth and final voyage to the New World, Christopher Columbus anchored just offshore from present-day Limón. Whether he actually gave the country its name—"the rich coast"—is open to debate, but the Spaniards never did find much gold or many minerals to exploit here.

The earliest Spanish settlers found strong resistance in Costa Rica. Still, due to their small numbers, scattered villages, and tribal differences, the local indigenous peoples were quickly overcome by superior firepower and European diseases. When the fighting ended, however, the European colonizers in Costa Rica found that very few Indians were left to force into servitude. Some settlers were compelled to till their own lands, a situation unheard of in other parts of Central America. It didn't take long for Costa Rica's few Spanish settlers to head for the hills, where they found rich volcanic soil and a climate that was less oppressive than in the lowlands. **Cartago,** the colony's first capital, was founded in 1563, but it was not until the 1700s that additional cities were established in this agriculturally rich region. In the late-18th century, the first coffee plants were introduced, and because these plants thrived in the highlands, Costa Rica began to develop its first cash crop. Unfortunately, it was a long and difficult journey transporting the coffee to the Caribbean coast and then onward to Europe, where the demand for coffee was growing.

From Independence to the Present Day

In 1821, Spain granted independence to its colonies in Central America. Costa Rica joined with its neighbors to form the Central American Federation; but in 1838, it withdrew to form a new nation and pursue its own interests. By the mid-1800s, coffee was the country's main export. Free land was given to anyone willing to plant coffee on it, and plantation owners soon grew wealthy and powerful, creating Costa Rica's first elite class.

This was a stormy period in Costa Rican history. In 1856, the country was invaded by **William Walker,** a soldier of fortune from Tennessee who, with the backing of U.S. President James Buchanan, was attempting to create a slave state in Central America (before his invasion of Costa Rica, he had invaded Nicaragua and Baja California). The people of Costa Rica, led by president Juan Rafael Mora Porras, marched against Walker and chased him back to Nicaragua.

The Little Drummer Boy

Costa Rica's national hero is Juan Santamaría. The legend goes that young Juan enlisted as a drummer boy in the campaign against William Walker. On April 11, 1865, when Costa Rican troops had a band of Walker's men cornered in a downtown hostel in Rivas, Nicaragua, Santamaría volunteered for a nearly certain suicide mission to set the building on fire. Although he was mortally wounded, Santamaría was successful in torching the building and driving out Walker's men, where they were swiftly routed. Today, April 11 is a national holiday.

In 1889, Costa Rica held what is considered the first free election in Central American history. The opposition candidate won the election, and the control of the government passed from the hands of one political party to those of another without hostilities. Costa Rica established itself as the region's first true democracy. In 1948, this democratic process was challenged by **Rafael Ángel Calderón,** who had served as the country's president from 1940 to 1944. After losing by a narrow margin, Calderón, who had the backing of the communist labor unions and the Catholic Church, refused to concede the country's leadership to the rightfully elected president, **Otilio Ulate,** and a civil war ensued. Calderón was eventually defeated by José "Pepe" Figueres. In the wake of this crisis, a new constitution was drafted; among other changes, it abolished Costa Rica's army so that such a revolution could never happen again.

In 1994, history seemed to repeat itself—peacefully this time—when **José María Figueres** took the reins of government from the son of his father's adversary, Rafael Angel Calderón. In 2010, Costa Rica elected its first female president, **Laura Chinchilla.** On April 6, 2014, former university professor Luis Guillermo Solís of the opposition Citizen's Action Party won a run-off election by a landslide over longtime San José mayor Johnny Araya. So far, Solis's presidency has been a mixed bag. He's had trouble moving legislation forward, and divisions within his own ruling coalition have been a large part of that problem. Longstanding structural issues have hampered attempts at addressing infrastructure and revenue problems.

RECOMMENDED READING

NATURAL HISTORY I think every visitor to Costa Rica should read *Tropical Nature* by Adrian Forsyth and Ken Miyata. It's a wonderfully written and lively collection of tales and adventures by two Neotropical biologists who spent quite some time in the forests of Costa Rica.

Mario A. Boza's beautiful *Costa Rica National Parks* has been reissued in an elegant coffee-table edition. Other worthwhile coffee-table books include *Rainforests: Costa Rica and Beyond* by Adrian Forsyth, with photographs by Michael and Patricia Fogden; and *Costa Rica: A Journey Through Nature* by Adrian Hepworth.

Two good choices for an introduction to Costa Rica's fauna are *The Wildlife of Costa Rica: A Field Guide* by Fiona Reid, Jim Zook, Twan Leenders, and Robert Dean; and *Costa Rica: Traveller's Wildlife Guides* by Les Beletsky. Both pack a lot of useful information into a concise package.

A Guide to the Birds of Costa Rica by F. Gary Stiles and Alexander Skutch is an invaluable guide for identifying the many birds you'll see during your stay. Most guides and nature lodges have a copy on hand. Bird-watchers might also consider *A Bird-Finding Guide to Costa Rica* by Barrett Lawson, which details the best birding sites throughout the country.

Other interesting natural-history books that survey the plants and animals of Costa Rica include *Costa Rica Natural History* by Daniel Janzen; *A Guide to Tropical Plants of Costa Rica* by Willow Zuchowsky; *The Natural History of Costa Rican Mammals* by Mark Wainwright; *A Guide to the Amphibians and Reptiles of Costa Rica* by Twan Leenders; and the classic *A Neotropical Companion* by John C. Kricher, reissued in an expanded edition with color photos.

GENERAL INTEREST For a look into Costa Rican society, pick up *The Ticos: Culture and Social Change* by Richard, Karen, and Mavis Biesanz, an examination of the country's politics and culture. Also worth checking out is *The Costa Rica Reader: History, Culture, Politics,* a broad selection of stories and essays by Costa Ricans from all walks of life.

For more about the life and culture of Costa Rica's Talamanca coast, an area populated by Afro-Caribbean people whose forebears emigrated from Caribbean islands in the early-19th century, read Paula Palmer's *What Happen: A Folk-History of Costa Rica's Talamanca Coast,* a collection of oral histories.

FICTION & POETRY *Costa Rica: A Traveler's Literary Companion,* edited by Barbara Ras and with a foreword by Oscar Arias Sánchez, is a collection of short stories by Costa Rican writers, organized by regions of the country. Entries include works by many of the country's leading literary lights, and the geographical breakdown makes it a good companion as you travel from place to place around Costa Rica.

Young adults will enjoy Kristin Joy Pratt's *A Walk in the Rainforest,* while younger children will like the beautifully illustrated *The Forest in the Clouds* by Sneed Collard and Michael Rothman, and *The Umbrella* by Jan Brett. Pachanga Kids (www.pachangakids.com) has published several illustrated bilingual children's books with delightful illustrations by Ruth Angulo, including *Mar Azucarada/Sugar Sea* by Roberto Boccanera, and *El Coyote y la Luciérnaga/The Coyote and the Firefly* by Yazmin Ross, which (full disclosure) I translated and which includes a musical CD that also features your humble author's singing.

One of the most important pieces in the Costa Rican canon, Carlos Luis Fallas's 1941 tome *Mamita Yunai* provides a stark look at the impact of the large banana giant United Fruit on the country. More recently, Fernando Contreras takes up where his predecessor left off in *Unico Mirando al Mar,* which describes the conditions of the poor, predominantly children, who scavenge Costa Rica's garbage dumps.

COSTA RICA IN POPULAR CULTURE

Music

Several musical traditions meet and mingle in Costa Rica. The northern Guanacaste region is a hotbed of folk music, strongly influenced by the marimba (wooden xylophone) traditions of Guatemala and Nicaragua, while also featuring guitars, maracas, and the occasional harp. On the Caribbean coast, you can hear traditional calypso sung by descendants of the original black workers brought over to build the railroads and tend the banana plantations. Roving bands play a mix of guitar, banjo, washtub bass, and percussion in the bars and restaurants of Cahuita and Puerto Viejo.

Costa Rica also has a healthy contemporary music scene. The jazz-fusion trio **Editus** has won two Grammy awards for its work with Panamanian salsa giant (and movie star) **Rubén Blades. Malpaís,** the closest thing Costa Rica had to a supergroup, suffered the sudden and tragic loss of its lead singer in

Cartago's Basilica.

2011, but still has several excellent discs out and occasionally performs with the surviving members.

Also look for music by **Cantoamérica,** which plays upbeat dance music ranging from salsa to calypso to merengue. Jazz pianist and former minister of culture **Manuel Obregón** (also a member of Malpaís) has several excellent solo albums out, including **Simbiosis** (2011)**,** on which he improvises along with the sounds of Costa Rica's wildlife, waterfalls, and weather.

Local label **Papaya Music ★★★** (www.papayamusic.com) has done an excellent job promoting and producing albums by Costa Rican musicians in a range of styles and genres. Their offerings range from the Guanacasteca folk songs of **Max Goldemberg** to the boleros of **Ray Tico** to the original calypso of **Walter "Gavitt" Ferguson.** You can find their CDs at gift shops and record stores around the country.

Art

Unlike Guatemala, Mexico, or even Nicaragua, Costa Rica does not have a strong tradition of local or indigenous arts and crafts. The strong suit of Costa Rican art is European- and Western-influenced, ranging from neoclassical to modern in style.

Deceased and living legends of the art world include **Rafa Fernández, Lola Fernández,** and **Cesar Valverde.** Also be on the lookout for works by **Max Jiménez** (1900–74), **Francisco Amighetti** (1907–98), **Manuel de la Cruz** (1909–86), and **Teodorico Quiros** (1897–1977). These early-20th-century painters were responsible for the first semi-important local art movement.

Contemporary artists making waves and names for themselves include **Fernando Carballo, Rodolfo Stanley, Lionel González, Manuel Zumbado,** and **Karla Solano.**

Sculpture is perhaps one of the strongest aspects of the Costa Rican art scene, with the large bronze works of **Francisco "Paco" Zuñiga** among the best of the genre. Meanwhile, the artists **José Sancho, Edgar Zuñiga,** and **Jiménez Deredia** are all producing internationally acclaimed pieces, many of monumental proportions. You can see examples by all these sculptors around the country, as well as at San José's downtown **Museo de Arte Costarricense (Costa Rican Art Museum)** ★★ (p. 82). I also enjoy the whimsical works of **Leda Astorga,** who sculpts and then paints a pantheon of plump and voluptuous figures in interesting, and at times compromising, poses.

You'll find excellent museums and galleries, including the **Museo de Arte Costarricense (Costa Rican Art Museum)** ★★ (p. 82) and **Galería 11–12** ★★★ (p. 87), in San José and the Central Valley, as well as, to a much lesser extent, in some of the country's larger and more popular tourist destinations.

Architecture

Costa Rica lacks the large-scale pre-Columbian ceremonial ruins found throughout much of the rest of Mesoamerica. The only notable early archaeological site is **Guayabo.** However, only the foundations of a few dwellings, a handful of carved petroglyphs, and some road and water infrastructure are still visible here.

Similarly, Costa Rica lacks the large and well-preserved colonial-era cities found throughout much of the rest of Latin America. The original capital of **Cartago** (p. 95) has some old ruins and a few colonial-era buildings, as well as the country's grandest church, the **Basílica de Nuestra Señora de los Ángeles (Basilica of Our Lady of the Angels)** ★★★ (p. 95), which was built in honor of the country's patron saint, La Negrita, or the Virgin of Guadalupe.

A few modern architects are creating names for themselves. **Ronald Zurcher,** who designed the Four Seasons Resort at Papagayo Peninsula and several other large hotel projects, is one of the shining lights of contemporary Costa Rican architecture. Zurcher is known for incorporating animal forms and motifs into his designs, with rooflines mimicking turtles or armadillos, for example.

EATING & DRINKING

Costa Rican food is not especially memorable, although some of the exotic fruits and vegetables served here certainly are. Creative chefs using fresh local ingredients have livened up the dining scene in San José and at most of the major tourist destinations, and a few are even turning out inventive takes on traditional Costa Rican classics. Outside of the capital and major tourist destinations, though, your options get very limited very fast; in fact, many destinations are so remote that you have no choice but to eat in the hotel's restaurant. At remote jungle lodges, the food is usually served buffet- or family-style; the quality can range from bland to inspired, depending on who's doing the cooking, and turnover in the kitchen is high.

Fortunately, eating in Costa Rica won't break your budget. At even the more expensive restaurants, it's hard to spend more than $50 a head unless you really splurge on drinks. It gets even cheaper outside the city and high-end hotels. But if you really want to save money, Costa Rican, or "típico," food is always the cheapest nourishment available. It's primarily served in *sodas,* Costa Rica's equivalent of diners.

Meals & Dining Customs

Rice and beans are the foundation of all Costa Rican meals, whether breakfast, lunch, or dinner. At breakfast, they're called *gallo pinto* and come with everything from eggs to steak to seafood. At lunch or dinner, rice and beans are an integral part of a *casado* (which translates as "married" and is the name for the local version of a blue-plate special). A *casado* usually consists of cabbage-and-tomato salad, fried plantains (a starchy, banana-like fruit), and a chicken, fish, or meat dish of some sort. On the Caribbean coast, rice and beans are cooked in coconut milk.

Dining hours in Costa Rica are flexible, but typically follow North American customs. Some downtown restaurants in San José are open 24 hours, but pricier spots tend to be open for lunch from 11am to 3pm and for dinner from 6 to 11pm.

APPETIZERS   Known as *bocas* in Costa Rica, appetizers are served with drinks in most bars. Often the *bocas* are free, but even if they aren't, they're very inexpensive. Popular *bocas* include *gallos* (tortillas piled with meat, chicken, cheese, or beans), ceviche (a marinated seafood salad), tamales (stuffed cornmeal patties steamed inside banana leaves), *patacones* (fried green plantain chips), and fried yuca.

SANDWICHES & SNACKS   Ticos love to snack, and a large variety of tasty little sandwiches and snacks are available on the street, at snack bars, and in sodas. *Arreglados* are little meat-filled sandwiches, as are *tortas,* which are served on little rolls with a bit of salad tucked into them. Tacos, tamales, *gallos* (see above), and empanadas (turnovers) also are quite common.

TICO etiquette & CUSTOMS

In general, Costa Ricans are easygoing, friendly, and informal. That said, Ticos tend to be conservative and, in conversation, relatively formal. When addressing someone, they use the formal "usted" in most instances, reserving the familiar "vos" for close friends, family, and children or teenagers.

Upon greeting or saying goodbye, both sexes shake hands, although across genders, a light kiss on one cheek is common.

Proud of their country's neutrality and lack of armed forces, everyday Costa Ricans are uncomfortable with confrontation. What may seem like playful banter or justified outrage to a foreign tourist may be taken very badly by a Tico.

In some cases, especially in the service industry, a Tico may tell you what he or she thinks you want to hear, just to avoid a confrontation—even if he or she knows there's little chance of follow-through or ultimate customer satisfaction. I've also had, on more than one occasion, Ticos give me wrong directions, rather than telling me they didn't know the way.

The two words mentioned at the start of this chapter—"pura vida"—will go a long way to endearing you to most Ticos. In conversation, "pura vida" is used as a greeting, exclamation, adjective, and general space filler. Feel free to sprinkle a "pura vida" or two into your conversations with locals.

Tico men dress conservatively. It is very rare to see Costa Rican men wear short pants except at the beach. In most towns and cities, tourists will stand out when wearing short pants, sandals, and other typical vacation wear (although it is considered acceptable). Costa Rican women, on the other hand, especially young women, do tend to show some skin. Still, be respectful in your dress, especially if you plan on visiting churches, small towns, or local families.

Women, no matter how they dress, may find themselves on the receiving end of whistles, honks, hoots, hisses, and catcalls. For more information on this manifestation of Costa Rican machismo, see "Women Travelers" on p. 281.

Punctuality is not a Costa Rican strong suit. Ticos often show up anywhere from 15 minutes to an hour or more late to meetings and appointments—this is known as la hora tica, or Tico time. That said, buses and local airlines, tour operators, movie theaters, and most businesses do tend to run on a relatively timely schedule.

MEAT   Costa Rica is beef country, having converted much of its rainforest land to pastures for raising beef cattle. Consequently, beef is cheap and plentiful, although it might be a bit tougher—and cut and served thinner—than it is back home. One typical local dish is *olla de carne,* a bowl of beef broth with large chunks of meat, local tubers, and corn. Spit-roasted chicken is also very popular and is surprisingly tender; I much prefer it to most steaks. Lamb is very sparsely used in Costa Rican cooking, although finer restaurants often have a lamb dish or two on the menu.

SEAFOOD   Costa Rica has two coasts, and, as you'd expect, plenty of seafood is available everywhere in the country. *Corvina* (sea bass) is the most commonly served fish and is prepared innumerable ways, including as

A typical casado.

ceviche. (**Be careful:** In many cheaper restaurants, particularly in San José, shark meat is often sold as *corvina.*) You will likely also come across *pargo* (red snapper), *dorado* (mahimahi), and tuna on some menus, especially along the coasts. Although Costa Rica is a major exporter of shrimp and lobster, both are relatively expensive and in short supply here.

VEGETABLES　On the whole, you'll find vegetables surprisingly lacking in the meals you're served in Costa Rica—usually nothing more than a little pile of shredded cabbage topped with a slice or two of tomato. For a much more satisfying and filling salad, order *palmito* (hearts of palm salad). The heart (actually the stalk or trunk of these small palms) is first boiled and then sliced into disks and served with other fresh vegetables, and topped with dressing. If you want something more than this, you'll have to order a side dish such as *picadillo,* a stew or puree of vegetables with meat in it.

　Although *plátanos* (plantains) are technically considered a fruit, these giant relatives of bananas are really more like vegetables and require cooking before they can be eaten. Green plantains have a very starchy flavor and consistency, but they become as sweet as candy as they ripen. Fried *plátano* is one of my favorite dishes. Yuca (manioc root or cassava in English) is another starchy staple root vegetable in Costa Rica.

One more vegetable worth mentioning is the *pejibaye,* a form of palm fruit that looks like a miniature orange coconut. Boiled *pejibayes* are frequently sold from carts on the streets of San José. When cut in half, a *pejibaye* reveals a large seed surrounded by soft, fibrous flesh. You can eat it plain, but it's usually topped with mayonnaise.

FRUITS   Costa Rica has a wealth of delicious tropical fruits. The most common are mangoes (the season begins in May), papayas, pineapples, melons, and bananas. Other fruits include *marañón,* which is the fruit of the cashew tree and has orange or yellow glossy skin; *granadilla,* or *maracuyá* (passion fruit); *mamón chino,* which Asian travelers will immediately recognize as rambutan; and carambola (star fruit).

DESSERTS   *Queque seco,* literally "dry cake," is the same as pound cake. *Tres leches* cake (three milks sponge cake), on the other hand, is so moist that you almost need to eat it with a spoon. Flan is a typical custard dessert. It often comes as either *flan de caramelo* (caramel) or *flan de coco* (coconut). Numerous other sweets are available, many of which are made with condensed milk and raw sugar. *Cajetas* are popular handmade candies, made from sugar and various mixes of evaporated, condensed, and powdered milk. They're sold at most *pulperías* (general stores) and streetside food stands.

Beverages

Frescos, refrescos, and *jugos naturales* are my favorite drinks in Costa Rica. They are usually made with fresh fruit and milk or water. Among the more common fruits used are mangoes, papayas, blackberries, and pineapples. You'll also come across *maracuyá* (passion fruit) and carambola (star fruit). Some of the more unusual *frescos* are *horchata* (made with rice flour and a lot of cinnamon) and *chan* (made with the seed of a plant found mostly in

Chifrijo: King of Costa Rican *Bocas*

Without a doubt, Costa Rica's most popular and famous *boca* is a bowl of *chifrijo.* The name is a phonetic abbreviation of its two most important ingredients: *chicharrones* (fried pork bellies) and *frijoles* (beans). A proper bowl of *chifrijo* will also have rice, *pico de gallo* (a tomato-based salsa), a few slices of avocado, and be adorned with some tortilla chips for scooping up all that goodness.

The creation was the brainchild of Miguel Cordero, who began serving it in his family bar in Tibas in the early 1980s.

The dish quickly spread like wildfire and can now be found in restaurants and bars around the country. Cordero had the foresight to trademark his dish, and in 2014 began taking legal action against competitors for trademark infringement. Thanks to Cordero's trademark claims, restaurant and bar owners have had to scramble. In most cases, you can still usually find *chifrijo* on the menu, only it might be called *frichijo* or *hochifri,* or some other variation on the theme.

Guanacaste—definitely an acquired taste). The former is wonderful; the latter requires an open mind (it's reputed to be good for the digestive system). Order *un fresco con leche sin hielo* (a fresco with milk but without ice) if you're avoiding untreated water (see "Dietary Red Flags" on p. 272 for more on this).

If you're a coffee drinker, you might be disappointed here. Most of the best coffee has traditionally been targeted for export, and Ticos tend to prefer theirs weak and sweet. Better hotels and restaurants are starting to cater to gringo tastes, serving superior blends.

For something different for your morning beverage, ask for *agua dulce,* a warm drink made from melted sugar cane and served either with milk or lemon, or straight. Kids love it, too.

Costa Rica has seen an amazing boom in craft beers and places to drink them in the past few years. **Costa Rica's Craft Brewing Company** (www.beer.cr) has led the way. Its Libertas Golden Ale and Segua Red Ale are available at more and more restaurants and bars around the country, and can be purchased at larger supermarkets. These folks offer tours of their brewery and have a small brewpub at their main facility in Ciudad Colon, a western suburb of San Jose. Other brews and breweries to look for include Ambar by **Cervecera del Centro** (www.cerveceradelcentro.com); Majadera Pale Ale and Japiendin Tropical Ale from **Treinta y Cinco** (www.treintaycinco.com); and Witch's Rock Pale Ale and Gato Malo Dark Ale by the **Volcano Brewing Company** (www.volcanobrewingcompany.com) in Tamarindo.

SHOPPING

Costa Rica is not known for shopping. Most of what you'll find for sale is pretty run-of-the-mill, mass-produced souvenir fare. So scant are its handicrafts offerings that most tourist shops sell Guatemalan clothing, Panamanian appliquéd textiles, El Salvadoran painted-wood souvenirs, and Nicaraguan rocking chairs. Still, Costa Rica does have a few locally produced arts and handicrafts to look out for, and a couple of towns and villages with well-deserved reputations for their unique works.

Perhaps the most famous of all towns for shopping is **Sarchí** ★ (p. 98), a Central Valley town filled with handicrafts shops. Sarchí is best known as the

Artist's workshop in Sarchí.

citadel of the colorfully painted Costa Rican **oxcart,** reproductions of which are manufactured in various scaled-down sizes. A lot of furniture is also made in Sarchí.

Up in Guanacaste, the small town of **Guaitíl** is famous for its pottery (see "Pretty Pots," on p. 135). A host of small workshops, studios, and storefronts ring the town's central park (which is actually a soccer field). Many of the low-fired ceramic wares here carry ancient local indigenous motifs, while others get quirky modern treatments. You can find examples of this low-fired simple ceramic work in many gift shops around the country, and even at road-side stands all across Guanacaste.

You might also run across **carved masks** ★★★ made by the indigenous **Boruca** people of southern Costa Rica. The small Boruca villages where these masks are carved are off-the-beaten path, but you will find masks for sale at some of the better gift shops around the country. These full-size wood masks are distinctive, with animal-based or "devil" faces. They come in a variety of styles, both painted and unpainted, and run anywhere from $20 to $150, depending on the quality of workmanship. The Boruca aren't the only Costa Rican indigenous group or local artisans to make masks, and you'll likely see a wide range of masks and crafts works for sale around the country. *Tip:* Don't be fooled. You'll see scores of mass-produced wooden masks at souvenir and gift shops, but real Boruca masks are unique indigenous art works, and the better ones are signed by their carvers.

In addition to the masks, quite a bit of Costa Rican woodwork is for sale, but it's mainly mass-produced wooden bowls, napkin holders, placemats, and the like. A couple of notable exceptions include the work of Barry Biesanz, proprietor of **Biesanz Woodworks** ★★ (p. 88), whose excellent hardwood creations are sold at better gift shops around the country, and the unique, large-scale sculptures created and sold at the **Original Grand Gallery** (p. 172), in La Fortuna.

Coffee remains my favorite gift item. It's a great deal, it's readily available, and Costa Rican coffee is some of the best in the world. See "Joe to Go" on p. 86 for tips on buying coffee in Costa Rica.

A few other items worth keeping an eye out for include reproductions of **pre-Columbian gold jewelry** and **carved-stone figurines.** The former are available as either solid gold, silver, or gold-plated. The latter, although interesting, can be extremely heavy.

Buyer, Be Aware!

International laws prohibit trade in **endangered wildlife,** so don't buy any plants or animals, even if they're readily for sale. Do not buy any kind of sea-turtle products (including jewelry); wild birds; lizard, snake, or cat skins; corals; or orchids (except those grown commercially). No matter how unique, beautiful, insignificant, or inexpensive it might seem, your purchase will directly contribute to the further hunting of these species.

In addition, be careful when buying **wood products.** Costa Rica's rainforest hardwoods are a finite and rapidly disappearing resource. Try to buy sustainably harvested woods, if at all possible.

Contemporary and **classic Costa Rican art** is another great option, both for discerning collectors and those looking for a unique reminder of their time in the country. San José has the greatest number of galleries and shops, but you will find good, well-stocked galleries in some of the more booming tourist destinations, including Liberia, Manuel Antonio, Jacó, and Monteverde. Throughout the book, I list my favorite galleries, and you can check out "Art," earlier in this chapter, for a list of some of the country's more prominent artists.

Finally, one item that you'll see at gift shops around the country is **Cuban cigars.** Although these are still illegal to bring into the United States, they are perfectly legal and readily available in Costa Rica.

WHEN TO GO

Costa Rica's high season for tourism runs from late November to late April, which coincides almost perfectly with the chill of winter in the United States, Canada, and Great Britain, and includes Christmas, New Year's, Easter, and most school spring breaks. The high season is also the dry season. If you want some unadulterated time on a tropical beach and a little less rain during your rainforest experience, this is the time to come. During this period (and especially around the Christmas holiday), the tourism industry operates at full tilt—prices are higher, attractions are more crowded, and reservations need to be made in advance.

Local tourism operators often call the tropical rainy season (May through mid-November) the "green season." The adjective is appropriate. At this time of year, even brown and barren Guanacaste province becomes lush and verdant. I personally love traveling around Costa Rica during the rainy season (but then again, I'm not trying to flee cold snaps in the U.S.). It's easy to find or at least negotiate reduced rates, there are far fewer fellow travelers, and the rain is often limited to a few hours each afternoon (although you can occasionally get socked in for a week at a time). *A drawback:* Some of the country's rugged roads become downright impassable without four-wheel-drive during the rainy season.

Weather

Costa Rica is a tropical country and has distinct wet and dry seasons. However, some regions are rainy all year, and others are very dry and sunny for most of the year. Temperatures vary primarily with elevations, not with seasons: On the coasts, it's hot all year; in the mountains, it can be cool at night any time of year. Frost is common at the highest elevations (3,000–3,600m/9,840–11,810 ft.).

Average Daytime High Temperatures & Rainfall in San José

	JAN	FEB	MAR	APR	MAY	JUNE	JULY	AUG	SEPT	OCT	NOV	DEC
Temp (°F)	75	76	79	79	80	79	77	78	79	77	77	75
Temp (°C)	24	24	26	26	27	26	25	26	26	25	25	24
Days of rain	1.3	1.5	2.2	4.2	11.5	14.5	13.7	14.5	18.1	17.9	8.6	2.3

Generally, the **rainy season** (or "green season") is from May to mid-November. Costa Ricans call this wet time of year their winter. The **dry season,** considered summer by Costa Ricans, is from mid-November to April. In Guanacaste, the dry northwestern province, the dry season lasts several weeks longer than in other places. Even in the rainy season, days often start sunny, with rain falling in the afternoon and evening. On the Caribbean coast, especially south of Limón, you can count on rain year-round, although this area gets less rain in September and October than the rest of the country.

In general, the best time of year to visit weatherwise is in December and January, when everything is still green from the rains, but the sky is clear.

Holidays

Because Costa Rica is a Roman Catholic country, most of its holidays are church-related. The biggies are Christmas, New Year's, and Easter, which are all celebrated for several days. Keep in mind that Holy Week (Easter week) is the biggest holiday time in Costa Rica, and many families head for the beach. Also, there is no public transportation on Holy Thursday or Good Friday. Government offices and banks are closed on official holidays, transportation services are reduced, and stores and markets might also close.

Official holidays in Costa Rica are **January 1** (New Year's Day), **March 19** (St. Joseph's Day), Thursday and Friday of Holy Week, **April 11** (Juan Santamaría's Day), **May 1** (Labor Day), **June 29** (St. Peter and St. Paul Day), **July 25** (annexation of the province of Guanacaste), **August 2** (Virgen de Los Ángeles Day), **August 15** (Mother's Day), **September 15** (Independence Day), **October 12** (Discovery of America/Día de la Raza), **December 8** (Immaculate Conception of the Virgin Mary), **December 24** and **25** (Christmas Eve/Christmas Day), and **December 31** (New Year's Eve).

Calendar of Events

Some of the events listed here might be considered more of a happening than an event—there's not, for instance, a Virgen de Los Ángeles PR Committee that readily dispenses information. If you don't see a contact number listed, your best bet is to call the **Costa Rican Tourist Board (ICT)** at ℂ **866/COSTA-RICA** in the U.S. and Canada, or 2223-1733 in Costa Rica, or visit **www.visitcostarica.com.**

JANUARY

Copa del Café (Coffee Cup), San José. Matches for this international event on the junior tennis tour are held at the Costa Rica Country Club (www.copacafe.com; ℂ **2228-9333**). First week in January.

Fiestas of Palmares, Palmares. Perhaps the largest and best organized of the traditional fiestas, it includes bullfights, a horseback parade (*tope*), and many concerts, carnival rides, and food booths (www.fiestas-palmares.com). First 2 weeks in January.

MARCH

Día del Boyero (Oxcart Drivers' Day), San Antonio de Escazú. Colorfully painted oxcarts parade through this suburb of San José, and local priests bless the oxen. Second Sunday in March.

National Orchid Show, San José. Orchid growers throughout the world gather to show their wares, trade tales and secrets, and admire the hundreds of species on display. Contact the Costa Rican Tourist Board for location and dates. Mid-March.

APRIL

Holy Week. Religious processions are held in cities and towns throughout the country. Week before Easter.

Juan Santamaría Day, Alajuela. Costa Rica's national hero is honored with parades, concerts, and dances. April 11.

JULY

Fiesta of the Virgin of the Sea, Puntarenas. A regatta of boats carrying a statue of the patron saint of Puntarenas marks this festival. A similar event is held at Playa del Coco. Saturday closest to July 16.

Annexation of Guanacaste Day, Liberia. Tico-style bullfights, folk dancing, horseback parades, rodeos, concerts, and other events celebrate the day when this region became part of Costa Rica. July 25.

AUGUST

Fiesta de la Virgen de Los Angeles, Cartago. This is the annual pilgrimage day of the patron saint of Costa Rica. Many people walk the 24km (15 miles) from San José to the basilica in Cartago. August 2.

SEPTEMBER

Costa Rica's Independence Day, nationwide. One of the most distinctive aspects of this festival is the nighttime marching-band parades of children in their school uniforms, who play the national anthem on steel xylophones. September 15.

International Beach Clean-Up Day. This is a good excuse to chip in and help clean up the beleaguered shoreline of your favorite beach. Third Saturday in September.

OCTOBER

Limón Carnival/Día de la Raza, Limón. A smaller version of Mardi Gras, complete with floats and dancing in the streets, commemorates Columbus's discovery of Costa Rica. Week of October 12.

DECEMBER

El Tope and Carnival, San José. The streets of downtown belong to horses and their riders in a proud recognition of the country's important agricultural heritage. The next day, those same streets are taken over by carnival floats, marching bands, and street dancers. December 26 and 27.

Festejos Populares, San José. Bullfights, carnival rides, games of chance, and fast-food stands are set up at the fairgrounds in Zapote (www.festejospopulares.net). Last week of December.

COSTA RICA'S NATURAL WORLD

4

Costa Rica occupies a central spot in the isthmus that joins North and South America. For millennia, this land bridge served as a migratory thoroughfare and mating ground for species native to the once-separate continents. It was also where the Mesoamerican and Andean pre-Columbian indigenous cultures met.

In any one spot in Costa Rica, temperatures remain relatively constant year-round. However, they vary dramatically according to altitude, from tropically hot and steamy along the coasts to below freezing at the highest elevations. These variations in altitude, temperature, and precipitation have given rise to a wide range of ecosystems and habitats.

For its part, the wide variety of ecosystems and habitats has blessed the country with a unique biological bounty. More than 10,000 identified species of plants, 880 species of birds, 9,000 species of butterflies and moths, and 500 species of mammals, reptiles, and amphibians are found here.

Thankfully, for visitors and the local flora and fauna alike, nearly one-quarter of Costa Rica's entire landmass is protected either as part of a national park or private nature reserve. This chapter includes a rundown and description of the most important national parks and bioreserves in the country.

THE LAY OF THE LAND
Costa Rica's Ecosystems
RAINFORESTS
Costa Rica's **rainforests** are classic tropical jungles. Some receive more than 500cm (197 in.) of rainfall per year, and their climate is typically hot and humid, especially in the lowland rainforests. Trees grow tall and fast, fighting for sunlight in the upper reaches. In fact, life and foliage on the forest floor are surprisingly sparse. The action is typically 30m (98 ft.) up, in the canopy, where long vines

Smiling brown-throated, three-toed baby sloth in the mangrove.

stream down, lianas climb up, and bromeliads grow on the branches and trunks of towering hardwood trees.

Some of the more indicative rainforest tree species include the parasitic strangler fig and the towering ceiba, which can reach some 60m (197 ft.). Mammal species that call the Costa Rican rainforests home include the jaguar, three-toed sloth, all four native monkey species, and Baird's tapir, while some of the more prominent birds you might spot are the harpy eagle, scarlet macaw, and the chestnut-mandibled toucan.

You can find these lowland rainforests along the southern Pacific coast and Osa Peninsula, as well as along the Caribbean coast. **Corcovado, Cahuita,** and **Manuel Antonio** national parks, as well as the **Gandoca–Manzanillo Wildlife Refuge,** are fine examples of lowland rainforests. Examples of mid-elevation rainforests include the **Braulio Carrillo National Park,** the forests around **La Selva** and the **Puerto Viejo de Sarapiquí** region, and those around the **Arenal Volcano** and **Lake Arenal.**

TROPICAL DRY FORESTS

In a few protected areas of Guanacaste, you'll still find examples of the otherwise vanishing **tropical dry forest.** During the long and pronounced dry

IN SEARCH OF turtles

Few places in the world have as many sea-turtle nesting sites as Costa Rica. Along both coasts, five species come ashore at specific times of the year to dig nests in the sand and lay their eggs. Sea turtles are endangered throughout the world due to over-hunting, accidental deaths in fishing nets, development of beaches that once served as nesting areas, and the collection and sale (often illegally) of their eggs. International trade in sea-turtle products is already prohibited by most countries (including the U.S.), but sea-turtle numbers continue to dwindle.

The species of sea turtles that nest on Costa Rica's beaches are the **olive ridley** (known for mass egg-laying migrations, or *arribadas*), **leatherback, hawksbill, green,** and **Pacific green turtle.** Excursions to see nesting turtles have become common, and they are fascinating, but please make sure that you and/or your guide do not disturb the turtles. Any light source (other than red-tinted flashlights) can confuse female turtles and cause them to return to the sea without laying their eggs. In fact, as more development takes place on the Costa Rican coast, hotel lighting may cause the number of nesting turtles to drop. Luckily, many of the nesting beaches have been protected as national parks.

Here are the main places to see nesting sea turtles: **Santa Rosa National Park** (near Liberia, olive ridleys nest here July–Dec, and to a lesser extent Jan–June); **Las Baulas National Marine Park** (near Tamarindo, leatherbacks nest here early Oct through mid-Feb); **Ostional National Wildlife Refuge** (near Playa Nosara, olive ridleys nest here July–Dec, and to a lesser extent Jan–June); and **Tortuguero National Park** (on the northern Caribbean coast, green turtles nest here July through mid-Oct, with Aug–Sept the peak period; in lesser numbers, leatherback turtles nest here Feb–June, peaking Mar–Apr).

season (late Nov to late Apr), no rain relieves the unabated heat. In an effort to conserve much-needed water, the trees drop their leaves but bloom in a riot of color: Purple jacaranda, scarlet poró, and brilliant orange flame-of-the-forest are just a few examples. Then, during the rainy season, this deciduous forest is transformed into a lush and verdant landscape.

Other common dry forest trees include the guanacaste, with its broad, shade canopy, and the distinctive pochote, whose trunk is covered with thick, broad thorns.

Because the foliage is less dense than that found in cloud forests and rainforests, dry forests are excellent places to view a variety of wildlife. Howler monkeys are commonly seen in the trees, and coatimundis, pumas, and coyotes roam the ground. Costa Rica's remaining dry forests are most prominently found in **Santa Rosa, Guanacaste, Rincón de la Vieja,** and **Palo Verde** national parks.

CLOUD FORESTS

At higher altitudes, you'll find Costa Rica's famed **cloud forests.** Here the steady flow of moist air meets the mountains and creates a nearly constant

Green and black poison dart frog.

mist. Epiphytes—resourceful plants that live cooperatively on the branches and trunks of other trees—grow abundantly in the cloud forests, where they must extract moisture and nutrients from the air. Because cloud forests are found in generally steep, mountainous terrain, the canopy here is lower and less uniform than in lowland rainforests, providing better chances for viewing elusive fauna.

The **resplendent quetzal** is perhaps the most famous and sought-after denizen of Costa Rica's cloud forests, but you'll also find a broad and immense variety of flora and fauna, including a dozen or more hummingbird species, wild cats, monkeys, reptiles, and amphibians. **Orchids,** many of them epiphytic, thrive in cloud forests, as do mosses, ferns, and a host of other plants, many of which are cultivated and sold as common household plants throughout the rest of the world.

Costa Rica's most spectacular cloud forest is the **Monteverde Cloud Forest Biological Reserve,** but you can also explore Monteverde's neighbor, the **Santa Elena Cloud Forest Reserve,** or, closer to San José, the **Poás Volcano.**

MANGROVES & WETLANDS

Along the coasts, primarily where river mouths meet the ocean, you will find extensive **mangrove forests, wetlands,** and **swamps.** Mangroves, in

monkey BUSINESS

No trip to Costa Rica would be complete without at least one monkey sighting. Home to four distinct species of primates, Costa Rica offers the opportunity for one of the world's most gratifying wildlife-viewing experiences. Just listen for the deep guttural call of a howler or the rustling of leaves overhead—telltale signs monkeys are near.

Costa Rica's most commonly spotted monkey is the white-faced or **capuchin monkey** (*mono cara blanca* in Spanish), which you might recognize as the infamous culprit from the film *Outbreak* (though, in reality, they don't live in Africa). Capuchins are agile, medium-size monkeys that make good use of their long, prehensile tails. They inhabit a diverse collection of habitats, ranging from the high-altitude cloud forests of the central region to the lowland mangroves of the Osa Peninsula. It's almost impossible not to spot capuchins at Manuel Antonio, where they have become sadly dependent on feedings by tourists. Please do not feed wild monkeys (and try to keep your food away from them—they're notorious thieves), and boycott establishments that try to attract both monkeys and tourists with daily feedings.

Howler monkeys (*mono congo* in Spanish) are named for their distinct and eerie call. Large and mostly black, these monkeys can seem ferocious because of their physical appearance and deep, resonant howls that can carry for more than

a mile. Biologists believe that male howlers mark the bounds of their territories with these sounds. In the presence of humans, however, howlers are actually timid and tend to stay higher up in the canopy than their white-faced cousins. Howlers are easy to spot in the dry tropical forests of coastal Guanacaste and the Nicoya Peninsula.

More elusive are **spider monkeys** (*mono araña* in Spanish). These long, slender monkeys are dark brown to black and prefer the high canopies of primary rainforests. Spiders are very adept with their prehensile tails, but actually travel through the canopy with a hand-over-hand motion frequently imitated by their less graceful human cousins on playground monkey bars around the world. I've had my best luck spotting spider monkeys along the edges of Tortuguero's jungle canals.

The rarest and most endangered of Costa Rica's monkeys is the tiny **squirrel monkey** (*mono tití* in Spanish). These small brown monkeys have dark eyes surrounded by large white rings, white ears, white chests, and very long tails. In Costa Rica, squirrel monkeys can be found only at Manuel Antonio and the Osa Peninsula. These seemingly hyperactive monkeys are predominantly fruit eaters and often feed on banana and other fruit trees near hotels. Squirrel monkeys usually travel in large bands, so if you do see them, you'll likely see quite a few.

particular, are an immensely important ecological phenomenon. Around the intricate tangle of mangrove roots exists one of the most diverse and rich ecosystems on the planet. All sorts of fish and crustaceans live in the brackish tidal waters. Many larger saltwater and open-ocean fish species begin life in the nutrient rich and relatively safe and protected environment of a mangrove swamp.

Mangrove swamps and wetlands are havens for and home to scores of water birds: **cormorants, magnificent frigate birds, pelicans, kingfishers, egrets, ibises,** and **herons.** The larger birds tend to nest up high in the canopy, while the smaller ones nestle in the underbrush. And in the waters, **caimans** and **crocodiles** cruise the maze of rivers and unmarked canals.

Mangrove forests, swamps, and wetlands exist all along both of Costa Rica's coasts. Some of the prime areas that can be explored by tourists include the areas around the **Sierpe River** mouth and **Diquis Delta** near the **Golfo Dulce** in the southern zone, **Palo Verde National Park** and the **Tempisque River** basin in Guanacaste, and the **Gandoca–Manzanillo Wildlife Refuge** on the Caribbean coast.

PARAMO

At the highest reaches, the cloud forests give way to **elfin forests** and **páramos.** More commonly associated with the South American Andes, a páramo is a barren plain characterized by a variety of tundralike shrubs and grasses, with a scattering of twisted, windblown trees. Reptiles, rodents, and raptors are the most common residents here, and since the vegetation is so sparse, they're often easier to spot. **Mount Chirripó, Chirripó National Park,** and

The Irazú Volcano in Cordillera Central.

the **Cerro de la Muerte (Mountain of Death)** are the principal areas of páramo in Costa Rica.

VOLCANOES

Costa Rica is a land of high volcanic and seismic activity. The country has three major **volcanic mountain ranges,** and many of the volcanoes are still active, allowing visitors to experience the awe-inspiring sight of steaming **fumaroles,** sky-lighting **eruptions,** and intense **lava flows** during their stay. In ecological terms, cooled-off lava flows are fascinating laboratories, where you can watch pioneering lichen and mosses eventually give way to plants and shrubs, and eventually trees and forests.

The top spot to see steady volcanic activity, in the form of mud pots, fumaroles, and hot springs, is in the **Rincón de la Vieja National Park.** Closer to San José, the **Poás** and **Irazú volcanoes** are currently active, although relatively quiet. **Arenal Volcano** is the country's most famous and most visited volcano, and while there are still hot springs around its base, the volcano itself has been dormant for the past several years.

Costa Rica's Top National Parks & Bioreserves

Costa Rica has 34 national parks and reserves, protecting more than 12% of the country. Scores of other private reserves bring the total protected area up to some 23% of the national territory. Official state-protected parks range in size from the 212-hectare (524-acre) Guayabo National Monument to the 189,696-hectare (468,549-acre) La Amistad National Park. Many of these national parks are undeveloped tropical forests, with few services or facilities available for visitors. Others, however, offer easier access to their wealth of natural wonders.

Most of the national parks charge a $12 to $15 per-person per-day fee for any foreigner, although Chirripó National Park costs $18 per day and Isla del Coco is $50 per day. Costa Ricans and foreign residents continue to pay much, much less. At parks where camping is allowed, an additional charge of around $2 per person per day usually applies.

This section is not a complete listing of all of Costa Rica's national parks and protected areas, but rather a selective list of those parks that are of greatest interest and accessibility. They're popular, and they're also among the best. You'll find detailed information about food and lodging options near some of the individual parks in the regional chapters that follow. As you'll see from the descriptions, Costa Rica's national parks vary greatly in terms of attractions, facilities, and accessibility.

If you're looking for a camping adventure or an extended stay in one of the national parks, I recommend **Santa Rosa, Rincón de la Vieja, Chirripó,** or **Corcovado.** Any of the others are better suited for day trips or guided hikes, or in combination with your travels around the country.

For more information, call the national parks information line at ☎ **1192,** or the main office at ☎ **2283-8004.**

THE CENTRAL VALLEY

Irazú Volcano National Park ★ Irazú Volcano is the highest (3,432m/11,260 ft.) of Costa Rica's four active volcanoes and a popular day trip from San José. A paved road leads right up to the crater, and the lookout also has a view of both the Pacific and the Caribbean on a clear day. The volcano last erupted in 1963 on the same day U.S. President John F. Kennedy visited the country. There are picnic tables, restrooms, an information center, and a parking area here. **Location:** 55km (34 miles) east of San José.

Poás Volcano National Park ★★   Poás is the other active volcano close to San José. The main crater is more than 1.6km (1 mile) wide, and it is constantly active with fumaroles and hot geysers. I slightly prefer Poás to Irazú because Poás is surrounded by dense cloud forests and has some nice gentle trails to hike. Although the area around the volcano is lush, much of the growth is stunted due to the gases and acid rain. On January 8, 2009, a 6.1-magnitude earthquake struck Costa Rica, with its epicenter very close to Poás. The park was closed for several days, and an uptick in volcanic activity was noted. The park still sometimes closes when the gases get too feisty. There are picnic tables, restrooms, and an information center. **Location:** 37km (23 miles) northwest of San José.

GUANACASTE & THE NICOYA PENINSULA

Palo Verde National Park ★   A must for bird-watchers, Palo Verde National Park is one of Costa Rica's best-kept secrets. This part of the Tempisque River lowlands supports a population of more than 50,000 waterfowl and forest bird species. Various ecosystems here include mangroves, savanna brush lands, and evergreen forests. There are camping facilities, along with an information center and some rustic, dorm-style accommodations at the Organization for Tropical Studies (OTS) research station here. **Location:** 200km (124 miles) northwest of San José. Be warned that the park entrance is 28km (17 miles) off the highway down a very rugged dirt road; it's another 9km (5½ miles) to the OTS station and campsites. For more information, call the OTS (www.threepaths.co.cr; © **2524-0607**).

Rincón de la Vieja National Park ★★
This large tract of parkland experiences high volcanic activity, with numerous fumaroles and geysers, as well as hot springs, cold pools, and mud pots. You'll find excellent

hikes to the upper craters and to several waterfalls. You should hire a guide for any hot-spring or mud-bath expeditions; inexperienced visitors have been burned. Camping is permitted at two sites, each with an information center, a picnic area, and restrooms. **Location:** 266km (165 miles) northwest of San José.

Santa Rosa National Park ★   Occupying a large section of Costa Rica's northwestern Guanacaste province, Santa Rosa has the country's largest area of tropical dry forest, important turtle-nesting sites, and the historically significant La Casona monument. The beaches are almost always deserted and have basic camping facilities. While the waves make them quite popular with surfers, most arrive for the day, and often by boat. An information center, a picnic area, and restrooms are at the main campsite and entrance. Additional campsites are located on pristine and undeveloped beaches here. **Location:** 258km (160 miles) northwest of San José. For more information, you can call the park office at © **2666-5051**.

THE NORTHERN ZONE

Arenal National Park ★★   This park, created to protect the ecosystem that surrounds Arenal Volcano, has a couple of good trails and a prominent lookout point that is extremely close to the volcano. The main trail here will take you through a mix of transitional forest, rainforest, and open savanna, before an invigorating scramble over a massive rock field formed by a cooled-off lava flow. **Location:** 129km (80 miles) northwest of San José.

Caño Negro National Wildlife Refuge ★
A lowland swamp and drainage basin for several northern rivers, Caño Negro is excellent for bird-watching. A few basic *cabinas* and lodges are in this area, but the most popular way to visit is on a combined van and boat trip from the La Fortuna/Arenal area. **Location:** 20km (12 miles) south of Los Chiles, near the Nicaraguan border.

Monteverde Cloud Forest Biological Reserve ★★★   This private reserve might be the most famous patch of forest in Costa Rica. It covers some 10,520 hectares (26,000 acres) of primary forest, mostly mid-elevation cloud forest, with a rich variety of flora and fauna. Epiphytes thrive in the cool, misty climate. The most renowned resident is the spectacular resplendent quetzal. There is a well-maintained trail system, as well as some of the best-trained and most experienced guides in the country. Nearby, you can visit both the Santa Elena and Sendero Tranquilo reserves. **Location:** 167km (104 miles) northwest of San José.

CENTRAL PACIFIC COAST

Carara National Park ★★ Located just off the highway near the Pacific coast, on the road to Jacó, this is one of the best places in Costa Rica to see scarlet macaws. Several trails run through the park, including one that's wheelchair accessible. The park is comprised of various ecosystems, ranging from rainforests to transitional forests to mangroves. **Location:** 102km (63 miles) west of San José.

Manuel Antonio National Park ★★ Though relatively small, Manuel Antonio is the most popular national park and supports the largest number of hotels and resorts. This lowland rainforest is home to a healthy monkey population, including the endangered squirrel monkey. The park is best known for its splendid beaches. **Location:** 129km (80 miles) south of San José.

THE SOUTHERN ZONE

Corcovado National Park ★★★ The largest single block of virgin lowland rainforest in Central America, Corcovado National Park receives more than 500cm (200 in.) of rain per year. It's increasingly popular, but still very remote. (It has no roads; only dirt tracks lead into it.) Scarlet macaws live here, as do countless other Neotropical species, including two of the country's largest cats, the puma and the endangered jaguar. Camping facilities and trails are throughout the park. **Location:** 335km (208 miles) south of San José, on the Osa Peninsula.

THE CARIBBEAN COAST

Cahuita National Park ★★ A combination land and marine park, Cahuita National Park protects one of the few remaining living coral reefs in the country. The topography here is lush lowland tropical rainforest. Monkeys and numerous bird species are common. **Location:** On the Caribbean coast, 42km (26 miles) south of Limón.

Tortuguero National Park ★★ Tortuguero National Park has been called the Venice of Costa Rica due to its maze of jungle canals that meander through a dense lowland rainforest. Small boats, launches, and canoes carry visitors through these waterways, where caimans, manatees, and numerous bird and mammal species are common. The extremely endangered great green macaw lives here. Green sea turtles nest on the beaches every year between June and October. The park has a small but helpful information office and well-marked trails. **Location:** 258km (160 miles) northeast of San José.

COSTA RICAN WILDLIFE

For such a small country, Costa Rica is incredibly rich in biodiversity. With just .03% of the earth's landmass, the country is home to some 5% of its biodiversity. Whether you come to Costa Rica to check off 100 or more species on your lifetime list, or just to check out of the rat race for a week or so, you'll be surrounded by a rich and varied collection of flora and fauna.

In many instances, the prime viewing recommendations should be understood within the reality of actual wildlife-viewing. Most casual visitors and even many dedicated naturalists will never see a wild cat or kinkajou. However, anyone working with a good guide should be able to see a broad selection of Costa Rica's impressive flora and fauna.

Scores of good field guides are available; two of the best general guides are *The Field Guide to the Wildlife of Costa Rica* by Carrol Henderson, and *Costa Rica: Traveller's Wildlife Guides* by Les Beletsky. Bird-watchers will want to pick up one or both of the following two books: *A Guide to the Birds of Costa Rica* by F. Gary Stiles and Alexander Skutch, and *Birds of Costa Rica* by Richard Garrigues and Robert Dean. Other specialized guides to mammals, reptiles, insects, flora, and more are also available. Zona Tropical (www.zonatropical.net) is a Costa Rica–based publishing house that specializes in field guides and wildlife books.

Searching for Wildlife

Animals in the forests are predominantly nocturnal. When they are active in the daytime, they are usually elusive and on the watch for predators. Birds are easier to spot in clearings or secondary forests than they are in primary forests. Unless you have lots of experience in the tropics, your best hope for enjoying a walk through the jungle lies in employing a trained and knowledgeable guide. (By the way, if it's been raining a lot and the trails are muddy, a good pair of rubber boots comes in handy. These are usually provided by the lodges or at the sites, where necessary.)

Here are a few helpful hints:

○ **Listen.** Pay attention to rustling in the leaves; whether it's monkeys up above or racoon-like *pizotes* on the ground, you're most likely to hear an animal before seeing one.

○ **Keep quiet.** Noise will scare off animals and prevent you from hearing their movements and calls.

○ **Don't try too hard.** Soften your focus and allow your peripheral vision to take over. This way you can catch glimpses of motion and then focus in on the animal you're observing.

○ **Bring binoculars.** It's also a good idea to practice a little first to get the hang of them. It would be a shame to be fiddling around and staring into space while everyone else in your group oohs and aahs over a quetzal.

○ **Dress appropriately.** You'll have a hard time focusing your binoculars if you're busy swatting mosquitoes. Light, long pants and long-sleeved shirts are your best bet. Comfortable hiking boots are a real boon, except where heavy rubber boots are necessary. Avoid loud colors; the better you blend in with your surroundings, the better your chances are of spotting wildlife.

○ **Be timely.** Your best shots at seeing forest fauna are in the very early morning and late afternoon hours.

○ **Read up.** Familiarize yourself with what you're most likely to see. Most nature lodges and hotels have a copy of a few wildlife field guides, although it's always best to have your own. A good all-around book to use is Carrol Henderson's *The Field Guide to the Wildlife of Costa Rica*.

TIPS ON HEALTH, SAFETY & ETIQUETTE IN THE WILDERNESS

Although most tours and activities are safe, risks are involved in any adventure activity. Know and respect your own physical limits before undertaking any strenuous activity. Be prepared for extremes in temperature and rainfall and for wide fluctuations in weather. A sunny morning hike can quickly become a cold and wet ordeal, so it's a good idea to carry along some form of rain gear when hiking in the rainforest, or to have a dry change of clothing waiting at the end of the trail. Bring along plenty of sunscreen when you're not going to be protected by the forest canopy.

If you do any backcountry packing or camping, remember that it really is a jungle out there. Don't go poking under rocks or fallen branches. Snakebites are very rare, but don't do anything to increase the odds. If you encounter a snake, stay calm, don't make any sudden movements, and do not try to handle it. Also avoid swimming in major rivers unless a guide or local operator can vouch for their safety. Although white-water sections and stretches in mountainous areas are generally safe, most mangrove canals and river mouths in Costa Rica support healthy crocodile and caiman populations.

Bugs and bug bites will probably be your greatest health concern in the Costa Rican wilderness, and even they aren't as big of a problem as you might expect. Mostly, bugs are an inconvenience, although mosquitoes can carry malaria or dengue. A strong repellent and proper clothing minimize both the danger and the inconvenience; you might also want to bring along some cortisone or Benadryl cream to soothe itching. ***And remember:*** Whenever you enter and enjoy nature, you should tread lightly and try not to disturb the natural environment. The popular slogan well known to most campers certainly applies here: "Leave nothing but footprints; take nothing but memories." If you must take home a souvenir, take photos. Do not cut or uproot plants or flowers. Pack out everything you pack in, and please do not litter.

RESPONSIBLE TOURISM

Costa Rica is one of the planet's prime ecotourism destinations. Many of the hotels, isolated nature lodges, and tour operators around the country are pioneers and dedicated professionals in the sustainable tourism field. Many other hotels, lodges, and tour operators are honestly and earnestly jumping on the bandwagon and improving their practices, while still others are simply "green-washing," using the terms "eco," "green," and "sustainable" in their promo materials, but doing little real good in their daily operations.

In 2014, Costa Rica was ranked 54th globally in the Environmental Performance Index (EPI; http://epi.yale.edu). This was a huge drop from just 2 years earlier, when it was ranked 5th. Despite its reputation, the substantial amount of good work being done, and ongoing advances being made in the field, Costa Rica is by no means an ecological paradise free from environmental and social threats. Untreated sewage is dumped into rivers, bays, oceans, and watersheds at an alarming rate. Child labor and sexual exploitation are rampant, and certain sectors of the tourism trade only make these matters worse.

Over the last decade or so, however, Costa Rica has taken great strides toward protecting its rich biodiversity. Thirty years ago, it was difficult to find a protected area anywhere, but now more than 11% of the country is protected within the national park system. Another 10% to 15% of the land enjoys moderately effective preservation as part of private and public reserves, indigenous reserves, and wildlife refuges and corridors. Still, Costa Rica's precious tropical hardwoods continue to be harvested at an alarming rate, often illegally, while other primary forests are clear-cut for short-term agricultural gain. Many experts predict Costa Rica's unprotected forests could be gone within the early part of this century.

While you can find hotels and tour operators using comprehensive sustainable practices all across Costa Rica—even in the San José metropolitan area—a few prime destinations are particular hot spots for sustainable tourism practices. Of note are the remote and wild Osa Peninsula and Golfo Dulce area of southern Costa Rica; the rural northern zone that includes both Monteverde and the Arenal Volcano and Lake Arenal attractions; and the underdeveloped Caribbean coast, with the rainforest canals of Tortuguero, Cahuita National Park, and the Manzanillo-Gandoca Wildlife Refuge.

In addition to focusing on wildlife-viewing and adventure activities, ecolodges in these areas tend to be smaller, often lacking televisions, air-conditioning, and other typical luxury amenities. The more remote lodges usually depend largely or entirely on small solar and hydro plants for their power consumption. That said, some of these hotels and lodges provide levels of comfort and service that are quite luxurious.

In Costa Rica, the government-run tourism institute (ICT) provides a sustainability rating for a host of hotels and tour agencies under its **Certificate of Sustainable Tourism Program (CST).** You can look up the ratings at www.turismo-sostenible.co.cr.

Bear in mind that this program is relatively new and the list is far from comprehensive. Many hotels and tour operators in the country haven't completed the extensive review and rating process. Moreover, die-hard ecologists find some of these listings and the criteria used somewhat suspect. Still, this list and the rating system are a good start, and they're improving and evolving constantly.

A parallel program, **"The Blue Flag,"** is used to rate specific beaches and communities in terms of their environmental condition and practices. The Blue Flags are reviewed and handed out annually. Find current listings of Blue Flag–approved beaches and communities at www.visitcostarica.com.

SAN JOSÉ

Founded in 1737, San José was a forgotten backwater of the Spanish empire until the late-19th century, when it boomed with the coffee business. Sure, the city has its issues: gridlock traffic, poorly maintained sidewalks, and street crime. But, at 1,125m (3,690 ft.) above sea level, San José enjoys springlike temperatures year-round, and its location in the Central Valley—the lush Talamanca Mountains to the south, and the Poás, Barva, and Irazú volcanoes to the north—makes it both stunning and convenient as a base of exploration.

ESSENTIALS

Arriving

BY PLANE

Juan Santamaría International Airport (www.fly2sanjose.com; *℃* **2437-2626** for 24-hr. airport information; airport code SJO) is near the city of Alajuela, about 20 minutes from downtown San José. A taxi into town costs between C14,000 and C28,000, and a bus is only C585. The Alajuela–San José buses run frequently and will drop you off anywhere along Paseo Colón or at a station near the Parque de la Merced (downtown, btw. calles 12 and 14 and avs. 2 and 4). There are two separate lines: **Tuasa** (*℃* **2442-6900**) buses are red; **Station Wagon** (*℃* **2442-3226**) buses are beige/yellow. At the airport, the bus stop is directly in front of the main terminal, beyond the parking structure. Be sure to ask whether the bus is going to San José, or you'll end up in Alajuela. If you have a lot of luggage, you probably should take a cab.

Most car-rental agencies have desks and offices at the airport, although if you're planning to spend a few days in San José itself, I personally think a car is a liability. (If you're heading off immediately to the beach, though, it's much easier to pick up your car here than at a downtown office.)

Tip: Chaos and confusion greet arriving passengers as they step out of the terminal. You must abandon your luggage carts just before exiting the building and then run a gauntlet of aggressive taxi drivers, shuttle drivers waving signs, and people offering to

San José

ATTRACTIONS ●

Mercado Central **8**

Museo de Arte Costarricense
(Costa Rican Art Museum) **2**

Museo de Jade Marco Fidel Tristán
(Jade Museum) **20**

Museo de Los Niños (Children's Museum) **9**

Museo Nacional de Costa Rica
(National Museum) **19**

Museos del Banco Central de Costa Rica
(Gold Museum) **14**

Parque La Sabana **2**

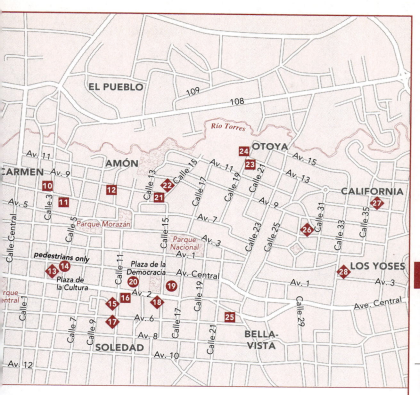

HOTELS ■

Aldea Hostel **6**
Costa Rica Backpackers **25**
Hostel Pangea **10**
Hotel Aranjuez **24**
Hotel Cacts **7**
Hotel Colonial **16**
Hotel Don Carlos **12**
Hotel Grano de Oro **5**
Hotel Rincón de San José **21**
Hotel Santo Tomás **11**
Kap's Place **23**
Tryp Sabana by Windham **4**

RESTAURANTS ◆

Alma de Café **13**
Café Mundo **22**
Grano de Oro Restaurant **5**
Kalú **26**
La Esquina de Buenos Aires **15**
Mantras Veggie Café and Tea House **27**
Olio **28**
Park Café **1**
Restaurante Nuestra Tierra **18**
Soda Tapia **3**
Tin Jo **17**

Inset map: NICARAGUA / CARIBBEAN SEA / SAN JOSÉ / The Central Valley / PACIFIC OCEAN / PANAMA

Volcán Platanar

Juan Castr Blanco Nat'l Park

Los Angeles Cloud Forest Reserve

Tilarán Range

15

Zarcero

Naranjo

Sarchí 1

San Ramón

Grecia

Palmares

Pan-American Highw

1

← To Puntarenas

La Garita

Atenas

11

11

27

Caldera

27

Orotiná

Gulf of Nicoya

Carara Nat'l Park

To Jacó

Ark Herb Farm **6**
Basílica de Nuestra Señora de los Angeles **12**
Café Britt Farm **7**
Chaverri Oxcart Factory **1**
Doka Estate **4**
Else Kientzler Botanical Garden **1**
INBio Park **8**

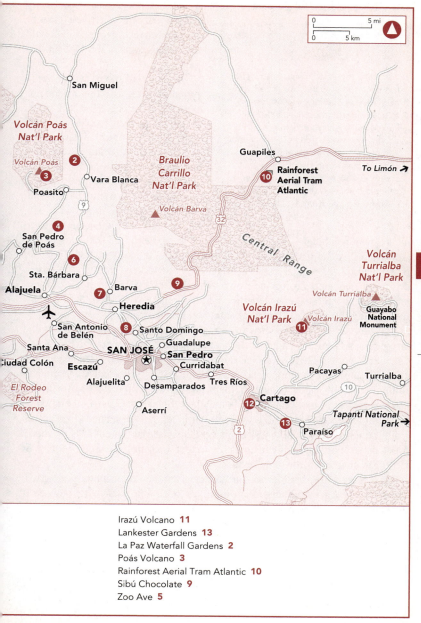

0   5 mi
0   5 km

San Miguel

Volcán Poás Nat'l Park

Volcán Poás   2

3   Poasito

Vara Blanca

Braulio Carrillo Nat'l Park

Guapiles

10   **Rainforest Aerial Tram Atlantic**

To Limón ↗

Volcán Barva

9

32

4

San Pedro de Poás

6

Sta. Bárbara

Central Range

Volcán Turrialba Nat'l Park

Volcán Turrialba

Alajuela

7   Barva

9

Heredia

8   **Santo Domingo**

Guayabo National Monument

Volcán Irazú Nat'l Park

Volcán Irazú

11

✈

San Antonio de Belén

Santa Ana

SAN JOSÉ

Guadalupe

San Pedro

Ciudad Colón   **Escazú**

Curridabat

Pacayas

Turrialba

Alajuelita

Desamparados

Tres Ríos

10

El Rodeo Forest Reserve

Aserrí

12   **Cartago**

13   **Paraíso**

Tapantí National Park →

2

5

SAN JOSÉ | Essentials

Irazú Volcano **11**
Lankester Gardens **13**
La Paz Waterfall Gardens **2**
Poás Volcano **3**
Rainforest Aerial Tram Atlantic **10**
Sibú Chocolate **9**
Zoo Ave **5**

carry your bags. Note that often there's really nowhere for the latter to have to carry your bags, because the line of waiting taxis and shuttles is just steps away. Keep a very watchful eye on your bags: Thieves have historically preyed on newly arrived passengers and their luggage. You should tip porters about C200 to C300 per bag.

In terms of taxis, you should probably stick with the official airport taxi service, **Taxis Unidos Aeropuerto** (www.taxiaeropuerto. com; ✆ **2221-6865**), which operates a fleet of orange vans and sedans. These folks have a kiosk in the no man's land just outside the exit door for arriving passengers. Here they will assign you a cab. These taxis use meters, and fares to most downtown hotels should run between C13,500 and C25,000. Despite the fact that Taxis Unidos has an official monopoly at the airport, you'll usually find a handful of regular cabs (in traditional red sedans) and "pirate" cabs, driven by freelancers using their own vehicles. You could use either of these latter options ("pirate" cabs tend to charge a dollar or two less), but I recommend using the official service for safety and standardized prices.

You have several options for **exchanging money** when you arrive at the airport. An ATM in the baggage claim area is connected to both the PLUS and Cirrus networks. There's also a **Global Exchange** (www.globalexchange. co.cr; ✆ **2431-0686**) money exchange booth just as you clear Customs and Immigration. It's open whenever there are arriving flights; however, these folks exchange at more than 10% below the official rate. There's a branch of the **Banco de San José** inside the main terminal, on the second floor across from the airline check-in counters, as well as a couple more ATMs up there. Most taxis and all rental-car agencies accept U.S. dollars. See "Money & Costs" in chapter 11 for more details.

Tip: There's no pressing need to exchange money the minute you arrive. Taxis Unidos accepts dollars. Wait until you settle into your hotel and see if the hotel will give you a good rate of exchange, or use one of the many downtown banks or ATMs.

BY BUS

If you're coming to San José by bus, where you disembark depends on where you're coming from. The different bus companies have their offices—and, thus, their drop-off points—all over downtown San José. When you buy your ticket, ask where you'll be let off. Buses arriving from Panama pass first through Cartago and San Pedro before letting passengers off in downtown San José; buses arriving from Nicaragua generally enter the city on the west end of town, on Paseo Colón. If you're staying here, you can ask to be let off before the final stop.

Visitor Information

The **Costa Rican National Tourism Chamber** (**CANATUR;** www.canatur. org; © **2440-1676**) has a desk at the Juan Santamaría International Airport, the baggage claims area, just before Customs. You can pick up maps and browse brochures, and they might even lend you a phone to make or confirm a reservation. It is usually open for all arriving flights.

City Layout

Downtown San José is laid out on a grid. *Avenidas* (avenues) run east and west, while *calles* (streets) run north and south. The center of the city is at **Avenida Central** and **Calle Central.** To the north of Avenida Central, the avenidas have odd numbers beginning with Avenida 1; to the south, they have even numbers beginning with Avenida 2. Likewise, calles to the east of Calle Central have odd numbers, and those to the west have even numbers. The main downtown artery is **Avenida 2,** which merges with Avenida Central on

SEARCHING FOR addresses

This is one of the most confusing aspects of visiting Costa Rica, in general, and San José, in particular. Although downtown San José often has street addresses and building numbers for locations, they are almost never used. Addresses are given as a set of coordinates such as "Calle 3 between avenidas Central and 1." It's then up to you to locate the building within that block, keeping in mind that the building could be on either side of the street. Many addresses include additional information, such as the number of meters from a specified intersection or some other well-known landmark. (These "meter measurements" are not precise but are a good way to give directions to a taxi driver. In basic terms, 100m = 1 block, 200m = 2 blocks, and so on.) These landmarks are what become truly confusing for visitors to the city because they are often simply restaurants, bars, and shops that would be familiar only to locals.

Things get even more confusing when the landmark in question no longer exists. The classic example of this is "the Coca-Cola," one of the most common landmarks used in addresses in the blocks surrounding San José's main market. The trouble is, the Coca-Cola bottling plant that it refers to is no longer there; the edifice is long gone, and one of the principal downtown bus depots stands in its place. Old habits die hard, though, and the address description remains. You might also try to find someplace near the *antiguo higuerón* (old fig tree) in San Pedro. This tree was felled over a decade ago. In outlying neighborhoods, addresses can become long directions, such as "50m (½ block) south of the old church, then 100m (1 block) east, then 20m (two buildings) south."

either side of downtown. West of downtown, Avenida Central becomes **Paseo Colón,** which ends at Parque La Sabana and feeds into the highway to Alajuela, the airport, Guanacaste, and the Pacific coast. East of downtown, Avenida Central leads to San Pedro and then to Cartago and the Interamerican Highway heading south. **Calle 3** takes you out of town to the north, onto the Guápiles Highway that leads to the Caribbean coast.

The Neighborhoods in Brief

San José is divided into dozens of neighborhoods, known as *barrios*. Most of the listings in this chapter fall within the main downtown area, but there are a few outlying neighborhoods you'll need to know about. In addition, the nearby suburbs of Escazú and Santa Ana are so close that they could almost be considered part of San José.

Downtown In San José's busy downtown, you'll find most of the city's museums, as well as a handful of small urban parks and open-air plazas, and the city's main cathedral. Many tour companies, restaurants, and hotels are located here. Unfortunately, traffic noise and exhaust fumes make this one of the least pleasant parts of the city. Streets and avenues are usually crowded with pedestrians and vehicular traffic, and street crime is most rampant here. Still, the sections of Avenida Central between calles 6 and 7, as well as Avenida 4 between calles 9 and 14, have been converted into pedestrian malls, greatly improving things on these stretches.

Barrio Amón/Barrio Otoya These two picturesque neighborhoods, just north and east of downtown, are the site of the greatest concentration of historic buildings in San José. Some of these have been renovated and turned into boutique hotels and atmospheric restaurants. If you're looking for character and don't mind the noise and exhaust fumes from passing cars and buses, this neighborhood makes a good base for exploring the city.

La Sabana/Paseo Colón Paseo Colón, a wide boulevard west of downtown, is an extension of Avenida Central and ends at Parque La Sabana. It has several good, small hotels and numerous restaurants. This is also where several of the city's car-rental agencies have their in-town offices. Once the site of the city's main airport, Parque La Sabana (La Sabana Park) is San José's largest public

park, with ample green areas, recreation facilities, the National Stadium, and the Museo de Arte Costarricense (Costa Rican Art Museum).

San Pedro/Los Yoses Located east of downtown San José, Los Yoses is an upper-middle-class neighborhood that is home to many diplomatic missions and embassies. San Pedro is a little farther east and is the site of the University of Costa Rica. Numerous college-type bars and restaurants are all around the edge of the campus, while more upscale and refined restaurants and boutique hotels can be found in the residential sections of both neighborhoods.

Escazú/Santa Ana Located in the hills west of San José, Escazú and Santa Ana are fast-growing suburbs. Although the area is only 15 minutes from San José by car, it feels much farther away because of its relaxed and suburban atmosphere. This area also has a large expat community with many bed-and-breakfast establishments and several of the city's restaurants.

Heredia/Alajuela/Airport Area Heredia and Alajuela are two colonial-era cities that lie closer to the airport than San José. Alajuela is closest to the airport; Heredia is about midway between Alajuela and the capital. For more information on Heredia, see "Day Trips from San José" on p. 93. Several quite unique, high-end boutique hotels are in this area, and several large hotels and chain hotels are located on, or just off, the Interamerican Highway close to the airport.

GETTING AROUND

By Bus

Bus transportation around San José is cheap—the fare is usually somewhere around C195 to C475—although the Alajuela/San José buses that run in from the airport cost C555. The most important buses are those running east along Avenida 2 and west along Avenida 3. The **Sabana/Cementerio** bus runs from Parque La Sabana to downtown and is one of the most convenient buses to use. You'll find a bus stop for the outbound Sabana/Cementerio bus near the main post office on Avenida 3 near the corner of Calle 2, and another one on Calle 11 between avenidas Central and 1. This bus also has stops all along Avenida 2. **San Pedro** buses leave from the end of the pedestrian walk on Avenida Central between calles 9 and 11, and take you out of downtown heading east.

You pay as you board the bus. The city's bus drivers can make change, although they don't like to receive large bills. Be especially mindful of your wallet, purse, or other valuables because pickpockets often work the crowded buses.

By Taxi

Although taxis in San José have meters (*marías*), the drivers sometimes refuse to use them, particularly with foreigners, so you'll occasionally have to negotiate the price. Always try to get them to use the meter first (say, *"ponga la maría, por favor"*). The official rate at press time is C640 per kilometer (½-mile). Wait time is charged at C3,650 per hour, and is prorated for smaller increments.

Depending on your location, the time of day, and the weather (rain places taxis at a premium), it's relatively easy to hail a cab downtown. You'll always find taxis in front of the Teatro Nacional (albeit at high prices) and around the Parque Central at Avenida Central and Calle Central. Taxis in front of hotels and the El Pueblo tourist complex usually charge more than others, although this is technically illegal. Most hotels will gladly call you a cab. You can also get a cab by calling **Coopetaxi** (✆ 2235-9966), **Coopeirazu** (✆ 2254-3211), **Coopetico** (✆ 2224-7979), or **Coopeguaria** (✆ 2226-1366). **Cinco Estrellas Taxi** (✆ 2228-3159) is based in Escazú but services the entire metropolitan area and airport, and claims to always have an English-speaking operator on call.

On Foot

Downtown San José is very compact. Nearly every place you might want to go is within a 15×4-block area. Because of traffic congestion, you'll often find it faster to walk than to take a bus or taxi. Be careful when walking the streets any time of day or night. Flashy jewelry, loosely held handbags or backpacks, and expensive camera equipment tend to attract thieves. **Avenida Central** is a pedestrian-only street from calles 6 to 7, and has been redone with interesting paving stones and the occasional fountain in an attempt to create a comfortable pedestrian mall. A similar pedestrian-only walkway runs along **Avenida 4,** between calles 9 and 14.

By Train

San José has very sporadic and minimal urban commuter train service, and it is geared almost exclusively to commuters. There are three major lines. One line connecting the western neighborhood of Pavas with the eastern suburb of San Pedro passes right through the downtown, with prominent stops at, or near, the U.S. Embassy, Parque La Sabana, the downtown court area, and the Universidad de Costa Rica (University of Costa Rica) and Universidad Latina (Latin University). This train runs commuter hours roughly every hour from 5 to 8:30am and 4 to 7:30pm.

Another line runs between downtown San José and Heredia. This train runs roughly every 30 minutes from 5:30 to 8am, and 3:30 to 7:30pm.

A third line runs between downtown San Jose and Cartago. This train runs roughly every 30 minutes from 6:30 to 8am, and 3:30 to 7:30pm. This later route is potentially useful for tourists, but again, the train is predominantly for local commuters, and not geared toward tourists. You cannot purchase tickets in advance, and trains often fill up, leaving you waiting 30 minutes or more for the next train.

Fares range from C420 to C550, depending on the length of your ride.

By Car

It will cost you between $45 and $150 per day to rent a car in Costa Rica (the higher prices are for 4WD vehicles). Many car-rental agencies have offices at the airport. If not, they will usually either pick you up or deliver the car to any San José hotel. If you decide to pick up your rental car in downtown San José, be prepared for some very congested streets.

The following companies have desks at Juan Santamaría International Airport, as well as offices downtown: **Adobe Rent A Car** (www.adobecar.com; ✆ **2542-4800**); **Avis** (www.avis.com; ✆ **800/633-3469** in the U.S. and 800/879-2847 in Canada, or 2293-2222 central reservation number in Costa Rica); **Budget** (www.budget.com; ✆ **800/472-3325** in the U.S. and Canada, or 2255-4240 in San José); **Dollar** (www.dollar.com; ✆ **800/800-6000** in the U.S. and Canada, or 2257-1585 in San José); **Hertz** (www.hertz.com; ✆ **800/654-3131** in the U.S. and Canada, or 2221-1818 in San José); **National Car Rental** (www.nationalcar.com; ✆ **877/222-9058** in the U.S. and Canada, 2221-4700 in San José); and **Payless Rent A Car** (www.paylesscar.com; ✆ **800/729-5377** in the U.S. and Canada, or 2432-4747 in Costa Rica).

Dozens of other smaller, local car-rental agencies are in San José, and most will arrange for airport or hotel pickup or delivery. Some of the more dependable local agencies are **Hola! Rent A Car** (www.hola.net; ✆ **2520-0100**); **Toyota Rent A Car** (www.toyotarent.com; ✆ **2256-5713**); and **Vamos Rent**

A Car ★★ (www.vamosrentacar.com; ℂ **800/950-8426** in the U.S. and Canada, or 2432-5258 in Costa Rica). Vamos gets especially high marks for customer service and transparency.

[FastFACTS] SAN JOSÉ

ATMs/Banks You'll find an extensive network of banks and ATMs around San José. Banks are usually open Monday through Friday from 9am to 4pm, although many have begun to offer extended hours. Due to crime directed at folks just as they are withdrawing cash from an ATM, some of the banks disable their ATM networks at night.

Dentists Call your embassy (p. 273), which will have a list of recommended dentists. Because treatments are so inexpensive in Costa Rica, dental tourism has become a popular option for people needing extensive work (p. 294).

Doctors Contact your embassy for information on doctors in San José, or see "Hospitals," below.

Drugstores San José has countless pharmacies and drugstores. Many of them deliver at little or no extra cost. The pharmacy at the **Hospital Clínica Bíblica,** Avenida 14 between calles Central and 1 (ℂ **2522-1000**), is open daily 24 hours, as is the **Hospital CIMA** pharmacy (ℂ **2208-1080**) in Escazú. **Farmacia Fischel** (www.fischel.co.cr; ℂ **800/347-2435** toll-free in Costa Rica) has scores of branches around the metropolitan area.

Embassies & Consulates See chapter 11.

Emergencies In case of any emergency, dial ℂ **911** (which should have an English-speaking operator); for an ambulance, call ℂ **1028;** and to report a fire, call ℂ **1118.**

Hospitals Clínica Bíblica, Avenida 14 between calles Central and 1 (www.clinicabiblica.com; ℂ **2522-1000**), is conveniently close to downtown and has several English-speaking doctors. The **Hospital CIMA** (www. hospitalcima.com; ℂ **2208-1000**), located in Escazú on the Próspero Fernández Highway, which connects San José and the western suburb of Santa Ana, has the most modern facilities in the country.

Internet Access Internet cafes are all over San José. Rates run between C400 and C3,000 per hour. Many hotels have their own Internet cafe or allow guests to send and receive e-mail. And many have added wireless access, either for free or a small charge.

Police Dial ℂ **911** or 2295-3272 for the police. They should have someone available who speaks English.

Post Office The main post office (*correo*) is on

Calle 2 between avenidas 1 and 3 (www.correos.go.cr; ℂ **2223-9766**). See "Mail" on p. 274 for more information.

Restrooms Public restrooms are rare to nonexistent, but most big hotels and public restaurants will let you use their restrooms. Downtown, you can find public restrooms at the entrance to the Museos del Banco Central de Costa Rica (p. 81).

Safety Pickpockets and purse snatchers are rife in San José, especially on public buses, in the markets, on crowded sidewalks, near hospitals, and lurking outside bank offices and ATMs. Leave most of your money and other valuables in your hotel safe, and carry only as much as you really need when you go out. If you do carry anything valuable, keep it in a money belt or special passport bag around your neck. Day packs are a prime target of brazen pickpockets. One common scam involves someone dousing you or your pack with mustard or ice cream. Another scamster (or two) will then quickly come to your aid—they are usually much more interested in cleaning you out than cleaning you up.

Stay away from the red-light district northwest of

the Central Market. Also be advised that the Parque Nacional is not a safe place for a late-night stroll. Other precautions include walking around corner vendors, not between the vendor and the building. The tight space between the vendor and the building is a favorite spot for pickpockets. Never park a car on the street, and never leave anything of value in a car, even if it's in a guarded parking lot. Don't even leave your car unattended by the curb in front of a hotel while you dash in to check on your reservation. With these precautions in mind, you should have a safe visit to San José. Also, see "Safety" in chapter 11.

WHERE TO STAY

San José offers a wide range of hotel choices, from plush boutique hotels to budget pensions and backpacker hangouts. Many downtown hotels and small inns are housed in beautifully converted and restored old mansions. The vast majority of accommodations—and the best deals—are in the moderate price range, where you can find everything from elegant little inns to contemporary business-class chains. Staying in San José puts you in the center of the action and close to all of the city's museums, restaurants, and nightlife venues. However, it also exposes you to many urban pitfalls, including noise, traffic, pollution, and street crime.

The prices quoted here are for hotels' rack rates, the maximum that they charge; it is not always necessary, however, to pay that rate. You'll often find discounts of up to 20% for rooms when booking directly, or through websites such as Booking.com, Priceline.com, or Kayak.com. *Note:* Quoted discount rates often do not include breakfast, local taxes, or other applicable hotel fees.

Downtown San José/Barrio Amón

The urban center of San José is the city's heart and soul, with a wide range of hotels and restaurants and easy access to museums and attractions. It also has several popular public parks and plazas, and the atmospheric Barrio Amón, a charming neighborhood that's home to the city's greatest concentration of colonial-era architecture. The neighborhood's biggest drawbacks are the street noise, bus fumes, gridlock traffic, and petty crime.

INEXPENSIVE

In addition to the hotels listed below, the **Hotel Colonial ★**, Calle 11, between avenidas 4 and 6 (www.hotelcolonialcr.com; ✆ **2223-0109**), and **Hotel Rincón de San José ★** (www.hotelrincondesanjose.com; ✆ **2221-9702**), on the corner of Avenida 9 and Calle 15, are solid boutique options.

For those on an even tighter budget, **Kap's Place** (www.kapsplace.com; ✆ **2221-1169**), across from the Hotel Aranjuez on Calle 19 between avenidas 11 and 13, is another good choice, while real budget hounds might want to try **Hostel Pangea ★** (www.hostelpangea.com; ✆ **2221-1992**), on Avenida 7 and Calle 3, or **Costa Rica Backpackers** (www.costaricabackpackers.com; ✆ **2221-6191**), on Avenida 6 between calles 21 and 23.

Hotel Aranjuez ★★   Set on a quiet side street in the Barrio Amón neighborhood, five adjacent wooden homes have been joined in an intricate maze of hallways and courtyards to create one of the best and most unique budget lodgings in the country. These courtyards and hallways overflow with mature trees, tropical flowers, and potted ferns. There are quiet nooks for reading and a half-dozen or so common areas where guests gather to trade travel tales and play board games. Rooms vary greatly in size and isolation; but most feature high ceilings and antique wood or tile floors. Some of the nearly century-old walls in these homes are fairly thin, and noise can be a problem for some. The massive buffet breakfast is a real plus, and the staff and owners are extremely helpful.

Calle 19, btw. avs. 11 and 13. www.hotelaranjuez.com. ✆ **2256-1825.** 35 units, 6 with shared bathroom. $38 double with shared bathroom; $53–$69 double with private bathroom. Rates include breakfast buffet. Free parking. **Amenities:** Several lounges; free Wi-Fi.

Hotel Don Carlos ★★   If you're looking for colonial-era charm and an unmistakably Costa Rican ambience, this is a good choice. The converted downtown home once belonged to a former Costa Rican president. The rooms and hallways are decorated with a wealth of local art and crafts, including large stone sculptures, painted oxcart wheels, antique oil paintings, and vivid stained glass works, as well as lush potted ferns, palms, orchids, and flowing fountains. The restaurant serves local cuisine that is best enjoyed at one of the marble tables with wrought-iron chairs set on a covered patio. The rooms here can vary tremendously in size, so ask before you book. The hotel's Boutique Annemarie gift shop (p. 88) is one of the most extensive and best stocked in the country.

779 Calle 9, btw. avs. 7 and 9, San José. www.doncarloshotel.com. ✆ **866/675-9259** in the U.S. and Canada, or 2221-6707 in Costa Rica. 30 units. $85 double, $95–$100 suites. Rates include continental breakfast. Free parking. **Amenities:** Restaurant; bar; room service; free Wi-Fi.

Hotel Santo Tomás ★★   This quaint boutique hotel is in the heart of downtown in a restored coffee-baron mansion. Owner Thomas (Tomás) Douglas runs a tight ship. All rooms are clean and well maintained, although it's worth the splurge for the superior and deluxe rooms, which are more spacious and located inside a newer annex, farther away from the street noise and city bustle. The best of these have private balconies. There's a small kidney-shaped pool in a courtyard garden, with a Jacuzzi set above it on a mock stone volcano. The two are joined by a short curving waterslide. The hotel's Oasis restaurant serves excellent Continental cuisine, with a healthy dose of Italian pastas and main dishes, alongside local dishes and spa-style healthy cuisine.

Av. 7, btw. calles 3 and 5. www.hotelsantotomas.com. ✆ **2255-0448.** 30 units. $60–$83 double. Rates include breakfast. Parking $12. **Amenities:** Restaurant; bar; lounge; outdoor pool; exercise room; Jacuzzi; free Wi-Fi.

La Sabana/Paseo Colón

Located on the western edge of downtown, La Sabana Park is San José's largest city park, and Paseo Colón is a broad commercial avenue heading straight into the heart of the city. Stay in this neighborhood if you're looking for fast, easy access to the highways heading to Escazú, Santa Ana, the Pacific coast, and the airport and northern zone. Since it's on the edge of town, the area can be pretty dead at night.

EXPENSIVE

In addition to the hotel below, **Tryp Sabana by Windham ★** (www.tryphotels. com; ☎ **800/468 3261** in the U.S. and Canada, or 2547-2323 in Costa Rica), inside the Centro Colón building on Avenida 3, between calles 38 and 40, is a well-located business-class hotel, with a very good restaurant and excellent amenities.

Hotel Grano de Oro ★★★   This is the standard-bearer for luxury boutique hotels in San José. A combination of restoration and expansion has transformed this grand colonial-era mansion into a refined refuge in the center of a busy city. The signature suite is the most opulent of the hotel's rooms and is reached by a private stairwell. Elegantly decorated to evoke a bygone era, with wood-paneled walls, it has at its center a carved antique bed in deep

The Jacuzzi terrace at Hotel Grano de Oro.

wood, most inviting for an afternoon doze. If you can bear to get out of bed, you could plunge into the private Jacuzzi with views of the city skyline through massive picture windows. But don't worry, if that's beyond your budget, there are standard rooms too, and the chic rooftop patio with its two large Jacuzzi spas will almost make you forget you are in bustling San José. The sophisticated courtyard restaurant is among the best in the city for fine dining (p. 77). A final reason to visit: Your money will do good. The owners, Eldon and Lori Cook, support a range of social and environmental causes.

Calle 30, no. 251, btw. avs. 2 and 4, 150m (1½ blocks) south of Paseo Colón. www. hotelgranodeoro.com. © **2255-3322.** 40 units. $158–$285 double; $295–$480 suite. Free parking. **Amenities:** Restaurant; bar; lounge; spa services; 2 Jacuzzis; room service; free Wi-Fi.

INEXPENSIVE

In addition to the place mentioned below, **Aldea Hostal** (www.aldeahostel costarica.com; © **2233-6365**), is a popular hostel option, with a bustling little pizza restaurant attached.

Hotel Cacts ★   This is a solid budget lodging housed in a converted home on a side street about 2 blocks in from the busy Paseo Colón. There's a hostel-like vibe to the operation, but you also get niceties like a small pool and Jacuzzi. The staff is incredibly friendly and helpful. My favorite feature here, however, is the open-air rooftop patio, which has some chairs and chaise longues, and offers up a spectacular view of the city and surrounding mountains.

Av. 3 bis, no. 2845, btw. calles 28 and 30, San José. www.hotelcacts.com. © **2221-2928** or 2221-6546. 25 units. $80 double. Rates include breakfast buffet. Free parking. **Amenities:** Lounge; outdoor pool; Jacuzzi; free Wi-Fi.

San Pedro/Los Yoses

Located just east of downtown, Los Yoses is home to numerous foreign embassies and consulates, and was one of the city's early upper-class outposts, while San Pedro is home to the University of Costa Rica, and provides a distinct, college-town vibe. Staying here, you'll be close to much of the city's action but still enjoy some peace and quiet. If you've rented a car, be sure your hotel provides secure parking or you'll have to find (and pay for) a nearby lot.

MODERATE

Hotel Milvia ★   Housed in a converted old wooden plantation home, this boutique hotel is the handiwork of Steve Longrigg and Florencia Urbina. Steve has decades in the hospitality industry in Costa Rica, and Florencia is one of the country's more prominent artists and the former director of the Costa Rican Art Museum (p. 82). Rooms, hallways, and common areas feature a varied and striking collection of contemporary Costa Rican art by

Urbina and her friends and cohorts. The simply styled rooms offer plenty of natural light and most lead out onto a veranda or common courtyard sitting area. All of these common areas overflow with tropical plants and flowers and striking artwork. This hotel is close to the Universidad Latina and one of the city's few train lines, so street noise can be a problem at times.

1 block north and 2 blocks east of Muñoz y Nanne Supermarket, San Pedro. www.hotelmilvia.com. ✆ **2225-4543.** 9 units. $69 double. Rates include continental breakfast. **Amenities:** Lounge; free Wi-Fi.

Escazú & Santa Ana

Located about 15 to 20 minutes west of San José and about the same distance from the international airport, these affluent suburbs are popular with the Costa Rican professional class and North American retirees and expatriates, and quite a few hotels have sprung up to cater to their needs. It's relatively easy to commute between Escazú or Santa Ana and downtown via bus or taxi. Taxi fare should run around $10 to $20, each way. A bus costs around C300 to C400.

MODERATE

In addition to the hotel below, the **Courtyard San José** (www.marriott.com; ✆ **888/236-2427** in the U.S. and Canada, or 2208-3000 in Costa Rica); **Residence Inn San José Escazú** (www.marriott.com; ✆ **888/236-2427** in the U.S. and Canada, or 2588-4300 in Costa Rica); and **Holiday Inn Express** (www.hiexpress.com; ✆ **888/465-4329** in the U.S. and Canada, or 2506-5000 in Costa Rica) are all modern business-class hotels a few miles from each other, right on the western Próspero Fernández Highway connecting Santa Ana and Escazú with San José.

For a great boutique option in Escazu, try **Casa de las Tias** (www.casadelastias.com. ✆ **2289-5517**), which is owned and run by Xavier and Pilar, a very personable husband-wife team.

Alta Hotel ★★   The Alta is a hacienda-flavored, spectacularly *romántica* collection of arches, ramps, catwalks, and spiral stairs layered across a lush hillside out in the ritzy (well, ritz*ier*) western 'burbs, and we think it's a top choice. The glass-tiled oval pool out back shares sweeping valley views with a nearby Jacuzzi, a small spa, a pretty good little gym, and an on-site restaurant, La Luz, that is among the top dining experiences in the country. All of the above makes it sound like the Alta is some big, sprawling resort, when it's actually got all of 23 rooms. They are much cozier than the public spaces, with an upscale-rustic feel and earth-tone palette: terra-cotta floors, old-fashioned-tile counters in the bathrooms, and arches all over, from windows to alcoves. Most feature wonderful private balconies to take in the view. Because of the odd shape of the building, a few of the rooms do, unfortunately, have unusually small bathrooms.

Alto de las Palomas, old road to Santa Ana. www.thealtahotel.com. ✆ **888/388-2582** in the U.S. and Canada, or 2282-4160. 23 units. $140 double; $170–$280 suite. Rates include continental breakfast. Free parking. **Amenities:** Restaurant; bar; outdoor pool; exercise room; Jacuzzi; sauna; concierge; room service; free Wi-Fi.

Heredia & Alajuela (Airport Area)

Alajuela and Heredia, two colonial-era cities that lie much closer to the airport than San José, are great places to find small, distinct, and charming hotels. To learn more about Heredia, see "Day Trips from San José," later in this chapter. If you plan to get yourself to a remote beach or rainforest lodge as quickly as possible, using San José and the Central Valley purely as a transportation hub, or if you just detest urban clutter, noise, and pollution, you might do well to choose one of the hotels listed below.

EXPENSIVE

Finca Rosa Blanca Coffee Plantation & Inn ★★★ This fanciful boutique hotel is the loving creation of its amiable owners Glen and Teri Jampol. All rooms here are either junior suites, suites, or villas, and no two are alike. The large Rosa Blanca Suite with its master bedroom in a tall turret is one of the highlights, but I also love some of the more intimate options, like the second-floor El Guarumo with its free-form tile tub in a corner nook with great evening views over the central valley. Set on a high hillside on the flank of the Barva volcano, the inn maintains 14 hectares (35 acres) of prize-winning organic coffee under cultivation, and they offer an excellent in-house coffee tour. Organic gardens and greenhouses supply the produce for their wonderful organic farm-to-table restaurant, **El Tigre Vestido.** As the name implies, an award-winning organic coffee plantation is on-site, and excellent, informative tours and tastings are offered. The owners here are committed environmentalists and leaders in the local sustainable tourism field.

Santa Bárbara de Heredia. www.fincarosablanca.com. ✆ **305/395-3042** in the U.S., or 2269-9392 in Costa Rica. 15 units. $320–$565 double. Rates include breakfast. Free parking. **Amenities:** Restaurant; bar; lounge; outdoor pool; spa; concierge; room service; free Wi-Fi.

Marriott Costa Rica Hotel ★★★ Designed to resemble a colonial-era mansion, this is the best large-scale resort hotel in the city. The hotel is close enough to the airport to be considered an "airport hotel," yet it feels like an isolated country retreat. The entryway lets out onto a massive central courtyard meant to mimic Havana's Plaza de Armas. The elegant, traditional-style rooms are large and have views to the surrounding hillsides, suburbs, and coffee fields. There are several distinct dining choices, and the Casa de Café coffee house and restaurant actually fronts a small working coffee field. Be sure to check the online booking engine, as good deals are frequently offered there.

San Antonio de Belén. www.marriott.com. ✆ **2298-0000.** 299 units. $199–$249 double; $279–$329 executive level. Valet parking $6/day. **Amenities:** 3 restaurants; 2 bars; 2 outdoor pools; golf driving range; 2 tennis courts; spa; Jacuzzi; sauna; concierge; room service; free Wi-Fi in lobby, $10–$16/day in-room.

Peace Lodge ★★★   Part of the popular **La Paz Waterfall Gardens** (p. 84), Peace Lodge is about 45 minutes from the airport, near the Poás Volcano. The rooms and villas are huge and feature faux rustic decor, including massive four-poster log beds and river stone fireplaces. All come with a Jacuzzi on their private balcony, but the deluxe rooms also feature an immense bathroom with a second indoor Jacuzzi backed by a full wall of orchids, flowers, and bromeliads, with a working waterfall. The steep rates here get you not only these fanciful rooms, but also unlimited access to the attached Waterfall Gardens.

6km (3¾ miles) north of Varablanca on the road to San Miguel. www.waterfallgardens. com. ✆ **954/727-3997** in the U.S., or 2482-2720 in Costa Rica. 17 units. $395–$470 double; $605–$810 villa. Rates include entrance to La Paz Waterfall Gardens. **Amenities:** Restaurant; bar; 2 outdoor pools; Jacuzzi; free Wi-Fi.

MODERATE

If you want a classic airport hotel, with regular shuttle service, both the **Courtyard by Marriott** ★ (www.marriott.com; ✆ **888/236-2427** in the U.S. and Canada, or 2429-2700 in Costa Rica) and **Holiday Inn Express** ★ (www. hiexpress.com; ✆ **800/439-4745** in the U.S. and Canada, or 2443-0043 in Costa Rica) are solid U.S.-chain hotels located right across from the airport.

Hotel Bougainvillea ★   This well-run midsize hotel, about 15 to 20 minutes from the airport, has the feel and facilities of a larger resort hotel, but at a very affordable price. The signature features here are the large, lush, and varied gardens that surround the hotel. Rooms are large and well kept. Most come with a small private balcony overlooking either the gardens or the city below. Nice extras include a lovely pool and two lighted tennis courts.

In Santo Tomás de Santo Domingo de Heredia, 100m (1 block) west of the Escuela de Santo Tomás, San José. www.hb.co.cr. ✆ **866/880-5441** in the U.S. and Canada, or 2244-1414 in Costa Rica. 81 units. $119–$129 double; $135–$145 suites. Rates include breakfast buffet. Free parking. **Amenities:** Restaurant; bar; outdoor pool; 2 tennis courts; sauna; free Wi-Fi.

Pura Vida Hotel ★★   Located just 10 minutes from the airport, this homey little inn is run by the very genial couple of Bernie Jubb and Nhi Chu. Rooms and private *casitas* (little houses) are spread around a spacious compound and lush gardens. These overgrown and mature gardens feature vine-covered arbors, fruit trees, and exotic flowers, as well as quiet seating nooks, and a highly coveted hammock with a shade and rain cover. The two-bedroom casitas are great for families. Nhi is an amazing chef specializing in market-fresh Asian cuisine. Three-course fixed-menu meals are served around long communal tables and need to be booked in advance. The hotel is located just a kilometer or two north of downtown Alajuela.

Tuetal de Alajuela. www.puravidahotel.com. ✆ **2430-2929** or 8878-3899. 6 units. $99–$165 double. Rates include full breakfast and one-way airport transfer. **Amenities:** Restaurant; free Wi-Fi.

INEXPENSIVE

Villa San Ignacio ★★   Formerly the Orquideas Inn, this boutique hotel is only 10 minutes or so from the airport, on the road that leads to the summit of the Poás Volcano. After a major remodeling, this place has emerged as a quietly elegant option, with soft colors, plush appointments, and minimalistic decor, all at an amazing price. Street noise can be a little bit of a problem in some rooms. The hotel sits on 22 acres of land that are great for bird-watching, with tall native trees on a sloping hillside. And there's a refreshing mid-size rectangular pool off the main lobby and restaurant area, with low-lying Balinese-style chaise lounges. The 1920s-style Pandora restaurant serves excellent creative concoctions rooted in locally grown ingredients, and sometimes has live music on weekends. There are actually several routes to the top of the Poás Volcano and this hotel can be a bit hard to find, so be sure you're armed with good directions or a GPS.

Poas de Alajuela. www.villasanignacio.com. ⓒ **8492-1133.** 12 units. $85 double. Rates include full breakfast. Free parking. **Amenities:** Restaurant; bar; pool; free Wi-Fi.

WHERE TO EAT

San José has an excellent variety of restaurants serving cuisine from all over the world. You can find superb French, Italian, and contemporary fusion restaurants around the city, as well as Peruvian, Japanese, Swiss, and Spanish spots. The greatest concentrations and varieties of restaurants are in the downtown area and in the nearby Central Valley suburbs of Escazú and Santa Ana. If you're looking for cheap eats, you'll find them all across the city in little restaurants known as *sodas,* which are the equivalent of diners in the United States.

Fruit vendors stake out spots on almost every street corner in downtown San José. If you're lucky enough to be in town between April and June, you can sample more varieties of mangoes than you ever knew existed. I like buying them already cut up in a little bag; they cost a little more this way, but you don't get nearly as messy. Be sure to try a green mango with salt and chili peppers—it's guaranteed to wake up your taste buds. Another common street food is *pejibaye,* a bright orange palm nut about the size of a plum. They're boiled in big pots on carts; you eat them in much the same way you eat an avocado, and they taste a bit like squash.

Downtown San José
EXPENSIVE

La Esquina de Buenos Aires ★★ ARGENTINE/STEAKHOUSE   Frankly, the Argentines do steak much better than the Ticos, and this Argentine-themed steakhouse is one of the best in the city. The decor and ambience are pure Porteño, and the extensive menu features a long list of grilled meats, some very good pastas, and various seafood and poultry dishes. This place is festive and almost always full to the brim. Reservations are essential most nights.

Calle 11 and Av. 4. www.laesquinadebuenosaires.com. ✆ **2223-1909** or 2257-9741. Reservations recommended. Main courses C5,300–C13,800. Mon–Fri 11:30am–3pm and 6–10:30pm; Sat 12:30–11pm; Sun noon–10pm.

MODERATE

Restaurante Nuestra Tierra ★ COSTA RICAN   Okay, so this place is a bit touristy. Designed to re-create the feel of an old Costa Rican homestead kitchen, the waitstaff wear traditional garb, and guests sit on benches at heavy wooden tables overhung by bunches of bananas and onions and scores of painted enamel coffee mugs strung on wooden columns and beams. Typical Costa Rican meals are served on banana leaves set over large plates. The prices are high for what you get. On the plus side, service is prompt and pleasant, portions are large, and it does give one the feel of a typical Costa Rican restaurant from a bygone era.

Av. 2 and Calle 15. ✆ **2258-6500.** Main courses C6,000–C15,000. Daily 24 hrs.

Tin Jo ★★★ CHINESE/PAN-ASIAN   Costa Rica has a long history of Chinese immigration, and this family restaurant is on its second generation. However, the menu here wanders far beyond China, with traditional Szechuan and Cantonese plates sharing the stage with a mix of Thai, Japanese, Indian, and even Malay dishes. Despite this schizophrenic mix, this has long been one of the best and most popular restaurants in the city. Each of the various rooms features unique decor from one of the aforementioned countries or regions. There are tons of great vegetarian options, all clearly marked as to whether they are vegan and/or gluten-free.

Calle 11, btw. avs. 6 and 8. www.tinjo.com. ✆ **2221-7605** or 2257-3622. Reservations recommended. Main courses C6,000–C14,000. Mon–Fri 11:30am–2:30pm and 6–10pm (Fri 11pm); Sat noon–3pm and 6–11pm; Sun noon–9pm.

INEXPENSIVE

Alma de Café ★ CAFE/COFFEEHOUSE   Housed in a marble-floored, mural-ceilinged anteroom off the main lobby of the neo-baroque National Theater (Teatro Nacional), this coffee shop is a swell place for a light lunch or a cup of Costa Rican java and dessert (it's usually open after the shows let out, as well as during the day). The menu features healthful salads, quiches, sandwiches, and lasagna.

In the Teatro Nacional, Av. 2, btw. calles 3 and 5. ✆ **2010-1119.** Sandwiches C3,000– C6,200; main courses C4,000–C6,500. Mon–Sat 9am–7pm; Sun 9am–6pm.

Barrio Amón/Barrio Otoya

MODERATE

Café Mundo ★ INTERNATIONAL   A popular spot, set in the hallways, patios, terraces, and rooms of a remodeled old mansion, Café Mundo serves good food in an artsy setting. The menu features a solid selection of salads, pizzas, pastas, and a range of main dishes running the gamut from seafood-stuffed tenderloin to chicken in a honey-mustard sauce. The largest dining room here features floor-to-ceiling flowers painted by Costa Rican artist Miguel Casafont. Still, I generally try to grab a table at one of the outdoor patios, where I can enjoy a cool breeze on a hot tropical day or night.

Calle 15 and Av. 9, 200m (2 blocks) east and 100m (1 block) north of the INS Building. *C* **2222-6190.** Reservations recommended. Main courses C4,500–C20,000. Mon–Thurs 11am–10:30pm; Fri 11am–11:30pm; Sat 5–11:30pm.

Kalú ★★ CAFE/BISTRO   Costa Rican-born chef Camille Ratton, trained at the Cordon Bleu, has created a wonderfully casual little bistro restaurant and gallery in a converted 1950s-era Art Deco home in a quiet neighborhood. The menu features a range of light and healthful options like salads and lettuce wraps, as well as tacos, panini, burgers, and more. When I'm feeling a bit more famished, I order up some fresh mahimahi in a Romesco sauce. Don't miss out on the desserts, which, to my mind, are Camille's specialty—especially the *Tarta Cahuita,* an individual tartlette with a caramelized banana filling, grated lime peel, and chocolate ganache. The attached **Kiosco** (p. 88) is one of the better and more creative gift shops in the city.

Calle 31 and Av. 5. www.kalu.co.cr. *C* **2253-8426.** Reservations recommended. Main courses C4,850–C10,500. Tue–Fri noon–10pm; Sat 9am–10pm; Sun 9am-4pm.

La Sabana/Paseo Colón
EXPENSIVE

Grano de Oro Restaurant ★★★ INTERNATIONAL   It's no accident that the city's most elegant boutique hotel (p. 70) also has one of its most revered fine dining restaurants. The main dining room rings an open-air central courtyard, with a flowing fountain, tall potted trees, and large stained-glass features. French-born chef Francis Canal was classically trained, but he has never stopped evolving, combining traditional techniques from his homeland with local ingredients, tropical flavors, and contemporary Fusion elements. Start things off with a trio of savory crème brûlée—Gorgonzola, porcini, and goat cheese. For main dishes, I recommend the roasted lamb chops with cilantro sauce and sautéed fennel. Be sure to leave room for dessert. Their namesake pie is a silky layering of coffee and mocha mousse on a rich cookie crust.

Calle 30, no. 251, btw. avs. 2 and 4, 150m (1½ blocks) south of Paseo Colón. www.hotelgranodeoro.com. *C* **2255-3322.** Reservations recommended. Main courses C10,000–30,000. Daily 7am–10pm.

Park Café ★★ FUSION   While the Grano de Oro (see above) thrives on elegance and consistency, this place can be more hit and miss—but the payoff from British chef Richard Neat, who ran a two-star Michelin restaurant in London before moving to Costa Rica, can also be substantial. The restaurant is spread throughout the interior courtyard and garden of a stately old home that functions as an antiques and decorative arts shop by day. Giant carved doors from India and stone Buddhas from Bali add to the decor, and are also for sale. The menu changes seasonally, but always features creative, contemporary dishes with sometimes dazzling presentations, often in tapas-size portions to encourage sharing and broad samplings. Choices have included prosciutto-wrapped scallops topped with fried onion rings in a Malbec reduction, or a rabbit breast served with confit of rabbit-stuffed ravioli and grilled artichokes.

Sabana Norte, 1 block north of Rostipollos. www.parkcafecostarica.blogspot.com. ✆ **2290-6324.** Reservations recommended. Main courses C3,900–C7,000. Tues–Sat 5:30–9pm.

INEXPENSIVE

Soda Tapia ★ COSTA RICAN   This classic Costa Rican eatery serves up the cuisine of a typical Tico *soda* (diner) in a retro 1950s-style American diner, complete with bright lights and Formica tables. Still, this is a great place to come for some *típico* (typical) cooking. Its extended hours make it a good choice for a late-night bite. The main branch is just across from the popular La Sabana park and Museo de Arte Costarricense (p. 82). Other branches are around the Central Valley, including ones in Santa Ana (Centro Comercial Vistana Oeste, across from MATRA; ✆ 2203-7175) and Alajuela (Centro Comercial Plaza Real Alajuela; ✆ 2441-6033).

Calle 42 and Av. 2, across from the Museo de Arte Costarricense. www.sodatapia.com. ✆ **2222-6734.** Sandwiches C4,000–C4,400; main dishes C3,000–C5,000. Mon–Thurs 6am–2am; Fri–Sun 24 hrs.

San Pedro/Los Yoses

MODERATE

Olio ★★ MEDITERRANEAN   This dimly lit, intimate restaurant has a romantic vibe, with several small rooms and quiet nooks located off the main dining area. A laundry list of classic Greek, Italian, and Spanish dishes are served in tapas-size portions, alongside more hearty pasta and main-course options. The wine list ventures beyond the immediate shores of the Mediterranean to include offerings from Chile, Argentina, and even Bulgaria.

Barrio California, 200m (2 blocks) north of Bagelman's. ✆ **2281-0541.** Reservations recommended. Main courses C4,950–C13,750. Mon–Wed noon–11pm; Thurs–Fri noon–midnight; Sat 6pm–midnight.

INEXPENSIVE

Mantras Veggie Café and Tea House ★★ VEGETARIAN   With both indoor and garden patio seating, this is my (mostly) vegan wife's favorite vegetarian restaurant in the city, and I concur. I especially like the garden seating, under bright red canvas umbrellas. The menu features a broad mix of soups, salads, wraps, sandwiches, and main dishes. There are both vegan and

DINING UNDER THE stars

Although there are myriad unique experiences to be had in Costa Rica, one of my favorites is dining on the side of a volcano with the lights of San José shimmering below. These hanging restaurants, called *miradores,* are a resourceful response to the city's topography. Because San José is set in a broad valley surrounded on all sides by volcanic mountains, people who live in these mountainous areas have no place to go but up—so they do, building roadside cafes vertically on the slopes.

The food at most of these establishments is not spectacular, but the views often are, particularly at night, when the wide valley sparkles in a wash of lights. The town of **Aserrí,** 10km (6¼ miles) south of downtown San José, is the king of *miradores,* and **Mirador Ram Luna** (✆ **2230-3022**) is the king of Aserrí. Grab a window seat and, if you've got the fortitude, order a plate of

chicharrones (fried pork rinds). There's often live music. You can hire a cab for around $15 or take the Aserri bus at Avenida 6 between calles Central and 2. Just ask the driver where to get off.

You'll also find *miradores* in the hills above Escazú and in San Ramón de Tres Ríos and Heredia. The most popular is **Le Monastère** (www.monastere-restaurant.com; ✆ **2289-4404;** closed Sun), an elegant converted church serving somewhat overrated French and Belgian cuisine in a spectacular setting above the hills of Escazú. I recommend coming here just for the less formal **Cantina La Cava** ★, a bar and grill located under the main restaurant. I also like **Mirador Tiquicia** ★ (www.mirador tiquicia.com; ✆ **2289-7330**), which occupies several rooms in a sprawling old Costa Rican home and has live folkloric dance shows on Thursday.

raw offerings. Signature dishes here include the raw zucchini pasta with pesto and the pad Thai. As the name implies, they serve a broad selection of herbal teas, many grown on-site or purchased at local organic markets.

2 blocks east and ¼ block west of El Farolito, in Barrio Escalante. ✆ **2253-6715.** Main courses C3,850–C3,800. Mon–Sat 8:30am–5pm.

Escazú & Santa Ana

These two suburbs have the most vibrant restaurant scenes in the Central Valley, and much of the action takes place, oddly, in modern strip malls.

Two great one-stop options to consider are **Plaza Itskatzú,** just off the highway and sharing a parking lot with the Courtyard San José, and **Avenida Escazú,** which is anchored by the Marriott Residence Inn and is located next to the CIMA Hospital. My favorite options at Plaza Itskatzú include **Chancay** ★ (www.chancay.info; ✆ **2588-2327**), which serves Peruvian and Peruvian/Chinese cuisine; and **Samurai Fusion** ★ (✆ **2288-2240**), a fine sushi and teppanyaki joint.

Over on Avenida Escazú, you'll find **Saga** ★ (www.sagarestaurant.com; ✆ **2289-6615**), with a contemporary-casual bistro menu; **Terraza Toscana** ★★ (www.terrazzatoscanacr.com; ✆ **4000-2220**), an excellent and elegant Italian restaurant; and **L'Ile de France** ★★ (© **2289-7533**), a top-notch, high-end French restaurant.

EXPENSIVE

Bacchus ★★ ITALIAN   Set in an adobe home built in 1870, this classy restaurant is one of the best Italian options in the city. Paper-thin pizzas come out of the wood-burning oven (you'll see it in the open kitchen), and the pastas and raviolis are homemade. Of these, I really like the pappardelle with white wine, arugula, carrots, and crabmeat. Desserts are creative and delicious, like the banana and apple croquettes made of phyllo dough and topped with a Grand Marnier sauce. Bacchus' several dining rooms are decorated with regularly rotating art exhibits; or you can sit in the open-air (but covered) patio that overlooks the kitchen and pizza oven.

Downtown Santa Ana. www.bacchus.cr. © **4001-5418.** Reservations recommended. Main courses C6,500–C14,700. Mon–Fri noon–3pm and 6–11pm; Sat noon–11pm; Sun noon–9pm.

MODERATE

Product-C ★★ SEAFOOD   Although San José is inland, this fish market and restaurant makes daily pre-dawn runs to Puntarenas and other coastal supply points to get the freshest catch possible. They even set up the first and only oyster farm in Costa Rica, producing small, yet very tasty, bivalves. And it doesn't take much to make fish that were swimming the night before taste delish. The simple menu is scrawled on a chalkboard; most diners simply walk up to the display case, point, and ask for the style of cooking of their choice.

Av. Escazú. www.product-c.com. © **2288-5570.** Reservations recommended. Main courses C6,500–C13,000. Mon–Sat noon–11pm; Sun noon–6pm.

EXPLORING SAN JOSÉ

Some of the best and most modern museums in Central America are here, with a wealth of fascinating pre-Columbian artifacts. Standouts include the **Museo de Jade Marco Fidel Tristán (Jade Museum;** see below), and the **Museo de Arte Costarricense (Costa Rican Art Museum;** see below), which features a top-notch collection of Costa Rican art and a beautiful, open-air sculpture garden.

Just outside San José in the Central Valley are also several great things to see and do. With day trips out of the city, you can spend quite a few days in this region.

The Top Attractions
DOWNTOWN SAN JOSE

Museo de Jade Marco Fidel Tristán (Jade Museum) ★★ MUSEUM The Spanish conquistadors may have been gaga over gold, but the folks they

Tico sculptures in San José.

conquered were more into jade, so it's well worth ducking into this museum. Set on the western edge of the Plaza de la Democracia, the five-story building boasts more than 75,000 square feet of exhibition space, which, for the first time ever, is enough to display the museum's impressive 7,000-piece collection (it's the largest jade collection in Central America). Artifacts date from 500 B.C. to A.D. 1500. There are some pretty neat items in here, including mysterious stone spheres from the southern reaches of the country, and a terracotta incense burner in the shape of a mythological crocodile. The jadework reflects Olmec and Maya influences, with pieces that are almost modern-looking in their elegant simplicity, and that includes a couple of cases' worth of erotic pieces. Wall text is in both English and Spanish. Allow around 2 to 3 hours for a visit here.

Calle 13, btw. avs. Central and 2. ⓒ **2521-6610.** Admission $15; $5 students with valid ID, free for children 10 and under. Daily 10am–5pm.

Museos del Banco Central de Costa Rica (Gold Museum) ★★
MUSEUM   Housing some 1,600 gold pieces dating from 500 B.C. to A.D. 1500 and spread over three floors, this museum is directly underneath the downtown Plaza de la Cultura. Admirers of gold and jewels will definitely want to stop here. The collection features a wide range of artifacts from cast

animal figurines to jewelry and functional pieces. This museum is actually one of three housed in this complex (there are numismatic and philatelic museums here, as well), and the admission fee gets you in to all three. Admission is free every Wednesday. Allow around 2 hours to visit the museum.

Calle 5, btw. avs. Central and 2, underneath the Plaza de la Cultura. www.museosdel bancocentral.org. (?) **2243-4202.** Admission C5,500 adults, C4,000 students, free for children 11 and under. Free admission Wed. Daily 9:15am–5pm. Closed Jan 1, Holy Thursday, Good Friday, Easter Sunday, May 1, and Christmas.

Museo Nacional de Costa Rica (National Museum) ★★ MUSEUM

Head here for an erudite but fun overview of the archaeological, historical, and natural wonders of Costa Rica from pre-Columbian times to the present. Exhibits here include gold and jade artifacts like those you'd see at the Gold Museum (see above) or Jade Museum (see above), but obviously not in the quantity that you'd find in either of those two more specifically oriented institutions. In addition to all the historical exhibits, this museum has a large butterfly garden with more than 25 species fluttering about. Housed in a large former army barracks, the building features turrets and outside walls that still bear the bullet marks from fighting in the 1948 civil war. It takes a good 2 hours to see everything here.

Calle 17, btw. avs. Central and 2, on the Plaza de la Democracia. www.museocostarica. go.cr. (?) **2257-1433.** Admission $8 adults, $4 students and children 11 and under. Tues–Sat 8:30am–4:30pm; Sun 9am–4:30pm. Closed Jan 1, Holy Thursday, Good Friday, Easter, May 1, and Christmas.

LA SABANA/PASEO COLON

Museo de Arte Costarricense (Costa Rican Art Museum) ★★

ART MUSEUM   Originally the main terminal of San José's first international airport, this museum houses the largest and most important collection of works by Costa Rican artists from the colonial time to the present. All in all, more than 6,000 pieces grace its permanent collection, including works by Juan Manuel Sánchez, Max Jiménez, Francisco "Paco" Zuñiga, Francisco Amighetti, Lola Fernández, and more. On the back patio—which used to lead to the tarmac—is a large and varied sculpture garden, where you'll find everything from Francisco "Paco" Zuñiga's "Monumento al Argricultor" (Monument to the Farmer) to Jorge Jiménez Deredia's abstract "Imagin Cosmica" (Cosmic Image). This museum is free, and anchors the eastern edge of the large La Sabana city park, making it easy to combine a visit here with a walk in the park. Allow around 2 hours to visit the museum.

Calle 42 and Paseo Colón, Parque La Sabana Este. www.musarco.go.cr. (?) **2256-1281.** Free admission. Tues–Sun 9am–4pm.

Especially for Kids

Museo de Los Niños (Children's Museum) ★ MUSEUM   Housed

in a former prison (and yes, there *is* a place where you can pretend to lock up the kiddos if they're misbehaving), this massive museum gives families a whirlwind tour through Costa Rica, from the obvious (interactive exhibits and educational displays on the rainforest and pre-Columbian village life) to the "who knew?" The latter comes in the form of the interior of a spaceship, in honor of Costa Rican astronaut Franklin Chang. Also a favorite, for all ages: the simulated earthquake area. The museum site is home to the National Auditorium, and often features temporary exhibitions of contemporary art. Most visitors can easily spend 2 to 3 hours here. *One warning:* Take a taxi to get here, as the museum sits just in from a rather seedy section of the city's red-light district.

Calle 4 and Av. 9. www.museocr.org. © **2258-4929.** Admission C2,200 adults, free for children 15 and under. Tues–Fri 8am–4:30pm; Sat–Sun 9:30am–5pm.

Outside San José

Café Britt Farm ★ COFFEE FARM You'll know more than the baristas do after a visit to Café Britt, one of the largest coffee producers in Costa Rica (it's about 20 min. outside of San José). At the company's farm, visitors are treated to an informative tour and stage production, which covers how coffee is grown, how the coffee "cherry" is roasted into a delicious bean, and more. And get ready to get caffeinated: Tasting sessions allow visitors to experience the different qualities of coffee. The entire tour, including transportation, takes about 3 to 4 hours. Allow some extra time, and an extra $10, for a visit to the nearby working plantation and mill. You can even strap on a basket and go out coffee picking during harvest time . . . if you want.

North of Heredia on the road to Barva. www.coffeetour.com. © **2277-1600.** Admission $22 adults, $17 children 6–11; $39 adults and $34 children, including transportation from downtown San José. Add $15 for lunch buffet. Tours daily at 9:30 and 11am; 1:15 and 3:15pm. Store and restaurant daily 8am–5pm.

Doka Estate ★ COFFEE FARM Another large and long-standing coffee estate/farm in Alajuela, Doka's tour takes visitors from "seed to cup." Along the way, tourists get the full rundown of the processes involved in the growing, harvesting, curing, packing, and brewing of their award-winning coffee. This coffee tour is similar to that offered at Café Britt (see above), but is a little more down-home in feel. These folks also have a butterfly garden, a Bonsai tree, and orchid exhibit on-site. Allow about 2½ hours for the full tour.

Sabanilla de Alajuela. www.dokaestate.com. © **888/946-3652** in the U.S. and Canada, or 2449-5152 in Costa Rica. Admission $20 adults, $16 students with valid ID, $10 children 6–12, free for children 5 and under. Packages including transportation and breakfast or lunch available. Tours daily at 9, 10, and 11am; 1:30 and 2:30pm. Reservations required.

INBio Park ★★ MUSEUM/NATURE PARK Run by the National Biodiversity Institute (Instituto Nacional de Biodiversidad), INBio is part museum, part educational center, and part nature park. The visit begins with a 15-minute informational video; guests then tour two large pavilions explaining Costa Rica's biodiversity and natural wonders. Really ambitious tourists hike on trails that re-create the ecosystems of a tropical rainforest, dry forest, and premontane forest (a 2-hr. guided hike is included in the entrance fee; self-guided-tour booklets are also available). There's a good-size butterfly garden, as well as a Plexiglass viewing window into the small lagoon. There's a simple, cafeteria-style restaurant here for lunch, as well as a coffee shop and gift shop. You can easily spend 2 to 3 hours here.

400m (4 blocks) north and 250m (2½ blocks) west of the Shell station in Santo Domingo de Heredia. www.inbioparque.com. ℂ **2507-8107.** Admission $25 adults, $19 students, $15 children 12 and under. Fri 9am–3pm (last admission 2pm); Sat–Sun 9am–4pm.

La Paz Waterfall Gardens ★★ NATURAL ATTRACTION   The original attraction here consists of a series of trails through primary and secondary forests alongside La Paz River, with lookouts over a series of powerful falls, including the namesake La Paz Fall. In addition to an orchid garden and a hummingbird garden, you must visit the huge butterfly garden, which is easily the largest in Costa Rica. A small serpentarium, featuring a mix of venomous and nonvenomous native snakes, several terrariums containing various frogs and lizards, and a section of wild cats and local monkey species in large enclosures are added attractions. While the admission fee is a little steep, the trails and waterfalls are beautiful and the exhibits can be magical (especially the "storm" of butterflies). This is a good stop after a morning visit to the Poás Volcano. Plan to spend 3 to 4 hours here. The hotel rooms here at **Peace Lodge** (p. 74) are some of the most extravagant in the country.

6km (3¾ miles) north of Varablanca on road to San Miguel. www.waterfallgardens.com. ℂ**2482-2100.** Admission $40 adults, $24 children 3–12, free for children 2 and under. Daily 8am–5pm. No easy or regular bus service here, so arrive in rental car or taxi, or arrange transport with La Paz.

Sibú Chocolates ★★★ CAFE/CHOCOLATE FACTORY   Chocolate lovers will definitely want to visit this gourmet organic chocolate maker, which features a lovely small cafe, gift shop, and tours of its production facility. Tasting tours are offered at 10:30am, and last about 1 hour. The tour includes an informative presentation about the history and techniques of chocolate making, as well as several tempting tastings.

Outside Heredia. www.sibuchocolate.com. ℂ**2268-1335.** Tasting tours $24 (Tues–Sat at 10:30am; reservations essential). Gift shop and production facility Tues–Sat 8am–5pm.

Zoo Ave ★ ZOO   Dozens of scarlet macaws, reclusive owls, majestic raptors, several different species of toucans, and a host of brilliantly colored birds from Costa Rica and around the world make this one exciting place to visit. In total, more than 115 species of birds are on display, including some 80 species found in Costa Rica. There are also large iguana, deer, tapir, ocelot, puma, and monkey exhibits—and look out for the 3.6m (12-ft.) crocodile. Zoo Ave houses only injured, donated, or confiscated animals. It takes about 2 hours to walk the paths and visit all the exhibits here.

La Garita, Alajuela. www.zooavecostarica.org. ℂ **2433-8989.** Admission $20 adults, $15 students with valid ID. Daily 9am–5pm. Catch bus to Alajuela on Av. 2, btw. calles 12 and 14. In Alajuela, transfer to bus to Atenas and get off at Zoo Ave before La Garita. Fare 65¢.

Outdoor Activities & Spectator Sports

Because of the chaos and pollution, you'll probably want to get out of the city before undertaking anything too strenuous. But if you want to brave the elements, there are a few outdoor activities in and around San José. For information on horseback riding, hiking, and white-water-rafting trips from San José, see "Day Trips from San José," later in this chapter.

Parque La Sabana ★★ (La Sabana Park, at the western end of Paseo Colón), formerly San José's international airport, is the city's center for active sports and recreation. Here you'll find jogging trails, a banked bicycle track, soccer fields, a roller rink, a few public tennis courts, and the massive National Stadium. Aside from events at the National Stadium, all the facilities are free and open to the public. On weekends, you'll usually find free, public aerobic, yoga, or dancercise classes, with hundreds of folks taking part. Families gather for picnics, people fly kites, pony rides are available for the kids, and there's even an outdoor sculpture garden. If you really want to experience the local culture, try getting into a pickup soccer game here. Be careful in this park, however, especially at dusk or after dark, when it becomes a favorite haunt for youth gangs and muggers.

SOCCER (FUTBOL) ★   Ticos take their *fútbol* seriously. Costa Rican professional soccer is some of the best in Central America, and the national team, or "Sele" (*selección nacional*), qualified for the World Cup in 2002, 2006, and 2014, where they made it to the quarterfinals, losing in a penalty kick shoot-out to Holland, the eventual runner-up.

The local professional soccer season runs from August through June, with a break for Christmas and New Year's, and separate championship playoffs every December and July. The main San José team is Saprissa (affectionately called *El Monstruo,* or "The Monster"). **Saprissa's stadium** is in Tibás (www.saprissa.co.cr; ℂ **2240-4034;** take any Tibás bus from Calle 2 and Av. 5). Games are often held on Sunday at 11am, but are occasionally scheduled for Saturday afternoon or Wednesday evening. Check the local newspapers for game times and locations.

International and other important matches are often held in the **National Stadium** on the northeastern corner of Parque La Sabana.

Aside from major international matches at the National Stadium, you don't need to buy tickets in advance. Tickets generally run between C1,500 and C10,000. It's worth paying a little extra for *sombra numerado* (reserved seats in the shade). This will protect you from both the sun and the more rowdy aficionados (periodic violent incidents, both inside and outside the stadiums, have marred the sport here, so be careful). Other options include *sombra* (general admission in the shade), *palco* and *palco numerado* (general admission and reserved mezzanine), and *sol general* (general admission in full sun).

It is possible to buy tickets to most sporting events in advance from **E-Ticket** (www.eticket.cr); the site is, however, entirely in Spanish.

SHOPPING

Serious shoppers will be disappointed in San José. Aside from coffee and miniature oxcarts, there isn't much that's distinctly Costa Rican. To compensate for its own relative lack of goods, San José (and all of Costa Rica) does a brisk business in selling crafts and clothes imported from Guatemala, Panama, Ecuador, and China.

THE SHOPPING SCENE San José's central shopping corridor is bounded by avenidas 1 and 2, from about Calle 14 on the west to Calle 13 on the east. For several blocks west of the Plaza de la Cultura, **Avenida Central**

joe TO GO

Two words of advice: Buy coffee. Lots of it.

Coffee is the best shopping deal in all of Costa Rica. Although the best Costa Rican coffee is allegedly shipped off to North American and European markets, it's hard to beat the coffee that's roasted right in front of you here. Best of all is the price: One pound of coffee sells for $4 to $7. It makes a great gift and truly is a local product.

Café Britt is the big name in Costa Rican coffee. These folks have the largest export business in the country, and, although high-priced, their blends are very dependable. Café Britt is widely available at gift shops around the country, and at the souvenir concessions at both international airports. My favorites, however, are the coffees roasted and packaged in Manuel Antonio and Monteverde, by **Café Milagro** and **Café Monteverde.** If you visit either of these places, definitely pick up their beans.

In general, the best place to buy coffee is in a supermarket. Why pay more at a gift or specialty shop? If you buy prepackaged coffee in a supermarket in Costa Rica, the beans will be marked either *grano* (grain) or *grano entero* (whole bean). If you opt for ground varieties (*molido*), be sure the package is marked *puro;* otherwise, it will likely be mixed with a good amount of sugar, the way Ticos like it.

One good coffee-related gift to bring home is a coffee sock and stand. This is the most common mechanism for brewing coffee in Costa Rica. It consists of a simple circular stand, made out of wood or wire, which holds a sock. Put the ground beans in the sock, place a pot or cup below it, and pour boiling water through. You can find the socks and stands at most supermarkets and in the Mercado Central. In fancier crafts shops, you'll find them made out of ceramic. Depending on its construction, a stand will cost you between $1.50 and $15; socks run around 30¢, so buy spares.

is a pedestrian-only street mall where you'll find store after store of inexpensive clothes for men, women, and children. Depending on the mood of the police that day, you might find a lot of street vendors as well. Most shops in the downtown district are open Monday through Saturday from about 8am to 6pm. Some shops close for lunch, while others remain open (it's just the luck of the draw for shoppers). You'll be happy to find that sales and import taxes have already been figured into display prices.

Modern Malls

With globalization and modernization taking hold in Costa Rica, much of the local shopping scene has shifted to large megamalls. Modern multilevel affairs with cineplexes, food courts, and international brand-name stores are becoming ubiquitous. The biggest and most modern of these malls include the **Mall San Pedro, Multiplaza** (one each in Escazú and the eastern suburb of Zapote), and **Terra Mall** (on the outskirts of downtown on the road to Cartago). Although they lack the charm of small shops found around San José, they are a reasonable option for one-stop shopping; most contain at least one or two local galleries and crafts shops, along with a large supermarket, which is always the best place to stock up on local coffee, hot sauces, liquors, and other nonperishable foodstuffs.

Shopping A to Z

ART GALLERIES

Galería 11–12 ★★★   This outstanding gallery deals mainly in high-end Costa Rican art, from neoclassical painters such as Teodorico Quirós to modern masters such as Francisco Amighetti and Paco Zuñiga, to current stars such as Rafa Fernández, Rodolfo Stanley, Fernando Carballo, and Fabio Herrera. Plaza Itzkatzú, off the Próspero Fernández Hwy., Escazú. ✆ **2288-1975.**

Galería Kandinsky ★   Owned by the daughter of one of Costa Rica's most prominent modern painters, Rafa Fernández, this small gallery usually has a good selection of high-end contemporary Costa Rican paintings, be it the house collection or a specific temporary exhibit. Centro Comercial Calle Real, San Pedro. ✆ **2234-0478.**

Galería Valanti ★★   This is a gorgeous, well-lit, and expertly curated gallery. The collection here is ever evolving, but always includes a good mix of contemporary and classic Costa Rican and Latin American artists. Regular lectures, courses, and drawing classes are offered by regularly by prominent artists in the collection or local curators and historians. Av. 11, no. 3395, btw. calles 33 and 35, Barrio Escalante. www.galeriavalanti.com. ✆ **2253-1659.**

CHOCOLATE

Sibú Chocolate ★★★   Building on the success of their organic chocolate production and tour operation in the hills of Heredia, the folks from Sibú Chocolate have opened a small storefront in the Sabana Norte neighborhood.

Here you can pick up a mix of their wonderful truffles and bonbons, as well as cacao powder, chocolate bars, and cacao nibs (my family loves to sprinkle those on cereal and granola in the morning). This is also a great place to grab a cup of hot chocolate (or coffee) and a pastry. 2 blocks north of Rostipollos in Sabana Norte. www.sibuchocolate.com. ✆ **2220-0050.**

HANDICRAFTS

The range and quality of craftworks for sale here has improved greatly in recent years. In addition to the places listed below, you might want to check out the works of Lil Mena, a local artist who specializes in working with and painting on handmade papers and rough fibers, and **Cecilia "Pefi" Figueres ★★**, who creates brightly colored abstract and figurative ceramic bowls, pitchers, coffee mugs, and more. Works by both Mena and Figueres are sold at some of the better gift shops around the city.

Biesanz Woodworks ★★
Biesanz makes a wide range of high-quality wood items, including bowls, jewelry boxes, humidors, and some nifty sets of chopsticks. The company is actively involved in local reforestation, too. Bello Horizonte, Escazú. www.biesanz.com. ✆ **2289-4337.** Call for directions and off-hour appointments.

Boutique Annemarie ★
Occupying two floors at the Hotel Don Carlos (p. 69), this shop has an amazing array of wood products, leather goods, papier-mâché figurines, paintings, books, cards, posters, and jewelry. You'll see most of this stuff at the city's other shops, but not in such quantities or in such a relaxed and pressure-free environment. At the Hotel Don Carlos, Calle 9, btw. avs. 7 and 9. ✆ **2233-5343.**

Chietón Morén ★★★
Chietón Morén features Arts and Crafts from a dozen or so different Costa Rican indigenous communities, displayed in a space that is part museum and part showroom and market. Operating as a nonprofit and certified "fair trade" (the words *Chietón Morén* mean "fair deal" in the Boruca language), all the profits are given directly back to the artisans and their communities. Offerings include a wide range of textiles, carved masks, prints, and jewelry. Calle 1, btw. avs. 10 and 12. www.chietonmoren.org. ✆ **2221-0145.**

Galería Namu ★★★
Galería Namu offers quality Arts and Crafts, specializing in truly high-end indigenous works, including excellent Boruca and Huetar carved masks and "primitive" paintings. More modern Arts and Crafts pieces, including the ceramic work of Cecilia "Pefi" Figueres, are sold as well. The gallery also organizes tours to various indigenous tribes and artisans. Av. 7, btw. calles 5 and 7. www.galerianamu.com. ✆ **2256-3412.**

Kiosco ★★★
Attached to the restaurant Kalú (p. 77), this place features a range of original and one-off pieces of functional, wearable, and practical pieces made by contemporary Costa Rican and regional artists and designers. While the offerings are regularly changing, you'll usually find a selection of jewelry, handbags, shoes, dolls, furniture, and knickknacks. Often the pieces

are made with recycled or sustainable materials (but they don't look like it; they look luxe). Calle 31 and Av. 5, Barrio Escalante. www.kioscosjo.com. ✆ **2253-8426.**

Mercado Central ★   Although this tight maze of stalls is primarily a food market, vendors also sell souvenirs, leather goods, musical instruments, and many other items. Be especially careful with your wallet, purse, and prominent jewelry, as skilled pickpockets frequent the area. All of the streets surrounding the Mercado Central are jammed with produce vendors selling from small carts or loading and unloading trucks. It's always a hive of activity, with crowds of people jostling for space on the streets. Your best bet is to visit on Sunday or a weekday; Saturday is particularly busy. Btw. avs. Central and 1 and calles 6 and 8, San José. No phone.

Plaza de la Democracia ★★   Two long rows of outdoor stalls sell T-shirts, Guatemalan and Ecuadorian handicrafts and clothing, small ceramic ocarinas (a small wind instrument), and handmade jewelry. The atmosphere here is much more open than at the Mercado Central, which I find just a bit too claustrophobic. You might be able to talk prices down a bit, but bargaining is not a traditional part of the vendor culture here, so you'll have to work hard to save a few colones. On the west side of the Plaza de la Democracia, Calle 13 bis, btw. avs. Central and 2. No phone.

NIGHTLIFE

Catering to a mix of tourists, college students, and party-loving Ticos, San José has a host of options to meet the nocturnal needs of visitors and residents alike. You'll find plenty of fun clubs and bars, a range of theaters, and some very lively dance clubs.

To find out what's going on in San José while you're in town, check out the online, English-language *Tico Times* (www.ticotimes.net) or Spanish-language daily *La Nación.* The former is the place to find out where local expatriates are hanging out.

Tip: Several very popular nightlife venues are located in the upscale suburbs of Escazú and Santa Ana, as well as in Heredia (a college town) and Alajuela.

The Performing Arts

Visiting artists stop in Costa Rica on a regular basis. Recent concerts and performances have featured everyone from Aerosmith and Metallica to Cirque du Soleil. The **National Symphony Orchestra** is respectable by regional standards, although its repertoire tends to be rather conservative. Symphony season runs from March through November, with concerts roughly every other weekend at the **Teatro Nacional** (see below). Tickets cost between $3 and $30 and can be purchased at the box office.

Costa Rica's cultural panorama changes drastically every March when the country hosts large arts festivals. In odd-numbered years, **El Festival Nacional**

de las Artes reigns supreme, featuring purely local talent. In even-numbered years, the month-long fete is **El Festival Internacional de las Artes,** a nightly smorgasbord of dance, theater, and music from around the world. Most nights of the festival have between 4 and 10 shows. Many are free, and the most expensive ticket is usually around $5. For exact dates and details, you can contact the **Ministry of Youth and Culture** (www.mcj.go.cr; ℂ **2221-1022**), although information is in Spanish.

Teatro Nacional (National Theater) ★★ Costa Rica's most elegant and elaborate theater, the Teatro Nacional was opened in 1897. Funded with a special tax on coffee, and modeled on the Paris Opera House, this neo-baroque theater features marble floors and columns, numerous sculptures, and a beautiful fresco on the main auditorium's ceiling. It is home base for the National Symphony Orchestra, and site of numerous other cultural events. Av. 2, btw. calles 3 and 5. www.teatronacional.go.cr. ℂ **2010-1110.**

The Club, Music & Dance Scene

You'll find plenty of places to hit the dance floor in San José. Salsa and merengue are the main beats that move people here, and many of the city's dance clubs, discos, and salons feature live music on the weekends. You'll find a pretty limited selection, though, if you're looking to catch some small-club jazz, rock, or blues performances.

The daily "Viva" and Friday's "Tiempo Libre" sections of *La Nación* newspaper have weekly performance schedules. Some dance bands to watch for are Gaviota, Chocolate, Son de Tikizia, Taboga Band, and La Orquesta Son Mayor. While Ghandi, Akasha, and El Parque are popular local rock groups, Marfil is a good cover band, and the Blues Devils, Chepe Blues, and Las Tortugas are outfits that play American-style hard-driving rock and blues. If you're looking for jazz, check out Editus, El Sexteto de Jazz Latino, or pianist and former Minister of Culture Manuel Obregón. For something eclectic, look for Santos y Zurdo, Sonámbulo Psicotropical, or Cocofunk.

Most of the places listed below charge a nominal cover charge; sometimes it includes a drink or two.

Castro's ★ This is a classic Costa Rican dance club. The music varies throughout the night, from salsa and merengue to reggaeton and occasionally electronic trance. The rooms and various types of environments include some intimate and quiet corners, spread over a couple of floors, while the main dance floor features worn parquet flooring surrounded by fake palms. It's open daily from noon to anytime between 3 and 6am. Av. 13 and Calle 22, Barrio México. ℂ **2256-8789.**

Vértigo ★★ Tucked inside a nondescript office building and commercial center on Paseo Colón, this club remains one of the more popular places for rave-style late-night dancing and partying. The dance floor is huge and the ceilings are high, and electronic music rules the roost. It's open Friday and Saturday till 6am. Edificio Colón, Paseo Colón. www.vertigocr.com. ℂ **2257-8424.**

The Bar Scene

San José has something for every taste. Lounge lizards will be happy in most hotel bars downtown, while students and the young at heart will have no problem mixing in at the livelier spots around town. Sports fans have plenty of places to catch the most important games of the day, and a couple of brewpubs are drastically improving the quality and selection of the local suds.

The best part of the varied bar scene in San José is something called a *boca,* the equivalent of tapas in Spain: a little dish of snacks that arrives at your table when you order a drink. Although this is a somewhat dying tradition, especially in the younger, hipper bars, you'll still find *bocas* alive and well in the older, more traditional San José drinking establishments. The most traditional of these are known locally as *cantinas.* In most, the *bocas* are free, but in some, where the dishes are more sophisticated, you'll have to pay for the treats. You'll find drinks reasonably priced, with beer costing around $2 to $3 a bottle, and mixed drinks costing $4 to $10.

El Cuartel de la Boca del Monte ★★ This popular bar, one of San José's best, began life as an artist-and-bohemian hangout, and has evolved into a massive melting pot, attracting everyone from the city's young and well-heeled, to foreign exchange students and visitors. Artists still come, too.

One of the many bars on La Calle de Amargura in San Pedro.

Live music is usually Monday, Wednesday, and Friday nights, when the place is packed shoulder to shoulder. From Monday to Friday, it's open for lunch and again in the evenings; on weekends, it opens at 6pm. On most nights, it's open till about 1am, although the revelry might continue till about 3am on Friday or Saturday. Av. 1, btw. calles 21 and 23 (50m/½ block west of the Cine Magaly). © **2221-0327.**

El Sótano ★★ *El Sótano* translates as "the basement," and that's just where you'll find this tiny bar and performance space. On most nights, you'll find some of the city's best jazz and blues players holding forth, and on Tuesdays, there's an open jam session. A small menu of bar food and sandwiches is available. When there's no live band, the house music is entirely played from vinyl. Upstairs from El Sótano is a separate bar and lounge space, El Solar. It's open 6pm to 2am daily. Calle 3, btw. avs. 9 and 11. © **2221-2302.**

El Steinvorth ★★ This is one of San José's trendiest clubs, and one of the only places where you might find a line to get in, or be turned away because the doorman doesn't like how you're dressed or think you're cool enough. It's housed in an old brick building with a crumbling facade, and inside you'll find a large contemporary space with several rooms, art hanging on the walls, and a second-floor balcony area that looks down on one of the main dance spaces. DJs blast their best mixes through a strong sound system, with a heavy emphasis on contemporary electronic dance music. El Steinvorth is open Wednesday through Saturday from 9pm until at least 5am. www.elsteinvorth.com. Calle 1, btw. avs. Central and 1. No phone.

HANGING OUT IN SAN PEDRO

The funky 2-block stretch of **San Pedro** ★★ just south of the University of Costa Rica has been dubbed La Calle de Amargura, or the "Street of Bitterness," and it's the heart and soul of this eastern suburb and college town. Bars and cafes are mixed in with bookstores and copy shops. After dark, the streets are packed with teens, punks, students, and professors barhopping and just hanging around. You can walk the strip until someplace strikes your fancy—or you can try one of the places listed below. *Note:* La Calle de Amargura attracts a certain unsavory element. Use caution here. Try to visit with a group, and try not to carry large amounts of cash or wear flashy jewelry.

Jazz Café ★ The Jazz Café is one of the more happening spots in San Pedro, and is consistently a great spot to find live music. It remains one of my favorites, although low ceilings and poor air circulation make it almost unbearably smoky most nights. Wrought-iron chairs, sculpted busts of famous jazz artists, and creative lighting give the place ambience. There's live music here most nights. It's open daily till about 2am. Sister club **Jazz Café Escazú** (© **2288-4740**) is on the western end of town. Next to the Banco Popular on Av. Central. www.jazzcafecostarica.com. © **2253-8933.**

Mundoloco El Chante ★★ This club is the brainchild of DJ, radio host, and musician Bernal Monestel. I tend to start off meeting friends at the street-front open-air terrace, just off the entrance. A jukebox plays both English and Spanish-language rock from the 70s, 80s, and 90s. There's also a continuation of this casual pub-bar vibe just inside, before a separate entrance leading to a performance space and stage in back, where you'll find live music or DJs most nights—usually with a slight cover charge. Bands tend to be eclectic, with a tendency toward electronic and world music, in addition to homegrown rock and reggae outfits. Southeast corner of the Banco Popular on Av. Central. www.facebook.com/MundolocoElChante. ✆ **2253-4125.**

Casinos

Gambling is legal in Costa Rica, with casinos at several major hotels. However, some idiosyncrasies are involved in gambling "a la Tica."

If blackjack is your game, you'll want to play "rummy." The rules are almost identical, except that the house doesn't pay 1½ times on blackjack—instead, it pays double on any three of a kind or three-card straight flush.

If you're looking for roulette, what you'll find here is a bingo-like spinning cage of numbered balls. The betting is the same, but some of the glamour is lost.

You'll also find a version of five-card-draw poker, but the rule differences are so complex that I advise you to sit down and watch for a while and then ask questions before joining in. That's about all you'll find. There are no craps tables or baccarat.

There's some controversy over slot machines—one-armed bandits are currently outlawed—but you will be able to play electronic slots and poker games. Most casinos here are casual and small by international standards. You may have to dress up slightly at some of the fancier hotels, but most are accustomed to tropical vacation attire.

DAY TRIPS FROM SAN JOSÉ

San José makes an excellent base for exploring the beautiful Central Valley. For first-time visitors, the best way to make the most of these excursions is usually to take a guided tour, but if you rent a car, you'll have greater independence. Some day trips also can be done by public bus.

Guided Tours & Adventures

A number of companies offer a wide variety of primarily nature-related day tours out of San José. The most reputable include **Costa Rica Sun Tours** ★ (www.crsuntours.com; ✆ **866/271-6263** in the U.S. and Canada, or 2296-7757 in Costa Rica), **Horizontes Tours** ★★ (www.horizontes.com; ✆ **888/786-8748** in the U.S. and Canada, or 2222-2022 in Costa Rica), and **Swiss Travel Service** (www.swisstravelcr.com; ✆ **2282-4898**). Prices range from around $35 to $70 for a half-day trip, and from $70 to $160 for a full-day trip.

Before signing on for a tour of any sort, find out how many fellow travelers will be accompanying you, how much time will be spent in transit and eating lunch, and how much time will actually be spent doing the primary activity. I've had complaints about tours that were rushed, that spent too much time in a bus or on secondary activities, or that had a cattle-car, assembly-line feel to them. You'll find many tours that combine two or three different activities or destinations.

AERIAL TRAM The most popular canopy-style day trip destination from San José is the **Rainforest Aerial Tram Atlantic ★** (www.rainforesttram. com; © **866/759-8726** in the U.S. and Canada, or 2257-5961 in Costa Rica), built on a private reserve bordering Braulio Carrillo National Park. This pioneering tramway is the brainchild of rainforest researcher Dr. Donald Perry, whose cable-car system through the forest canopy at Rara Avis helped establish him as an early expert on rainforest canopies. On the 90-minute tram ride through the treetops, visitors have the chance to glimpse the complex web of life that makes these forests unique. Additional attractions include a butterfly garden, serpentarium, and frog collection. They also have their own zip-line canopy tour, and the grounds feature well-groomed trails through the rainforest and a restaurant—with all this on offer, a trip here can easily take up a full day. If you want to spend the night, 10 simple but clean and comfortable bungalows cost $125 per person per day (double occupancy), including three meals, a guided hike, taxes, the signature tram ride, and unlimited use of the rest of the facilities.

The cost for a full-day tour, including both the aerial tram and canopy tour, as well as all the park's other attractions, is $99 adults; students and those 17 and under pay $65. Packages, including round-trip transportation and lunch, are also available. Alternatively, you can drive or take one of the frequent Guápiles buses—they leave every half-hour throughout the day and cost C1,405—from the Caribbean bus terminal (Gran Terminal del Caribe) on Calle Central and Avenida 15. Ask the driver to let you off in front of the *teleférico* (cable car). If you're driving, head out on the Guápiles Highway as if driving to the Caribbean coast. Watch for the tram's roadside welcome center—it's hard to miss. Because this is a popular tour for groups, I highly recommend that you get an advance reservation in the high season and, if possible, a ticket; otherwise you could wait a long time for your tram ride or even be shut out. The tram handles only about 80 passengers per hour, so scheduling is tight; the folks here try to schedule as much as possible in advance.

DAY CRUISES Several companies offer cruises to lovely Tortuga Island in the Gulf of Nicoya. These full-day tours generally entail an early departure for the 1½-hour chartered bus ride to Puntarenas, where you board a vessel for a 1½-hour cruise to Tortuga Island. Then you get several hours on the uninhabited island, where you can swim, lie on the beach, play volleyball, or try a canopy tour.

The original and most dependable company running these trips is **Calypso Tours ★** (www.calypsocruises.com; © **855/855-1975** in the U.S. and Canada, or 2256-2727 in Costa Rica). The tour costs $145 per person and includes

Day Trips from San José

SAN JOSÉ

round-trip transportation from San José, Jacó, or Manuel Antonio, a buffet breakfast before embarking on the boat, all drinks on the cruise, and an excellent buffet lunch on the beach at the island. The Calypso Tours main vessel is a massive, motor-powered catamaran. They also run a separate tour to a private nature reserve at **Punta Coral** ★. The beach is much nicer at Tortuga Island, but the tour to Punta Coral is more intimate, and the restaurant, hiking, and kayaking are all superior here. These folks provide daily pickups from San José, Manuel Antonio, Jacó, and Monteverde, and you can use the day trip on the boat as your transfer or transportation option between any of these towns and destinations.

RAFTING, KAYAKING & RIVER TRIPS   Cascading down Costa Rica's mountain ranges are dozens of tumultuous rivers, several of which are very popular for white-water rafting and kayaking. If I had to choose just one day trip out of San José, it would be a white-water rafting excursion. For between $75 and $120, you can spend a day rafting through lush tropical forests; multiday trips are also available. Some of the most reliable rafting companies are **Aventuras Naturales** ★★ (www.adventurecostarica.com; ✆ **888/680-9031** in the U.S., or 2225-3939 in Costa Rica), **Exploradores Outdoors** ★ (www. exploradoresoutdoors.com; ✆ **646/205-0828** in the U.S. and Canada, or 2222-6262 in Costa Rica), and **Ríos Tropicales** ★★ (www.riostropicales.com; ✆ **866/722-8273** in the U.S. and Canada, or 2233-6455 in Costa Rica). These companies all ply a number of rivers of varying difficulty, including the popular Pacuare and Reventazón rivers. Moreover, any of these companies will drop you off in Arenal or on the Caribbean coast at the end of the rafting trip, essentially getting you an in-country transfer for the price of the rafting trip. For details, see "White-Water Rafting & Kayaking" in chapter 12.

Cartago & the Orosí Valley

These two regions southeast of San José can easily be combined into a day trip. You might also squeeze in a visit to the Irazú Volcano (see below for details).

CARTAGO

Located about 24km (15 miles) southeast of San José, **Cartago** ★ is the original capital of Costa Rica. Founded in 1563, it was Costa Rica's first city—and was, in fact, its only city for almost 150 years. Irazú Volcano rises up from the edge of town, and although it's quiet these days, it has not always been so peaceful. Earthquakes have damaged Cartago repeatedly over the years, so few of the colonial buildings are left standing. In the center of the city, a public park winds through **Las Ruinas,** the ruins of a large church that was destroyed in 1910 before it could be finished. Construction was abandoned after the quake, and today the ruins sit at the heart of a neatly manicured park, with quiet paths and plenty of benches. The ruins themselves are closed off, but the park around them is lovely. (The park is a free Wi-Fi hot spot as well.)

Cartago's most famous building is the **Basílica de Nuestra Señora de los Ángeles (Basilica of Our Lady of the Angels)** ★★★, which is dedicated to

HOLY SMOKE! FINDING THE RIGHT
volcano TRIP

Poás, Irazú, and Arenal volcanoes are three of Costa Rica's most popular destinations, and the first two are easy day trips from San José (see below). Although numerous companies offer day trips to Arenal, I don't recommend them because travel time is at least 3½ hours in each direction.

Most tour companies in the city and hotel tour desks can arrange a day trip to any of these volcanoes. Prices range from $30 to $50 for a half-day trip, and from $50 to $120 for a full-day trip.

The 3,432m (11,260-ft.) **Irazú Volcano ★** (℃ **2200-4222**) is historically one of Costa Rica's more active volcanoes, although it's relatively quiet these days. It last erupted on March 19, 1963, the day that President John F. Kennedy arrived in Costa Rica. There's a good paved road right to the rim of the crater, where a desolate expanse of gray sand nurtures few plants and the air smells of sulfur. The landscape here is often compared to that of the moon. There are magnificent views of the fertile Meseta Central and Orosí Valley as you drive up from Cartago, and if you're very lucky, you might be able to see both the Pacific Ocean and the Caribbean Sea. Clouds usually descend by noon, so get here as early in the day as possible.

The visitor center has info on the volcano and natural history. A short trail leads to the rim of the volcano's two craters, their walls a maze of eroded gullies feeding onto the flat floor far below. This is a national park, with an admission fee of $15 charged at the gate. Dress in layers; this might be the tropics, but it can be cold up top if the sun's not out. The park restaurant, at an elevation of 3,022m (9,915 ft.), with walls of windows looking out over the valley far below, claims to be the highest restaurant in Central America.

Poás Volcano ★★ (℃ **2482-1228**) is 37km (23 miles) from San José on narrow roads that wind through a landscape of fertile farms and dark forests. As at Irazú, there's a paved road right to the top, although you'll have to hike in about 1km (½ mile) to reach the crater. The volcano stands 2,708m (8,885 ft.) tall and is located within a national park, which preserves not only the volcano but also dense stands of virgin forest. Poás's crater, said to be the second largest in the world, is more than a mile across. Geysers in the crater sometimes spew steam and muddy water 180m (590 ft.) into the air, making this the largest geyser in the world. There's an information center where you can see a slideshow about the volcano, and there are well-groomed and -marked hiking trails through the cloud forest that rings the crater. About 15 minutes from the parking area, along a forest trail, is an overlook onto beautiful Botos Lake, which has formed in one of the volcano's extinct craters.

Be prepared when you come to Poás: This volcano is often enveloped in dense clouds. If you want to see the crater, it's best to come early and during the dry season. Moreover, it can get cool up here, especially when the sun isn't shining, so dress appropriately. Admission to Poás Volcano National Park is $15.

the patron saint of Costa Rica and stands on the east side of town. Within the walls of this Byzantine-style church is a shrine containing the tiny carved figure of **La Negrita,** the Black Virgin, which is nearly lost amid its ornate altar. Legend has it that La Negrita first revealed herself on this site to a peasant girl in 1635. The walls of the shrine are covered with a fascinating array of tiny silver images left as thanks for cures affected by La Negrita. Amid the plethora of diminutive silver arms and legs, there are also hands, feet, hearts, lungs, kidneys, eyes, torsos, breasts, and—peculiarly—guns, trucks, beds, and planes. There are even dozens of sports trophies that I assume were left as thanks for helping teams win big games. Outside the church, vendors sell a wide selection of these trinkets, as well as little candle replicas of La Negrita.

More than 1km (½ mile) east of Cartago, on the road to Paraíso, you'll find **Lankester Gardens** ★★ (see below) a botanical garden known for its orchids.

GETTING THERE **Lumaca** buses (✆ **2537-2320**) for Cartago leave San José every 3 to 5 minutes between 4:30am and 9pm, with slightly less frequent service until midnight, from Calle 5 and Avenida 10. You can also pick up one en route at any of the little covered bus stops along Avenida Central in Los Yoses and San Pedro. The length of the trip is 45 minutes; the fare is about $1.10. The Paraíso bus stop is 1 block south and ¾ block west of the Catholic church ruins in Cartago (the ride takes 30–40 min., and the fare is around 65¢).

Lankester Gardens ★★ GARDEN Costa Rica has more than 1,400 varieties of orchids, and almost 800 species are cultivated and on display at this botanical garden in Cartago province. Created in the 1940s by English naturalist Charles Lankester, the gardens are administered by the University of Costa Rica. The primary goal is to preserve the local flora, with an emphasis on orchids and bromeliads. Paved, well-marked trails meander from open, sunny gardens into shady forests. In each environment, different species of orchids are in bloom. There's an information center and gift shop. Plan to spend between 1 and 3 hours here if you're interested in flowers and gardening; you could run through it more quickly if you're not. You can easily combine a visit here with a tour at Cartago and/or the Orosí Valley and Irazú Volcano.

1km (½ mile) east of Cartago, on road to Paraíso de Cartago. www.jbl.ucr.ac.cr. ✆ **2511-7939.** Admission $8 adults, $5 children 6–16. Daily 8:30am–4:30pm.

OROSI VALLEY

The Orosí Valley, southeast of Cartago and visible from the top of Irazú on a clear day, is considered one of the most beautiful valleys in Costa Rica. The Reventazón River meanders through this steep-sided valley until it collects in the lake formed by the Cachí Dam. There are scenic overlooks near the town of Orosí, which is at the head of the valley, and in Ujarrás, which is on the banks of the lake. Near **Ujarrás** are the ruins of Costa Rica's oldest church (built in 1693), whose tranquil gardens are a great place to sit and gaze at the surrounding mountains. In the town of Orosí itself, there's yet another colonial church and convent, built in 1743. A small museum here displays religious artifacts.

Near the town of Cachí, you'll find **La Casa del Soñador (House of the Dreamer)** ★ (✆ **8955-7779**), the home and gallery of the late sculptor

Legend has it that Juana Pereira stumbled upon the statue of La Negrita, sitting atop a rock, while gathering wood. Juana took it home, but the next morning it was gone. She went back to the rock, and there it was again. This was repeated three times, until Juana took her find to a local priest. The priest took the statue to his church for safekeeping, but the next morning it was gone, only to be found sitting upon the same rock later that day. The priest eventually decided that the strange occurrences were a sign that the Virgin wanted a temple or shrine built to her upon the spot. And so work was begun on what would eventually become today's impressive basilica.

Miraculous healing powers have been attributed to La Negrita, and, over the years, a parade of pilgrims have come to the shrine seeking cures for their illnesses and difficulties. August 2 is her patron saint day. Each year, on this date, tens of thousands of Costa Ricans and foreign pilgrims walk to Cartago from San José and elsewhere in the country in devotion to this statue.

Macedonio Quesada and his sons, who carry on the family tradition. Quesada earned fame with his primitive sculptures of La Negrita (see above) and other religious and secular characters carved on coffee tree roots and trunks. You can see some of Macedonio's original work here, including his version of "The Last Supper" carved onto one of the walls of the main building. You can also shop its current collection of small sculptures, carved religious icons, and ornate walking sticks.

From the Orosí Valley, it's a quick shot to the entrance to the **Tapantí National Park** ★ (© **2206-5615;** daily 8am–4pm), where you'll find some gentle and beautiful hiking trails, as well as riverside picnic areas. Admission is $10.

If you're interested in staying out here, the charming little **Orosí Lodge** (www.orosilodge.com; © **2533-3578**) is right next to some simple hot spring pools.

GETTING THERE   If you're driving, take the road to Paraíso from Cartago, head toward Ujarrás, continue around the lake, and then pass through Cachí and on to Orosí. From Orosí, the road leads back to Paraíso. It is difficult to explore this whole area by public bus because this is not a densely populated region and connections are often infrequent or unreliable. However, there are regular buses from Cartago to the town of Orosí. These buses run roughly every half-hour and leave the main bus terminal in Cartago. The trip takes 30 minutes, and the fare is C310. There are also guided day tours of this area from San José (call any of the companies listed under "Guided Tours & Adventures," earlier in this chapter).

Heredia, Sarchí ★ & Zarcero

In the volcanic hillsides northwest of San José, the scenery is rich and verdant, and the small towns and scattered farming communities are truly representative of Costa Rica's agricultural heartland and *campesino* (peasant) tradition.

All of these cities and towns are northwest of San José and can be combined into a long day trip (if you have a car), perhaps in conjunction with a visit to Poás Volcano and/or the La Paz Waterfall Gardens. Sarchí and Zarcero can also be convenient stopping points on the way to La Fortuna and the Arenal Volcano area. This is a great area to explore on your own in a rental car, if you don't mind getting lost a bit (roads are narrow, winding, and poorly marked). The road to Heredia turns north off the highway from San José to the airport. If you're going to Sarchí, take the highway west toward Puntarenas. Turn north to Grecia and then west to Sarchí. There'll be plenty of signs.

HEREDIA

Set on the flanks of the impressive Barva Volcano, this city was founded in 1706. Heredia is affectionately known as "The City of Flowers." A colonial church inaugurated in 1763 stands in the central park—the stone facade leaves no questions as to the age of the church. The altar inside is decorated with neon stars and a crescent moon surrounding a statue of the Virgin Mary. In the middle of the palm-shaded park is a music temple, and across the street, beside several tile-roofed municipal buildings, is the tower of an old Spanish fort. Of all the cities in the Meseta Central, Heredia has the most colonial feel to it—you'll still see adobe buildings with Spanish tile roofs along narrow streets. Heredia is also the site of the **National Autonomous University,** and you'll find some nice coffee shops and bookstores near the school.

Surrounding Heredia is an intricate maze of picturesque villages and towns, including Santa Bárbara, Santo Domingo, Barva, and San Joaquín de Flores. San Isidro de Heredia has a lovely, large church with an ornate facade. However, the biggest attraction up here is **INBio Park ★★** (p. 83). Located on 5 hectares (12 acres) in Santo Domingo de Heredia, this place is part museum, part educational center, and part nature park. This is also where you'll find the **Café Britt Farm ★** (p. 83). Anyone with an interest in medicinal herbs should plan a visit to the **Ark Herb Farm ★** (www.arkherbfarm.com; © **8922-7599** or 2269-4847). These folks offer guided tours of their gardens, which feature more than 300 types of medicinal plants. The tour costs $12 per person, and includes a light snack and refreshments. Reservations are required.

Buses (© **2233-8392**) leave for Heredia every 10 minutes between 5am and 11pm from Calle 1, between avenidas 7 and 9, or from Avenida 2, between calles 12 and 14. Bus fare is C445.

SARCHÍ ★

Sarchí is Costa Rica's main artisan town. The colorfully painted miniature **oxcarts** that you see all over the country are made here. Oxcarts such as these were once used to haul coffee beans to market. Today, most are purely decorative. However, they remain a well-known symbol of Costa Rica. In addition to miniature oxcarts, many carved wooden souvenirs are made here with rare hardwoods from the nation's forests. There are dozens of shops in town, and all have similar prices. Perhaps your best one-stop shop in Sarchí is the large and long-standing **Chaverri Oxcart Factory ★** (© **2454-4411**), which is right in the center of things, but it never hurts to shop around and visit several of the stores.

Aside from handicrafts, you'll want to see the town's main **church ★**; built between 1950 and 1958, it's painted pink with aquamarine trim and looks strangely like a child's birthday cake. But my favorite attraction here is the **Else Kientzler Botanical Garden ★★** (see below).

While there are no noteworthy accommodations in Sarchí itself, the plush **El Silencio Lodge & Spa** (www.elsilenciolodge.com; © **2231-6122**) is about a 35-minute drive away in a beautiful mountain setting.

GETTING THERE   Tuan (© **2494-2139**) buses leave San José for Grecia, with connections to Sarchí from Calle 18 between avenidas 3 and 5. The fare is C985. Alternatively, you can take one of the Alajuela-Sarchí buses, leaving every 30 minutes from Calle 8 between avenidas Central and 1 in Alajuela.

Else Kientzler Botanical Garden ★★ GARDEN   Located on the grounds of an ornamental flower farm, on the outskirts of the tourist town Sarchí, these are extensive, impressive, and lovingly laid-out botanical gardens. More than 2.5km (1.5 miles) of trails run through a collection of more than 2,000 species of flora. All the plants are labeled with their Latin names, with some further explanations around the grounds in both English and Spanish. There's a topiary labyrinth, as well as a variety of lookouts, gazebos, and shady benches on the grounds. A children's play area features some water games, jungle gym setups, and a child-friendly, little zip-line canopy tour. More than 40% of the gardens are wheelchair accessible.

About 6 blocks north of the central football (soccer) stadium in the town of Sarchí, Alajuela. www.elsegarden.com. © **2454-2070.** Admission $12 adults, $9 students with valid ID and children 5–12. Fee includes 1-hour guided tour. Reservations recommended. Daily 8am–4pm.

ZARCERO

Beyond Sarchí, on picturesque roads lined with cedar trees, you'll find the town of Zarcero. In a small park in the middle of town is a **menagerie of sculpted shrubs** that includes a monkey on a motorcycle, people and animals dancing, an ox pulling a cart, a man wearing a top hat, and a large elephant. Behind all the topiary is a wonderful rural **church.** It's not really worth the drive just to see this park, but it's a good idea to take a break on the way to La Fortuna and Arenal Volcano to walk the gardens in Zarcero.

Daily **buses** (© **2255-0567**) for Zarcero leave from San José hourly from the Atlántico del Norte bus station at Calle 12, avenidas 14 and 18. This is actually the Ciudad Quesada–San Carlos bus. Just tell the driver that you want to get off in Zarcero, and keep an eye out for the topiary. The ride takes around 1½ hours, and the fare is around C1,870.

GUANACASTE & THE NICOYA PENINSULA

Guanacaste and the Nicoya Peninsula are Costa Rica's "Gold Coast"—and not because this is where the Spanish conquistadors found vast quantities of the brilliant metal ore. Instead, it's because more and more visitors to Costa Rica are choosing this region as their first—and often only—stop. Beautiful beaches abound along this coastline. Several are packed with a mix of hotels and resorts, some are still pristine and deserted, and others are backed by small fishing villages. Beaches range from long, broad sections of sand stretching on for miles, to tiny pocket coves bordered by rocky headlands.

This is Costa Rica's most coveted vacation destination and the site of its greatest tourism development. The international airport in Liberia receives daily direct flights from several major U.S. and Canadian hub cities, allowing tourists to visit some of Costa Rica's prime destinations without having to go through San José.

This is also Costa Rica's driest region. The rainy season starts later and ends earlier, and overall it's more dependably sunny here than in other parts of the country. Combine this climate with a coastline that stretches south for hundreds of miles, from the Nicaraguan border all the way to the Nicoya Peninsula, and you have an equation that yields beach bliss.

One caveat: During the dry season (mid-Nov to Apr), when sunshine is most reliable, the hillsides in Guanacaste turn browner than the chaparral of Southern California. Dust from dirt roads blankets the trees in many areas, and the vistas are far from tropical. Driving these dirt roads without air-conditioning and with the windows rolled up tight can be extremely unpleasant.

On the other hand, if you happen to visit this area in the rainy season (particularly May–Aug), the hillsides are a beautiful, rich green, and the sun usually shines all morning, giving way to an afternoon shower—just in time for a nice siesta.

Inland from the beaches, Guanacaste remains Costa Rica's "Wild West," a land of dry plains populated with cattle ranches and cowboys, who are known here as *sabaneros,* a name that derives from the Spanish word for "savanna" or "grassland." If it weren't for those rainforest-clad volcanoes in the distance, you might swear you were in Texas.

Guanacaste is home to several active volcanoes and some beautiful national parks, including **Santa Rosa National Park** ★, the site of massive sea-turtle nestings and of a major battle to maintain independence; **Rincón de la Vieja National Park** ★★, which features hot springs and bubbling mud pots, pristine waterfalls, and an active volcanic crater; and **Palo Verde National Park** ★, a beautiful expanse of mangroves, wetlands, and savanna.

Heading south from Guanacaste takes you to the Nicoya Peninsula, where you'll find the beach towns of **Playa Sámara, Playa Nosara, Montezuma, Malpaís,** and **Santa Teresa.** The beaches of the Nicoya Peninsula don't get nearly as much attention or traffic as those to the north in Guanacaste. However, they are just as stunning, varied, and rewarding.

With easy access via paved roads and the time-saving La Amistad Bridge, Playa Sámara is one of the coastline's more popular destinations, especially with Ticos looking for a quick and easy weekend getaway. Just north of Sámara, Nosara and its neighboring beaches remain remote and sparsely visited, thanks in large part to the horrendous dirt road that separates these distinctly different destinations. However, Nosara is widely known and coveted as one of the country's top **surf spots,** with a host of different beach and point breaks from which to choose.

Down on the tip of the peninsula sit Montezuma, Malpaís, and Santa Teresa. Montezuma, with its jungle waterfalls and gentle surf, is the original beach destination out this way. However, it has been eclipsed by the up-and-coming hot spots of Malpaís and Santa Teresa, two adjacent beach areas popular with surfers, sun seekers, and a host of A-list celebrities.

PLAYA HERMOSA ★, PLAYA PANAMÁ ★ & PAPAGAYO ★

258km (160 miles) NW of San José; 40km (25 miles) SW of Liberia

While most of Costa Rica's coast is highly coveted by surfers, the beaches here are mostly protected and calm, making them good destinations for families with kids. Plus, they are the closest beaches to the **Daniel Oduber International Airport** in Liberia.

Playa Hermosa ★ means "beautiful beach," which is an apt moniker for this pretty crescent of sand. Surrounded by steep, forested hills, this curving gray-sand beach is long and wide, and the surf is usually quite gentle. Fringing the beach is a swath of trees that stays surprisingly green even during the dry season. The shade provided by these trees, along with the calm, protected waters, is a big part of the beach's appeal. Rocky headlands jut out into the surf at both ends of the beach, and at the base of these rocks are fun tide pools to explore.

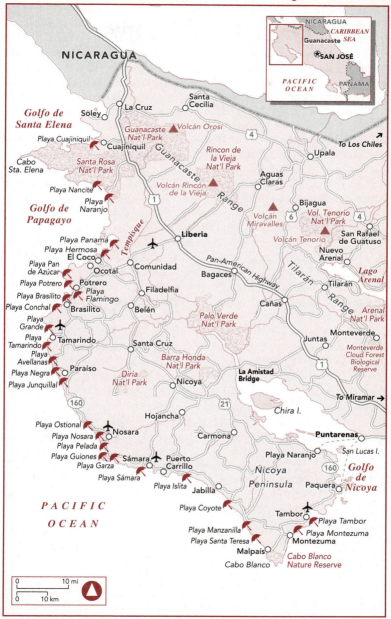

NICARAGUA

CARIBBEAN SEA

Guanacaste

PACIFIC OCEAN

★SAN JOSÉ

PANAMA

NICARAGUA

Golfo de Santa Elena

Soley

La Cruz

Santa Cecilia

Guanacaste Nat'l Park

Volcán Orosi

4

To Los Chiles

Playa Cuajiniquil

Cuajiniquil

Cabo Sta. Elena

Santa Rosa Nat'l Park

1

Rincon de la Vieja Nat'l Park

Upala

Volcán Rincón de la Vieja

Aguas Claras

Playa Nancite

Playa Naranjo

Golfo de Papagayo

Volcán Miravalles

Bijagua

Vol. Tenorio Nat'l Park

4

Volcán Tenorio

San Rafael de Guatuso

Playa Panamá

Playa Hermosa

El Coco

Ocotal

Liberia

Nuevo Arenal

Playa Pan de Azúcar

Comunidad

Pan-American Highway

Bagaces

Lago Arenal

Tilarán

Playa Potrero

Potrero

Filadelfia

Playa Brasilito

Playa Flamingo

Playa Conchal

Belén

Brasilito

Cañas

Arenal Nat'l Park

Playa Grande

Palo Verde Nat'l Park

Monteverde

Playa Tamarindo

Tamarindo

Santa Cruz

Juntas

Monteverde Cloud Forest Biological Reserve

Playa Avellanas

Barra Honda Nat'l Park

Playa Negra

Paraíso

La Amistad Bridge

1

Playa Junquillal

Diria Nat'l Park

Nicoya

To Miramar

160

Chira I.

21

Playa Ostional

Hojancha

Playa Nosara

Nosara

Puntarenas

Playa Pelada

Carmona

San Lucas I.

Playa Guiones

Sámara

Puerto Carrillo

Playa Naranjo

160

Golfo de Nicoya

Playa Garza

Nicoya Peninsula

Paquera

Playa Sámara

Playa Islita

Jabilla

PACIFIC OCEAN

Playa Coyote

Tambor

Playa Tambor

Playa Manzanilla

Playa Montezuma

Playa Santa Teresa

Montezuma

Malpaís

Cabo Blanco

Cabo Blanco Nature Reserve

0   10 mi

0   10 km

Golfo de Santa Elena — Guanacaste Range — Tempisque — Tilarán Range

Beyond Playa Hermosa, you'll find **Playa Panamá** ★ and, farther on, the calm waters of **Bahía Culebra** ★, a large, protected bay dotted with small, private patches of beach and ringed with mostly intact dry forest. Around the north end of Bahía Culebra is the **Papagayo Peninsula** ★, home to two large, all-inclusive resorts and one championship golf course. This peninsula has a half-dozen or so small to midsize beaches, the nicest of which might just be **Playa Nacascolo** ★★★, which is inside the domain of the Four Seasons Resort here—but all beaches in Costa Rica are public, so you can visit, albeit after passing through security and parking at the public parking lot.

Essentials

GETTING THERE & DEPARTING   By Plane: The **Daniel Oduber International Airport** (✆ **2668-1010;** airport code LIR) in Liberia receives a steady stream of scheduled commercial and charter flights throughout the year. Major North American airlines have direct links to Liberia. In addition, numerous commercial charter flights from various North American cities fly in throughout the high season. Check with your travel agent.

Sansa (www.flysansa.com; ✆ **877/767-2672** in the U.S. and Canada, or 2290-4100 in Costa Rica) and **Nature Air** (www.natureair.com; ✆ **800/235-9272** in the U.S. and Canada, or 2299-6000 in Costa Rica) both have several flights daily to Liberia. Fares run between $105 and $155 each way.

From the airport, you can hire a taxi to bring you to any of the beach destinations in this area. The ride should take between 25 and 30 minutes and cost $40 to $60.

The following car rental companies all have local agencies: **Adobe** (✆ 2667-0608), **Alamo** (✆ 2668-1115), **Avis** (✆ 2668-1196), **Budget** (✆ 2668-1118), **Dollar** (✆ 2668-1001), **Hertz** (✆ 2668-1179), **Thrifty** (✆ 2665-0787), and **Toyota** (✆ 2668-1212). You can also reserve with these and most major international car-rental companies via their San José and international offices.

By Car: From San José, you can either take the Interamerican Highway (CR1) north all the way to Liberia from downtown San José, or first head west out of the city on the San José–Caldera Highway (CR27). When you reach Caldera, follow the signs to Puntarenas, Liberia, and the Interamerican Highway (CR1). This latter route is a faster and flatter drive.

Once you reach the main intersection of CR1 at the crossroads of Liberia, turn left on to CR21 toward Santa Cruz and the beaches of Guanacaste. The turnoff for the Papagayo Peninsula is prominently marked 8km (5 miles) south of the Liberia airport. At the corner here, you'll see a massive Do It Center hardware store and lumberyard.

If you are going to a hotel along the Papagayo Peninsula, turn at the Do It Center and follow the paved road out and around the peninsula. If you are going to Playa Panamá or Playa Hermosa, you should also turn here and take the access road shortcut that leads from a turnoff on the Papagayo Peninsula road, just beyond the Do It Center, directly to Playa Panamá. When you reach Playa Panamá, turn left for Playa Hermosa.

To get to Playa Hermosa, you can also continue on a little farther west on CR21 and, just past the village of Comunidad, turn right. In about 11km (6¾ miles), you'll come to a fork in the road; take the right leg.

These roads are all relatively well marked, and a host of prominent hotel billboards should make it easy enough to find the beach or resort you are looking for. The drive takes about 4 to 4½ hours from San José.

By Bus: A **Tralapa** express bus (© **2221-7202**) leaves San José daily at 3:30pm from Calle 20 and Avenida 3, stopping at Playa Hermosa and Playa Panamá, 3km (1¾ miles) farther north. The one-way fare for the 5-hour trip is around C5,500.

Gray Line (www.graylinecostarica.com; © **800/719-3105** in the U.S. and Canada, or 2220-2126 in Costa Rica) and **Interbus** (www.interbusonline. com; © **4100-0888**) both have two daily buses leaving San José for all beaches in this area, one in the morning and one in the afternoon. The fare is around $50. Both companies will pick you up at most San José–area hotels, and they make connections to most other major tourist destinations in Costa Rica.

You can also take a bus from San José to Liberia and then take a bus from Liberia to Playa Hermosa and Playa Panamá. **Pulmitan** express buses (© **2222-1650** in San José, or 2666-0458 in Liberia) leave San José roughly every hour between 6am and 8pm from Calle 24 between avenidas 5 and 7. The ride to Liberia takes around 4 hours. A one-way fare costs C4,000. **Transportes La Pampa** buses (© **2665-7530**) leave Liberia for Playa Hermosa and Playa Panamá at least a half-dozen times daily between 4:30am and 5:30pm. The trip lasts 40 minutes because the bus stops frequently to drop off and pick up passengers. The one-way fare costs C750. These bus schedules change from time to time, so it's best to check in advance. During the high season and on weekends, extra buses from Liberia are sometimes added. You can also take a bus to Playa del Coco, from which playas Hermosa and Panamá are a relatively quick taxi ride away. Taxi fare should run C8,000 to C10,000.

Where to Stay
EXPENSIVE

In addition to the Four Seasons, the **Andaz Peninsula Papagayo Resort ★★★** (http://papagayo.andaz.hyatt.com; © **800/233-1234** in the U.S. and Canada, or 2690-1234 in Costa Rica) is another excellent, large-scale luxury resort on the Papagayo Peninsula.

Four Seasons Resort Costa Rica ★★★   It can get hot in Guanacaste, but you'll always be greeted here with a chilled damp towel with a citrus scent. The Four Seasons is set near the narrowest point along a long peninsula with pristine, white sand beaches on either side. Ronald Zucher's architecture is meant to evoke images of turtles and armadillos, particularly the roof lines. Rooms are large and plush, as you would expect, but you can also choose suites and villas with multiple rooms, full kitchens, and private infinity-effect pools. Four restaurants offer up the top-notch dining experience you'd expect from the Four Seasons—and the famed service remains peerless. The Arnold Palmer–designed championship golf course is my favorite in the country, with ocean views from the tees, greens, and fairways of 15 of its 18 holes. In addition to providing all this luxury, the Four Seasons has been awarded "4 Leaves" by the CST Sustainable Tourism program.

Papagayo Peninsula, Guanacaste. www.fourseasons.com/costarica. *C* **800/332-3442** in the U.S., or 2696-0000. 154 units. $750–$1,000 double; $1,075 and up suites and villas. Children stay free in parent's room. **Amenities:** 4 restaurants; 2 bars; lounge; 3 outdoor pools; golf course; 5 tennis courts; spa; watersports equipment; children's programs; concierge; room service; babysitting; free Wi-Fi.

Hotel Playa Hermosa Bosque del Mar ★★★   Sitting on the quiet southern end of Playa Hermosa, this is my favorite beachfront boutique hotel in the area. Rooms and suites are spread around the free-form pool with a sculpted waterfall amid the shade of tall trees. Old-growth trees (which are inhabited by iguanas and troops of monkeys) pop up through decking and roofs in the main lobby and one even passes right through the center of a balcony of one of the junior suites. The oceanfront suites come with a Jacuzzi on the private balcony where you can soak as you listen to the sounds of the waves or watch the sun set through coconut palms.

Playa Hermosa, Guanacaste. www.hotelplayahermosa.com. *C* **2672-0046.** 32 units. $226–$339 suite; $678 and up penthouse suites. **Amenities:** Restaurant; bar; Jacuzzi; outdoor pool; free Wi-Fi.

INEXPENSIVE

Villa del Sueño Hotel ★★   Tall trees and mature gardens give this sprawling complex of hotel rooms and condo units a cool and refreshing feel, even on the hottest and driest of Guanacaste's summer days. A thatch-roof Tiki bar just off the main pool also helps beat the heat. As soon as you arrive, French-Canadian owners Claude and Sylvia make you feel part of the family. Red tile floors and bright tropical paintings and wall hangings give the rooms a cheery feel, and guests in the second-floor rooms enjoy higher ceilings. The in-house restaurant is one of the best in town.

Playa Hermosa, Guanacaste. www.villadelsueno.com. *C* **800/378-8599** in the U.S., or 2672-0026 in Costa Rica. 43 units. $89–$149 double; $159–$289 suite. Free for children 12 and under. Rates include taxes. **Amenities:** Restaurant; bar; 2 outdoor pools; room service; free Wi-Fi.

Where to Eat

In addition to the places listed below, the restaurant at **Villa del Sueño Hotel** (see above) is consistently one of the best in the area.

Abbocato ★★★ FUSION/BISTRO   Husband-and-wife chefs Andrea and Paola create two distinct nightly tasting menus. One typically features Asian-inspired flavors and preparations, and the other is Mediterranean in style. It's anybody's guess which of the two is behind any one dish. No matter, everything is sublime. On the Asian side, you might get some home-smoked fresh tuna in a light ginger dressing with homemade pickles; on the Mediterranean side, it could be mushroom sausage in a phyllo quiche shell with pesto and Fontina cheese. The dining room has Travertine tile floors, heavy wooden tables, walls of glass and sliding French doors, and high peaked ceilings with exposed wood beams. The whole thing opens onto a broad patio and pool area that overlooks the Pacific Ocean and provides great sunset views.

Inside Hacienda del Mar, 1km (½ mile) inland from Playa Panamá. www.abbocatocr. com. ℂ **2672-0073** or 8820-2576. Reservations necessary for dinner. Main courses $10–$35. Four-course prix-fixe dinner $45. Tues–Sat noon–9pm.

Ginger ★★ INTERNATIONAL/TAPAS   From the angular open architecture to the creative cocktails and wide-ranging tapas menu, this is easily the hippest place to drink and dine in the Papagayo area. The menu demonstrates international influences as diverse and distinct as Thailand, Spain, and Italy. I especially like the firecracker shrimp and the shredded pork lettuce wraps in a mango-tamarind sauce. Friday night is "Martini Night," featuring $3 martinis.

On the main road, Playa Hermosa. www.gingercostarica.com. ℂ **2672-0041.** Tapas $5–$13. Tues–Sun 5–10pm.

Exploring Playa Hermosa, Playa Panamá & Papagayo

Most of the beaches up here are usually quite calm and good for swimming. If you want to do some diving, check in with one of the companies listed in the Playa del Coco and Playa Ocotal section below.

In the middle of Playa Hermosa, **Aqua Sport** (ℂ 2672-0050) is where to go for watersports equipment rentals. Kayaks, sailboards, canoes, bicycles, beach umbrellas, snorkel gear, and parasails are all available at fairly reasonable rates. You'll also find a small supermarket, public phones, and a restaurant.

Because the beaches in this area are relatively protected and generally flat, surfers should look into boat trips to nearby **Witch's Rock** ★★ and **Ollie's Point** ★, two world-class surf spots primarily accessed by boat. **Costa Rica Surf Charters** (www.crsurfcharters.com; ℂ **8935-2538**) and **Aqua Sport** (ℂ **2672-0050**) provide trips for up to six surfers ($60–$120 per hour).

Most of these companies mentioned above also have fishing trips for two to four anglers for $400 to $1,200. **Dream On Sportfishing** ★★ (www.dreamonsportfishing.com; ℂ **8735-3121**) or **North Pacific Tours** ★ (www.northpacifictours.com; ℂ **2670-1564**) are two excellent fishing operators.

Charlie Don't Surf, but Ollie Does

Ollie's Point is named after Oliver North, the famous and felonious former lieutenant colonel at the center of the Iran-Contra scandal. The beaches and ports of northern Guanacaste were a staging ground for supplying the Nicaraguan Contra rebels. Legend has it that during a news broadcast of an interview with North, some surfers noticed a fabulous point break going off in the background. Hence, the discovery and naming of Ollie's Point.

If you're interested in sailing, check in with any of the sailboat charter outfits listed in the Playa del Coco section below. All have a range of full- and half-day tours, with snorkel stops, as well as sunset cruises.

Both **Charlie's Adventures** ★ (www.charliesadventure.com; ℂ **2672-0317**) and **Swiss Travel Service** (www.swisstravelcr.com; ℂ **2668-1020**) have a wide range of activities and tours, including trips to Santa Rosa or Rincón de la Vieja national parks, and rafting on the Corobicí River. These operations have desks at several of the hotels around here and will pick you up at any hotel in the area.

The best zip-line canopy tour in this area is the **Witch's Rock Canopy Tour** ★★ (www.witchsrockcanopytour.com; ℂ **2696-7101**), a bit before the main entrance to the Four Seasons Resort. For $75, the 1½-hour tour covers 3km (1¾ miles) of cables touching down on 24 platforms and crossing three suspension bridges.

PLAYA DEL COCO & PLAYA OCOTAL ★

253km (157 miles) NW of San José; 35km (22 miles) W of Liberia

Playa del Coco is one of Costa Rica's busiest and most developed beach destinations. A large modern mall and shopping center anchor the eastern edge of town. You'll pass through a tight jumble of restaurants, hotels, and souvenir shops for several blocks before you hit the sand and sea; homes, condos, and hotels have sprouted up along the beach in either direction. This has long been, and remains, a popular destination with middle-class Ticos and weekend revelers from San José. It's also a prime jumping-off point for some of Costa Rica's best scuba diving. The beach, which has grayish-brown sand and gentle surf, is quite wide at low tide and almost nonexistent at high tide. The crowds that come here like their music loud and late, so if you're in search of a quiet retreat, stay away from the center of town. Still, if you're looking for a beach with a variety of hotels, lively nightlife, and plenty of cheap food and beer close at hand, you'll enjoy Playa del Coco.

More interesting still, in my opinion, is **Playa Ocotal** ★, which is a couple of miles to the south. This tiny pocket cove features a small salt-and-pepper beach bordered by high bluffs and is quite beautiful. When it's calm, there's good snorkeling around some rocky islands close to shore here.

Essentials

GETTING THERE & DEPARTING   By Plane: The nearest airport with regularly scheduled flights is in Liberia. From there, you can hire a taxi to take you to Playa del Coco or Playa Ocotal, about a 25-minute drive, for $35 to $60.

By Car: From Liberia, head west on CR21 toward Santa Cruz. Just past the village of Comunidad, turn right. In about 11km (6¾ miles), you'll come to a fork in the road. Take the left leg. The right leg goes to Playa Hermosa. The drive takes about 4 hours from San José.

By Bus: Pulmitan express buses (www.pulmitandeliberia.com; ✆ **2222-1650** in San José, or 2670-0095 in Playa del Coco) leave San José for Playa del Coco at 8am and 2 and 4pm daily from Calle 24 between avenidas 5 and 7. Allow 5 hours for the trip. A one-way ticket is C4,350. From Liberia, buses (✆ **2666-0458**) to Playa del Coco leave regularly throughout the day between 5am and 7pm. A one-way ticket for the 40-minute trip costs around C850. Bus schedules change frequently, so it's always best to check in advance. During the high season and on weekends, extra buses from Liberia are sometimes added. The direct bus for San José leaves Playa del Coco daily at 4 and 8am and 2pm. Local buses for Liberia leave daily between 5am and 7pm.

Depending on demand, the Playa del Coco buses sometimes go as far as Playa Ocotal; check beforehand. Otherwise, a taxi should cost around C3,000 to C5,000.

Gray Line (www.graylinecostarica.com; ✆ **800/719-3105** in the U.S. and Canada, or 2220-2126 in Costa Rica) and **Interbus** (www.interbusonline.com; ✆ **4031-0888**) both have two daily buses leaving San José for Playa del Coco and Ocotal. The fare is around $50.

Both companies will pick you up at most San José–area hotels and have connections to most other tourist destinations around Costa Rica.

GETTING AROUND   You can rent cars from any number of rental companies. Most are based in Liberia, or at the airport. See p. 104.

If you can't flag down a **taxi** on the street, call ✆ **2670-0408.**

CITY LAYOUT   Playa del Coco is a compact and busy beach town. At the center of town, running for a few hundred meters in either direction is a seafront walkway, or *malecón.* You'll find benches scattered along this walkway, as well as patches of grass and a basketball court. Most of the town's hotels and restaurants are on the water, on the road leading into town, or on the road that heads north, about 100m (330 ft.) inland from and parallel to the beach.

Playa Ocotal, which is south of Playa del Coco on a paved road that leaves the main road about 180m (600 ft.) before the beach, is a small collection of vacation homes, condos, and a couple of hotels. It has one bar and one restaurant on the beach.

FAST FACTS   The nearest major hospital is in Liberia (✆ **2690-2300**). For the local **health clinic,** call ✆ **2670-1717;** for the local **pharmacy,** call ✆ **2670-2050.** For local **police,** dial ✆ **2670-0258.** You'll find several banks and ATMs.

Where to Stay
MODERATE
Coco Beach Hotel & Casino ★   If you want to be in the center of the action, this is the place for you. Set right in the heart of Playa del Coco's busiest restaurant, bar, and commercial strip, this place has clean, cool, contemporary rooms that are fairly plain, but get a shot of life and color with bright multicolor paintings based on local indigenous designs. Thatch-roof shade structures ring the pool area. These thatch roofs and a small strip mall separate

the rooms from the street and also help to block the blazing Guanacaste sun, which was a problem when this place first opened. The beach is about 2 blocks away.

Playa del Coco, Guanacaste. www.cocobeachhotelandcasinocr.com. ⓒ **2670-0494.** 32 units. $145–$186 double. Rates include full breakfast. **Amenities:** Restaurant; bar; outdoor pool; free Wi-Fi.

El Ocotal Beach Resort ★

This small resort has an enviable location, perched on a steep hillside overlooking the Pacific Ocean and a series of tiny offshore islands. The views are mesmerizing all day, and the sunsets are spectacular. Most rooms enjoy these wonderful views. If you get one that doesn't, the open-air deck off the main restaurant and bar is a prime oceanview spot. The rooms and facilities here are a mixed bag, and service and upkeep can be lax at times. Some of the rooms are quite well done and well kept, while others show their age. Each of the bungalow duplex units shares a small plunge pool. These folks have one of the best and longest-running dive operations in the area.

Playa del Coco, Guanacaste. www.ocotalresort.com. ⓒ **2670-0321.** 42 units (including 12 bungalows and 3 suites). $185–$220 double; $230–$265 bungalow and suite. Rates include full breakfast. Children 11 and under stay free in parent's room. **Amenities:** 2 restaurants; 3 outdoor pools; lighted tennis court; exercise room; spa; Jacuzzi; free Wi-Fi.

Where to Eat

A clutch of basic open-air *sodas* (diners) are at the traffic circle in the center of El Coco village. These restaurants serve standard Tico fare, with an emphasis on fried fish. Prices are quite low—and so is the quality, for the most part.

You can get excellent Italian food at **Soda Mediterránea ★** (ⓒ **8742-6553**) in the little El Pueblito strip mall on the road running north and parallel to the beach, and a good mix of Mediterranean and Peruvian cuisine at the beachfront **Donde Claudio & Gloria ★** (www.dondeclaudioygloria.com; ⓒ **2670-1514**). For a quick or light meal, try **Le Coq** (ⓒ **2670-0608**), an open-air Lebanese restaurant on the main drag in the center of town.

Right on the main strip, you'll also find members of the Papagayo restaurant group: **Papagayo Seafood ★** (ⓒ **2670-0298**), **Papagayo Steak House ★** (ⓒ **2670-0605**), and **Papagayo Sushi Boat ★** (ⓒ **2670-0298**).

MODERATE

Citron ★★★ FUSION/INTERNATIONAL Even though it's set in a small contemporary strip mall, this is easily the town's most elegant and creative restaurant. White brick walls greet you upon entering. The natural colors, local cane ceiling, and soft lighting will put you at ease, and the attentive wait staff will make sure you stay that way. I especially like the tenderloin and portobello risotto in red-wine reduction. However, being this close to the ocean, I often choose the freshly caught local sea bass served over orzo pasta, with a Catalan-inspired sauce. Be sure to save room for the desserts, especially the vanilla crème brûlée, which is made with local organic vanilla.

In the Pacífico Mall, on the main road into town. Playa del Coco. www.citroncoco.com. ✆ **2670-0942.** Main courses $12–$19. Mon–Sat 5:30–10pm.

Father Rooster ★ SEAFOOD/BAR A casual, open-air beachfront bar, Father Rooster sits just a few steps from the water on tiny Playa Ocotal. Burgers, tacos, and beer-battered fish or shrimp, as well as nachos and other typical bar fare fill the menu. The building itself is a rustic wood affair painted a haphazard mix of primary colors. There's a pool table in one room, and seating all around the veranda and out onto the sand, where you can grab a table under the shade of canvas umbrellas and a tall mango tree. On the weekends, you'll sometimes catch a live band here.

On the beach, Playa Ocotal. www.fatherrooster.com. ✆ **2670-1246.** Main courses C6,500–C9,000. Daily 11:30am–10pm.

The Lookout ★ SEAFOOD/BAR It's worth the short drive or taxi ride to this rooftop bar restaurant on the outskirts of Playas del Coco, for the outstanding sunsets and upscale pub food. Menu standouts include the tuna poke nachos and the lobster grilled cheese, both with locally sourced seafood. These folks also have a wide-ranging selection of Costa Rican craft beers, as well as fresh locally farmed oysters.

On the outskirts of Playas del Coco, inside the Hotel Chantel. www.thelookoutcoco. com. ✆ **8755-7246.** Main courses C3,000–C8,500. Tues-Sun 3–10pm.

Exploring Playa del Coco & Playa Ocotal

Plenty of boats are anchored at Playa del Coco, and that means plenty of opportunities to go fishing, diving, or sailing. Still, the most popular activities, especially among the hordes of Ticos who come here, are lounging on the beach, walking along the *malecón,* hanging out in the *sodas,* and cruising the bars and discos at night. If you're interested, you might be able to join a soccer match. (The soccer field is in the middle of town.) You can also arrange horseback rides; ask at your hotel.

BEACH CLUB If you're staying at a hotel without a pool, or just want a sense of exclusivity on the beach, consider **Café de Playa Beach & Dining Club** (www.cafedeplaya.com; ✆ **2670-1621**). In addition to having an excellent restaurant, it offers a $15 day pass that grants access to the pool and private grassy lawn fronting the beach, which is filled with comfortable teak chaise lounges. There are also watersports equipment rentals and tours, as well as a small spa.

CANOPY TOUR Set in a stand of thick, tropical dry forest, **Congo Trail Canopy Tour** ★ (✆ **2666-4422**) is on the outskirts of Playa del Coco, along a dirt road that leads to Playa Pan de Azúcar. In addition to the zip-line tour, these folks have a small butterfly farm and a few zoo enclosures with monkeys and reptiles. Tours run daily, 8am to 5pm, and cost $35 for the canopy tour ($5 extra to see the animals).

SAILING Several cruising sailboats and longtime local salts offer daily sailing excursions. The 47-foot ketch-rigged *Kuna Vela* (www.kunavela.com;

© **8301-3030**) and the 45-foot ketch *Seabird* (www.seabirdsailingexcursions. com; © **8880-6393**) both ply the waters off Playa del Coco. They also provide half- and full-day and sunset sailing trips, with snorkel stops and an open bar.

SCUBA DIVING   Scuba diving is the most popular watersport in the area, and dive shops abound. **Sirenas Diving Costa Rica ★★** (www.costarica diving.net; © **2670-0603**), **Summer Salt ★** (www.summer-salt.com; © **2670-0308**), and **Rich Coast Diving ★★** (www.richcoastdiving.com; © **2670-0176**) are the most established and offer equipment rentals and dive trips. A two-tank dive, with equipment, should cost between $85 and $150 per person, depending on the distance to the dive site. The more distant dive sites visited include the Catalina Islands and Bat Island. All of these operators also offer PADI certification courses.

SPORTFISHING   Full- and half-day sportfishing excursions can be arranged through any of the hotel tour desks, or with **Dream On Sportfishing ★★** (www.dreamonsportfishing.com; © **8735-3121**) or **North Pacific Tours ★** (www.northpacifictours.com; © **2670-1564**). A half-day of fishing (the boat, captain, food, and tackle,) should cost around $500 to $900 for two to four passengers; a full day should run $700 to $1,200.

SURFING   Playa del Coco has no surf whatsoever, but is a popular jumping-off point for boat trips to Witch's Rock (Roca Bruja), and Ollie's Point up in Santa Rosa National Park (p. 125). *Note:* Both Witch's Rock and Ollie's Point are technically within Santa Rosa National Park. Permits are sometimes required, and boats without permits are sometimes turned away. If you decide to go, be sure your boat captain is licensed and has cleared access to the park. You may also have to pay the park's $15 fee.

  Single Fin Surf Charters (www.singlefinsurfcharters.com; © **8935-2583**) offers a plush trip out to these surf spots at $235 per person for a full-day trip. But if you ask around town, you should be able to find one of the local skippers, who tend to offer trips for up to six surfers for much less.

  Alternately, you can contact **Pacific Coast Stand Up Paddle & Surf Trips** (www.pacificcoastsuptours.com; © **8359-8115**). The calm waters off Playa del Coco are great for stand-up paddling. These folks give lessons and guided outings for traditional surfing and also for those looking to try out stand-up paddling.

Entertainment & Nightlife

Playa del Coco is one of Costa Rica's liveliest beach towns after dark. Most of the action is centered along a 2-block section of the main road into town, just before you hit the beach. Here you'll find the **Lizard Lounge ★** (© **2670-0307**), which has a raucous party vibe. Just across the street is the large, open-air **Zi Lounge ★★** (© **2670-1978**). Those looking for a gringo-influenced sports-bar hangout can try **Coconutz ★** (www.coconutz-costarica.com; © **2670-1982**).

  Just off the beach, at the center of town, is **Beach Bums Bar & Grill ★** (© **2671-0110**). This is a very popular spot, with frequent live bands and DJs.

On the south end of the beach, reached via a rickety footbridge over the estuary, you'll find **La Vida Loca** ★ (lavidalocabeachbar.com; ✆ **2670-0181**), a lively beachfront bar with a pool table, Ping-Pong table, *foosball* (table football) table, and live bands.

En Route: Between Playas del Coco & Playa Flamingo

Hotel Sugar Beach ★★   If you're looking for an isolated boutique getaway in Guanacaste, it's hard to beat this place. The hotel is spread over a gently curved, forested hillside that cradles Playa Pan de Azúcar (Sugar Beach). The grounds are rich in wildlife, and it's not uncommon to find troops of howler monkeys in the trees here—so be prepared for some unrequested early wake-up calls. While there are no private beaches in Costa Rica, for all intents and purposes, the beach here is the nearly exclusive playground of the hotel guests. In addition, the rocky outcroppings just off and around this beach are often good for snorkeling.

Playa Pan de Azúcar, Guanacaste. www.sugar-beach.com. ✆ **2654-4242.** 32 units. $158–$198 double; $277–$280 suite; $575-$667 3-bedroom villa. Rates include breakfast and taxes. **Amenities:** Restaurant; bar; pool; free Wi-Fi.

PLAYAS CONCHAL ★★, BRASILITO, FLAMINGO ★★ & POTRERO

280km (174 miles) NW of San José; 67km (42 miles) SW of Liberia

Playa Conchal ★★ is the first in a string of beaches stretching north along this coast. It's almost entirely backed by the massive Westin Playa Conchal resort and Reserva Conchal condominium complex. The unique beach here was once made up primarily of soft, crushed shells—a shell-collectors' heaven. Unfortunately, as Conchal has developed, unscrupulous builders have brought in dump trucks to haul away the namesake seashells for landscaping and construction, and the impact is noticeable.

Just beyond Playa Conchal to the north, you'll come to **Playa Brasilito,** a tiny beach town and one of the few real villages in the area. The soccer field is the center of the village, and around its edges are a couple of little *pulperías* (general stores). The long stretch of gray-sand beach has a quiet, undiscovered feel to it.

Playa Flamingo ★★ is one of the loveliest beaches in the area—a broad stretch of pinkish-white sand, located on a long spit of land that forms part of Potrero Bay. If you continue along the road from Brasilito without taking the turn for Playa Flamingo, you'll come to **Playa Potrero.** The sand here is a brownish gray, but the beach is long, clean, deserted, and very calm for swimming. Drive a little farther north and you'll find the still-underdeveloped beaches of **Playa La Penca** ★ and, finally, **Playa Pan de Azúcar (Sugar Beach)** ★ (see above).

Playas Conchal, Brasilito, Flamingo & Potrero | GUANACASTE & THE NICOYA PENINSULA

Essentials

GETTING THERE & DEPARTING **By Plane:** The nearest airport with regularly scheduled flights is in Tamarindo (see "Playa Tamarindo & Playa Langosta: Getting There & Departing: By Plane" on p. 127), although it is also possible to fly into Liberia. From either of these places, you can arrange for a taxi to drive you to any of these beaches. Playas Brasilito and Conchal are about 25 minutes from Tamarindo and 40 minutes from Liberia. A taxi from Tamarindo should cost around $35 to $50, and between $50 and $70 from Liberia.

By Car: Two major routes go to the beaches. The most direct is by way of the La Amistad Bridge over the Tempisque River. Take the Interamerican Highway west from San José; 47km (29 miles) past the turnoff for Puntarenas, you'll see signs for the turnoff to the bridge. After crossing the Tempisque River, follow the signs for Nicoya, continuing north to Santa Cruz. About 16km (10 miles) north of Santa Cruz, just before the village of Belén, take the turnoff for playas Conchal, Brasilito, Flamingo, and Potrero. After another 20km (12 miles), at the town of Huacas, you'll come to a fork; take the right leg to reach these beaches. The drive takes about 4½ hours.

Alternatively, you can drive here via Liberia. When you reach Liberia, turn west and follow the signs for Santa Cruz and the various beaches. Just beyond the town of Belén, take the turnoff for playas Flamingo, Brasilito, and Potrero, and continue following the directions given above. This route takes around 5 hours.

By Bus: Tralapa express buses (© 2221-7202 in San José, or 2654-4203 in Flamingo) leave San José daily at 8 and 10:30am and 3pm from Calle 20, between avenidas 3 and 5, stopping at playas Brasilito, Flamingo, and Potrero, in that order. The ride takes around 5 hours. A one-way ticket costs C6,290.

Alternatively, the same company's buses to Santa Cruz (© **2680-0392**) connect with one of the several buses from Santa Cruz to Playa Potrero. Buses depart San José for Santa Cruz daily roughly every 2 hours between 7am and 6pm from Calle 20, between avenidas 3 and 5. The trip is around 4 hours; the fare is C5,425. From Santa Cruz, the ride is about 90 minutes; the fare is C1,500.

Gray Line (www.graylinecostarica.com; © **800/719-3105** in the U.S. and Canada, or 2220-2126 in Costa Rica) and **Interbus** (www.interbusonline.com; © **4031-0888**) both have two daily buses leaving San José for the beaches in this area, one in the morning and one in the afternoon. The fare is around $50. Both companies will pick you up at most San José–area hotels and have connections to most other tourist destinations around Costa Rica.

Express buses depart **Playa Potrero** for San José at 3 and 9am and 2pm, stopping a few minutes later in playas Flamingo and Brasilito. Ask at your hotel where to catch the bus. Buses to **Santa Cruz** leave Potrero at regular intervals throughout the day and take about 90 minutes. If you're heading north toward Liberia, get off the bus at Belén and wait for a bus going north. Buses leave Santa Cruz for San José roughly every other hour between 6am and 6pm.

Where to Stay

EXPENSIVE

Westin Playa Conchal Resort & Spa ★★★

Easily the best large-scale, all-inclusive resort in Costa Rica, the Westin sits on one of the country's prettiest beaches, to boot (its massive, free-form swimming pool is also a marvel). Not enough? There's also a Robert Trent Jones II–designed 18-hole golf course and pro shop here. Every room is considered a suite and comes with either one king-size or two double beds, set in a raised sleeping room. Only a handful of the rooms actually have ocean views, however. A casino is on the premises. You choose from several restaurants, and there's a steady stream of food, beverages, and organized activities on tap all day and night.

Playa Conchal, Guanacaste. www.westinplayaconchal.com. ✆ **800/937-8461** in the U.S., or 2654-3442. 406 units. $740 double; $850 and up suite double; children 3–12 add $160–$185 per child per day; children 2 and under stay free in parent's room. Rates include all meals, drinks, taxes, some activities, and nonmotorized watersports equipment. Golf and spa services extra. **Amenities:** 6 restaurants; 5 bars; 2 lounges; 2 outdoor pools; golf course; 4 lighted tennis courts; exercise room; spa; Jacuzzi; watersports equipment rentals; bike rentals; children's programs; concierge; room service; babysitting; free Wi-Fi.

MODERATE

Bahía del Sol Beachfront & Boutique Hotel ★★

I like the low-key vibe and intimate feel of this small resort. I like the flowering ginger that overflows in its gardens, and I like lying in the shade of one of the thatch-roof *palapas* (open-sided huts) they've built near the sand. The hotel is set on a grassy patch of land just in from the center of Playa Potrero. The rooms are simple and plain, but very well kept and a good value. Studio apartments and suites with kitchenettes are perfect for families or for longer stays, but a good restaurant is also on the property. A small spa is set in a patch of thick gardens smack in the center of the resort, and daily yoga and Pilates classes are included. This hotel has received "4 Leaves" in the CST Sustainable Tourism program.

Playa Potrero, Guanacaste. www.bahiadelsolhotel.com. ✆ **866/223-2463** in the U.S. and Canada, or 2654-4671 in Costa Rica. 28 units. $189–$225 double; $330–$410 suite. Rates include breakfast. **Amenities:** Restaurant; bar; outdoor pool; spa; Jacuzzi; room service; free Wi-Fi.

INEXPENSIVE

A string of inexpensive *cabinas* line the main road leading into Brasilito, just before you hit the beach. It's also possible to camp on playas Potrero and Brasilito. At the former, contact **Maiyra's** (✆ **2654-4213**); at the latter, try **Camping Brasilito** (✆ **2654-4452**). Both of these places have some budget rooms as well. Each charges around C3,000 per person to make camp and use the basic restroom facilities, or around C5,000 to C10,000 per person to stay in a rustic room.

Conchal Hotel ★★

Burned to the ground in early 2013, this place was quickly rebuilt and is better than ever. Rooms are spacious and feature sturdy steel bed frames, white linens, and whitewashed walls offset with bright primary accents. Superior rooms come with large, flat-screen televisions and more space. Most rooms open onto a private or shared balcony or veranda fronting the small central pool and gardens. Despite its name, this hotel really should be considered part of Playa Brasilito, which is about a 2-block walk away. Owners Simon and Hilda are delightful and very hands-on. Service is very attentive and personal, and the hotel's tropical fusion Papaya restaurant (see p. 116) is one of the best in the area.

Playa Brasilito, Guanacaste. www.conchalcr.com. © **2654-9125.** 13 units. $96 double; $238 family suite. Rates include continental breakfast and taxes. Highly reduced rates available in off season. **Amenities:** Restaurant; bar; small pool; free Wi-Fi.

Hotel Brasilito This long-standing budget hotel provides clean, well-kept rooms in a pair of two-story wood buildings just a stone's throw from the water. Snag a room with a balcony and you'll be in budget heaven. The owners have an excellent in-house tour operation, and their open-air restaurant, El Oasis, is equally nice.

Playa Brasilito, Guanacaste. www.hotelbrasilito.com. © **2654-4237.** 15 units. $44–$84 double. **Amenities:** Restaurant; free Wi-Fi.

Where to Eat

You can't go wrong at **El Coconut Beach Club** ★★ (www.elcoconut-tamarindo.com; © **2654-4300**; see "A Beach Club," below).

EXPENSIVE

Camarón Dorado ★ SEAFOOD The quintessential beach restaurant, complete with plastic lawn furniture set in the sand and tiki torches. (You can also sit in an open-air, but covered, dining area on a concrete slab if you don't want sand in your shoes.) From either section, you are able to enjoy the ocean views and nightly sunsets. The extensive seafood-centric menu features a plethora of preparations of fresh local fish, lobster shrimp and shellfish, as well as filet mignon, fried chicken, and hamburgers. Everything is very well done, although popularity has led the prices to be jacked up a bit above what you should be paying in what is essentially a simple, beachfront fish shack.

Playa Brasilito. © **2654-4028.** Reservations recommended in high season. Main courses C5,000–C17,000. Daily 11am–10pm.

MODERATE

Marie's ★★ COSTA RICAN/SEAFOOD Marie has been serving up good, fresh, fairly priced food for decades, and her restaurant is justifiably popular. You can get a typical *casado* (blue plate special), as well as burritos and quesadillas, or some simple grilled fish or chicken. Be sure to check for daily specials. The large, open-air restaurant features extremely high ceilings pocked with slow-turning ceiling fans.

Playa Flamingo. www.mariesrestaurantincostarica.com. © **2654-4136.** Main courses C3,800–C13,000. Daily 6:30am–9:30pm.

Papaya ★★★ INTERNATIONAL/SEAFOOD A great spot for any meal of the day, this is easily the best restaurant in the Brasilito/Conchal area.

Occupying a large, open-air, second-floor space overlooking the pool and gardens of the Conchal Hotel, it specializes in fresh, vibrant food and friendly, personal service. Pacific Rim fusion and Nuevo Latino flavors stand out on the small menu, which is always augmented with daily chalkboard specials. My faves include fresh mahimahi in a coconut crust and local lobster tails seasoned with Chinese five spice. At night, dim ambient lighting and table-top candles make this a romantic spot.

Playa Brasilito. ℂ **2654-9125.** Main courses C8,500–C11,400. Thurs–Tues 7am–8:30pm.

INEXPENSIVE

Coco Loco ★★★ COSTA RICAN/SEAFOOD   While many still bemoan the closing of Mar y Sol, there's plenty of reason to rejoice, now that chef Jean-Luc Taulere has opened up this casual beachfront bar and restaurant. Teak-wood tables under white canvas umbrellas are spread on the sand, at the far southern end of Playa Flamingo. The menu features a blackened swordfish wrap and fresh yellowfin tuna tacos. Meat lovers can opt for the slow-cooked pork ribs in a pineapple barbecue sauce. This is a great spot for sunsets. There's an extensive bar and cocktail menu, and there's often live music or DJs at night.

South end of Playa Flamingo. www.cocolococostarica.com. ℂ **2654-6242.** Main courses C3,400–C5,700. Daily 11am–9pm.

Exploring Playas Conchal, Brasilito, Flamingo & Potrero

Playa Conchal ★★ is a lovely looking beach, but the drop-off is quite steep, making it notorious for strong riptides. The water at **Playa Brasilito,** however, is often fairly calm, which makes it a good swimming choice. This is also a great jumping-off point for visiting other nearby and less popular beaches, like **Playa La Penca** ★★ and **Playa Pan de Azúcar** ★★, both of which are north of here.

   Playa Flamingo is one of the prettiest beaches in the region. A long, broad stretch of pinkish white sand, it's on a long spit of land that forms part of Potrero Bay. At the northern end of the beach is a high rock outcropping upon which most of Playa Flamingo's hotels and vacation homes are built. This rocky hill has great views.

   If you continue along the road from Brasilito without taking the turn for Playa Flamingo, you'll come to **Playa Potrero,** which sits in a broadly curving bay, protected by the Flamingo headlands. The sand here is a brownish gray, but the beach is long, clean, deserted, and very calm for swimming. You can see the hotels of Playa Flamingo across the bay. Drive a little farther north and you'll find the still-underdeveloped beaches of **Playa Prieta** ★, **Playa La Penca** ★, and finally **Playa Pan de Azúcar (Sugar Beach)** ★★.

   Tip: All beaches in Costa Rica are public property. But the land behind the beaches is not, and the Westin hotel owns almost all of it in Playa Conchal, so the only public access is along the soft-sand road that follows the beach south from Brasilito. Before the road reaches Conchal, you'll have to ford a small river and then climb a steep, rocky hill, so four-wheel-drive is recommended.

A Day Trip to El Viejo Wetlands

Located a bit inland from the Guanacaste agricultural town of Filadelfia and bordering the Palo Verde National Park, **El Viejo Wildlife Refuge & Wetlands** ★★ (www.elviejowetlands.com; 🕿 2296-0966) is a unique and intriguing choice for a day tour. The principal attraction here is the wildlife, which is abundant and viewed both from open-air, safari-style vehicles and small boats on the Tempisque River. You'll see scores of water birds, and probably a crocodile or two. The main hacienda-style building at the heart of this operation dates to 1870, and is where they serve up excellent Costa Rican lunches. Additional tour options include a zip-line and a visit to the on-site organic farm and sugar cane–processing *trapiche* (sugar mill). Rates run from $60 to $130, depending on how many activities or tours you take, and whether or not you need transportation. All tours include lunch.

WATERSPORTS You can rent jet skis and Wave Runners on the beach in Playa Conchal from **Dorado Jet Ski Tours** (🕿 8824-4293). They also take guided snorkel tours out to the Catalina Islands, as well as wet and wild "Banana Boat" rides, where a group of friends and family get pulled behind a speed boat on a giant, inflatable banana boat.

You can rent jet skis, boogie boards, skim boards, and stand-up paddleboards on Playa Flamingo from **Playa Vida** (🕿 2654-4444), located on the south side of the Flamingo Beach Resort. They take guided snorkel tours out to the Catalina Islands, in addition to renting out beach chairs and shade umbrellas.

A BEACH CLUB If your hotel doesn't have a pool or beach access, head to **El Coconut Beach Club** (www.elcoconut-tamarindo.com; 🕿 2654-4300). Located right on Playa Potrero, it has a pool and a mess of chaise lounges and chairs. You can enjoy the facilities as long as you eat and drink at their excellent restaurant.

LEARN THE LANGUAGE The **Centro Panamericano de Idiomas** (www.cpi-edu.com; 🕿 2265-6306), which has schools in San José and Monteverde, has a branch in Flamingo, across from the Flamingo Marina, facing Potrero Bay. A 1-week program with 4 hours of class per day and a homestay with a local family costs $730.

SCUBA DIVING Scuba diving is quite popular here. **Costa Rica Diving** (www.costarica-diving.com; 🕿 2654-4148) has a shop in Flamingo and offers trips to Catalina Island for around $85.

SPORTFISHING & SAILBOAT CHARTERS Although the Flamingo Marina remains in a state of legal limbo and turmoil, you still have plenty of sportfishing and sailboat charter options here. Jim McKee, the former force behind the Flamingo Marina, manages a fleet of boats. Contact him via his company, **Oso Viejo** (www.flamingobeachcr.com; 🕿 8827-5533 or 2653-8437). Full-day fishing excursions cost between $700 and $2,200, depending on the size and quality of the boat and the distance traveled. Half-day trips cost between $500 and $700.

If you're looking for a full- or half-day sail or sunset cruise, check in with **Oso Viejo** (see above) to see what boats are available, or ask about the 52-foot cutter *Shannon.* Prices range from around $65 to $120 per person, depending on the length of the cruise. Multiday trips are also available.

Another option is to head down the beach at Playa Potrero to the **Costa Rica Sailing Center** (www.learntosailcr.com; © **8699-7289**). These folks give sailing lessons and rentals, with a wide range of small sailcraft from which to choose. They also rent out stand-up paddle boards, kayaks, fishing gear, and snorkel equipment.

Entertainment & Nightlife

Pretty much all of the nightlife in Playa Conchal happens at the large Westin resort (see above), which has a range of bars, nightly entertainment, and a casino. Over in Brasilito, you might see if there's any live music or sporting events on the televisions at the **Tiki's Seaside Grille** (© **2654-9028**). With both a disco and casino, **Amberes** (© **2654-4001**), just slightly up the hill at the north end of town, is the undisputed hot spot in this area.

Over in Potrero, there's sometimes live music on the rooftop bar at **La Terraza de los Mariscos** (© **2654-4379**). However, my favorite bar here is **Bar La Perla** ★(© **2654-4500**) a simple concrete slab construction with a corrugated zinc roof and mostly open walls using chain link fencing for window screens. Located on a dusty corner, this is a very typical Costa Rican-style cantina, but it draws a good mixed crowd of locals, expats, and tourists alike.

RINCÓN DE LA VIEJA NATIONAL PARK ★★

242km (150 miles) NW of San José; 25km (16 miles) NW of Liberia

This sprawling national park begins on the flanks of the Rincón de la Vieja Volcano and includes this volcano's namesake active crater. Down lower is an area of geothermal activity similar to that of Yellowstone National Park in the United States. Fumaroles, geysers, and hot pools cover this small area, creating a bizarre, otherworldly landscape. In addition to hot springs and mud pots, you can explore waterfalls, a lake, and volcanic craters. The bird-watching here is very rewarding, and the views across the pasturelands to the Pacific Ocean are stunning.

> ### What's in a Name?
>
> *Rincón de la Vieja* translates literally as "the old lady's corner." In this case, *la vieja* means a witch or hag, while *rincón* is better interpreted as a "lair" or "hangout." The smoking, belching volcanic crater and mud pots gave rise to this name.

Essentials

GETTING THERE   By Car: You'll first need to get to Liberia, the largest city of northern Guanacaste. It sits at the intersection of the Interamerican

Rincón de la Vieja National Park.

Highway (CR1) and the CR21, which connects Liberia to the Guanacaste beaches. From Liberia, head north on CR1 toward Peñas Blancas and the Nicaraguan border.

To reach the **Las Pailas (Las Espuelas) entrance,** drive about 5km (3 miles) north of Liberia and turn right on the dirt road to the park. The turnoff is well marked. In about 12km (7½ miles), you'll pass through the small village of Curubandé. Continue on this road for another 6km (3¾ miles) until you reach the Hacienda Guachipelín. The lodge is private property, and the owners charge vehicles a C700 toll to pass through their gate and continue on to the park. I'm not sure if this is legal or mandatory, but it's not worth the hassle to protest. Pay the toll, pass through the gate, and continue for another 4km (2½ miles) until you reach the park entrance.

Two routes lead to the **Santa María entrance.** The principal route heads out of the northeastern end of Liberia toward the small village of San Jorge. This route is about 25km (16 miles) long and takes about 45 minutes. A four-wheel-drive vehicle is required. Alternatively, you can reach the entrance on a turnoff from the Interamerican Highway at Bagaces. From here, head north through Guayabo, Aguas Claras, and Colonia Blanca. Though the road is paved up to Colonia Blanca, a four-wheel-drive vehicle is required for the final, very rough 10km (6¼ miles) of gravel road.

Where to Stay & Eat

In addition to the hotel listed below, a couple of other good choices are near the park. On the Cañas Dulces road, **Buena Vista Lodge** ★ (www.buenavista lodgecr.com; ⓒ **2690-1414**) is set on the edge of the national park and offers a wide range of activities and attractions, including its own waterslide and canopy tour.

If you're looking for a little luxury in this area, check out the **Hotel Borin-quen Mountain Resort** ★★ (www.borinquenresort.com; ☎ **2690-1900**).

In the area around Aguas Claras, **Finca La Anita** ★★ (laanitarainforest ranch.com; ☎ **8388-1775** or 2466-0228) is a remote and rustic, yet very cozy lodge, with a series of wooden cabins set on a working farm, on the edge of lush rainforests and cloud forests. The area around the lodge is home to several hot springs; it provides easy access to the seldom-used Santa María sector of Rincón de la Vieja National Park.

Hacienda Guachipelín ★★   This working cattle and horse ranch affords easy access to the hiking and adventures in the Rincón de la Vieja area. To find this place, just follow the directions/signs to Curubandé and Rincón de la Vieja National Park. Most of the rooms are set in a large horseshoe around an ample garden and lawn area a short walk from the main lodge and restaurants. The rooms themselves are large and airy, although simple and plain. A few standard rooms are still housed in some of the ranch's older buildings. Plenty of hikes, tours, and adventure activities are offered—"see "One-Stop Adventure Shop," below. Staff members even run a free shuttle several times a day to the national park entrance, as well as to their own, wonderful hot springs. The owners are deeply committed to sustainable tourism and the conservation of this region.

Rincón de la Vieja (23km/14 miles northeast of Liberia). www.guachipelin.com. ☎ **888/730-3840** in the U.S. and Canada, 2690-2900 for reservations in Costa Rica, or 2666-8075 at the lodge. 54 units. $102 double; $121 superior double; $189 suite. Rates include taxes and breakfast. Rates higher during peak periods. **Amenities:** Restaurant; outdoor pool; spa; free Wi-Fi.

Horseback riding at Hacienda Guachipelín.

Exploring Rincón de la Vieja National Park

Rincón de la Vieja National Park has several excellent trails. The easiest hiking is on the gentle **Las Pailas Loop ★**, a 3km (1.75-mile) trail just off the Las Espuelas park entrance. It passes by several bubbling mud pots and steaming fumaroles. This gentle trail crosses a river, so you'll have to either take off your shoes or get them wet. The whole loop is 3.2km (2 miles) and takes around 2 hours at a leisurely pace.

My favorite hike here is to the **Blue Lake and La Cangrejo Waterfall ★★**. Along this well-marked 9.6km (6-mile) round-trip trail, you'll pass through several different ecosystems, including tropical dry forest, transitional moist forest, and open savanna. You are likely to spot a variety of birds and mammals and have a good chance of coming across a group of coatimundi—a raccoon-like local mammal. While not requiring any great climbs or descents, the hike is nonetheless arduous. Pack a lunch; at the end of your 2-hour hike in, you can picnic at the aptly named Blue Lake, where a 30m (100-ft.) waterfall empties into a small pond with amazing crystal-blue hues.

Due to volcanic activity and the extreme nature of the hike, the summit trail has been closed to visitors since late 2013. If it's reopened, more energetic hikers can tackle the **summit ★** and explore the several craters and beautiful lakes up here. On a clear day, you'll be rewarded with a fabulous view of the plains of Guanacaste and the Pacific Ocean below. The trail is 16.6km (10.3 miles) round-trip and should take about 7 hours (the trail head is at the ranger station). It heads pretty much straight up the volcano and is pretty steep in places. Along the way, you'll pass through several different ecosystems, including sections of tropical moist and tropical cloud forests, while climbing some 1,000m (3,280 ft.) in altitude. After about 6km (3.7 miles), the trail splits. Take the right-hand fork to the Crater Activo (Active Crater). Filled with rainwater, this crater is some 700m (2,300 ft.) in diameter and still active. Off to the side is the massive Laguna Jigueros. Because this crater emits large amounts of sulfur and acid gases, it's not recommended that you linger here long. If you have the energy, a side trail leads to the Von Seebach Crater.

The park entrance fee is $15 per person per day, and the park is open Tuesday to Sunday from 8am to 4pm.

Camping will cost you an extra $2 per person per day. There are actually two entrances and camping areas here: **Santa María** and **Las Pailas** (also called Las Espuelas; ℂ **2666-5051**) ranger stations. Las Pailas is by far the more popular and accessible, and it's closer to the action. These small camping areas are near each other. I recommend the one closer to the river, although the restroom and shower facilities are about 90m (300 ft.) away, at the other site. For those seeking a less rugged tour of the park, several lodges around the park perimeter give guided hikes, horseback rides into the park.

More Adventures Around Rincón de la Vieja

ONE-STOP ADVENTURE SHOP

Hacienda Guachipelín (see above) provides a range of adventure-tour options, including horseback riding, hiking, white-water inner-tubing, a waterfall canyoning and rappel tour, and two distinct traditional zip-line canopy tours. There's also a butterfly garden and serpentarium on-site. The most popular way to experience this is with the hacienda's **1-Day Adventure pass** ★★, which allows you to choose as many of the hotel's different tours as you can fit into an adventure-packed day. The price for this is $85, including a buffet lunch and transportation. Almost all Guanacaste beach hotels and resorts offer day trips here, or you can book directly with the lodge. *Be forewarned:* During the high season, the whole operation can have a bit of a cattle-car feel, with busloads of day-trippers coming in from the beach.

HOT SPRINGS & MUD BATHS

The active Rincón de la Vieja volcano has blessed this area with several fine hot springs and mud baths. Even if you're not staying at the **Hacienda Guachipelín** (see above) or the **Hotel Borinquen Mountain Resort** (see below), you can take advantage of their hot-spring pools and hot mud baths. Both have on-site spas offering massages, facials, and other treatments.

Up the road from their lodge, Hacienda Guachipelín has opened the **Río Negro Hot Springs** ★★ (© 2666-8075). A $15 entrance fee gets you access to the pools and an application of the hot volcanic mud. For $62, you can take a horseback ride from the main lodge to the springs. A wide range of massages, mud wraps, facials, and other treatments are available at reasonable prices.

At the **Hotel Borinquen Mountain Resort,** a $25 entrance fee allows you access to its range of **hot spring–fed pools** ★, which vary from tepid to very hot, as well as its fresh volcanic mud bath area and large freshwater pool.

Finally, **Vandara Hot Springs** ★★ (www.vandarahotsprings.com; © 4000-0660) is an excellent spa and adventure center run by the folks at Buena Vista Lodge, with a lovely man-made pool fed by natural hot springs. Unlike the other pools mentioned above, this one has no sulfuric smell. Entrance to the pool runs about $30, but various packages, with a canopy tour, horseback ride, or other adventure activity, are available. Meals and spa treatments are also provided.

A Side Trip to a Waterfall

Located about 25km (16 miles) south of Liberia, the **Llanos del Cortés Waterfall** ★ is a beautiful and wide jungle waterfall with an excellent pool at the base for swimming. At roughly 12m (40 ft.) wide, the falls are actually slightly wider than they are tall. This is a great spot for a picnic. The turnoff for the dirt road to the falls is well marked and about 3km (1¾ miles) north of the crossroads for Bagaces. From the turnoff, you must drive a rough dirt road to the parking area and then hike down a short steep trail to the falls. Admission is C1,000 and goes to support the local school. Even though there are guards, be careful about leaving anything of value in your car.

Especially for Kids

Since the landscape is postcard-perfect, especially in the dry season, you shouldn't be too surprised to see antelopes, zebras, giraffes, and elands roaming

Shady Business

This province gets its name from the abundant guanacaste (*Enterolobium cyclocarpum*), Costa Rica's national tree. Known for its broad, full crown, it provides welcome shade on the Guanacaste's hot plains and savannas. The guanacaste is also known as the elephant-ear tree, because of the distinctive shape of its large seedpods. Its fragrant white flowers bloom between February and April.

the grassy plains of Guanacaste. **Africa Safari Adventure Park** (www.africasafaricostarica.com; ☎ **2288-1000**) offers safari-style open-jeep tours through its 100-hectare (247-acre) private reserve populated with a wide range of non-native (predominantly African) species. All the animals are herbivores, so don't expect to see any lions, hyenas, or cheetahs. The trip does provide some sense of being on the Serengeti or some other African plain, and the animals have plenty of room to roam. Admission, which is $100 for adults, and $50 for children 11 and under, includes a 90-minute guided tour and safari-style tractor ride through the park. These folks also offer a separate ATV tour, and full-day passes are available. Africa Safari Adventure Park is located just off the Interamerican Highway, 8km (5 miles) south of Liberia. The park is open daily from 9am to 5pm.

Birding

The **Río Tempisque Basin ★**, southwest of town, is one of the best places in the country to spot marsh and stream birds by the hundreds. This area is an important breeding ground for gallinules, jacanas, and limpkins, as well as numerous heron and kingfisher species and the roseate spoonbill. Several tour operators offer excursions and a wide range of tours in the region. **Swiss Travel Services** (www.swisstravelcr.com; ☎ **2282-4898**) is the largest and most reliable of the major operators here.

One of the most popular tours is a boat tour down the Bebedero River to **Palo Verde National Park ★**, which is south of Cañas and is best known for its migratory bird populations. Some of the best bird-watching requires no more than a little walking around the Biological Station in the park.

You can get a similar taste of these waterways and bird-watching opportunities at **El Viejo Wetlands** (p. 118) and **Rancho Humo** (p. 140).

Rafting Trips

Leisurely raft trips (with little white water) are offered by **Ríos Tropicales ★★** (www.riostropicales.com; ☎ **2233-6455**), about 40km (25 miles) south of Liberia. Its 2-hour ($110) float trips are primo for families and bird-watchers. Along the way, you'll likely see many of the area's more exotic animal residents: howler monkeys, iguanas, caimans, coatimundis, otters, and toucans, parrots, motmots, trogons, and many other species of birds. Aside from your binoculars and camera, a bathing suit and sunscreen are the only things you'll need. Ríos Tropicales is based out of the Restaurant Rincón Corobicí, which is located right on the Interamerican Highway (CR1).

For a much wetter and wilder ride, the folks at **Hacienda Guachipelín** (see above) offer white-water inner-tube trips on the narrow Río Negro.

Exploring Santa Rosa National Park ★

Known for its remote, pristine beaches (reached by several kilometers of hiking trails or a 4WD vehicle), **Santa Rosa National Park** ★ (www.acguanacaste.ac.cr; ✆ **2666-5051**) is a great place to camp on the beach, surf, bird-watch, or (if you're lucky) watch sea turtles nest. Located 30km (19 miles) north of Liberia and 21km (13 miles) south of La Cruz on the Interamerican Highway, Costa Rica's first national park blankets the Santa Elena Peninsula. Unlike other national parks, it was founded not to preserve the land but to save a building, known as **La Casona,** which played an important role in Costa Rican independence. It was here, in 1856, that Costa Rican forces fought the decisive Battle of Santa Rosa, forcing the U.S.-backed soldier of fortune William Walker and his men to flee into Nicaragua. La Casona was completely destroyed by arson in 2001, but it has been rebuilt, very accurately mimicking the original building, and now houses a small museum, detailing the political history of the ranch house and housing rotating temporary art exhibits. The museum descriptions, however, are in Spanish only.

La Casona has a few nearby hiking trails. The best for most visitors is the **Indio Desnudo (Naked Indian) trail,** a 2.6km (1.5-mile) loop trail that should take you about 45 minutes. It leads through a small patch of tropical dry forest and into overgrown former pastureland. If you're lucky, you might spot a white-tailed deer, coatimundi, black guan, or mantled howler monkey along the way.

Park entrance is $15 per person; day visitors can access the park daily from 8am to 3:30pm. Camping is allowed at several sites within the park. A campsite costs $19 per person, per day. Camping is near the entrance, the principal ranger station, La Casona, and by playas Naranjo and Nancite.

THE BEACHES ★★   Eight kilometers (5 miles) west of La Casona, down a rugged road that's impassable during the rainy season (it's rough on 4WD vehicles even in the dry season), is **Playa Naranjo.** Four kilometers (2½ miles) north of Playa Naranjo, along a hiking trail that follows the beach, you'll find **Playa Nancite. Playa Blanca** is 21km (13 miles) down a dirt road from Caujiniquil, which itself is 20km (12 miles) north of the park entrance. None of these three beaches has shower or restroom facilities. (Playa Nancite does have some facilities, but they're in a reservations-only camping area.) Bring along your own water, food, and anything else you'll need, and expect to find things relatively quiet and deserted.

Playa Nancite is known for its *arribadas* ("arrivals," or grouped egg-layings) of olive ridley sea turtles, which come ashore to nest by the tens of thousands each year in October. Playa Naranjo is legendary for its perfect surfing waves. In fact, this spot is quite popular with day-trippers who come in by boat from the Playa del Coco area to ride the waves that break around **Witch's Rock,** which lies just offshore.

On the northern side of the peninsula is **Playa Blanca,** a beautiful, remote, white-sand beach with calm waters. This beach is reached by way of the small village of Caujiniquil and is accessible only during the dry season.

If you reach Caujiniquil and then head north on a rugged dirt road for a few kilometers, you'll come to a small annex to the national park system at **Playa Junquillal ★** (© 2666-5051), not to be confused with the more-developed beach of the same name farther south in Guanacaste. This is a lovely little beach that is also often good for swimming. You'll have to pay the park entrance fee ($10) to use the beach, and $2 more to camp here. There are basic restroom and shower facilities.

Río Celeste ★★ & the Tenorio Volcano

A crystalline turquoise pool at the foot of a forest waterfall, with nearby hot springs and volcanic mud, make **Río Celeste ★★** a must-see. With attractions and activities similar to Rincón de la Vieja, this is a much less-visited and more remote-feeling area. Río Celeste, which means "blue river," is inside the **Parque Nacional Volcán Tenorio (Tenorio Volcano National Park; © 2206-5369).** The hike takes about 2 hours each way and is steep in places. Above the main pool and waterfall, a loop trail will take you along the river to a few spots where underground hot springs bubble up into the blue waters. Locals have made some well-worn pools at the spots best for soaking. Along the riverbanks here, you can find volcanic mud deposits perfect for a free, mid-hike facial treatment. The park is open daily from 8am until 4pm, and the entrance fee is $12.

If you want easy access to the Tenorio Volcano and Río Celeste, I recommend the humble, yet delightful, **La Carolina Lodge ★** (www.lacarolina lodge.com; © 843/343-4201 in the U.S. and Canada, or 2466-6393 in Costa Rica), which is on a working farm, next to a clear flowing river. Another good option is the **Celeste Mountain Lodge ★** (www.celestemountainlodge.com; © 2278-6628), a handsome, sustainable lodge, with great views of the surrounding volcanoes. Finally, the most luxurious option in these parts is the **Río Celeste Hideaway ★★** (www.riocelestehideaway.com; © 800/320-3541 in the U.S. and Canada, or 2206-5114 in Costa Rica), which is actually located on the "back side" of the Tenorio National Park, and reached via the road connecting Upala to the small town of Guatuso.

Getting There: Tenorio National Park is located near the small town of Bijagua. The road to Bijagua (CR6) heads north off the Interamerican Highway about 5km (3 miles) northwest of Cañas. From here, it's another 30km (19 miles) to Bijagua, and yet another 12km (7½ miles) to the park entrance. The last part is on rough dirt roads.

Near Miravalles Volcano

Part of a string of active volcanoes running down the spine of the country, Miravalles Volcano has long been a major energy supplier for the country's electric grid, but a rather forgotten and undiscovered area for tourism. **Río Perdido ★★** (www.rioperdido.com; © 888/236-5070 in the U.S. and Canada, or 2673-3600 in Costa Rica) aims to change all that. With a beautiful setting amongst rolling hills and striking rock formations, this hotel, spa, and adventure center features lovely rooms and a gorgeous hot spring complex. The hot springs here range from a modern pool structure fed by warm mineral waters up near the main lodge, to a beautiful natural river with pools of clear water and varied temperatures. The lodge also has a zip-line canyon tour and an extensive mountain bike park, as well as white-water-river tubing.

PLAYA TAMARINDO ★ & PLAYA LANGOSTA ★★

295km (183 miles) NW of San José; 73km (45 miles) SW of Liberia

Tamarindo is the biggest boomtown in Guanacaste—and in some ways, the boom has gone too far, too fast. The main road into Tamarindo is a helter-skelter jumble of strip malls, surf shops, hotels, and restaurants. Ongoing development is spreading up the hills inland from the beach and south to Playa Langosta. None of it seems regulated or particularly well planned.

Still, the array of accommodations, numerous restaurants, and active night-life, along with very dependable surf, have established Tamarindo as one of the most popular beaches on this coast. The swell beach here is a long, wide swath of white sand that curves gently from one rocky headland to another. Fishing boats bob at their moorings and brown pelicans fish just beyond the breakers. A sandy islet off the southern end of the beach makes a great destination if you're a strong swimmer; if you're not, it makes a great foreground for sunsets. Tamarindo is very popular with surfers, who ply the break right here or use the town as base for visiting other beach and point breaks at playas Grande, Langosta, Avellanas, and Negra.

Essentials

GETTING THERE & DEPARTING **By Plane:** Both **Nature Air** (www. natureair.com; ℂ **800/235-9272** in the U.S. and Canada, or 2299-6000 in Costa Rica) and **Sansa** (www.flysansa.com; ℂ **877/767-2672** in the U.S. and Canada, or 2290-4100 in Costa Rica) have several daily direct flights throughout the day to the small airstrip on the outskirts of Tamarindo. Fares run $141 to $158. During the high season, additional flights are sometimes added. Nature Air also connects Tamarindo and Arenal, Liberia, and Quepos.

Whether you arrive on Sansa or Nature Air, a couple of cabs or minivans are always waiting for arriving flights. It costs C5,000 to C10,000 for the ride into town.

If you're flying into Liberia, a taxi should cost around $120. Alternatively, you can use **Tamarindo Transfers & Tours** (www.tamarindoshuttle.com; ℂ **929/800-4621** in the U.S., or 2653-4444 in Costa Rica), which charges $20 per person, one-way. These folks also have a variety of tours and transfer services.

By Car: The most direct route is by way of the La Amistad Bridge. From San José, you can either take the Interamerican Highway (CR1) north from

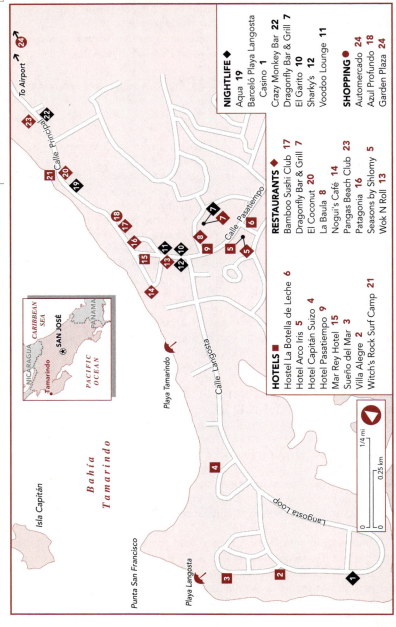

NIGHTLIFE ◆
Aqua **19**
Barceló Playa Langosta
Casino **1**
Crazy Monkey Bar **22**
Dragonfly Bar & Grill **7**
El Garito **10**
Sharky's **12**
Voodoo Lounge **11**

SHOPPING ●
Automercado **24**
Azul Profundo **18**
Garden Plaza **24**

RESTAURANTS ◆
Bamboo Sushi Club **17**
Dragonfly Bar & Grill **7**
El Coconut **20**
La Baula **8**
Nogui's Café **14**
Pangas Beach Club **23**
Patagonia **16**
Seasons by Shlomy **5**
Wok N Roll **13**

HOTELS ■
Hostel La Botella de Leche **6**
Hotel Arco Iris **5**
Hotel Capitán Suizo **4**
Hotel Pasatiempo **9**
Mar Rey Hotel **15**
Sueño del Mar **3**
Villa Alegre **2**
Witch's Rock Surf Camp **21**

To Airport

Calle Principal

Calle Pasatiempo

Calle Langosta

Langosta Loop

Bahía Tamarindo

Isla Capitán

Punta San Francisco

Playa Tamarindo

Playa Langosta

NICARAGUA
CARIBBEAN SEA
SAN JOSÉ
PANAMA
PACIFIC OCEAN
Tamarindo

1/4 mi
0.25 km

downtown San José, or first head west out of the city on the San José–Caldera Highway (CR27) until it meets up with the Interamerican Highway near Puntarenas. This latter route is a faster and flatter drive. At 47km (29 miles) north of the Puntarenas exit on the Interamerican Highway, you'll see signs for the turnoff to the bridge. After crossing the river, follow the signs for Nicoya and Santa Cruz. Continue north out of Santa Cruz, until just before the village of Belén, where you will find the turnoff for Tamarindo. In another 20km (12 miles) you will come to a fork; take the left leg for Playa Tamarindo at Huacas and continue on until the village of Villareal, where you make your final turn into Tamarindo. The trip should take around 4 hours.

You can save a little time, especially in the dry season, by taking a more direct but rougher route: You turn left just after passing the main intersection for Santa Cruz at the turnoff for playas Junquillal and Ostional. The road is paved until the tiny village of Veintisiete de Abril. From here, it's about 20km (12 miles) on a rough dirt road until the village of Villareal, where you make your final turn into Tamarindo.

Alternatively, you can drive here via Liberia. When you reach Liberia, turn west and follow the signs for Santa Cruz and the various beaches. Just beyond the town of Belén, take the turnoff for playas Flamingo, Brasilito, and Tamarindo, and then follow the directions for the second option above. This route takes around 5 hours.

By Bus: Alfaro express buses (www.empresaalfaro.com; ⓒ **2222-2666** in San José, or 2653-0268 in Tamarindo) leave San José daily for Tamarindo at 11:30am and 3:30pm, departing from Calle 14 between avenidas 3 and 5. **Tralapa** (ⓒ **2221-7202**) also has two daily direct buses to Tamarindo leaving at 7:15am and 4pm from its main terminal at Calle 20 between avenidas 3 and 5. The trip takes around 5 hours, and the one-way fare is about C5,730.

You can also catch a bus to Santa Cruz from either of those bus companies. Buses leave both stations for Santa Cruz roughly every 2 hours between 6am and 6pm. The 4-hour, one-way trip is around C5,650. Buses leave Santa Cruz for Tamarindo roughly every 1½ hours between 5:45am and 10pm; the one-way fare is C685.

Gray Line (www.graylinecostarica.com; ⓒ **800/719-3105** in the U.S. and Canada, or 2220-2126 in Costa Rica) and **Interbus** (www.interbusonline.com; ⓒ **4031-0888**) both have two daily buses leaving San José for Tamarindo (one in the morning, one in the afternoon); the fare is $50. Both companies will pick you up at most San José–area hotels, and have connections to most other major tourist destinations in Costa Rica.

Direct buses leave Tamarindo for San José daily at 3:30 and 5:30am (except on Sun) and 2 and 4pm. Buses to Santa Cruz leave roughly every 2 hours between 4:30am and 8:30pm. In Santa Cruz, you can transfer to one of the frequent San José buses.

GETTING AROUND   **Adobe** (ⓒ 2542-4800), **Alamo** (ⓒ 2653-0727), **Budget** (ⓒ 2436-2000), **Economy** (ⓒ 2653-0752), **Hertz** (ⓒ 2653-1358), and **Thrifty** (ⓒ 2653-0829) have rental car offices in Tamarindo.

The town itself is very compact and you should be able to walk most places. It's really not even that far of a walk from Playa Langosta. Still, a large fleet of taxis cruise around town, or hang out at principal intersections and meeting points. If you need to, you can contact **PDQ Taxi** (www.tamarindo-taxi.com; ✆ **8918-3710**).

CITY LAYOUT   The road leading into town runs parallel to the beach and ends in a small cul-de-sac just past the Mar Rey Hotel. A major side road off this main road leads farther on, to Playa Langosta, from just before the Mar Rey Hotel. A variety of side roads branch off this road. To reach playas Avellanas, Negra, and Junquillal, you have to first head out of town and take the road toward Santa Cruz.

FAST FACTS   The local **police** can be reached at ✆ **2653-0283**. A **Banco Nacional** branch is at the little mall across from the Hotel Tamarindo Diria, and a branch of the **Banco de Costa Rica** is in the Plaza Conchal mall. Several Internet cafes and a couple of pharmacies are also in town. You'll find **Back Wash Laundry** (✆ **2653-0870**) just past the turnoff for Playa Langosta.

Where to Stay

In addition to the hotels listed below, beach houses and condos may be rented (by the night, week, or month) in Tamarindo, Playa Langosta, and Playa Grande. Check out **RE/MAX Tamarindo** (www.remax-oceansurf-cr.com; ✆ **866/976-8898** in the U.S. and Canada, or 2653-0073 in Costa Rica) or **RPM Vacation Rentals** (www.rpmvacationrentals.com; ✆ **2653-0738**) for more on these places.

EXPENSIVE

In addition to the places listed below, **Villa Alegre ★** (www.villaalegre costarica.com; ✆ **2653-0270**) is a lovely little B&B on the beach in Playa Langosta.

Hotel Capitán Suizo ★★★   This is my favorite hotel in Tamarindo, located right on the beach at the quieter far southern end of Tamarindo. The grounds are lush and beautiful, service is top-notch, and the rooms are large, well kept, and thoroughly inviting. Private balconies and patios open onto exuberant tropical gardens, where squirrels, monkeys and magpie jays are common. The hotel's free-form pool is one of the biggest and best in town. *Note:* There are no TVs in the room, if that matters, and about half are cooled simply by fans and well-designed cross-ventilation.

Playa Tamarindo, Guanacaste. www.hotelcapitansuizo.com. ✆ **2653-0075.** 28 units, 6 bungalows. $250–$280 double; $360–$440 bungalow; $440–$680 suite. Rates include breakfast buffet. **Amenities:** Restaurant; bar; 2 outdoor pools; spa; free Wi-Fi.

MODERATE

Hotel Arco Iris ★★   Set about 300m (100 ft.) inland from the beach, this small complex of rooms and bungalows sits on shady grounds. It's worth a small splurge for the larger deluxe rooms, with their private patios or balconies and contemporary granite bathrooms with glass-enclosed showers. The

American owner Richard is frequently on hand and makes sure everything is in great shape. There's a small pool, and the restaurant here, **Seasons by Shlomy** (see below), is excellent.

Playa Tamarindo, Guanacaste. www.hotelarcoiris.com. ✆ **2653-0330.** 13 units. $160–$210 double, $130 bungalow. Rates include breakfast. **Amenities:** Restaurant; bar; outdoor pool; free Wi-Fi.

Sueño del Mar ★★
This intimate bed-and-breakfast has built a loyal following and gained plenty of local fame with its well-designed rooms, personalized service, gorgeous sunsets, and spectacular breakfasts. A quiet setting on Playa Langosta doesn't hurt, either. The second-floor Luna Suite is the prime room in the house and is worth the splurge if it's available. The standard rooms feature cute, open-air showers with small gardens and plantings providing privacy. There are hammocks strung under shade trees and wooden chairs in the sand set facing the waves, where guests gather every night around sunset with cool drinks in hand.

Playa Langosta, Guanacaste. www.sueno-del-mar.com. ✆ **2653-0284.** 4 units, 2 casitas. $155–$204 double; $185–$310 suite or casita. Rates include full breakfast. Children 12 and under not allowed. **Amenities:** Outdoor pool; watersports equipment; free Wi-Fi.

INEXPENSIVE

In addition to the hotels listed below, **Hostel La Botella de Leche** ★ (www.labotelladeleche.com; ✆ **2653-0189**) bills itself as a "5 star" hostel and is a popular backpacker option. The beachfront **Witch's Rock Surf Camp** ★ (www.witchsrocksurfcamp.com; ✆ **888/318-7873** in the U.S. and Canada, or 2653-1262 in Costa Rica) caters to young, budget-minded surfers.

Hotel Pasatiempo ★★
This lovely small resort, located a few blocks inland from the water, has rooms that are spacious and well maintained, with cool tile floors and a relaxed, tropical decor. Each room is named after a distinct and different local beach, and comes with a hammock, chaise lounge, or wooden Adirondack chairs on a private patio. The central pool is quite inviting, featuring a broad deck area and tall shade trees all around. The hotel's bar and restaurant is one of the livelier spots in town. Wednesday nights are especially fun with an open mic.

Playa Tamarindo, Guanacaste. www.hotelpasatiempo.com. ✆ **2653-0096.** 18 units. $89–$99 double; $129 suite. Rates include breakfast. **Amenities:** Restaurant; bar; pool; free Wi-Fi.

Mar Rey Hotel ★
With an enviable location on a prominent corner right in the heart of Tamarindo, this family-run operation delivers clean, cozy rooms at great prices. It's worth the small splurge for a room with air-conditioning and TV. There's a small, free-form pool for cooling off, but the beach is literally just steps away, across the street. For decades, this place was known as Hotel Zully Mar, and the change is really in name only.

Playa Tamarindo, Guanacaste. www.hotelmarrey.com. ✆ **2653-0028.** 22 units. $61–$69 double. **Amenities:** Outdoor pool; spa; free Wi-Fi.

Where to Eat

Tamarindo has a glut of excellent restaurants. **El Coconut** ★ (www.elcoconut-tamarindo.com; © **2653-0086**), right on the main road into town, is a long-standing option, with a large menu, specializing in fresh seafood.

Nogui's Café ★ (www.noguistamarindo.com; © **2653-0029**) is one of the more popular places in town—and rightly so. This simple, open-air cafe just off the beach on the small traffic circle serves hearty breakfasts and well-prepared salads, sandwiches, burgers, and casual meals. There are even a few tables and chairs on the beach, in front of the main restaurant.

Wok N Roll ★ (© **2653-0156**), a half-block inland from the Mar Rey Hotel (see above) along the road that leads to Playa Langosta, is a cheery, open-air affair, with a big menu of healthy, fresh Asian cuisine. For pizza, I recommend **La Baula** ★ (© **2653-1450**), a delightful open-air place on the road to Dragonfly (see below). If you want sushi, head to the **Bamboo Sushi Club** ★ (© **2653-4519**), on the main road, near the turnoff for Langosta. And, for good steaks and Argentinean fare, try **Patagonia** (© **2653-0612**), located right across from the Tamarindo Diria Hotel.

Dragonfly Bar & Grill ★★ INTERNATIONAL/FUSION   Set down a back street a little bit away from the action, this open-air restaurant has a casual-chic vibe and a menu that features spices and flavors from around the world with prominent influences from the Pacific Rim and southwestern United States. The thick-cut pork loin comes crusted in *panko* (Japanese breadcrumbs) and served with a brandy Dijon cream sauce. Portions are huge. The bar serves up primo cocktails, and there's occasionally live music.

Down a dirt road behind Hotel Pasatiempo. www.dragonflybarandgrill.com. © **2653-1506.** Reservations recommended. Main courses C5,500–C9,500. Mon–Sat 6–9:30pm.

Pangas Beach Club ★★★ SEAFOOD/INTERNATIONAL   Chef Jean-Luc Taulere had a very successful run at Mar y Sol in Playa Flamingo, but real-estate issues forced him to close up shop there—much to the betterment of the dining scene in Tamarindo. Located on the main road near the northern end of town, Pangas lets out onto the beach, right about where the ocean meets the estuary. Heavy wooden tables are spread on hard-packed sand under tall coconut trees, which are strung with simple lights to give this place a tropically romantic feel by night. While fresh seafood is the specialty here, I also love the steak tenderloin served on a hot volcanic stone to be cooked at the table. Breakfast and lunch are also served.

On the waterfront, north end of Tamarindo. © **2653-0024.** Reservations recommended. Main courses C7,500–C18,000. Daily 9am–10pm.

Seasons by Shlomy ★★ INTERNATIONAL   Cordon Bleu–trained chef and owner Shlomy Koren serves up his tasty Mediterranean-inspired cuisine out of a small kitchen at the Hotel Arco Iris (see above). It's not exactly a show kitchen, but there is a small service window and the door is always open, so it's possible and fun to watch Shlomy and crew at work. I recommend pretty much anything and everything on the menu, but find myself going back for the rice-paper-wrapped red snapper with a sun-dried-tomato tapenade and lemon-chili sauce. Still, it's hard to get too attached to any one dish, as the menu changes, well, seasonally.

Inside the Hotel Arco Iris. www.seasonstamarindo.com. ✆ **8368-6983.** Reservations recommended. Main courses $18–$19. No credit cards. Mon–Sat 6–10pm.

Exploring Tamarindo

Tamarindo is a long, white-sand beach. Still, you have to be careful when and where you swim. The calmest water and best swimming are always down at the far southern end of the beach, toward Punta Langosta. Much of the sea just off the busiest part of the town is best for surfing. When the swell is up, you'll find scores of surfers in the water here. *Be careful:* Rocks are just offshore in several places, some of which are exposed only at low tide. An encounter with one of these rocks could be nasty, especially if you're bodysurfing. I also advise that you avoid swimming near the estuary mouth, where the currents can carry you out away from the beach.

There is a host of good tour operators in Tamarindo. My favorites include **Xplore CR ★** (www.xplorecostarica.com; ✆ **844/278-6877** in U.S. and Canada, or 2653-4130 in Costa Rica), **Tamarindo Shuttle & Tours ★** (www.tamarindoshuttle.com; ✆ **2653-4444**), and **Iguana Surf** (www.iguanasurf.net; ✆ **2653-0613**). All offer a range of half- and full-day trips, including outboard or kayak tours through the nearby estuary and mangroves, excursions to Santa Cruz and Guaitíl, raft floats on the Corobicí River, and tours to Palo Verde and Rincón de la Vieja national parks. Rates run between $50 and $185, depending on the length of the tour and group size.

All of the hotel desks and tour operators in the area have **turtle nesting tours** to neighboring Playa Grande, in season, or you can contact **ACOTAM** (✆ **2653-1687**), a specialized local operator.

CANOPY TOURS There's no canopy tour available right in Tamarindo, but the **Monkey Jungle Canopy Tour** (www.canopymonkeyjungle.com; ✆ **2653-1172**) and **Cartagena Canopy Tour ★** (www.canopytourcartagena.com; ✆ **2675-0801**) are nearby. Both charge $50 per person and include transportation from Tamarindo. Of these two, the Monkey Jungle operation is much closer, but I prefer the Cartagena tour, which has a much more lush forest setting. Still, I think your best bet is to take a day trip to Hacienda Guachipelín (p. 122) and do the zip-line and canyoning tours there.

HORSEBACK RIDING Although some will be disappointed, I think it's a very good thing that horses are no longer allowed on the beach. Fortunately, you'll find plenty of opportunities to ride in the hills and forests around Tamarindo. Most tour operators offer horseback-riding options, but I recommend you go riding with **Casagua Horses ★** (www.paintedponyguestranch.com; ✆ **2653-8041** or 8871-9266). Rates for horse rental, with a guide, are around $25 to $40 per hour.

SAILBOAT CHARTERS Several boats take cruises offshore from Tamarindo; the 40-foot catamaran *Blue Dolphin ★* (www.bluedolphinsailing.com;

© 855/842-3204 in the U.S., or 8842-3204 in Costa Rica) and 66-foot cata-maran *Marlin del Rey* (www.marlindelrey.com; © 877/827-8275 in the U.S., or 2653-1212 in Costa Rica) are both good choices. A half-day snorkel or shorter sunset cruise should cost $70 to $85 per person, and a full day should run between $100 and $150 per person. This usually includes an open bar and snacks on the half-day and sunset cruises, and all of that plus lunch on the full-day trip.

SPORTFISHING   A host of captains offer anglers a chance to go after the "big ones" that abound in the offshore waters. From the Tamarindo estuary, it takes only 20 minutes to reach the edge of the continental shelf, where the waters are filled with mostly marlin and sailfish. Although fishing is good all year, the peak season for billfish is between mid-April and August. Contact **Tamarindo Sportfishing** (www.tamarindosportfishing.com; © 2653-0090), **Capullo Sportfishing** ★ (www.capullo.com; © 2653-0048), or **Osprey Sportfishing** (www.osprey-sportfishing.com; © 8754-9292).

WATERSPORTS   If you want to try snorkeling, surfing, or sea kayaking in Tamarindo, **Iguana Surf** (see above) rents all the necessary equipment. It has half-day and hourly rates for many of these items.

Tamarindo has a host of surf shops and surf schools, if you want to learn to catch a wave while in town. Tamarindo's got a great wave to learn on, although it can get very crowded at the popular beginners' breaks. You can shop around town, or check in with the **Kelly's Surf Shop** ★ (www.kellys surfshop.com; © 888/710-4746 in the U.S. and Canada, or 2653-1355 in Costa Rica), **Tamarindo Surf School** (www.tamarindosurfschool.com; © 2653-0923), or **Witch's Rock Surf Camp** ★ (www.witchsrocksurfcamp. com; © 888/318-7873 in the U.S. and Canada, or 2653-1262 in Costa Rica).

A sailboat cruise near Tamarindo.

The lack of any long-standing local Arts and Crafts tradition across Costa Rica is often lamented. One of the outstanding exceptions to this rule is the small village of Guaitíl, located on the outskirts of the provincial capital of Santa Cruz. The small central plaza—actually a soccer field—of this village is ringed with crafts shops and artisan stands selling ceramic wares. Most are low-fired, relatively soft clay pieces, with traditional Chorotega indigenous design motifs. All of the local tour agencies offer day trips to Guaitíl, or you can drive there yourself, by heading first to Santa Cruz, and then taking the well-marked turnoff for Guaitíl, just south of the city, on the road to Nicoya.

Especially for Kids

If your kids have had too much beach or pool time, you can head to **Bolas Locas Mini Golf** (www.bolaslocas.com; ℂ 2653-1178) located next to Dragonfly Bar & Grill (see above). Open daily from 9am until 11pm, this 18-hole course features a wave wall, as well as a waterfall and traditional Costa Rican oxcart as obstacles. A round of golf costs $7 for adults, and $5 for children 9 and under.

Shopping

Tamarindo's main boulevard is awash in souvenir stands, art galleries, jewelry stores, and clothing boutiques. For original beachwear and jewelry, try **Azul Profundo** ★ (www.azulprofundoboutique.com; ℂ 2653-0395) in the Plaza Tamarindo shopping center. The modern **Garden Plaza** shopping center, near the entrance to town, has several high-end shops, as well as a massive **Automercado** (supermarket).

Entertainment & Nightlife

As a popular surfer destination, Tamarindo has a sometimes raging nightlife. The most happening bars in town are **El Garito** ★★ (ℂ 2653-2017), located about a block inland, on the road leading toward Playa Langosta, and **Aqua** ★ (ℂ 8934-2896), on the main road through town. Other popular spots throughout the week include the **Crazy Monkey Bar** at the Best Western Tamarindo Vista Villas (ℂ 2653-0114) and the **Dragonfly Bar & Grill** (p. 132). For a chill-out dance scene, try the **Voodoo Lounge** (ℂ 2653-0100), while those looking for a rocking sports bar can head to **Sharky's** ★★ (ℂ 8918-4968). These latter two places are just across from each other, a little up the road that heads to Playa Langosta.

The best casino in town is at the **Barceló Playa Langosta** (ℂ 2653-0363) resort down in Playa Langosta.

En Route South: Playa Avellanas & Playa Negra

Heading south from Tamarindo are several as-yet-undeveloped beaches, most of which are quite popular with surfers. Beyond Tamarindo and Playa

Langosta are **Playa Avellanas** and **Playa Negra.** The one and only major development here is the Hacienda Pinilla development, which features an 18-hole **golf course ★★**, a range of vacation homes and condo developments, and the large, luxurious **JW Marriott Guanacaste Resort & Spa ★★★** (see below).

WHERE TO STAY

JW Marriott Guanacaste Resort & Spa ★★★
This large resort is built around a massive free-form pool—claimed to be the largest in Central America--and fronts a gorgeous—but decidedly small and rocky—patch of soft white sand beach. The rooms are ample and well equipped, with dark stained furnishings and rectangular red tiles set in a herringbone pattern. Every room has a large balcony or patio. Dining options include a semiformal steakhouse and contemporary Asian Fusion restaurant. A regular shuttle takes guests to nearby Playa Langosta, where they get access to a small beach club with a pool, showers, bathrooms, a restaurant and bar, as well as boogie board and surfboard rentals.

Hacienda Pinilla, Guanacaste. www.marriott.com. ☎ **888/236-2427** in the U.S. and Canada, or 2681-2000. 310 units. $554–$635 double; $695 and up suite. **Amenities:** 4 restaurants; 1 bar; lounge; outdoor pool; access to nearby golf course; access to nearby tennis courts; health club; spa; watersports equipment; children's programs; concierge; room service; babysitting; free Wi-Fi in public areas, $10–$16/day in-room.

WHERE TO EAT

In addition to the place listed below, the restaurants inside the **JW Marriott** resort are open to the general public.

Lola's ★★★
INTERNATIONAL/SEAFOOD   This quintessential beach bar and restaurant sits on a patch of land and sand fronting the quiet and underdeveloped Playa Avellanas beach. The Belgian and American owners serve up solid, healthful food on homemade heavy wooden tables and chairs underneath the shade of palm trees and large linen umbrellas. The fresh seared tuna can be prepared in a sandwich on thick, freshly baked focaccia, or atop a large salad with an Asian dressing. This place is extremely popular, especially on weekends, so be prepared to wait occasionally for food or a table (sorry, no reservations). When you're finished, and if you're really lucky, you might snag a siesta in one of the hammocks strung between the many coconut palms. This place gets its name from the owners' pet pig, which you can meet in its large pen, and sometimes catch playing in the waves.

On the beach, Playa Avellanas. ☎ **2652-9097.** Main courses $12–$18. Tues–Sun 9am–sunset.

PLAYA SÁMARA ★

35km (22 miles) S of Nicoya; 245km (152 miles) W of San José

Playa Sámara is a long, broad beach on a gently curved horseshoe-shaped bay. Unlike most of the other beaches along this stretch of the Pacific coast, the water here is usually calm and perfect for swimming because an offshore island and rocky headlands break up most of the surf. Playa Sámara is popular both with Tico families seeking a quick and inexpensive getaway and with young Ticos looking to do some serious beach partying. On weekends, in particular, Sámara can get crowded and rowdy. Still, the calm waters and steep cliffs on the far side of the bay make this a very attractive spot, and the beach is so long that the crowds are usually well dispersed. Moreover, if you drive along the rugged coastal road in either direction, you'll discover some truly spectacular and isolated beaches.

Essentials

GETTING THERE & DEPARTING   **By Car:** Head west out of San José on the San José–Caldera Highway (CR27). When you reach Caldera, follow the signs to Puntarenas and the Interamerican Highway (CR1). At 47km (29 miles) after you get on the Interamerican Highway heading north, you'll see signs and the turnoff for La Amistad Bridge (CR18). After crossing the bridge, continue on CR18 until it hits CR21. Take this road north to Nicoya. Turn in to the town of Nicoya, and head more or less straight through town until you see signs for Playa Sámara. From here, it's a well-marked and paved road (CR150) all the way to the beach.

To drive to Sámara from Liberia, head out of town on the main road to the Guanacaste beaches, passing through Filadelfia, Santa Cruz, and Nicoya. Once you reach Nicoya, follow the directions outlined above.

By Bus: Alfaro express buses (www.empresaalfaro.com; ✆ **2222-2666**) leave San José daily at noon and 5pm from Avenida 5 between calles 14 and 16. The trip lasts 5 hours; the one-way fare is C4,620. Extra buses are sometimes added on weekends and during peak periods, so it's always wise to check.

You can also take a bus from this same station to Nicoya and then catch a second bus from Nicoya to Sámara. **Alfaro** buses leave San José nearly every hour between 5:30am and 5pm. The fare is C4,045. The trip can take 4 to 5½ hours, depending if the bus goes via Liberia or La Amistad Bridge. The latter route is much faster and more frequent. **Empresa Rojas** (✆ **2685-5032**) buses leave Nicoya for Sámara and Carrillo regularly throughout the day, between 5am and 9pm. The trip's duration is 1½ hours. The fare to Sámara is C1,135; the fare to Carrillo is C1,300.

An express bus to San José leaves daily at 4am. Buses for Nicoya leave throughout the day between 5am and 6pm. Buses leave Nicoya for San José nearly every hour between 3am and 5pm.

Interbus (www.interbusonline.com; ✆ **4031-0888**) has a daily bus that leaves San José for Playa Sámara at 8am. The fare is $50, and they will pick you up at most San José–area hotels.

GETTING AROUND   If you need a ride around Sámara, or to one of the nearby beaches, have your hotel call you a taxi. Rides in town should cost $2 to $5; rides to nearby beaches might run $10 to $25, depending upon the distance.

VISITOR INFORMATION The website **www.samarabeach.com** is an excellent, all-around resource for information about Playa Sámara and the vicinity.

CITY LAYOUT Sámara is a busy little town at the bottom of a steep hill. The main road heads straight into town, passing the soccer field before coming to an end at the beach. Just before the beach is a road to the left that leads to most of the hotels listed below. This road also leads to Playa Carrillo (see below) and onward to the remote luxury resort **Hotel Punta Islita.** If you turn right 3 blocks before the beach, you'll hit the coastal road that goes to playas Buena Vista, Barrigona, and eventually Nosara.

> ### Learn the Language
>
> If you want to acquire or polish some language skills while here, check in with the **Sámara Language School** (www.samaralanguageschool.com; ☎ **866/978-6668** in the U.S. and Canada, or 2656-3000 in Sámara). These folks have a range of programs and private lessons and can arrange for a homestay with a local family. The facility even features classes with ocean views, although that might be a detriment to your language learning.

FAST FACTS To reach the local police, dial ☎ **2656-0436.** Sámara has a small **medical clinic** (☎ **2656-0166**). A branch of **Banco Nacional** (☎ **2656-0089**) is on the road to Playa Buena Vista, just as you head out of town. For full-service laundry, head to **Green Life Laundry** (☎ **2656-1051**), 3 blocks west of the Banco Nacional.

Where to Stay

MODERATE

The Hideaway Hotel ★★ This two-story boutique hotel has the feel of a converted home. The guest rooms are all large, contemporary, and cool, featuring white tile floors and white painted walls, offset with bold blue curtains and linens. The color theme continues outside where bright blue chairs and lounges ring a crescent-shaped pool. The hotel is set about a block or so inland from the far southern end of Playa Sámara, and a rental car is very helpful to get to and from the many restaurants, bars, and shops in town.

Playa Sámara, Nicoya, Guanacaste. www.thehideawayplayasamara.com. ☎ **2656-1145.** 12 units. $139 double. Rates include full breakfast. **Amenities:** Restaurant; bar; outdoor pool; free Wi-Fi.

INEXPENSIVE

In addition to the places listed below, **Tico Adventure Lodge** ★ (www.ticoadventurelodge.com; ☎ **2656-0628**) is another good option, about 2 blocks from the beach, in the heart of town.

Hotel Belvedere ★ It's a few blocks from the beach, but you can't beat this German-run hotel for value and cleanliness. Rooms are actually housed in two separate complexes, each located across a dirt road from the other. Each complex has its own pool. I prefer the newer rooms in the annex a bit uphill from the original hotel, where you'll find a larger pool and more exuberant gardens. It's just a 1-block walk down into the heart of town and 2 blocks to the beach.

Playa Sámara. www.belvederesamara.net. ✆ **2656-0213.** 24 units. $75–$90 double, $80–$120 apartment. Rates include breakfast. **Amenities:** Lounge; 2 outdoor pools; Jacuzzi; free Wi-Fi.

Sámara Tree House Inn ★★   It's not possible to find a room closer to the waves in Playa Sámara. While not true treehouses, four raised-stilt wooden cabins are supported by columns made from whole tree trunks set in a tight line facing the ocean. They have prized ocean views from the elevated perch of their large sitting rooms, although the bedrooms do feel a bit small and spartan by comparison, and there's no air-conditioning. Every unit here does come with a full kitchenette, as well as a large area underneath the living area equipped with a varnished wood table and chairs, and a couple of woven hammocks. There's a postage stamp–size round pool at the center of the complex, and a few chaise lounges on a patch of well-tended grass facing the beach.

Playa Sámara, Guanacaste. www.samaratreehouse.com. ✆ **2656-0733.** 6 units. $89–$145 double. Rates include breakfast. **Amenities:** Jacuzzi; outdoor pool; free Wi-Fi.

Where to Eat

Sámara has numerous inexpensive *sodas,* and most of the hotels have their own restaurants. In addition to the places mentioned below, **El Ancla ★** (✆ **2656-0716**), located a bit south of downtown, serves up good, simple meals, with a beach view.

El Lagarto ★ STEAK/GRILL   A massive fire churns out a stream of hot wood-burning coals to feed the large, long barbecue grill stations at this restaurant and bar. Tables are made from massive heavy planks or crosscut sections of local hardwood trees, and the food is served on huge, crosscut blocks of wood, which adds to the rustic, homey vibe. Grilled meats, seafood, and other goodies are the heart of the long menu here. These folks pride themselves on using grass-fed beef aged in-house for 3 weeks and only organic vegetables.

North end of Playa Sámara. www.ellagartobbq.com. ✆ **2656-0750.** Reservations recommended. Main courses $8–$32. Daily 3–11pm.

Gusto Beach ★★ ITALIAN/BISTRO   This simple, Italian-run restaurant is basically a beachfront trattoria—and then some. Three meals daily are served at a mix of tables, chairs, couches, and bar stools at high cocktail tables, all set in the sand underneath coconut palms strung with rope lighting. You can get excellent pastas, panini, and thin-crust pizzas, as well as sushi, sashimi, and curries. During the day, you can join a beach volleyball game right out front, and at night there's often live music or DJs. You can rent chaise lounges with shade for the day and even use on-site showers and bathrooms, making this into a full-service beach club, of sorts.

On the beach, north end of Playa Sámara. ✆ **2656-0252.** Reservations recommended. Main courses C4,900–C14,000. Daily 9am–11pm.

Exploring Playa Sámara

Aside from sitting on the sand and soaking up the sun, the main activities in Playa Sámara seem to be hanging out in the bars and *sodas* and dancing into the early morning hours. But if you're looking for something more, there's horseback riding either on the beach or through the bordering pastureland and forests. Other options include surfing, sea kayaking in the calm waters off Playa Sámara, sportfishing, snorkeling, scuba diving, boat tours, mountain biking, and tours to Playa Ostional to see the mass nesting of olive ridley sea turtles. You can inquire about and book any of these tours at your hotel.

You'll find that the beach is nicer and cleaner down at the south end. Better yet, head about 8km (5 miles) south to **Playa Carrillo ★★**, a long crescent of soft, white sand. With almost no development, the beach here is nearly always deserted. Loads of palm trees provide shade. If you've got a good four-wheel-drive vehicle, set off in search of the hidden gems of **Playa Buena Vista** and **Playa Barrigona ★★**, which are north of Sámara, and less than a half-hour drive away.

All the hotels here can help you arrange any number of tour options, including horseback rides, boat trips, sea kayaking, scuba diving, and snorkeling outings. You might also contact **Carrillo Adventures** (www.carrillo adventures.com; ✆ 2656-0606), an excellent all-around local tour company.

CANOPY TOURS   The folks at **Wingnuts Canopy Tours** (www.wingnuts canopy.com; ✆ 2656-0153) offer zip-line and harness canopy tours. The 2-hour outing costs $60 per person or $45 for those 11 and under. If you want to repeat the adventure, they offer a 50% discount on your second tour. Their office is by the giant strangler fig tree (*matapalo*) toward the southern end of the beach.

SPORTFISHING   Almost every hotel in the area can arrange sportfishing trips, or contact **Kingfisher ★** (www.costaricabillfishing.com; ✆ **800/783-3817** in U.S., or 8358-9561 in Costa Rica). Rates run from $300 to $850 for a half-day and $700 to $1,400 for a full-day outing.

SURFING   To learn how to surf or to rent a board, check in with **C&C Surf Shop and School** (www.cncsurfsamara.webs.com; ✆ **5006-0369**) or **Choco's Surf School** (www.chocossurfschool.com; ✆ **8937-5246**). Surfboard rentals run around $10 to $15 per day. Private lessons cost $30 to $50 per hour.

ULTRALIGHT FLYING   For a bird's-eye view of the area, head over to the **Flying Crocodile** (www.flying-crocodile.com; ✆ **2656-8048** or 8330-3923) in Playa Buena Vista. The folks here also give flights on a two-seat (one for you, one for the pilot) Gyrocopter, the ultralight equivalent of a helicopter. Although it might feel like little more than a modified tricycle with a nylon wing and lawnmower motor, these winged wonders are very safe. A 20-minute flight will run you $110, while a 1-hour tour costs $230.

WILDLIFE-VIEWING   Located near Barra Honda National Park (see below), **Rancho Humo ★** (www.ranchohumo.com; ✆ **2233-2233**) is a private wildlife reserve with fabulous bird-watching and wildlife-viewing opportunities along the Tempisque River basin and surrounding wetlands. The area is rich in waterbird species, shore lizards, and crocodiles. A full-day tour ($95) here includes a river boat trip, a tour of the reeds and lowland forest in a motorized safari-style vehicle, and a tour of the neighboring cattle ranching operations, as well as lunch. Transportation can be provided, and you can choose a half-day tour that takes in only one or two of the elements of the full-day tour.

Going Down Under

Spelunkers will want to head 62km (38 miles) northeast of Playa Sámara on the road to La Amistad Bridge. If you don't have a car, your best bet is to get to Nicoya, which is about a half-hour away by bus, and then take a taxi to the park, which should cost about $25. Here, at **Barra Honda National Park ★** (© **2659-1551**), is an extensive system of caves, some of which reach more than 200m (650 ft.) in depth. Human remains and indigenous relics have been found in other caves, but those are not open to the public. The park is open daily from 8am to 5pm; admission is $12, but the last tour into the caves starts at 1pm.

If you plan to descend the one publicly accessible cave, you'll need to hire a local guide at the park entrance station. These guides are always available and will provide harnesses, helmets, and flashlights. Depending upon your group size and bargaining abilities, expect to pay between $30 to $40 per person for a visit to the **Terciopelo Cave,** including the guide, harness, helmet, and flashlight. Furthermore, the cave is open only during the dry season (mid-Nov to Apr). You begin the roughly 3-hour tour with a descent of 19m (62 ft.) straight down a wooden ladder with a safety rope attached. Inside you'll see plenty of impressive stalactites and stalagmites while visiting several chambers of varying sizes. Even if you don't descend, the trails around Barra Honda and its prominent limestone plateau are great for hiking and bird-watching. Be sure to make a stop at **La Cascada,** a gentle waterfall that fills and passes through a series of calcium and limestone pools, some of them large enough to bathe in. The entire operation is slightly reminiscent of Ocho Rios in Jamaica.

Entertainment & Nightlife

After dark, the most happening place in town is **Bar Arriba ★** (no phone), a second-floor affair with a contemporary vibe a couple of blocks inland from the beach on the main road into town. You might also check out what's going on at **Gusto Beach ★★** (see above), **La Vela Latina** (© **2656-2286**), or **Tabanuco** (© **2656-1056**), all on the beach or fronting the water, right near the center of the action, on the main road running parallel to the beach from the center of town.

PLAYA NOSARA ★★

55km (34 miles) SW of Nicoya; 266km (165 miles) W of San José

As is the case in Malpaís, **Playa Nosara** is a bucket term used to refer to several neighboring beaches, spread along an isolated stretch of coast. In addition to the namesake beach, **Playa Guiones, Playa Pelada, Playa Garza,** and (sometimes) **Playa Ostional** are lumped into this area. In fact, the village of Nosara itself is several kilometers inland from the beach. Playa Nosara marks the northern limit of the Nicoya Peninsula, has a large expat community, and less of a honky-tonk feel than some of the Guanacaste beach areas.

Playa Guiones is one of Costa Rica's most dependable beach breaks, and surfers come here in good numbers throughout the year. However, the waves are still much less crowded than you would find in and around Tamarindo.

The best way to get to Nosara is to fly, but, with everything so spread out, that makes getting around difficult after you've arrived. The roads to, in, and around Nosara are almost always in very rough shape, and there's little sign that this will improve anytime soon.

Essentials

GETTING THERE & DEPARTING   By Plane: Sansa (www.flysansa.com; ✆ 877/767-2672 in the U.S. and Canada, or 2290-4100 in Costa Rica) and **Nature Air** (www.natureair.com; ✆ 800/235-9272 in the U.S. and Canada, or 2299-6000 in Costa Rica) both have several flights daily to **Nosara airport** (NOB; no phone). Fares run between $110 and $160 each way.

It's usually about a 5- to 10-minute drive from the airport to most hotels. Taxis wait for every arrival, and fares range between C3,000 and C6,000 to most hotels in Nosara.

By Car: Follow the directions for getting to Playa Sámara (see "Playa Sámara," earlier in this chapter), but watch for a well-marked fork in the road a few kilometers before you reach that beach. The right-hand leg leads to Nosara over another 22km (14 miles) of rough dirt road.

By Bus: An **Alfaro** express bus (www.empresaalfaro.com; ✆ 2222-2666 in San José, or 2682-0064 in Nosara) leaves San José daily at 5:30am from Avenida 5 between calles 14 and 16. The trip's duration is 5½ hours; the one-way fare is C4,805.

You can also take an Alfaro bus from San José to Nicoya and then catch a second bus from Nicoya to Nosara. **Alfaro** buses leave San José nearly every hour between 6am and 5pm. The fare is C3,950. The trip can take between 4 and 5½ hours, depending on whether the bus goes via Liberia or La Amistad Bridge. The latter route is much faster and more frequent. **Empresa Rojas** buses (✆ 2685-5352) leave Nicoya for Nosara daily at 4:45 and 10am, and 12:30, 3, and 5:30pm. The trip is about 2 hours, and the one-way fare is C1,870.

A direct Alfaro bus from Nosara to San José leaves daily at 12:30pm. Buses to Nicoya leave Nosara daily at 4:45 and 10am, noon, and 3 and 5:30pm. Buses leave Nicoya for San José nearly every hour between 3am and 5pm.

GETTING AROUND   If you want to rent a car, both **Economy** (www.economyrentacar.com; ✆ 877/326-7368 in the U.S. and Canada, or 2582-1246 in Costa Rica) and **National** (www.natcar.com; ✆ 2242-7878) have offices here. Because demand often outstrips supply, I recommend you reserve a car in advance. Alternatively, you can rent an ATV from several operators around town, including **Iguana Expeditions** (see below) and **Boca Nosara Tours** (see below). If you need a taxi, call **Taxi Freddy** (🕿 8662-6080) or **Gypsy Cab Company** (www.gypsycabnosara.com; 🕿 8302-1903).

VILLAGE LAYOUT The village of Nosara is about 5km (3 miles) inland from the beach. The small airstrip runs pretty much through the center of town; however, most hotels listed here are on or near the beach itself.

This area was originally conceived and zoned as a primarily residential community. The maze of dirt roads and lack of any single defining thorough-fare can be confusing for first-time visitors. Luckily, a host of hotel and restaurant signs spread around the area helps point lost travelers in the direction of their final destinations.

FAST FACTS You'll find the **post office** and **police station** (🕿 2682-1130) right at the end of the airstrip. An EBAIS **medical clinic** (🕿 2682-0266) and a couple of **pharmacies** are in the village as well. Both **Banco Popular** and **Banco Nacional** have offices in Nosara with **ATMs.** There's even a tiny **strip mall** at the crossroads to Playa Guiones.

Where to Stay

In addition to the places listed below, the **Nosara Beach House** ★ (www.thenosarabeachhouse.com; 🕿 2682-0019) on Playa Guiones has clean, comfortable rooms and a swimming pool—and it's right on the beach, to boot. For an intimate lodging that's also a very good deal, check out the **Nosara Retreat** ★ (www.nosararetreat.com; 🕿 2682-0209).

EXPENSIVE

Harmony Hotel & Spa ★★★ With an enviable setting right on Playa Guiones, this is by far the best hotel choice in Nosara. Well-heeled surfers and yogis flock here, and it's often hard to get a room. The "Coco" rooms feature high peaked wood ceilings, queen-size beds, and a private, enclosed garden deck area with an outdoor shower. The bungalows are even larger and have king beds. A short path through thick foliage leads to the waves. There's an excellent on-site spa and yoga facility, and the restaurant serves top-notch locally sourced fare and healthful spa cuisine. This hotel was awarded "5 Leaves" from the CST Sustainable Tourism program.

Playa Guiones. www.harmonynosara.com. 🕿 **2682-4114.** 25 units. $210–$330 double; $280–$380 bungalow; $560–$690 2-bedroom suite. Rates include breakfast and 1 yoga class. **Amenities:** Restaurant; bar; outdoor pool; spa; surfboard rentals; bikes; free Wi-Fi.

MODERATE

Harbor Reef Surf Resort ★ This sprawling mini-resort features a mix of rooms and suites at excellent prices, and it's quite popular with the surf crowd. All of the rooms are spacious and clean, if on the spartan side. Some of the suites come with full kitchens, and several fully equipped houses can be rented for longer stays. The grounds have tall trees and lush gardens and two swimming pools—one with a swim-up bar and the other with a stone waterfall that forms a small, private, grotto-like area underneath. Hammocks are strung from some of those tall trees. The beach and popular surf break at Playa Guiones are about a 3-minute walk away.

Playa Guiones. www.harborreef.com. ✆ **2682-5049.** 23 units. $120–$165 double; $175–$280 suite. Rates include continental breakfast. **Amenities:** Restaurant; bar; 2 outdoor pools; free Wi-Fi.

INEXPENSIVE

In addition to the places mentioned below, **Kaya Sol ★** (www.nosarahotel kayasol.com; ✆ **2682-1459**) is a popular budget choice and surfer hangout.

The Gilded Iguana ★   Located in the heart of Playa Guiones, about 200m (600 ft.) inland from the beach, this place features a mix of rooms, a refreshing kidney-shaped pool, and one of the best restaurant and bar scenes in the area (see below). The most economical rooms here are simple and road-worn. I think it's worth a splurge for the newer rooms with air-conditioning. The downside to the restaurant and bar's popularity is that it can be noisy here, especially when there's a live band or major sporting event going on.

Playa Guiones. www.thegildediguana.com. ✆ **2682-0450.** 12 units. $60–$65 double; $85–$110 suite. **Amenities:** Restaurant; bar; outdoor pool; free Wi-Fi.

Lagarta Lodge ★★   Geared slightly more to nature lovers than surfers, this small lodge sits on a high hilltop overlooking the Nosara River. Standard rooms feature red tile floors and textured concrete walls meant to look like painted river stones. The superior rooms or suites (they use both terms inter-changeably), have a more contemporary feel and provide the lodge's signature view over the river and rainforests and beyond to the long stretch of Ostional Beach in the distance. Guests gather at the open-air deck off the restaurant to admire this view, and to look for birds and monkeys. It's only a 10- to 15-min-ute jaunt down to the beach, but it's a pretty steep and strenuous hike back up to the hotel. The owners of this hotel own 35 hectares (86 acres) of land bor-dering the Nosara River, which they've converted into a private reserve. Guests here get unlimited access to the trails of the reserve, which pass through tropical lowland rainforests and mangrove forests.

Playa Nosara. www.lagarta.com. ✆ **2682-0035.** 12 units. $80–$125 double. **Amenities:** Restaurant; bar; outdoor pool; free Wi-Fi.

Where to Eat

In addition to the places mentioned below, **Marlin Bill's** (✆ **2682-0458**) is a popular and massive open-air haunt on the hillside on the main road, just across from **Café de Paris** (see below). You can expect to get good, fresh seafood and American classics here. **La Dolce Vita ★★** (✆ **2682-0107**), on the out-skirts of town on the road to Playa Sámara, serves up solid Italian fare nightly.

If you're looking to beat the heat, head to **Robin's Ice Cream ★** (www. robinsicecream.com; ✆ **2682-0617**) for homemade ice cream. It also serves breakfast, lunch, and dinner.

Café de Paris ★ BAKERY/BISTRO   Located right at the crossroads head-ing down to Playa Guiones, Café de Paris has a small storefront bakery for takeout and a more formal restaurant around the side and to the rear. I like to stop here for a freshly baked croissant and cup of coffee before an early morning surf session—and often return for a full breakfast afterward. But it's also worthwhile for lunch (think burgers, nachos, or wraps) or dinner—both the steak au poivre and fish curry are excellent. A pool and children's play set just off the main dining area make this a good choice for families with young kids.

On the main road into Nosara. www.cafedeparis.net. © **2682-0087.** Main courses C6,500–C10,000. Daily 7am–5pm.

The Gilded Iguana ★★ SEAFOOD/GRILL   With excellent food and fresh fish perfectly prepared, this casual, open-air spot is one of the most popular in the Nosara area. The food here is "bar-food-plus" with all the regular bar-food staples you'd expect—burgers, nachos, quesadillas, fajitas, and wings—as well as more substantial (chicken Parmesan) or eclectic (Thai shrimp) fare. The menu also features vegetarian, gluten-free, and low-calorie dishes. The fresh fish is provided daily by Chiqui, the owner's husband, a Nosara-born fisherman and tour guide. There's live music here Tuesdays and Fridays, and sporting events are shown on a series of flatscreen TVs hung from the low ceilings, and projected onto the largest wall.

About 90m (295 ft.) inland from the beach at Playa Guiones. www.thegildediguana. com. © **2682-0259.** Main courses C4,000–C9,000. Daily 7am–10pm.

La Luna ★★ INTERNATIONAL   This funky, oceanfront bistro has the best setting of any restaurant in Nosara. Enjoying a grassy perch right above Playa Pelada, you can watch surfers just below from one of the outdoor tables or long couches with overstuffed pillows. This is also a great place to catch the sunset. Wood oven–fired pizzas and Mediterranean fare are the specialties here, but nightly chalkboard specials might feature anything from pad Thai to chicken curry. Start things off with the feta quinoa salad, fresh ceviche, or some tuna tartare. For lunch, I really like the fish tacos.

Playa Pelada. © **2682-0122.** Main courses C6,700–C11,200. Daily noon–9pm.

Exploring Playa Nosara

Among the several beaches at Nosara are the long, curving **Playa Guiones ★★**, **Playa Nosara ★**, and the diminutive **Playa Pelada ★**. Because the village of Nosara is several miles inland, these beaches tend to be clean, secluded, and quiet. Surfing and bodysurfing are good here, particularly at Playa Guiones, which is garnering quite a reputation as a consistent beach break with a good ride. Pelada is a short, white-sand beach with three deep scallops, backed by sea grasses and mangroves. There isn't too much sand at high tide, so you'll want to hit the beach when the tide's out. At either end of the beach, rocky outcroppings reveal tide pools at low tide.

When the seas are calm, you can do some decent snorkeling around the rocks and reefs just offshore. Masks, snorkels, and fins can be rented at **Café de Paris** (p. 144) or **Coconut Harry's Surf Shop** (see below). Bird-watchers should explore the mangrove swamps around the estuary mouth of the Río

Nosara. Just walk north from Playa Pelada and follow the riverbank to explore the paths into the mangroves. In addition to numerous water, shore, and sea-bird species, you're apt to spot a range of hawks and other raptors, as well as toucans and several parrot species.

FISHING   All the hotels in the area can arrange fishing charters for $200 to $500 for a half-day, or $400 to $1,200 for a full day. These rates are for one to four people and vary according to boat size and accouterments.

HIKING & WILDLIFE-VIEWING   Located on land surrounding the Nosara River mouth, the **Nosara Biological Reserve** (www.lagarta.com; ℭ **2682-0035**) features a network of trails and raised walkways through tropical transitional forests and mangrove swamps. More than 270 species of birds have been spotted here. This private reserve is owned and managed by the folks at the **Lagarta Lodge** (see above), and the trails start right at the hotel. Admission is $6. Guided tours and guided boat tours are also available.

HORSEBACK-RIDING & QUAD TOURS   The folks at **Boca Nosara Tours** (www.bocanosaratours.com; ℭ **2682-0280**) have a large stable of well-cared-for horses and a range of beach, jungle, and waterfall rides to choose from. They also run similar tours on motorized off-road quads. Rates run between $40 and $70 per person, depending on the size of your group and the length of the tour.

Another good option for ATV tours and rentals is **IQuad** (www.iquad nosara.com; ℭ **8629-8349**).

SEA TURTLE–WATCHING   If you time your trip right, you can do a night tour to nearby **Playa Ostional** to watch nesting olive ridley sea turtles. These turtles come ashore by the thousands in a mass egg-laying phenomenon known as an *arribada*. The *arribadas* are so difficult to predict that no one runs regularly scheduled turtle-viewing trips, but when the *arribada* is in full swing, several local guides and agencies offer tours. These *arribadas* take place 4 to 10 times between July and December; each occurrence lasts between 3 and 10 days. Consider yourself very lucky if you happen to be around during this fascinating natural phenomenon. Your best bet is to ask the staff at your hotel or check in with the **Associacion de Guias de Ostional** ★ (Ostional Local Guide Association; asoc.guiasostional@hotmail.com; ℭ **2682-0428**). Tours are generally run at night, but because the turtles come ashore in such numbers, you can sometimes catch them in the early morning light as well. Even if it's not turtle-nesting season, you might want to look into visiting Playa Ostional just to have a long, wide expanse of beach to yourself. However, be careful swimming here because the surf and riptides can be formidable. This beach is part of **Ostional National Wildlife Refuge** (ℭ **2682-0428**). At the northwest end of the refuge is **India Point,** which is known for its tide pools and rocky outcrops.

SURFING   With miles of excellent beach breaks and relatively few crowds, this is a great place to surf or learn how to surf. If you want to try to stand up for your first time, check in with the folks at **Coconut Harry's Surf Shop**

Yo Quiero Hablar Español

You can brush up on or start up your Spanish at the **Rey de Nosara Language School** (www.reydenosara.itgo.com; ℅ **2682-0215**), which gives group and private lessons according to demand and can coordinate week- or multiweek-long packages.

(www.coconutharrys.com; ℅ **2682-0574**), **Del Mar Surf Camp** (www.delmarsurfcamp.com; ℅ **855/833-5627** in the U.S. and Canada, or 2682-1433 in Costa Rica), or **Safari Surf School** (www.safari surfschool.com; ℅ **866/433-3355** in the U.S. and Canada, or 2682-0113 in Costa Rica). All of them give hourly solo or group lessons, along with multiday packages with accommodations and meals included, and board rentals.

YOGA & MORE   If you want to spend some time getting your mind and body together, check in with the **Nosara Yoga Institute ★★** (www.nosara yoga.com; ℅ **866/439-4704** in the U.S. and Canada, or 2682-0071 in Costa Rica), an internationally recognized retreat and teacher training center. The institute offers intensive and daily yoga classes, teacher trainings, and a host of custom-designed "retreat" options. Its daily 90-minute classes are open to the public and cost just $15 (loaner mat included).

Check the Harmony Hotel & Spa (p. 143) for more yoga options.

Entertainment & Nightlife

When evening rolls around, don't expect a major party scene. **Kaya Sol** (℅ **2682-1459**) has a lounge-style bar popular with surfers, and the **Gilded Iguana** (see above) often has live music. In "downtown" Nosara, you'll probably want to check out either the **Tropicana** (℅ **2682-0140**), the town's longstanding local disco, or the **Legends Bar** (℅ **2682-0184**), an American-style bar with big flatscreen TVs and pool and *foosball* tables.

North of Nosara

Just north of Nosara lies Playa Ostional, famous for its massive nestings of olive ridley sea turtles (see above). This is a very underdeveloped beach village and there are only a few hotels. The best of these is **Hotel Luna Azul ★** (www.hotellunaazul.com; ℅ **2682-1400**), which features beautiful individual bungalows and a great view of the ocean—although the beach is a good distance away. If you come to Ostional to surf, try the **Ostional Turtle Lodge** (www.surfingostional.com; ℅ **2682-0131**), a basic, hostel-type place right on the beach.

PLAYA MONTEZUMA ★★

166–184km (103–114 miles) W of San José (not including the ferry ride); 36km (22 miles) SE of Paquera; 54km (33 miles) S of Naranjo

For decades, this remote village and its surrounding beaches, forests, and waterfalls have enjoyed near-legendary status among backpackers, UFO seekers, hippie expatriates, and European budget travelers. Although it maintains its alternative vibe, Montezuma is a great destination for all manner of travelers looking for a beach retreat surrounded by some stunning scenery. Active pursuits abound, from hiking in the Cabo Blanco Absolute Nature Reserve to horseback riding to visiting a beachside waterfall. The natural beauty, miles of almost abandoned beaches, rich wildlife, and jungle waterfalls here are what first made Montezuma famous, and they continue to make this one of my favorite beach towns in Costa Rica.

Essentials

GETTING THERE & DEPARTING   By Plane: Sansa (www.flysansa.com; ✆ **877/767-2672** in the U.S. and Canada, or 2290-4100 in Costa Rica) and **Nature Air** (www.natureair.com; ✆ **800/235-9272** in the U.S. and Canada, or 2299-6000 in Costa Rica) both have several flights daily to a small airstrip in **Tambor airport** (TMU; no phone), which is 17km (11 miles) from Montezuma. The flight is about 30 minutes, and one-way fares range from $99 to $115.

Some of the hotels listed below might pick you up in Tambor for a reasonable fee. If not, you'll have to hire a taxi, which could cost anywhere between $40 and $50. **Taxis** are generally waiting to meet most regularly scheduled planes, but if they aren't, you can call **Gilberto** (✆ **8826-9055**).

By Car: The traditional route here is to first drive to Puntarenas and catch the ferry to Paquera. Montezuma is about 30 minutes south of Tambor, 1 hour south of Paquera.

Naviera Tambor (www.navieratambor.com; ✆ **2661-2084**) car ferries to Paquera leave Puntarenas roughly every 2 to 3 hours daily between 5am and 8:30pm, with one early trip at 5am. The trip takes 1½ hours. The fare is C11,400 per car, including the driver; C810 for each additional adult; and C485 for children. I recommend arriving early during the peak season and on weekends, because lines can be long; if you miss the ferry, you'll have to wait 2 hours or more for the next one. Moreover, the ferry schedule changes frequently, with fewer ferries during the low season, and the occasional extra ferry added during the high season to meet demand. It's always best to check in advance.

The car ferry from Paquera to Puntarenas leaves roughly every 2 to 3 hours between 5:30am and 8pm. *Note:* If you have to wait for the ferry, do not leave your car unattended, as break-ins are common here.

Another option is to drive via La Amistad Bridge over the Tempisque River. I recommend this route only when the ferries are on the fritz, or when the wait for the next car ferry is over 3 hours. (When the lines are long, you may not find room on the next departing ferry.) Although heading farther north and crossing the bridge is more circuitous, you will be driving the whole time, which beats waiting around in the midday heat of Puntarenas. To go this route, take the Interamerican Highway west from San José. At 47km (29 miles) past the turnoff for Puntarenas, turn left for La Amistad Bridge. After you cross the Tempisque River, head to Quebrada Honda and then south to Route 21, following signs for San Pablo, Jicaral, Lepanto, Playa Naranjo, and Paquera.

To drive to Montezuma from Liberia, head out of town on the main road to the Guanacaste beaches, passing through Filadelfia, Santa Cruz, and Nicoya on

A Time-Saving Route

By far the fastest route is the daily speedboat shuttle between Montezuma and Jacó (actually Playa Herradura). This 1-hour shuttle departs Montezuma for Playa Herradura at 9am and makes the return trip from Playa Herradura to Montezuma at 11am. The folks at **Coco-Zuma Traveller** (www.cocozuma.com; © **2642-0911**) or **Zuma Tours** (www.zumatours.net; © **2642-0024**) can help book this, including connecting shared shuttle service to or from San Jose, Manuel Antonio, Malpaís, and other destinations. The boat shuttle itself is $40 per person, one-way.

your way toward the turnoff for La Amistad Bridge. Continue straight at this turnoff, and follow the directions for this route as listed above.

By Bus & Ferry: Transportes Cobano (© **2642-1112**) runs two daily direct buses between San José and Montezuma. The buses leave from the Coca-Cola bus terminal at Calle 12 and Avenida 5 at 6am and 2pm. The fare is C7,500, including the ferry ride, and the trip takes a little over 5 hours.

Alternatively, it takes two buses and a ferry ride to get to Montezuma. **Empresarios Unidos Puntarenas** express buses (© **2222-0064**) to Puntarenas leave San José daily every hour between 6am and 7pm from Calle 16 and Avenida 12. The trip takes 2 hours; the fare is C2,640. From Puntarenas, you can take the ferry to Paquera. A bus south to Montezuma will be waiting to meet the ferry when it arrives in Paquera. The bus ride takes about an hour; the fare is C1,800. Be careful not to take the Naranjo ferry, because it does not meet with regular onward bus transportation to Montezuma.

Buses are met by hordes of locals trying to corral you to one of the many budget hotels. Remember, they get a commission for everybody they bring in, so their information is biased. Not only that, but they are also often flat-out lying when they tell you the hotel where you wanted to stay is fully booked.

When you're ready to head back, direct buses leave Montezuma daily at 6:30am and 2:30pm. Regular local buses to Paquera leave Cóbano roughly every 2 hours throughout the day starting around 4am. Buses to San José leave Puntarenas daily every hour between 6am and 7pm.

CITY LAYOUT   As the winding mountain road that descends into Montezuma bottoms out, you turn left onto a small dirt road that defines the village proper. On this 1-block road, you will find El Sano Banano Village Cafe and, across from it, a small shady park with plenty of tall trees, as well as a basketball court and children's playground. The bus stops at the end of this road. From here, hotels are scattered up and down the beach and around the village's few sand streets.

Around the center of town are several tour agencies and Internet cafes among the restaurants and souvenir stores.

Where to Stay
EXPENSIVE
Ylang Ylang Beach Resort ★★   This small rainforest resort does an excellent job of blending tropical fantasy with hints of luxury. The whole

complex is set just off the beach in a dense patch of forest and flowering gardens. Lodgings range from "glamping" (glamorous camping) style tent cabins to individual bungalows and geodesic domes, with outdoor garden showers. There are no roads, nor is there regular vehicular access to the resort, so check-in is handled at the sister El Sano Banano Village Cafe (see below) in the town, and you and your bags are shuttled in via Jeep or dune buggy. The owners, Lenny and Patricia, have been here for decades and have done much to promote and protect the area.

Montezuma, Cóbano de Puntarenas. www.ylangylangresort.com. ℂ **888/795-8494** in the U.S. and Canada, or 2642-0636 in Costa Rica. 22 units. $190–$360 tent cabin, $220–$360 double. Rates include breakfast and dinner. **Amenities:** Restaurant; bar; outdoor pool; spa; free Wi-Fi.

MODERATE

Amor de Mar ★★   This has long been one of my favorite hotels in Montezuma. With simple rooms spread throughout a two-story wooden building, the real draw here is the setting. A large lawn leads from the main building down to the sea, where a coral-and-rock outcropping forms a swimming pool–size tide pool at high tide. Between this pool and the rooms is a small grove of mango trees and coconut palms strung with hammocks. The best rooms are on the second floor, with either private or shared oceanview balconies; two fully equipped vacation homes on the adjacent property are available for rent.

Montezuma, Cóbano de Puntarenas. www.amordemar.com. ℂ **2642-0262.** 11 units. $120–$150 double; $250–$270 villa. **Amenities:** Restaurant; free Wi-Fi.

INEXPENSIVE

The folks at Ylang Ylang (see above) also run the in-town **El Sano Banano B&B** (www.elbanano.com; ℂ **866/332-3590** in the U.S. and Canada, or 2642-0636 in Costa Rica), just off their popular restaurant (see below). The rooms here feature air-conditioning (which, because of the design, you are basically forced to use) and satellite televisions. Double rooms are $75 to $95.

Hotel La Aurora ★   Located right at the entrance to the village, this three-story budget hotel gives you clean and spacious rooms at a great price. Rooms come with low wooden beds and rather thin mattresses. Still, the German owner Angela Kock runs a tight ship here, and things are kept as close to immaculate as possible. The best rooms have air-conditioning and private balconies. A friendly, hostel-like vibe pervades the whole operation. There's a communal kitchen that gets a lot of use, along with several common areas.

Montezuma, Cóbano de Puntarenas. www.hotelaurora-montezuma.com. ℂ **2642-0051.** 20 units. $40 double; $50–$60 suites. **Amenities:** Lounge; free Wi-Fi.

Hotel Lucy ★   For a budget hotel, this place has some serious location cache. It's set right on the beach, a short walk south of the village, and close to the Montezuma Waterfall trail entrance. However, the rooms here are incredibly basic and sporadically maintained, and the service and personal attention provided are minimal. Still, it's very inexpensive and right on the beach. You have the option of private bathrooms or shared dorm-style rooms. Spend a few extra dollars for the private bathroom.

Montezuma, Cóbano de Puntarenas. ℂ **2642-0273.** 17 units, 6 with bathroom. $24 double with shared bathroom; $28 double with private bathroom. Rates include taxes. **Amenities:** Free Wi-Fi.

Where to Eat

In addition to the places listed below, you'll find several basic *sodas* and casual restaurants right in the village. You might also want to check out the varied international fare at **Cocolores ★** (ℂ 2642-0348). Just outside of downtown proper, the Israeli-owned **Puggo's ★** (ℂ 2642-0325) serves up an eclectic menu that ranges from falafel to ceviche to focaccia and beyond.

For breakfast, coffee, and light meals, **Orgánico ★** (ℂ 2642-1322) is a good option, with a range of healthful sandwiches, daily specials, and freshly baked goods. The **Bakery Café ★** (ℂ 2642-0458) is another good choice, serving everything from gourmet coffee drinks to full meals from the massive menu.

Finally, the restaurant at **Ylang Ylang Beach Resort ★★** (see above) is excellent.

El Sano Banano Village Cafe ★★ INTERNATIONAL/VEGETARIAN

This is one of Montezuma's main social hubs, and it's not hard to see why: The food is tasty, the smoothies are refreshing, and it has a lively bar scene and nightly movies (at 7:30pm; $6 minimum). The menu is heavy on healthful vegetarian and vegan fare, but you can also get fish and chicken plates. Fresh ceviche is often on the menu, and the seafood quesadilla is delish.

On main road into village. ℂ **2642-0944.** Main courses C4,000–C8,500. Daily 7am–10pm.

Playa de los Artistas ★★★ ITALIAN/MEDITERRANEAN

A few tables spread around a covered patio and backyard, and onto the sand just steps away from the waves. Candles and dim lighting for romance. A nightly changing menu that always features a range of fresh fish carpaccio and thin-crust pizzas cooked in an outdoor wood-fired oven. Can you tell I really like this place? That oven and an open-air grill are used to turn out perfectly cooked fresh fish and seafood dishes (served on freshly cut banana leaves draped over thick, wooden plates). What could be better?

Across from Hotel Los Mangos. ℂ **2642-0920.** Reservations recommended. No credit cards. Main courses C6,000–C10,000. Mon–Sat 5–9:30pm. **Note:** Hours here are seasonal, with lunch sometimes served during high season.

Exploring Montezuma

The ocean here is a gorgeous royal blue, and beautiful beaches stretch out along the coast on either side of town. Be careful, though: The waves can occasionally be too rough for casual swimming, and you need to be aware of stray rocks at your feet. Be sure you know where the rocks and tide are before doing any bodysurfing. Given the prevailing currents and winds here,

Montezuma also has experienced several severe and long-lasting red tide episodes in recent years. During these periods of massive algae bloom, the ocean is reddish-brown in color and not recommended for swimming.

The best places to swim are a couple of hundred meters north of town in front of **El Rincón de los Monos,** or several kilometers farther north at Playa Grande.

If you're interested in more than simple beach time, head for the **Montezuma Waterfall** ★★ just south of town—it's one of those tropical fantasies where water comes pouring down into a deep pool. It's a popular spot, and it's a bit of a hike up the stream. Along this stream are a couple of waterfalls, but the upper falls are by far the more spectacular. You'll find the trail to the falls just over the bridge south of the village (on your right, just across from Amor de Mar). At the first major outcropping of rocks, the trail disappears and you have to scramble up the rocks and river for a bit. A trail occasionally reappears for short stretches. Just stick close to the stream and you'll eventually hit the falls.

Note: Be very careful when climbing close to the rushing water, and also if you plan on taking any dives into the pools below. The rocks are quite slippery, and several people each year get very scraped up, break bones, and otherwise hurt themselves here.

Another popular local waterfall is **El Chorro** ★, located 8km (5 miles) north of Montezuma. This waterfall cascades down into a tide pool at the edge of the ocean. The pool here is a delightful mix of freshwater and seawater, and you can bathe while gazing out over the sea and rocky coastline. When the water is clear and calm, this is one of my favorite swimming holes in all of Costa Rica. However, a massive landslide in 2004 filled in much of this pool and also somewhat lessened the drama and beauty of the falls. Moreover, the pool here is dependent upon the tides—it disappears entirely at very high tide. It's about a 2-hour hike along the beach to reach El Chorro. Alternatively, you can take a horseback tour here with any of the tour operators or horseback riding companies in town.

A range of guided tour and adventure trips is available in Montezuma. **CocoZuma Traveller** (www.cocozuma.com; ✆ **2642-0911**) and **Sun Trails** (www.montezumatraveladventures.com; ✆ **2642-0808**) can both arrange horseback riding, boat excursions, scuba-dive and snorkel tours, ATV outings, and rafting trips; car and motorcycle rentals; airport transfers; international phone, fax, and Internet service; and currency exchange.

A UNIQUE CANOPY TOUR   One popular tour here is the **Waterfall Canopy Tour** ★ (www.montezumatraveladventures.com; ✆ **2642-0808**), which is built right alongside Montezuma's famous falls. The tour, which features nine cables connecting 13 platforms, includes a swim at the foot of the falls and costs $45 per person. Tours are given daily at 9am and 1 and 3pm.

HORSEBACK RIDING   Several people around the village will rent you horses for around $10 to $20 an hour, although most people choose to do a guided 4-hour horseback tour for $30 to $50. Any of the hotels or tour agencies in town can arrange it for you, or you can contact Marvin at **El Pinto Expeditions** (www.elpintoexpeditions.com; © **8492-3249**).

OTHER ACTIVITIES   Some shops in the center of the village rent bicycles by the day or hour, as well as boogie boards and snorkeling equipment (although the water must be very calm for snorkeling).

An Excursion to Cabo Blanco Absolute Nature Reserve ★★

As beautiful as the beaches around Montezuma are, the beaches at **Cabo Blanco Absolute Nature Reserve ★★** (© **2642-0093**), 11km (6¾ miles) south of the village, are even more stunning. At the southernmost tip of the Nicoya Peninsula, Cabo Blanco is a national park that preserves a nesting site for brown pelicans, magnificent frigate birds, and brown boobies. The beaches are backed by a lush tropical forest that is home to howler monkeys. The main trail here, Sendero Sueco (Swiss Trail), is a rugged and sometimes steep hike through thick rainforest. The trail leads to the beautiful Playa Balsita and Playa Cabo Blanco, two white-sand stretches that straddle either side of the namesake Cabo Blanco point. The beaches are connected by a short trail. It's 4km (2.5 miles) to Playa Balsita. Alternatively, you can take a shorter 2km (1.25-mile) loop trail through the primary forest here. This is Costa Rica's oldest official bioreserve and was set up thanks to the pioneering efforts of conservationists Karen Mogensen and Nicholas Wessberg. Admission is $10; the reserve is open Wednesday through Sunday from 8am to 4pm.

On your way out to Cabo Blanco, you'll pass through the tiny village of **Cabuya.** There are a couple of private patches of beach to discover in this area, off some of the deserted dirt roads, and a small offshore island serves as the town's picturesque cemetery. Snorkel and kayak trips to this island are provided out of Montezuma.

Shuttle buses head from Montezuma to Cabo Blanco roughly every 2 hours beginning at 8am, and then turn around and bring folks from Cabo Blanco to Montezuma; the last one leaves Cabo Blanco around 5pm. The fare is $3 each way. These shuttles often don't run during the off season. Alternatively, you can share a taxi: The fare is around $15 to $20 per taxi, which can hold four or five passengers. Taxis tend to hang around Montezuma center. One dependable *taxista* (taxi driver) is **Gilberto Rodríguez** (© **8826-9055**).

Entertainment & Nightlife

The local after-dark action seems to base itself either at **Chico's Bar ★** (© **2642-0526**) or the bar at **Hotel Moctezuma** (www.hotelmoctezuma.com; © **2642-0058**). Both are located on the main strip in town facing the water. If your evening tastes are mellower, **El Sano Banano Village Cafe** (see above) doubles as the local movie house, with nightly late-run features projected on a large screen.

MALPAÍS & SANTA TERESA ★★

150km (93 miles) W of San José; 12km (7½ miles) S of Cóbano

Malpaís (or Mal País) translates as "badlands," and, while this may have been an apt moniker several years ago, it no longer accurately describes this booming beach area. Malpaís is often used to refer to a string of neighboring beaches running from south to north, and including Malpaís, Playa Carmen, Santa Teresa, Playa Hermosa, and Playa Manzanillo. These beaches are long, wide expanses of light sand dotted with rocky outcroppings. This is one of Costa Rica's hottest spots, and development is ongoing here, especially in Santa Teresa. Still, it will take quite some time before this place is anything like more developed destinations such as Jacó, Tamarindo, or Manuel Antonio. In Malpaís and Santa Teresa, you'll find a mix of beach hotels and resorts, restaurants, shops, and private houses, as well as miles of often deserted beach, and easy access to some nice jungle.

Essentials

GETTING THERE & DEPARTING **By Plane: Sansa** (www.flysansa. com; ☎ **877/767-2672** in the U.S. and Canada, or 2290-4100 in Costa Rica) and **Nature Air** (www.natureair.com; ☎ **800/235-9272** in the U.S. and Canada, or 2299-6000 in Costa Rica) both have several flights daily to a small airstrip at **Tambor airport** (TMU; no phone), which is 17km (11 miles) from Montezuma. The flight duration is around 30 minutes, and fares range from $99 to $115, one-way. Some of the hotels listed below might be willing to pick you up in Tambor for a reasonable fee. If not, you'll have to hire a taxi, which will cost between $60 and $70. **Taxis** are generally waiting to meet most regularly scheduled planes, but if they aren't, you can call **Richard** (☎ **8360-8166** or 2640-0099) for a cab.

By Car: Follow the directions above to Montezuma (see "Playa Montezuma," earlier in this chapter). At Cóbano, follow the signs to Malpaís and Playa Santa Teresa. It's another 12km (7½ miles) down a rough dirt road that requires four-wheel-drive much of the year, especially during the rainy season.

To drive to Malpaís from Liberia, head out of town on the main road to the Guanacaste beaches, passing through Filadelfia, Santa Cruz, and Nicoya on your way toward the turnoff for La Amistad Bridge. Continue straight at this turnoff, and follow the directions for this route as listed above.

By Bus & Ferry: Transportes Cobano (☎ **2642-1112**) has two daily buses to Malpaís and Santa Teresa departing from Avenida 9 and Calle 12. The buses leave at 6am and 2pm, and the fare is C7,535, including the ferry passage. The ride takes around 6 hours. The return buses leave Santa Teresa at 5:15am and 2pm.

Alternately, you can follow the directions above for getting to Montezuma, but get off in Cóbano. From Cóbano, there are several daily buses for Malpaís and Santa Teresa running throughout the day. The fare is C950. *Be forewarned:* These bus schedules are subject to change according to demand, road conditions, and the whim of the bus company.

If you miss the bus connection in Cóbano, you can hire a cab to Malpaís for around $25 to $30.

GETTING AROUND If you need a taxi, call **Richard** (© 8317-7614 or 2640-0099). If you want to do the driving yourself, you can contact the local offices of **Alamo** (www.alamocostarica.com; © 2640-0526) or **Budget Rent A Car** (www.budget.co.cr; © 2640-0500). Or you can head to **Quads Rental Center** (© 2640-0178), which has a large stock of ATVs.

ORIENTATION Malpaís and Santa Teresa are two tiny beach villages. As you reach the ocean, the road forks: Playa Carmen is straight ahead, Malpaís is to your left, and Santa Teresa is to your right. If you continue beyond Santa Teresa, you'll come to the even-more-deserted beaches of playas Hermosa and Manzanillo (not to be confused with beaches of the same names to be found elsewhere in the country). To get to playas Hermosa and Manzanillo, you have to ford a couple of rivers, which can be tricky during parts of the rainy season.

Where to Stay

EXPENSIVE

In addition to the places listed below, **Latitude 10** ★★ (www.latitude10 resort.com; © 8309-2943) is a lovely, boutique beachfront resort, while **Casa Chameleon** ★★ (www.hotelcasachameleon.com; © 888/705-0274 in the U.S. and Canada, or 2288-2879 in Costa Rica) is a collection of plush, individual villas, each with a private pool, set on a steep hillside overlooking Malpaís.

If you're looking to combine beachfront luxury with some serious yoga and healthful eating, **Pranamar Villas & Yoga Retreat** ★★ (www.pranamar villas.com; © 2640-0852) on the northern end of Santa Teresa is a great option, built and run by the original owners and builders of Florblanca Resort (see below).

Florblanca Resort ★★★ This is the premier boutique luxury beach resort in this area, which is saying a lot. A collection of massive private villas are spread around lush and exuberant gardens. This foliage is so thick and abundant that I often get lost on the stone walkways that weave through the resort and connect everything. Only a few villas have ocean views. Still, all feature massive amounts of living space, and large, open-air bathrooms with outdoor showers and bathtubs amidst private garden settings. There's a gorgeous full-service spa; a large, two-tier swimming pool; and a spacious, wood-floor yoga studio with regular classes and workshops. The Nectar restaurant here is also excellent.

Playa Santa Teresa. www.florblanca.com. © 800/683-1031 in the U.S. and Canada, or 2640-0232 in Costa Rica. 11 units. $400–$500 double; $550–$675 1-bedroom villa, $725–$925 2-bedroom villa for 4; $775–$925 honeymoon house. Children 5 and under not allowed. **Amenities:** Restaurant; bar; outdoor pool; health club; spa; watersports equipment rentals; room service; free Wi-Fi.

Pranamar Villas & Yoga Retreat ★★

This intimate beach resort and yoga retreat feels like a small village, with tight windy paths overflowing with tropical foliage weaving between thatch-roofed buildings, with wood and bamboo walls. As is common on this coast, there's a heavy dose of Balinese, Thai, and Indonesian artwork, crafts, and furnishings, but mixed in with elements from Mexico, Guatemala, and Ecuador, as well. As the name suggests, yoga is an integral part of the program here, with regular daily classes, a steady stream of visiting workshops and a large and lovely yoga studio. The hotel's Buddha Eyes restaurant specializes in healthy and vegetarian cuisine, without skimping on creativity or flavor. This hotel is located on the far northern edge of Santa Teresa, right where it becomes Playa Hermosa.

Playa Santa Teresa, Cóbano de Puntarenas. www.pranamarvillas.com. ✆ **2640-0852.** 10 units. $250–$425 double, $370 house. Rates include breakfast and daily yoga class. Rates lower in the off season; higher during peak periods. **Amenities:** Restaurant; bar; saltwater pool; spa treatments; free Wi-Fi.

MODERATE

Trópico Latino Lodge ★★

This delightful little beachfront resort is set on a prime patch of sand in Santa Teresa. You can opt for the large and economical garden units, or splurge for a beachfront room or bungalow. The expansive grounds here are covered with tall pochote trees that are often frequented by roaming bands of howler monkeys. There's a small pool and beautiful oceanfront yoga studio and spa. The Shambala restaurant is excellent. Some of the most coveted surf spots in Santa Teresa are directly in front of this resort.

Playa Santa Teresa, Cóbano, Puntarenas. www.hoteltropicolatino.com. ✆ **800/724-1235** in the U.S. and Canada, or 2640-0062 in Costa Rica. 21 units. $135–$260 double; $730 suite. **Amenities:** Restaurant; bar; outdoor pool; spa; Jacuzzi; free Wi-Fi.

INEXPENSIVE

In addition to the hotels listed below, hardcore budget travelers can check out **Tranquilo Backpackers ★** (www.tranquilobackpackers.com; ✆ **2640-0589**), which is located a bit inland off the road running toward Santa Teresa and has a mix of dorm-style and private rooms.

Hotel Oasis ★

This place is aptly named. Individual bungalows and studio apartments are spread around shady grounds, just a short walk from the beach and some of Malpaís's most popular surf breaks. All units have a full kitchenette. The bungalows are great for families, with separate master and kids' rooms. However, only the two studios have air-conditioning. There's a small pool, and the owners are very hands-on and attentive.

Malpaís, Cóbano de Puntarenas. www.oasis.cr. ✆ **2640-0259.** 8 units. $75–$140 double. **Amenities:** Outdoor pool; free Wi-Fi.

Malpaís Surf Camp & Resort ★

This is a fun, multifaceted, budget-conscious resort with a wide range of rooms and price points. You can opt for anything from a bunk-bed room with shared bathroom to a private poolside villa. You can also pitch a tent here, if you so desire. A good-size, free-form pool sits at the center of the complex, which itself is about a 5-minute walk from the waves.

Malpaís, Cóbano de Puntarenas. www.malpaissurfcamp.com. ℗ **2640-0031.** 16 units, 8 with shared bathroom. $10 per person, camping; $25 double with shared bathroom; $35 double with private bathroom; $65 villa. **Amenities:** Restaurant; bar; outdoor pool; health club; watersports equipment rental; free Wi-Fi.

Where to Eat

In addition to the places listed below, you might try **Mary's** ★ (www.marys-costarica.com; ℗ **2640-0153**), a very popular, open-air joint that features wood oven–baked pizzas and fresh seafood, located toward the northern end of Malpaís.

Right at the Playa Carmen Commercial Center, at the crossroads at the entrance to town, you'll find a small food court with a wide range of options, including the bistro-style **Chop It – Holy Cow Burger** ★★ (℗ **2640-0000**). My favorite option here, however, is **Product C** ★★ (℗ **2640-1026**), a seafood retail outlet that also cooks up the daily catch, makes fresh ceviche, and serves fresh, farm-grown, local oysters. Just across the street, you'll find **The Bakery** ★★ (℗ **2640-0560**), which serves an amazing array of fresh pastries and baked goods, as well as sandwiches, pizzas, and more.

Out in Santa Teresa, the **Nectar** ★★ restaurant at Florblanca Resort (see above) is a great spot for a fine, romantic meal. If you drive a bit farther north, to Playa Hermosa, expect excellent sushi and Japanese fare at **Koji** ★ (℗ **2640-0815**).

INEXPENSIVE

Caracolas ★★ SEAFOOD/COSTA RICAN/MEXICAN   Set on a tree-covered hillside sloping down to the sea, you can dine at large communal tables close to the water or in one of the intimate pop-up shade structures and rustic thatch-roof *palapas* (open-sided huts) spread around the grounds. When you're finished with your meal, feel free to stretch out in one of the hammocks hung between the coconut palms. The ceviche here is made daily with locally caught fish and seafood, and you can't go wrong with a grilled filet of dorado in garlic sauce. Caracolas is also a perfect choice for sunset cocktails and appetizers.

On the beach, about 1km south of main crossroads in Malpaís. ℗ **2291-1470.** Main courses C4,950–C9,500. Daily 7am–10pm.

Exploring Malpaís & Santa Teresa

If you decide to do anything here besides sunbathe on the beach and play in the waves, your choices include nature hikes, horseback riding, ATV tours, scuba diving, and snorkeling, which most hotels can help arrange. Surfing is a major draw, with miles of beach breaks to choose from and a few points, to boot. If you want to rent a board or take a lesson, you can find a host of surf shops in Malpaís, Playa Carmen, and Santa Teresa, all of which rent boards and give lessons. I recommend **Costa Rica Surf & SUP** (www.costarica surfandsup.com; © **2640-0328**), **Surfing Costa Rica Pura Vida** (www. surfingcostaricapuravida.com; © **8333-7825**), and **Del Soul Surf School** (www.surfvacationcostarica.com; © **8878-0880**).

If you've been beaten up by the waves, or are sore from paddling out, you'll find several excellent spas in town. The best and most extensive (and most expensive) of these is at the **Florblanca Resort** (see above). But you might also check into the **Pranamar Villas & Yoga Retreat** (see above), which is located on the beach, at the northern end of Santa Teresa.

For canopy adventures, head to **Canopy del Pacífico** (www.canopy malpais.com; © **2640-0360**), which is toward the southern end of Malpaís and just slightly inland. A 2-hour tour over the nearly 2km (1 mile) of cables touches down on 11 platforms, features two rappels, and offers good views of both the forest and the ocean below. The cost is $45. Round-trip transportation from an area hotel is just another $5 per person.

Finally, any hotel in the area can arrange a horseback-riding or ATV trip into the hills and along the beaches of this region, a guided hike through **Cabo Blanco Nature Reserve,** or a trip over to Montezuma. For fishing, wildlife-viewing, and bird-watching, I highly recommend **Sapoa Adventures** ★★ (www.sapoaadventures.com; © **8996-9000**).

Entertainment & Nightlife

The most popular bar in the area is **Coco Loco** ★ (no phone), which is right on the beach in Malpais and features a mix of live bands and DJs, with weekly reggae and Latin nights, as well as a monthly full moon party. Thursday nights in Santa Teresa belong to the punk-ska-reggae band that holds forth at **Kika** (© **2640-0408**). Also in Santa Teresa, **La Lora Amarilla** (© **2640-0134**) is a classic local nightspot. This is definitely the place to come on Saturday night to dance some salsa and merengue with the locals. For a mellower scene, guests and fellow travelers tend to gather in the evenings at **Malpaís Surf Camp** (see above).

THE NORTHERN ZONE

Costa Rica's northern zone is a fabulous destination for all manner of adventurers, naturalists, and down-to-earth travelers. The region is home to several prime ecotourist destinations, including the majestic **Arenal Volcano ★★** and the misty **Monteverde Cloud Forest Biological Reserve ★★★**. Changes in elevation create unique microclimates and ecosystems throughout the region. You'll find rainforests and cloud forests, jungle rivers and waterfalls, mountain lakes, and vast wetlands, all boasting an unbelievable wealth of birds and other wildlife. In addition to these natural wonders, this region provides an intimate glimpse into the rural heart and soul of Costa Rica. Small, isolated lodges flourish, and towns and villages remain predominantly small agricultural communities.

This area is also a must for adventure travelers. The northern zone has one of the best windsurfing spots in the world, on **Lake Arenal ★**, as well as excellent opportunities for mountain biking, hiking, canyoning, and river rafting. Zip-line canopy tours and suspended forest bridges abound. And if you partake in any number of adventure activities (or even if you don't), you'll also find several soothing natural hot springs in the area where you can soak your tired muscles.

ARENAL VOLCANO ★★ & LA FORTUNA ★★

140km (87 miles) NW of San José; 61km (38 miles) E of Tilarán

In July 1968, Arenal Volcano, which had lain dormant for hundreds of years, surprised everybody by erupting with sudden violence. The nearby village of Tabacón was destroyed, and nearly 80 of its inhabitants were killed. At 1,670m (5,479-ft.) high, Arenal was for several decades afterward one of the world's most regularly active volcanoes. Sometime around December 2010, it entered into a relatively quiet phase. Gone are the nightly light shows and the glow of flowing lava. No one knows how long this may last. Still, rising to a near-perfect cone, the volcano itself remains majestic to gaze upon. And the area offers a rich variety of primary rainforests, rushing jungle rivers and waterfalls, lush natural hot springs, and plenty of adventure activities.

Lying at the eastern foot of this natural spectacle is the town of **La Fortuna.** Once a humble little farming village, La Fortuna has become a magnet for adventure tourists.

Arenal Volcano.

Essentials
GETTING THERE
BY PLANE **Nature Air** (www. natureair.com; ℂ **800/235-9272** in the U.S. and Canada, or 2299-6000 in Costa Rica) and **Sansa** (www.fly sansa.com; ℂ **877/767-2672** in the U.S. and Canada, or 2290-4100 in Costa Rica) both have daily flights to Arenal/La Fortuna (airport code: FON) from Juan Santamaría International Airport in San José (airport code: SJO).

Taxis are sometimes waiting for arriving flights. If not, you can call one at ℂ **2479-9605.** The fare to La Fortuna runs around C6,000.

BY CAR Several routes connect La Fortuna and San José. The most popular is to head west on the Interamerican Highway (CR1) from San José and then turn north at Naranjo, continuing north through Zarcero to Ciudad Quesada on CR141. From Ciudad Quesada, CR141 passes through Florencia, Jabillos, and Tanque on its way to La Fortuna. This route affords wonderful views of the San Carlos valley as you come down from Ciudad Quesada; Zarcero, with its topiary gardens and quaint church, makes a good place to stop, stretch your legs, and snap a few photos.

You can also stay on the Interamerican Highway (CR1) until San Ramón (west of Naranjo) and then head north through La Tigra on CR142. The travel time on any of the above routes is roughly 3 to 3½ hours.

A new highway connecting San Ramón with Ciudad Quesada/San Carlos is expected to open in mid-2016. However, if history is any indication, I'd expect it to be delayed by at least a year.

BY BUS Buses (ℂ **2255-0567** or 2255-4318) leave San José for La Fortuna at 6:30, 8:30, and 12:30pm from the **Atlántico del Norte** bus station at Avenida 9 and Calle 12. The trip lasts 4 hours; the fare is C2,575. The bus you take might be labeled TILARÁN. Make sure it passes through Ciudad Quesada. If so, it passes through La Fortuna; if not, you'll end up a long way from La Fortuna.

Alternatively, you can take a bus from the same station to Ciudad Quesada and transfer there to La Fortuna. These buses depart roughly every 30 minutes between 5am and 7:30pm. The fare for the 2½-hour trip is C1,860. Local buses between Ciudad Quesada and La Fortuna run regularly through the day,

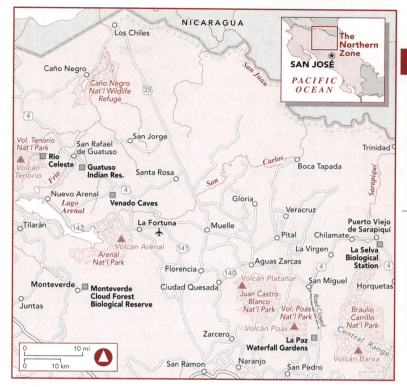

although the schedule changes frequently, depending on demand. The trip lasts an hour; the fare is C1,300.

Buses depart La Fortuna for San José roughly every 2 hours between 5am and 6pm; in most cases, you'll transfer in Ciudad Quesada to a bus to San José (they're frequent).

Gray Line (www.graylinecostarica.com; ☏ **800/719-3105** in the U.S. and Canada, or 2220-2126 in Costa Rica) and **Interbus** (www.interbusonline. com; ☏ **4031-0888**) both have two buses daily leaving San José for La Fortuna. The fare is around $50. Both companies will pick you up at most San José–area hotels. Both companies also run routes from La Fortuna with connections to most other major destinations in Costa Rica.

ORIENTATION

GUIDED SIGHTSEEING Desafío Expeditions ★★ (www.desafio costarica.com; ☏ **855/818-0020** in the U.S. and Canada, or 2479-0020 in Costa Rica), **Jacamar Tours** (www.arenaltours.com; ☏ **2479-9767**), and **Pure Trek Canyoning ★★** (www.puretrek.com; ☏ **866/569-5723** in the U.S.

boats, HORSES & TAXIS

You can travel between La Fortuna and Monteverde by boat and taxi, or you can add a horseback ride to the mix. A 10- to 20-minute boat ride across Lake Arenal cuts out the long drive around its shores. From La Fortuna, it is about a 25-minute taxi ride to the rocky beach on the shores of Lake Arenal, where you board (or disembark) the 15- to 20-passenger, covered ferryboat. The drive from the other embankment to Monteverde is around 1½ to 2 hours, over rugged dirt roads. The total trip should take about 2½ hours (as compared to 4 hours or more to drive around the lake). These trips can be arranged in either direction for between $28 and $35 per person,

and include door-to-door service from your hotels in each destination. There are daily fixed departures in each direction at 8am and 2pm. All of the hotels and tour agencies in the region can book this for you.

You can also add on a horseback ride on the Santa Elena/Monteverde side of the lake. **Desafío Expeditions** ★★ (www.desafiocostarica.com; ☎ 855/818-0020 in the U.S. and Canada, or 2479-0020 in Costa Rica) is one of the more reputable operators. They will even drive your rental car around for you while you take the scenic route. This trip costs $89, and takes around 5 hours.

and Canada, or 2479-1313 in Costa Rica) are the main tour operators in the area. All offer most of the tours listed in this section, as well as fishing and sightseeing excursions on the lake, and transfers to and from other destinations around Costa Rica.

CITY LAYOUT   As you enter La Fortuna from the east, you'll see the massive volcano directly in front of you. The main road into town, CR142, passes through the center of La Fortuna and then out toward Tabacón and the volcano. The town is only a few streets wide, with most hotels, restaurants, and shops clustered along the main road and around the small central park, which fronts the Catholic church.

GETTING AROUND   If you don't have a car, you'll need to either take a cab or go on an organized tour if you want to visit the hot springs or view the volcano. La Fortuna has tons of taxis (you can flag one down practically anywhere, or dial ☎ 2479-9605), and a line of them is always ready and waiting along the main road beside the central park. Another alternative is to rent a car when you get here. **Alamo** (www.alamocostarica.com; ☎ 2479-9090) has an office in downtown La Fortuna.

SPECIAL EVENTS   Each year, starting around February 1, La Fortuna pulls out all the stops for a 2-week celebration called "Fiestas Cívicas" (City Celebrations). There are horse parades, bullfights, mechanical rides, food stands, and concerts.

FAST FACTS   You'll find several information and tour-booking offices and Internet cafes, as well as a couple of pharmacies, general stores, banks, and launderettes, within a few blocks of the town's central park and church. If you need assistance, call the **Tourist Police** at ☎ 2479-7257.

Where to Stay in La Fortuna

INEXPENSIVE

Right in La Fortuna, you'll find a score of backpacker budget lodgings. One of the better choices is **Arenal Backpackers Resort** (www.arenalbackpackers resort.com; ☎ **2479-7000**), which bills itself as a "five-star hostel." It has shared-bathroom dorm rooms and more upscale private rooms, but even backpackers get to enjoy the large pool, Wi-Fi, and volcano views.

Hotel La Fortuna ★ I've been around long enough to remember when this was a simple, two-story, wood-and-zinc hostel. But a fire changed all of that, and now it's a modern, five-story property in the heart of downtown La Fortuna. The best rooms have volcano-facing balconies; of these, those on the top floors are preferable. The restaurant here is only open for breakfast, but you're right in the heart of downtown and close to all of the restaurants.

1 block south of the gas station, downtown La Fortuna, San Carlos. www.fortunainn.com. ☎ **415/315-9595** in the U.S. and Canada, or 2479-9197 in Costa Rica. 40 units. $80–$92 double. Rates include continental breakfast and taxes. **Amenities:** Restaurant; free Wi-Fi.

Where to Stay Near the Volcano

While La Fortuna is the major gateway town to Arenal Volcano, for my money, the best places to stay are located on the road between La Fortuna and the National Park.

EXPENSIVE

Nayara Hotel, Spa & Gardens ★★★ Intimate, romantic, and pampering—those words best describe the experience of staying at the individual cabins of Nayara. All are large and luxurious, with private, volcano-facing balconies featuring large, two-person Jacuzzis. Lush gardens provide privacy and good bird-watching. The dining options here are varied and all well executed, from the classy wine and tapas bar to the Peruvian-influenced sushi bar to the main international restaurant. However, unlike most of the other lodgings in this price category, there is no natural hot springs on-site. That can be remedied if you opt for one of the opulent villas in the **Nayara Springs** (www.nayarasprings.com) section of this resort. The villas here are massive and stunningly designed, and each features a spring-fed private pool and personal concierge service.

On the main road btw. La Fortuna and Lake Arenal. www.arenalnayara.com. ☎ **888/332-2961** in the U.S. and Canada, or 2479-1600 in Costa Rica. 66 units. $285 deluxe; $395 suite; $590 Springs villas. Rates include buffet breakfast. **Amenities:** 4 restaurants; 2 bars; 2 outdoor pools; exercise room; spa; 3 Jacuzzis; room service; free Wi-Fi.

Tabacón Grand Spa Thermal Resort ★★★ A swank, luxury hotel, Tabacón has the bonus of being just across the street from the best, most beautiful, and most extensive hot springs in the area (p. 173). Staying at the resort gets you unlimited access to that hot springs complex, with slightly extended hours and exclusive use of a private, hotel-guests-only section of the hot springs dubbed Shangri-La. If you take into account the hefty entrance fee to the springs, this place is practically a bargain. Not all of the rooms have

Arenal National Park & La Fortuna

ATTRACTIONS ●
Arenal National Park **4**
Athica Canopy **7**
Baldi Hot Springs **17**
Eco Termales **18**
Ecoglide **19**
El Silencio Mirador
   y Senderos **5**
La Fortuna Catholic Church **31**
Mistico Arenal
   Hanging Bridges **6**
Río Fortuna Waterfall **3**
Sky Adventures **1**
Tabacón Hot Springs **8**
Termales los Laureles **16**
The Springs Resort & Spa/
   Club Rio **12**

SHOPPING ●
Original Grand Gallery **20**
Art Shop Onirica **26**

HOTELS ■
Arenal Backpackers Resort **22**
Arenal Kokoro **13**
Arenal Observatory Lodge **2**
Cabinas Los Guayabos **11**
Hotel La Fortuna **29**
Hotel Silencio del Campo **15**
Nayara Hotel, Spa & Gardens **14**
Tabacón Grand Spa Thermal Resort **9**

RESTAURANTS ◆
Anch'io **23**
Cafe Mediterranea **21**
Don Rufino **30**
El Novillo del Arenal **10**
La Choza de Laurel **24**
Lava Lounge **25**
Rancho La Cascada **27**
Restaurante Nene's **28**

volcano views, and they maddeningly won't guarantee a volcano-view room, no matter how much you beg. On the plus side, management has a deep commitment to locally sustainable development and environmental conservation.

On the main road btw. La Fortuna and Lake Arenal, Tabacón. www.tabacon.com. ⓒ 855/822-2266 in the U.S. and Canada, 2479-2099 for reservations in San José, or 2479-2000 at the resort. 102 units. $240–$370 double; $375–$850 suite. **Amenities:** 2 restaurants; 3 bars; exercise room; nearby spa; Jacuzzi; outdoor pool; room service; free Wi-Fi.

MODERATE

Arenal Kokoro ★ For the best bang for your buck, at least in this area, choose these individual eco-cabinas. All are spacious and inviting and most have volcano views and a small private balcony. The casona rooms are a bit more basic and housed in two-story blocks of four rooms. It's definitely worth the slight splurge for an eco-cabina. Inside you'll find a mix of locally milled wood-plank paneling and painted concrete walls—some with hand-painted murals of birds, butterflies, and fanciful trees. The hotel has a pool and a small natural hot springs complex.

On the main road btw. La Fortuna and Lake Arenal. www.arenalkokoro.com. ⓒ 800/649-5913 in the U.S. and Canada, or 2479-1222 in Costa Rica. 30 units. $115–$140 double. Rates include breakfast. **Amenities:** Restaurant; bar; outdoor pool; spa; free Wi-Fi.

Arenal Observatory Lodge ★★ Originally a scientific observatory associated with the Smithsonian to monitor volcanic activity, this is one of the closest hotels to the Arenal Volcano, so the views are simply spectacular. The lodge is nicely isolated from the rest of the hustle and bustle of this busy region, and is graced with a large, private reserve and an excellent network of trails. The best rooms and views are found in the suites and private villas set below the main lodge building and restaurant, although those in the "Smithsonian" block also have great views. Given the remote location, I wouldn't recommend staying here without a rental car, as taxi rides to town are a bit long and expensive.

On the flanks of Arenal Volcano. www.arenalobservatorylodge.com. ⓒ 877/804-7732 in the U.S. and Canada, 2290-7011 for reservations in San José, or 2479-1070 at the lodge. 48 units. $97 La Casona double; $133 standard double; $171 Smithsonian; $195 junior suite. Rates include taxes and breakfast buffet; lower off-season rates. **Amenities:** Restaurant; bar; outdoor pool; spa; Jacuzzi; free Wi-Fi.

Hotel Silencio del Campo ★★ This friendly, family-run resort features a small collection of individual cabins oriented to take in the volcano view. All are quite spacious and perfectly maintained, with air-conditioning, TV, and a minifridge. They're a little bit close together, but not cramped, and large tropical flowers and palms planted all around give a sense of privacy. Still, try for one farthest from the main road. The best feature here is the lovely pool and hot springs complex, by far the best hotel hot springs complex in this price range. Service is extremely personalized and attentive.

On the main road btw. La Fortuna and Lake Arenal. www.hotelsilenciodelcampo.com. ⓒ 2479-7055. 23 units. $173–$182 double. Rates include full breakfast. **Amenities:** Restaurant; bar; outdoor pool; free Wi-Fi.

INEXPENSIVE

In addition to the inexpensive options in La Fortuna, if you have a car, **Cabinas Los Guayabos** ★ (www.cabinaslosguayabos.com; ✆ **2479-1444**) is a good value, with views and a location that rival the pricier lodgings listed above.

Where to Eat in & Around La Fortuna

Dining in La Fortuna is nowhere near as inspiring as the area's natural attractions, but given the town's booming tourist business, options abound. Popular places in downtown La Fortuna include **Rancho La Cascada** (✆ 2479-9145), **La Choza de Laurel** (✆ 2479-7063), and **Restaurante Nene's** (✆ 2479-9192) for Tico fare. For good pizza and Italian cuisine, try either **Café Mediterranea** (✆ 2479-7497), just outside town on the road to the La Fortuna waterfall, or **Anch'io** (✆ 2479-7560), just beyond Las Brasitas, on the road toward Tabacón and the national park entrance.

Don Rufino ★★ COSTA RICAN Don Rufino is the semi-official social center of town, with a popular open-air bar overlooking the main street of La Fortuna. The decor has rustic touches, but this is clearly a modern restaurant with contemporary fusion flourishes at every turn. In addition to great steaks and local staples, the long menu here features everything from Szechuan chicken to Cajun shrimp pasta. Prices are on the high end for La Fortuna, but, to my mind, worth it.

Main road through downtown La Fortuna, 2 blocks east of the church. www.donrufino. com. ✆ **2479-9997.** Main courses $10–$50. Daily 11am–10:30pm. Reservations recommended in high season.

El Novillo del Arenal ★ COSTA RICAN/STEAKHOUSE If you want some local steaks or well-prepared grilled chicken, but don't need fancy ambience, this is your spot. The restaurant is a simple affair set on a plain concrete slab under a very high, open-air, corrugated-zinc-roof structure. When it's clear, you get an excellent view of the volcano. Portions are hearty and the prices are right.

On the road to Tabacón, 10km (6¼ miles) outside of La Fortuna. ✆ **2479-1910.** Main courses C4,000–C12,000. Daily 11am–10pm.

Lava Lounge ★ INTERNATIONAL California meets Costa Rica at this popular downtown restaurant. Much of the main dining room is filled with wooden picnic tables with bench seating. If there are just two of you, consider sharing the table with some fellow travelers. The menu here ranges from glorified bar food—think nachos, quesadillas, wings, and wraps—to a hearty Costa Rican blue-plate special, or *casado,* with dishes such as a thick-cut grilled pork chop or coconut shrimp with spicy mango salsa. There are also burgers and pizzas.

Downtown La Fortuna, on the main road. www.lavaloungecostarica.com. ✆ **2479-7365.** Main courses $11–$25. Daily 11am–11pm.

Where to Stay & Eat Farther Afield

All the hotels listed in the following sections are at least a half-hour drive from La Fortuna and the volcano. Most, if not all, provide tours to Arenal and Tabacón, but they also hope to attract you with their own natural charms.

SOUTH OF LA FORTUNA

In addition to the places listed below, **Finca Luna Nueva Lodge** ★ (www.fincalunanuevalodge.com; ✆ **800/903-3470** in the U.S., or 2468-4006 in Costa Rica) is a fascinating sustainable farm and tourism project, and proud local advocate for the international "Slow Foods" movement.

Chachagua Rainforest Hotel & Hacienda ★★ This boutique rainforest lodge is set on 100 hectares (247 acres) of land, much of which is primary rainforest. While the rooms are certainly comfortable and cozy, I recommend splurging a bit more for one of the individual wooden bungalows, which are much roomier, and come with their own large covered-deck area. If you need modern conveniences like a TV and Jacuzzi tub, opt for one of the deluxe bungalows. On-site are miles of excellent trails through the rainforest; the owners can also book adventure tours and activities.

The small village of Chachagua sits 10km (6 miles) south of La Fortuna, on the road to San Ramón. The lodge itself is another 2km (1¼ miles) along a dirt road from the village. The entrance is well-marked and easy to spot.

Chachagua, Alajuela. www.chachaguarainforesthotel.com. ✆ **2468-1011.** 28 units. $179 double; $229–$259 bungalows. Rates include breakfast. **Amenities:** Restaurant; bar; outdoor pool; spa; mountain bike rentals; concierge; free Wi-Fi.

Villa Blanca Cloud Forest & Spa ★★ Once the country retreat and family-run hotel of former Costa Rican President Rodrigo Carazo Odio, this lovely little mountain resort is made up of individual small houses, or *casitas,* with clay-tile roofs, whitewashed stucco walls, rustic tile floors, and open-beam and cane ceilings. Each has a working wood-burning fireplace, which comes in handy in the cool, moist climate here. The deluxe *casitas* and suites have Jacuzzi tubs. The hotel's own private reserve borders the Los Angeles Cloud Forest Reserve, a lush area and ecosystem, very similar to that found in Monteverde. In fact, lucky visitors even have spotted the elusive resplendent quetzal here. A member of the "Green Hotels of Costa Rica," this lodge has earned "5 Leaves" in the CST Sustainable Tourism program.

To reach this hotel, you must first drive to the mountain city of San Ramón, which sits on the Interamerican highway (CR1), northwest of San José. From here, you'll drive north on CR142 toward Los Angeles, following signs to Villa Blanca.

San Ramón, Alajuela. www.villablanca-costarica.com. ✆ **877/256-8399** in the U.S. and Canada, or 2461-0300 in Costa Rica. 35 units. $205 double; $255 superior; $230 deluxe. Rates include full breakfast. **Amenities:** Restaurant; bar; spa; free Wi-Fi.

NORTH OF LA FORTUNA

Caño Negro Natural Lodge ★ Serious bird-watchers, nature lovers, and fishermen might consider this very remote little spot in the tiny lagoon-side village of Caño Negro. Bordering the area's namesake Caño Negro Wildlife Refuge, this simple lodge allows easy access to the lakes, lagoons, and waterways of this beautiful, low-lying wetlands area. The rooms here are large, clean, and cool, and the expansive grounds include lovely, well-tended gardens. To get there, drive toward the town of Los Chiles, and just before reaching Los Chiles, follow the well-marked signs for Caño Negro Natural Lodge. The final 18km (11 miles) is on a flat, but rugged, dirt road.

Caño Negro. www.canonegrolodge.com. © **2471-1426.** 42 units. $125 double. Rates include continental breakfast. **Amenities:** Restaurant; bar; outdoor pool; free Wi-Fi.

Exploring Arenal Volcano & La Fortuna

While in the town of La Fortuna, be sure to spend some time simply people-watching from a bench or grassy spot on the central plaza. It's also worth a quick visit to tour the town's **Catholic church.** This contemporary church was designed by famous Costa Rican artist Teodorico Quirós and features a soaring concrete steeple and clock tower.

EXPERIENCING THE VOLCANO ★★★

As I mentioned earlier, for the past couple of years the Arenal Volcano has been very quiet, with no loud eruptions or pyroclastic blasts. Still, the actual volcano remains a stunning sight to behold, and the natural park and surrounding trails and activities make this a great destination. That said, Arenal is surrounded by cloud forests and rainforests, and the volcano's cone is often socked in by clouds and fog. Many people come to Arenal and never see the exposed cone.

Although it's counterintuitive, the **rainy season** is often a better time to see the exposed cone of Arenal Volcano. But the bottom line is, catching a glimpse of the volcano's cone is never a sure thing.

Despite its current state of dormancy, climbing Arenal Volcano is neither common nor recommended. Over the years, many daredevil climbers have lost their lives, and others have been severely injured. The most recent fatalities occurred in August 2000. This is still a very "alive" volcano, with steam vents and a molten core.

ARENAL NATIONAL PARK ★★

Arenal National Park (© **2461-8499**) comprises an area of more than 2,880 hectares (7,115 acres), which includes the viewing and parking areas closest to the volcano. The park is open daily from 8am to 3:30pm; admission is $15 per person. The trails through forest and over old lava flows inside the park are gorgeous and fun—but be careful climbing on those volcanic boulders.

The principal trail inside the park, **Sendero Coladas (Lava Flow Trail) ★★**, is just under 2km (1.25 miles) and passes through secondary forest and open savanna. At the end of the trail, a short natural stairway takes you to a broad, open lava field left in the wake of a massive 1992 eruption. Scrambling over the cooled lava is a real treat, but be careful, as the rocks can be sharp in places. The closest view of the volcano can be found at **El Mirador (The Lookout) ★**, where you also can hear it rumble and roar on occasion. From the parking lot near the trailhead for the Lava Flow Trail, you have the option of hiking or driving the 1km (½-mile) to El Mirador.

OUTDOOR ACTIVITIES

Aside from the impressive volcanic activity, the area around Arenal Volcano is packed with other natural wonders.

ATV Several operators around town offer guided ATV tours. I like **Original Arenal ATV** (www.originalarenalatv.com; ✆ 2479-7522) which gives a 2½-hour ATV tour along the area around the lake and National Park. The cost is $99 per person, or $130 for two people riding tandem.

CANOPY TOURS CANYONING You have numerous ways to get up into the forest canopy here. Perhaps the simplest is to hike the trails and bridges of **Mistico Arenal Hanging Bridges** ★ (www.misticopark.com; ✆ 2479-1170). Located just over the Lake Arenal dam, this attraction is a complex of gentle trails and suspension bridges through a beautiful tract of primary forest. It's open daily from 7:30am to 4pm; admission is $36. These folks have also begun offering a night tour, departing at 5:30pm every evening.

Another option is the **Sky Tram** ★★ (www.skyadventures.travel; ✆ 844/468-6759 in the U.S., or 2479-4100 in Costa Rica), an open, gondola-style ride that begins near the shores of Lake Arenal and rises up, providing excellent views of the lake and volcano. From here, you can hike the series of trails and suspended bridges. In the end, you can hike down, take the gondola, or strap on a harness and ride the zip-line canopy tour down to the bottom. The zip-line tour here features several very long and very fast sections, with some impressive views of the lake and volcano. The cost is $93 for the combined tram ride up, a guided hike to the trails and hanging bridges, and the zip-line tour back down. It's $44 to ride the tram round-trip. The tram runs daily from 7:30am to 3pm. These folks also have butterfly and orchid garden exhibits on-site, as well as a range of other adventure tours.

Ecoglide ★ (www.arenalecoglide.com; ✆ 2479-7120) and **Athica Canopy** (www.athicacanopy.com; ✆ 2479-1405) are two other good zip-line canopy tour operations close to La Fortuna.

CANYONING If you'd like a bigger rush than the canopy tours offer, you could go "canyoning" with **Pure Trek Canyoning** ★★ (www.puretrek.com; ✆ 866/569-5723 in the U.S. and Canada, or 2479-1313 in Costa Rica) or **Desafío Expeditions** ★★★ (www.desafiocostarica.com; ✆ 855/818-0020 in the U.S. and Canada, or 2479-0020 in Costa Rica). This adventure sport is a mix of hiking through and alongside a jungle river, punctuated with periodic rappels through and alongside the faces of rushing waterfalls. Pure Trek's trip is probably better for first-timers and families with kids, while Desafío's tour is just a bit more rugged and adventurous. Both companies charge around $100 for the canyoning tour, and have various full-day excursions, mixing canyoning with other adventure tours, with two or three daily departures.

In 2015, Desafío added a new, more extreme canyoning tour that it calls **Gravity Falls** ★★★. Although it features only one major rappel, it consists of a series of leaps off high rocks into river pools below. The cost of this tour is $125. I've done it, and it's a lot of fun. However, I'm a bit torn about which I'd recommend for first-timers, and in the end I think the "traditional" canyoning tour might be a better fit for most travelers.

FISHING   With Lake Arenal just around the corner, fishing is a popular activity. The big fish to catch is the guapote, a Central American species of rainbow bass. However, you can also book fishing trips to Caño Negro, where snook, tarpon, and other game fish can be stalked. Most hotels and adventure-tour companies arrange fishing excursions ($150–$250 per boat); a full day goes for around $250 to $500.

HIKING   **El Silencio Mirador y Senderos** ★ (www.miradorelsilencio.com; ✆ **2479-9900**) is a top place for hiking outside of the national park. This private reserve has four well-marked, well-groomed trails, one of which takes you to a patch of the 1968 lava flow. There's a pretty pond and excellent views of the volcano, as well. Open daily from 7am to 9pm; admission is $8 per person.

For a more strenuous hike, sign up to climb **Cerro Chato** ★★, a dormant volcanic cone on the flank of Arenal with a beautiful little crater lake. **Desafío Expeditions** ★★ (www.desafiocostarica.com; ✆ **855/818-0020** in the U.S. and Canada, or 2479-0020 in Costa Rica) leads a 5- to 6-hour hike for $85, including lunch.

HORSEBACK RIDING   Horseback riding is a popular activity in this area, and there are scores of good rides on dirt back roads and through open fields and dense rainforest. Volcano and lake views come with the terrain on most rides. Horseback trips to the Río Fortuna waterfall are perhaps the most popular tours, but remember, the horse will get you only to the entrance; from there, you'll have to hike a bit. A horseback ride to the falls should cost between $30 and $50, including the entrance fee. Alternatively, you can check in with the folks at **Cabalgata Don Tobías** ★ (www.cabalgatadontobias.com; ✆ **2479-1780**), which runs a 2½-hour tour on its private land—a mix of farmland and forest, with some great views of the volcano. Two daily tours leave at 8:30am and 1:30pm, and the cost is $65 per person.

MOUNTAIN BIKING   This region is very well suited for mountain biking. Rides range in difficulty from moderate to extremely challenging. You can combine a day on a mountain bike with a visit to one or more of the popular attractions here. **Bike Arenal** ★ (www.bikearenal.com; ✆ **866/465-4114** in the U.S. and Canada, or 2479-7150 in Costa Rica) provides top-notch bikes, equipment, and a range of tours.

Hard-core bikers will want to come in March for the **Vuelta al Lago** ★ (www.vueltaallago.net; ✆ **2695-5297**), an annual 2-day race around the lake.

RÍO FORTUNA WATERFALL   Leading the list of side attractions in the area is the impressive **Río Fortuna waterfall** ★★ (www.arenaladifort.com; ✆ **2479-8338**), located about 5.5km (3½ miles) outside town in a lush jungle setting. A sign in town points the way to the road out to the falls. You can drive or hike to just within viewing distance. When you get to the entrance to the

Río Fortuna waterfall.

lookout, you'll have to pay a $10 entrance fee to actually check out the falls. It's another 15- to 20-minute hike down a steep and sometimes muddy path to the pool formed by the waterfall—and remember, it's also a steep and vigorous hike back up. You can swim, but stay away from the turbulent water at the base of the falls—several people have drowned here (enjoy the calm pool just around the bend instead, or join the locals at the popular swimming hole under the bridge on the paved road, just after the turnoff for the road up to the falls). The trail to the falls is open daily from 8am to 5pm.

It's also possible to reach the trailhead down to the falls by horseback. Most tour operators in town, as well as the waterfall folks themselves, offer this option for around $45. The tour generally lasts around 3 to 4 hours. *Note:* Desafío Expeditions (see above) also offers this tour in combination with a visit to a Maleku indigenous village.

WHITE-WATER RAFTING & KAYAKING For adventurous tours of the area, check out **Desafío Expeditions ★★** (www.desafiocostarica.com; ✆ **855/818-0020** in the U.S. and Canada, or 2479-0020 in Costa Rica) or **Wave Expeditions ★★** (www.waveexpeditions.com; ✆ **888/224-6105** in the U.S. and Canada, or 2479-7262 in Costa Rica). Both companies offer daily raft rides of Class I to II, III, and IV to V rapids on different sections of the Toro, Peñas Blancas, and Sarapiquí rivers. For families, a gentle safari float on the Peñas Blancas is probably the best bet. A half-day float trip on a nearby river costs around $70 per person; a full day of rafting on some rougher water costs around $90 per person, depending on what section of river you ride. Both companies also have mountain biking and local guided trips.

> **What'SUP**
>
> **Stand-Up Paddling (SUP)** is a booming sport and fitness craze, and you can practice it on lovely Lake Arenal, in the shadow of the lake's namesake volcano, with the folks at Desafío Expeditions (see above).

OTHER OUTDOOR ACTIVITIES IN THE AREA
La Fortuna is a great base for a day trip to the **Caño Negro National Wildlife Refuge ★**. This vast network of marshes and rivers (particularly the Río Frío) is 100km (62 miles) north of La Fortuna near the town of Los Chiles. This refuge is best known for its abundance of bird life, including roseate

spoonbills, jabiru storks, herons, and egrets, but you can also see caimans and crocodiles. Bird-watchers should not miss this refuge, although keep in mind that the main lake dries up in the dry season (mid-Apr to Nov), which reduces the number of wading birds. Full-day tours to Caño Negro average $70 to $80 per person. Be aware that most of the tours run out of La Fortuna that are billed as Caño Negro never really enter the refuge, but instead ply sections of the nearby Río Frío, which features similar wildlife and ecosystems. If you're interested in staying in this area and really visiting the refuge, check out the **Caño Negro Natural Lodge** (p. 167).

You can also visit the **Venado Caverns ★★,** a 45-minute drive away. In addition to plenty of stalactites, stalagmites, and other limestone formations, you'll see bats and unique cave fish and crabs. This tour is not for the claustrophobic, and it includes wading through a river, scrambling over rocks, and passing through a few semi-tight squeezes. This cave system is quite extensive, although tourists only have access to around 10 chambers. Still, these are quite striking, with impressive stone formations and ceilings over 100 feet high in places. Tours here cost between $65 and $80, including the guide and headlamps. Be prepared to get wet and muddy.

All of the tour agencies and hotel tour desks can arrange or directly provide trips to Caño Negro and Venado Caverns.

SHOPPING

La Fortuna is chock-full of souvenir shops selling standard tourist fare, but it's also home to one of my favorite crafts shops. On the way out of town toward Tabacón, keep your eye on the right-hand side of the road. When you see a massive collection of wood sculptures and the **Original Grand Gallery** (✆ **8946-0928**), slow down and pull over. This local artisan and his family produce works in a variety of styles and sizes. They specialize in faces, many of them larger than a typical home's front door. You can also find a host of animal figures, ranging in style from purely representational to rather abstract. Another good shop, which features original oil paintings, one-off jewelry, and jade pieces, is **Art Shop Onirica** (www.galeriaoniricacr.com; ✆ **2479-7589**), located next to La Fortuna's post office.

ESPECIALLY FOR KIDS

Located a couple of miles outside of La Fortuna, the **Ecocentro Danaus ★** (www.ecocentrodanaus.com; ✆ **2479-7019**) is a private biological reserve and sustainable tourism project that gives educational and engaging tours. Among the attractions here are a butterfly garden and reproduction center, botanical and medicinal plant gardens, and a small museum honoring the local Maleku indigenous culture. It's open daily from 8am to 4pm, and admission is $17, including a 90-minute guided tour. Night tours ($37) are offered by reservation. Children 5 to 11 get a 50% discount on any tour, and children 4 and under are free.

Set along the banks of the Arenal River, **Club Rio ★★★** (www.thesprings costarica.com; ✆ **954/727-8333** in the U.S. and Canada, or 2401-3313 in Costa Rica) is a wonderful playground for parents and kids alike. You can go

A SOOTHING SOAK IN hot springs

Tabacón Grand Spa Thermal Resort ★★★ (www.tabacon.com; ☏ **2519-1900**) is the most luxurious, extensive, and expensive spot in the area to soak your tired bones. A series of variously sized pools, fed by natural springs, are spread out among lush gardens. One of the stronger streams flows over a sculpted waterfall, with a rock ledge beneath that provides a perfect place to sit and receive a free hydraulic shoulder massage. The pools and springs closest to the volcano are the hottest—makes sense, doesn't it? The resort also has an excellent spa on the grounds, offering professional massages, mud masks, and other treatments, as well as yoga classes (appointments required). Most of the treatments are conducted in lovely, open-air gazebos surrounded by the rich tropical flora. The spa here even has several permanent sweat lodges, based on a Native American traditional design. A full-service restaurant, garden grill, and a couple of bars round out the amenities.

Admission is $60 for adults and $10 for children 11 and under. If you enter after 6pm, the adult fee drops to $45. A range of packages, including some with meals, are available. The hot springs are open daily from 10am to 10pm. The pools are busiest between 2 and 6pm. Management enforces a policy of limiting visitors, so reservations (which can be made online or by phone) are recommended.

Baldi Hot Springs (www.baldicostarica.cr; ☏ **2479-2190**) are the first hot springs you'll encounter on the drive from La Fortuna toward Tabacón. Baldi has a series of pools and slides, plus bars and restaurants spread around the expansive grounds. Frankly, I find this place far less attractive than the others mentioned here and it has much more of a party vibe, with loud music often blaring at some of the swim-up bars, and a heavy dose of large-bus and tour-group traffic. Admission is $34.

Just across the street from Baldi is the entrance to one of my favorite local hot springs, **Eco Termales** ★★ (www.ecotermalesfortuna.cr; ☏ **2479-8787**). Smaller and more intimate than Tabacón, this series of pools set amid lush forest and gardens is almost as picturesque and luxurious, although it has far fewer pools, lacks a view of the volcano, and the spa services are less extensive. Reservations are essential here, and admission is limited so that it never gets crowded. The admission fee is $34. An on-site restaurant serves basic local fare, but I recommend just coming for the springs.

Termales Los Laureles (www.termalesloslaureles.com; ☏ **2479-1395**) is located between Baldi and Eco Termales and Tabacón. This is the area's most local-feeling spot, and by far the most economical, charging just C6,000 for adults.

Finally, you can also enjoy the hot springs, pools, and facilities at the **Springs Resort & Spa** ★★ (www.thespringscostarica.com; ☏ **2401-3313**). In addition to the main pools by the hotel, they have a few more beautiful pools at the Club Rio riverfront area about 1km (½ mile) away.

inner tubing on the river, ride a horse through the forest trails, visit the midsize zoo, and take a shot at the three-story climbing wall. There's also a series of naturally fed hot springs sculpted alongside the river, as well as a restaurant and some simple chaise lounges for relaxing. It's part of the **Springs Resort & Spa** (see above), but you don't have to be staying at the resort to enjoy the activities and facilities here. A day pass ($99 adult; $75 children 12 and under) gets you access to the facilities and two of the above-mentioned adventure activities, as well as free run of all the pools and waterslides at the resort itself.

Finally, the newest attraction on the block is the **Kalambu Hot Springs & Water Park** ★ (www.kalambu.com; ✆ **2479-0170**). While most of the other hot springs in the area might have a waterslide or two, this place is a true water park, with several large waterslides and a massive and very entertaining children's play area and pools. The latter includes a giant bucket that is constantly filled and then dumped on everyone below. There are also a few quieter pool and hot spring areas, but this is the place to come if you're looking for more of a water park experience. Kalambu is open daily from 9am to 10pm. Entrance fees are $32 for adults and $16 for children. If you enter after 5pm, the entrance fees are $20 for adults and $10 for children.

ALONG THE SHORES OF LAKE ARENAL ★

200km (124 miles) NW of San José; 20km (12 miles) NW of Monteverde; 70km (43 miles) SE of Liberia

Despite its many charms, this area remains one of the least-developed tourism regions in Costa Rica. Lake Arenal, the largest lake in Costa Rica, is a long, beautiful body of water surrounded by rolling hills that are partly pasture and partly forested. Loads of activities and adventures are enjoyed both on the lake and in the hills and forests around it. While the towns of Tilarán and Nuevo Arenal remain quiet rural communities, several excellent hotels spread out along the shores of the lake.

Locals here used to curse the winds, which often come blasting across this end of the lake at 60 knots or greater. However, since the first sailboarders caught wind of Lake Arenal's combination of warm, fresh water, along with steady breezes and spectacular scenery, those blasts have brought a good number of visitors to the area.

The lake's other claim to fame is its rainbow-bass fishing. These fighting fish are known in Central America as guapote and are large members of the cichlid family. Their sharp teeth and fighting nature make them a real challenge.

Essentials

GETTING THERE & DEPARTING   By Car: From San José, you can either take the Interamerican Highway (CR1) north all the way from San José to Cañas, or first head west out of San José on the San José–Caldera Highway (CR27). When you reach Caldera, follow the signs to Puntarenas and the Interamerican Highway (CR1). You will actually follow signs for Liberia and San José, which are, in fact, leading you to the unmarked entrance to CR1. This road (CR23) ends when it hits the Interamerican Highway. You'll want to pass under the bridge and follow the on-ramp, which will put you on the highway heading north. This latter route is a faster and flatter drive, with no windy mountain switchbacks to contend with. In Cañas, turn east on CR142 toward Tilarán. The drive takes 3 to 4 hours. If you're continuing on to Nuevo Arenal, follow the signs in town, which will put you on the road that skirts the shore of the lake. Nuevo Arenal is about a half-hour drive from Tilarán. You can also drive here from La Fortuna, along a scenic road that winds around the lake. From La Fortuna, it's approximately 1 hour to Nuevo Arenal and 1½ hours to Tilarán.

By Bus: Transportes Tilarán buses (✆ **2222-3854**) leave San José for Tilarán roughly five times throughout the day between 7:30am and 6:30pm from Calle 20 and Avenida 3. The trip lasts from 4 to 5½ hours, depending on road conditions, and the fare is C4,400.

The daily bus from **Monteverde** (Santa Elena) leaves at 7am. The fare for the 2-hour trip is C1,150. Buses from **La Fortuna** leave for Tilarán daily at 8am and 12:15 and 5:30pm, returning at 7am and 12:20 and 4:30pm. The trip takes around 2 hours, and the fare is C2,300.

Direct buses to San José leave from Tilarán beginning at 5am. Buses to Puntarenas leave at 6am and 1pm daily. The bus to Santa Elena (Monteverde) leaves daily at 12:30pm. Buses also leave regularly for Cañas, and can be caught heading north or south along the Interamerican Highway.

GETTING AROUND   Both Tilarán and Nuevo Arenal are very small towns, and you can easily walk most places in the compact city centers. If you need a taxi to get to a lodge on Lake Arenal, call **Taxis Unidos Tilarán** (✆ **2695-5324**) in Tilarán, or **Taxis Nuevo Arenal** (✆ **8388-3015**) in Nuevo Arenal.

Where to Stay

In addition to the places listed below, **La Mansion Inn Arenal** ★ (www.lamansionarenal.com; ✆ **877/660-3830** in the U.S. and Canada, or 2692-8018 in Costa Rica) is an upscale option with a great setting and cozy cabins.

MODERATE

Mystica ★★   An Italian-owned hilltop retreat, rooms here are austere but immaculate, with wood or tile floors, large windows, and a shared common lakeview veranda. The best digs are the private villa and the individual cabin, which have more space and a greater sense of privacy. For families or small groups, there's also a two-bedroom house, with a full kitchen and hot tub. The expansive grounds and gardens are handsome, and there's a lovely river-stone pool and open-air yoga platform, as well as a massage room located in a tree house. The hotel's in-house Italian restaurant is a real plus here as well.

On the road btw. Tilarán and Nuevo Arenal. www.mysticacostarica.com. ✆ **2692-1001.** 9 units. $120 double; $140–$165 villa or cabin; $275 2-bedroom house. Rates include breakfast, except for the house. **Amenities:** Restaurant; bar; pool; spa; free Wi-Fi.

Villa Decary ★★   This intimate, lakeview lodging offers up a wonderfully cozy and friendly bed-and-breakfast experience. The rooms in the main building feature large picture windows and private balconies with wonderful views of Lake Arenal over well-tended gardens and patches of forest. There are also three private casitas, or little houses, with full kitchens and more space. These all have excellent lake views as well. Bright Guatemalan bedspreads provide a burst of color and walls are adorned with wildlife photos and primitive-style nature paintings. The original owners were hard-core palm enthusiasts, and the grounds and gardens are planted with scores of unique palm species. These lush grounds and gardens make for some fabulous bird- and wildlife-watching without even leaving the hotel.

Nuevo Arenal. www.villadecary.com. ☎ **800/556-0505** in the U.S. and Canada, or 2694-4330 in Costa Rica. 5 units, 3 casitas. $109 double; $142–$164 casita for 2. Rates include full breakfast. Extra person $15. **Amenities:** Free Wi-Fi.

INEXPENSIVE

Lucky Bug Bed & Breakfast ★★   Set back from the road, on a small hill above a small lake, this intimate bed-and-breakfast is a great lodging in the area. The rooms don't have any view to speak of, but they are spacious, cheery, and creative. Named for an element of rainforest flora or fauna, all feature handmade furniture, hand-painted tiles, and unique artwork based on the room's name, and created by the owner and her triplet daughters. The Butterfly and Frog rooms are my favorites, each with small private balconies. Over on the other side of the lake is an excellent restaurant and unique, well-stocked gift shop featuring a host of creations made by your host family.

Nuevo Arenal. www.luckybugcr.net. ☎ **2694-4515.** 5 units. $89–$109 double. Rates include full breakfast. **Amenities:** Restaurant; free Wi-Fi.

Where to Eat

The town of Tilarán has numerous inexpensive places to eat, including the restaurant at **Hotel La Carreta** (☎ **2695-6593**) and **Cabinas Mary** (☎ **2695-5479**). Another good option is the restaurant at **Mystica** (see above), which serves up excellent wood-oven pizzas and Italian specialties.

In Nuevo Arenal, **Tom's Pan German Bakery** (www.tomspan.com; ☎ **2694-4547**) is a popular spot for breakfast, snacks, lunch, and baked goods.

Gingerbread ★★★   MEDITERRANEAN/INTERNATIONAL   This small lakeside restaurant serves up the best and most creative food in the area. That's due to Israeli-born chef Eyal Ben-Menachem, who seeks out the best and freshest local ingredients (he's also a gregarious and gracious host, which makes coming here fun). Portions are huge, often big enough to share. In fact, depending on your group size, you may just be served a family-style meal, with no menu—although the food will be abundant, with plenty of variety and pizzazz. The duck quesadillas, seared tuna salad, and shrimp risotto are a few regularly occurring specials. There's both indoor and patio seating, and a bar that stays open long after the kitchen has closed down.

On the road btw. Tilarán and Nuevo Arenal. www.gingerbreadarenal.com. ☎ **2694-0039.** Main courses $27–$32. No credit cards. Reservations recommended. Tues–Sat 5–9pm.

Moya's Place ★★   INTERNATIONAL/VEGETARIAN/PIZZA   This cozy spot features large open front walls that open onto a small row of terrace seats facing the tiny town's main street. Interior walls are covered with hand-painted murals of Mayan temples and a giant Aztec calendar. There's a laid-back air to the whole operation, and Moya and Robyn are engaging hosts. Their delicious wood-oven pizzas are the main draw here. I also really like the hearty and healthy wraps and large, fresh salads—both are served big and filling. These folks open early, and this is also a great breakfast place. Locals and visitors alike come to spend time here. There's a lending/exchange library, and if there's any live music happening in Nuevo Arenal, it's most likely to be happening here.

Downtown Nuevo Arenal. © **2694-4001.** Main courses $5–$12. Daily 6:30am–9pm.

Exploring Along the Shores of Lake Arenal

ARTS, CRAFTS & DOWN-HOME COOKING About halfway between Nuevo Arenal and Tilarán is **Casa Delagua ★** (© **2692-1324**), the studio, gallery, and coffee shop of Costa Rican artist Juan Carlos Ruiz. The **Lucky Bug Gallery ★★** is an excellent roadside Arts and Crafts and souvenir shop, attached to the **Lucky Bug Bed & Breakfast** (see above). This place sells a host of functional and decorative pieces produced locally.

FISHING If you want to try your hand at fishing for guapote, a half-day fishing trip should cost around $150 to $300 per boat, and a full day goes for around $300 to $500. The boats used will usually accommodate up to three people fishing. Try **Captain Ron** at **Arenal Fishing Tours** (www.arenal fishing.com; © **2694-4678**).

HORSEBACK RIDING Any of the hotels in the area can hook you up with a horseback-riding tour for around $10 to $20 per hour.

WAKEBOARDING Lake Arenal is a big lake with plenty of calm, quiet spots to practice wakeboarding, a contemporary variation on waterskiing using a short, wide single board. If you're interested in lessons, or just a reliable pull on a wakeboard or water skis, contact **Fly Zone** (www.flyzone-cr. com; © **8339-5876**). Pulls behind their specialized boat run around $125 per hour, including boards, skis, and any other necessary gear.

WINDSURFING, KITEBOARDING & STAND-UP PADDLING (SUP) If you want to try windsurfing or kiteboarding, check in with the folks at **Tico Wind ★** (www.ticowind.com; © **2692-2002**), which sets up shop on the shores of the lake each year from December 1 to the end of April, when the winds blow. Rates run around $88 per day, including lunch; multiday and lesson packages are also available. This is also the place to rent stand-up paddleboards and equipment.

MONTEVERDE ★★

167km (104 miles) NW of San José; 82km (51 miles) NW of Puntarenas

Monteverde, which translates as "Green Mountain," is one of the world's first and finest ecotourism destinations. The mist-enshrouded and marvelous Monteverde Cloud Forest Biological Reserve and extensive network of neighboring private reserves are both rich and rewarding. Bird-watchers flock here for a chance to spot the myth-inspiring resplendent quetzal, scientists study its bountiful biodiversity, and a bevy of attractions and adventures await everyone else.

Cloud forests are a mountaintop phenomenon. Moist, warm air sweeping in off the ocean is forced upward by mountain slopes, and as this moist air rises, it cools, forming clouds. The mountaintops around Monteverde are blanketed almost daily in dense clouds, and as the clouds cling to the slopes, moisture condenses on forest trees. This constant level of moisture has given rise to an incredible diversity of innovative life forms and a forest in which nearly every square inch of space has some sort of plant growing. Within the cloud forest, the branches of huge trees are draped with epiphytic plants: orchids, ferns, and bromeliads. This intense botanical competition has created an almost equally diverse population of insects, birds, and other wildlife. Beyond the **resplendent quetzal,** the Monteverde area boasts more than 2,500 species of plants, 450 types of orchids, 400 species of birds, and 100 species of mammals.

Essentials

GETTING THERE & DEPARTING

BY CAR The principal access road to Monteverde is located along the Interamerican Highway (CR1); about 20km (12 miles) north of the exit for Puntarenas, is a marked turnoff for Sardinal, Santa Elena, and Monteverde. From this turnoff, the road is paved for 15km (9½ miles), to just beyond the tiny town of Guacimal. From here, it's another 20km (12 miles) to Santa Elena, the gateway town to Monteverde. Four-wheel drive is not necessary for this trip, but it's recommended, mostly for the clearance, as opposed to a need for traction.

Another access road to Santa Elena is found just south of the Río Lagarto Bridge. This turnoff is the first you approach if driving from Liberia. From the Río Lagarto turnoff, it's 38km (24 miles) to Santa Elena, and the road is unpaved the entire way.

Once you arrive, the roads in and around Santa Elena are paved, including all the way to Cerro Plano, and about halfway to the Cloud Forest Reserve.

To drive from Monteverde to La Fortuna, head out of Santa Elena toward Sky Trek and the Santa Elena Cloud Forest Reserve. Follow signs for Tilarán, which are posted at most of the critical intersections. If there's no sign, stick to the most well-worn road. This is a rough dirt road, all the way to Tilarán. From Tilarán, you have mostly well-marked and paved roads around the lake, passing first through Nuevo Arenal, and then over the dam and through Tabacón, before reaching La Fortuna.

HOTELS ■

Arco Iris Lodge **8**
Hidden Canopy Treehouses **5**
Hotel Fonda Vela **30**
Hotel Poco a Poco **16**
La Colina Lodge **29**
Monteverde Cloud Forest
Biological Reserve **32**
Monteverde Country Lodge **21**
Monteverde Lodge & Gardens **17**
Pensión Santa Elena **7**

SHOPPING ●

Casa de Arte **20**
CASEM COOP **26**

NIGHTLIFE ◆

Bar Amigos **6**
La Taberna **13**

RESTAURANTS ◆

Café Caburé **23**
Choco Café Don Juan **12**
Las Orquídeas Café **11**
Monteverde Cheese
Factory **28**
Morpho's Restaurant **9**
Sabor Español **1**
Sabor Tico **3, 14**
Sofía **22**
Stella's Bakery **25**
Tramonti **24**

ATTRACTIONS ●

Bat Jungle **23**
Chocolate Tour **23**
Curicancha Reserve **27**
Don Juan Coffee Tour **2**
El Trapiche Tour **2**
Finca Modelo Canyoning
Tour **31**
Monteverde Butterfly
Garden **19**
Monteverde Cloud Forest
Biological Reserve **32**
Monteverde Serpentarium **18**
Monteverde Theme Park **15**
Orchid Garden **10**
Santa Elena Cloud Forest
Reserve **4**
Selvatura Park **4**
Sky Adventures **4**

CARIBBEAN SEA

NICARAGUA

★ SAN JOSÉ

PANAMA

● Monteverde

PACIFIC OCEAN

MONTEVERDE CLOUD FOREST BIOLOGICAL RESERVE

Park Entrance ■

MONTEVERDE

Gas Station ■

CERRO PLANO

Quebrada Máquina

Río Guacimal

CASEM

SANTA ELENA

Post Office

See inset

To San José

Santa Elena

Bus Terminal

0   1/2 mi
0   0.5 km

179

BY BUS   **Transmonteverde** express buses (✆ **2256-7710** in San José, or 2645-7447 in Santa Elena) leave San José daily at 6:30am and 2:30pm from Calle 12 between avenidas 7 and 9. The trip takes around 4 hours; the fare is C2,905. Buses arrive at and depart from Santa Elena. If you're staying at one of the hotels or lodges near the reserve, arrange pickup if possible, or take a taxi or local bus. Return buses for San José also depart daily at 6:30am and 2:30pm.

A daily bus from Tilarán (Lake Arenal) leaves at 12:30pm. Trip duration, believe it or not, is 2 hours (for a 40km/25-mile trip); the fare is C1,150. The Santa Elena/Tilarán bus leaves daily at 7am.

Gray Line (www.graylinecostarica.com; ✆ **800/719-3105** in the U.S. and Canada, or 2220-2126 in Costa Rica) and **Interbus** (www.interbusonline. com; ✆ **4031-0888**) both have two daily buses that leave San José for Monteverde at 8am and 2:30pm. The fare is around $50. Both companies will pick you up and drop you off at most area hotels. Both Gray Line and Interbus have routes with connections to most major destinations in Costa Rica.

GETTING AROUND

Five or so buses daily connect the town of Santa Elena and the Monteverde Cloud Forest Biological Reserve. The first bus leaves Santa Elena for the reserve at 6:15am, and the last bus departing the reserve leaves at 4pm. The fare is C500. Periodic van transportation also runs between the two. Ask around town and you should be able to find the current schedule and book a ride for around C1,000 per person. A **taxi** (✆ **2645-6969** or 2645-6666) between Santa Elena and either the Monteverde Reserve or the Santa Elena Cloud Forest Reserve costs around C5,500 for up to four people. Count on paying between C3,000 and C5,500 for the ride from Santa Elena to your lodge in Monteverde. Finally, several places around town rent ATVs, or all-terrain vehicles, for around $50 to $75 per day.

CITY LAYOUT   The tiny town of **Santa Elena** is the gateway to Monteverde and the Monteverde Cloud Forest Biological Reserve, which is located 6km (3¾ miles) outside of town along a winding road that dead-ends at the reserve entrance. As you approach Santa Elena, you will reach a fork in the

Alternative Transport

You can travel between Monteverde and La Fortuna by boat and taxi, or on a combination boat, horseback, and taxi trip. See "Boats, Horses & Taxis" on p. 162 for details. Any of the trips described there can be done in the reverse direction departing from Monteverde. Most hotels and **Desafío Expeditions** ★★ (www. desafiocostarica.com; ✆ **855/818-0020**

in the U.S. and Canada, or 2479-0020 in Costa Rica) can arrange this trip for you. Desafío also offers transfers to Pacific coast beach towns combined with a day of rafting on the Tenorio River and multiday hikes from Monteverde to Arenal. On the latter, you spend the night in rustic research facilities inside the Bosque Eterno de los Niños.

Peace, Love & Ecotourism

Monteverde was settled in 1951 by Quakers from the United States who wanted to leave behind the fear of war, as well as their obligation to support continued militarism through paying U.S. taxes. They chose Costa Rica, a country that had abolished its army a few years earlier, in 1948. Although

Monteverde's founders came here to farm the land, they wisely recognized the need to preserve the rare cloud forest that covered the mountain slopes above their fields, and to that end, they dedicated the largest adjacent tract of cloud forest as the Monteverde Cloud Forest Biological Reserve.

road; take the right leg if you're heading directly to Monteverde. If you continue straight, you'll come into the little town center of Santa Elena, which has a bus stop, health clinic, bank, supermarket, a few general stores, and a collection of simple restaurants, budget hotels, souvenir shops, and tour offices. Heading just out of town toward Monteverde is a large Megasuper supermarket. Monteverde is not a village in the traditional sense of the word. There's no center of town—only dirt lanes leading off from the main road to various farms. This main road dead-ends at the reserve entrance.

Where to Stay

When choosing a place to stay in Monteverde, be sure to check whether the rates include a meal plan. In the past, almost all the lodges included three meals a day in their prices, but this practice is waning. Don't assume anything.

EXPENSIVE

Hidden Canopy Treehouses ★★★   If you're looking for an intimate, unique, in-touch-with-nature experience, head here. While there are a couple of rooms off the main lodge building, you'll definitely want one of the individual "tree houses." Set on raised stilts and set into the cloud forest canopy, these are all large, individual units, awash in varnished hardwoods and featuring large picture windows and a balcony or outdoor deck. Owner Jennifer King is almost always on-site and really pays attention to the fine details. Hidden Canopy employs excellent in-house guides and provides very personalized service.

On the road to Santa Elena Cloud Forest Reserve. www.hiddencanopy.com. ✆ **2645-5447.** 7 units. $225 double; $285–$445 double tree house. Rates include breakfast and afternoon tea. Extra person $40. Children 14 and under not permitted. 2-night minimum. **Amenities:** Lounge; free Wi-Fi.

MODERATE

Hotel Fonda Vela ★★   This longstanding hotel is one of the closest you'll find to the Monteverde Cloud Forest Reserve, just a 15-minute or so walk away. Owner Paul Smith's paintings, stained-glass works, and large sculptures are scattered throughout the hotel and grounds, giving it real personality. Rooms have lovely hardwood floors and are housed in several separate blocks of buildings, many with views over the forests to the Gulf of

Nicoya. The upgrade-worthy junior suites are especially spacious. A short walk from the restaurant and rooms, you'll find a covered pool, a couple of Jacuzzis, pool and Ping-Pong tables, board games, and a casual bar.

On the road to Monteverde Cloud Forest Reserve. www.fondavela.com. ☎ **800/270-8091** in the U.S. and Canada, or 2645-5125 in Costa Rica. 40 units. $177 double; $244 junior suite. Extra person $17. Rates include taxes. **Amenities:** 2 restaurants; 2 bars; outdoor pool; Jacuzzi; free Wi-Fi.

Hotel Poco a Poco ★★

A good choice for families with kids, Poco a Poco provides clean, comfortable rooms with all the modern amenities, including TV/DVD systems and access to a massive DVD library. A pool, heated Jacuzzi, and small spa are housed under a large complex of atrium-style clear roofing. This is a hive of activity and the spot where most guests spend time when not out touring or active around Monteverde. The restaurant is excellent and features live music nightly. These folks take sustainable tourism seriously and have earned "4 Leaves" in the CST Sustainable Tourism program.

Santa Elena. www.hotelpocoapoco.com. ☎ **855/557-6262** in the U.S. and Canada, or 2645-6000 in Costa Rica. 30 units. $134–$154 double. Rates include breakfast. **Amenities:** Restaurant; bar; outdoor pool; spa; Jacuzzi; free Wi-Fi.

Monteverde Lodge & Gardens ★★★

Some things do get better with age, and that's certainly true of this pioneering ecolodge. Rooms are large and what I'd call rustic yet elegant, with hardwood floors, and a wall of windows or French doors opening out to views of the gardens and surrounding forests. There are well-groomed and well-marked trails on-site through the lush and beautiful gardens, and there's a midsize heated outdoor pool with slate decking all around, as well as butterfly, orchid, and hummingbird attractions. They also have one of the best guide and tour operations in the area.

Santa Elena. www.monteverdelodge.com. ☎ **2257-0766** San José office, or 2645-5057 at the lodge. 28 units. $99–$228 double. Rates include breakfast. **Amenities:** Restaurant; bar; outdoor pool; Jacuzzi; free Wi-Fi.

INEXPENSIVE

In addition to the hotels listed below, there are quite a few *pensión* (hostel) and backpacker specials in Santa Elena and spread along the road to the reserve. The best of the bunch is the **Pensión Santa Elena** ★ (www.pensionsantaelena.com; ☎ **2645-5051**). A step up from a *pensión*, **Monteverde Country Lodge** ★ (www.monteverdecountrylodge.com; ☎ **888/936-5696** in the U.S. and Canada, or 2645-7600 in Costa Rica) is a homey, inviting, great-value hotel run by the folks at Hotel Poco a Poco (see above).

It's also possible to stay in a room right at the **Monteverde Cloud Forest Biological Reserve** ★ (www.reservamonteverde.com; ☎ **2645-5122**). A bunk bed, shared bathroom, and three meals per day here run $70 per adult, $40 for kids. For an extra $11 (adults only; children's rate still $40), you can get a room with a private bathroom. Admission to the reserve is included in the price. Rooms here are fairly spartan, especially the shared-bath, bunk-bed rooms, but the service is friendly, and you are steps away from the trails inside the reserve.

Arco Iris Lodge ★★ This small boutique hotel is actually right in the town of Santa Elena, but you'd never know it. The sprawling grounds and gardens give it a great sense of isolation, while still being a short walk from a host of restaurants, shops, and attractions. The rooms are cozy and immaculately kept. They come in a variety of shapes and sizes from simple standard units, some with bunk beds, to individual cabins and superior rooms with a kitchenette and sleeping loft.

Santa Elena. www.arcoirislodge.com. ℭ **2645-5067.** 24 units. $42–$50 budget; $88–$145 double; $195 honeymoon cabin. Rates include taxes. **Amenities:** Lounge; free Wi-Fi.

La Colina Lodge ★ This rustic old lodge (originally the Pensión Flor Mar) is located fairly close to the Monteverde Cloud Forest Reserve and it radiates a friendly, homey vibe. Guests from all over the world gather in the common lounge area or cook together in the communal kitchen. Rooms are basic, but well kept and cozy. You have a choice of shared bathroom dorm accommodations or rooms with their own private bath. You can even pitch a tent on the grounds, while enjoying kitchen and bathroom privileges.

Monteverde. www.lacolinalodge.com. ℭ **2645-5009.** 11 units, 7 with private bathroom. $35 double with private bathroom; $25 double with shared bathroom; $8 per person camping. Rates include taxes. **Amenities:** Restaurant; free Wi-Fi.

Where to Eat

Because most visitors want to get an early start, they usually grab a quick breakfast at their hotel. It's also common for people to have their lodging pack them a bag lunch to take to the reserve, although there's a decent little *soda* (diner) at the reserve entrance.

In addition to the places listed below, you can get good pizza and pastas at **Tramonti** ★ (www.tramonticr.com; ℭ 2645-6120), along the road to the reserve, and great paella and other Spanish specialties at **Sabor Español** ★ (ℭ 2645-5387), located a few miles outside of Santa Elena on the road to Tilarán. Also, the restaurant at the **Hotel Poco a Poco** ★ (ℭ 2645-6000; see above) gets good marks.

A popular choice for lunch is **Stella's Bakery** ★ (ℭ 2645-5560), across from the CASEM gift shop. The restaurant is bright and inviting, with lots of varnished woodwork inside and a few outdoor tables. The selection changes regularly, but might include vegetarian quiche, eggplant parmigiana, and an assortment of salads.

Finally, it's worth stopping by the **Monteverde Cheese Factory** ★ (www.monteverde.net; ℭ 2645-5150) to pick up some of the best cheese in Costa Rica. (You can even watch cheese being processed and get homemade ice cream.) There's a simple coffee shop and cafe featuring its various products. The cheese factory is right on the main road about midway between Santa Elena and the reserve.

EXPENSIVE

Sofia ★★★ COSTA RICAN/FUSION The food here is based on classic Tico dishes and ingredients, but with interesting twists. I like the tenderloin in chipotle butter salsa and the guava-glazed chicken. Even the cocktails here are creative, including their signature mango-ginger *mojito,* which is both sweet and tangy. Try to grab a seat in front of one of the large arched picture windows overlooking lush cloud forest foliage.

Cerro Plano, just past the turnoff to the Butterfly Farm, on your left. ℂ **2645-7017.** Reservations recommended in high season. Main courses $14–$20. Daily 11:30am–9:30pm.

Moderate

Café Caburé ★★★ INTERNATIONAL/CHOCOLATES   Set on the second floor of a small complex also housing the Bat Jungle (p. 189), with open-air seating on a broad wooden veranda, this is a great spot for a meal . . . or a decadent dessert break. The main menu features a wide range of international dishes, with everything from chicken mole to shrimp curry to excellent sandwiches, wraps, and fresh empanadas (one of the owners is Argentinean). But the homemade chocolates and fancy flavored truffles are the standouts here. And if you want to learn more about the chocolate-making and -tempering process, be sure to take the chocolate tour (see below).

On the road btw. Santa Elena and the reserve, at the Bat Jungle. www.cabure.net. ℂ **2645-5020.** Reservations recommended in high season. Main courses C2,900–C9,500. Mon–Sat 9am–8:30pm.

Inexpensive

Morpho's Restaurant ★ COSTA RICAN/VEGETARIAN   Although it's moved around over the years, this place is a local institution, serving up hearty meals at great prices. The large and varied *casado* (a local blue-plate special) is quite popular, as are the fresh-fruit smoothies and home-baked desserts. For something a bit fancier, try the thick pork chop in a plum/cherry sauce. There's also a host of excellent vegetarian selections. You can't miss this place, with its painted exterior covered with oversize, fluttering blue morpho butterflies.

In downtown Santa Elena, next to the Orchid Garden. www.morphosrestaurant.com. ℂ **2645-5607.** Main courses C3,000–C12,000. Daily 11am–9pm.

Sabor Tico ★★ COSTA RICAN   The name of this place translates as "Tico Flavor," and that's what you get at this family-run, traditional joint. The portions are huge, and everything is extremely tasty and well prepared, although service can be slow (but friendly) when they are busy. The *casados, arroz con pollo* (chicken with rice), and fresh fruit juices are all excellent. I always try to snag one of the few tables on the front veranda overlooking the town's soccer field. These folks have opened a second location

> **Take a Break**
>
> If all the activities in Monteverde have worn you out, stop in at **Las Orquídeas Café** (ℂ 2645-6850) or the **Choco Café Don Juan ★** (ℂ 2645-7444), two excellent local coffee shops just off the main drag in Santa Elena. The latter is connected to the Don Juan Coffee Tour (p. 189) and has a small gift shop attached.

(© **2645-5968**) in the Centro Comercial Monteverde shopping plaza, but I much prefer the more casual and authentic vibe of the original location.

In downtown Santa Elena, across from the soccer field. © **2645-5827.** Main courses C2,700–C4,900. Daily 9am–9pm.

Exploring the Monteverde Cloud Forest Biological Reserve ★★★

The **Monteverde Cloud Forest Biological Reserve** (www.reservamonteverde. com; © **2645-5122**) is one of the most developed and well-maintained natural attractions in Costa Rica. Its trails are clearly marked, regularly traveled, and generally gentle in terms of ascents and descents. The cloud forest here is lush and largely untouched. Still, keep in mind that most of the birds and mammals are rare, elusive, and nocturnal. Moreover, to all but the most trained of eyes, those thousands of exotic ferns, orchids, and bromeliads tend to blend into one large mass of indistinguishable green. However, with a guide hired through your hotel, or on one of the reserve's official guided 2- to 3-hour hikes, you can see and learn far more than you could on your own. At $18 per person, the reserve's tours might seem like a splurge, especially after you pay the entrance fee, but I strongly recommend that you go with a guide to enhance your visit.

Perhaps the most famous resident of the cloud forests of Costa Rica is the quetzal, a robin-size bird with iridescent green wings and a ruby-red breast, which has become extremely rare due to habitat destruction. The male quetzal also has two long tail feathers that can reach nearly .6m (2 ft.) in length, making it one of the most spectacular birds on earth. The best time to see quetzals is early morning to midmorning, and the best months are February through April (mating season).

Howler monkey.

Other animals that have been spotted in Monteverde, although sightings are extremely rare, include jaguars, ocelots, and tapirs. After the quetzal, Monteverde's most famous resident used to be the golden toad (*sapo dorado*), a rare native species. However, the golden toad has disappeared from the forest and is feared extinct. Competing theories of the toad's demise include adverse effects of a natural drought cycle, the disappearing ozone layer, pesticides, and acid rain.

ADMISSION, HOURS & TOURS   The reserve is open daily from 7am to 4pm; the entrance fee is $20 for adults, $10 for students and children. Only 220 people are allowed into the reserve at any one time, so you might be forced to wait. Most hotels can reserve a guided walk and entrance to the reserve for you on the following day, or you can get tickets in advance directly at the reserve entrance. Night tours of the reserve leave every evening at 6:15pm. The cost is $17, and includes admission to the reserve, a 2-hour hike, and, most importantly, a guide with a high-powered searchlight. For an extra $5, they'll throw in transportation to and from your area hotel.

Some of the trails can be very muddy, depending on the season, so ask about current conditions.

Exploring Outside the Reserve
BIRD-WATCHING & HIKING

You'll find ample bird-watching and hiking opportunities outside the reserve boundaries. Avoid the crowds at Monteverde by heading 5km (3 miles) north from the village of Santa Elena to the **Santa Elena Cloud Forest Reserve ★★** (www.reservasantaelena.org; ✆ **2645-5390**). This 310-hectare (765-acre) reserve has a maximum elevation of 1,680m (5,510 ft.), making it the highest cloud forest in the Monteverde area. There are 13km (8 miles) of hiking trails and an information center. Because it borders the Monteverde Reserve, a similar richness of flora and fauna is found here, although quetzals are not nearly as common. The $14 entry fee at this reserve goes directly to support a variety of good causes, including conservation and improving the local schools. The reserve is open daily from 7am to 5pm. Three-hour guided tours are available for $15 per person, not including the entrance fee.

Located just before the Monteverde Cloud Forest Reserve, and sharing many of the same ecosystems and habitats, the **Curicancha Reserve ★★★**

A self-guided HIKE THROUGH TH[...]

As I've mentioned, the reserve is best explored by a guided tour, but if you're intent on exploring the reserve on your own, or heading back for more after your tour, I suggest starting off on the **Sendero El Río (River Trail)** ★★. This trail, which heads north from the reserve office, puts you immediately in the midst of dense primary cloud forest, where heavy layers of mosses, bromeliads, and epiphytes cover every branch and trunk. This very first section of trail is also a prime location for spotting a resplendent quetzal.

After 15 or 20 minutes, you'll come to a little marked spur leading down to a **catarata,** or waterfall. This diminutive falls fills a small, pristine pond and is quite picturesque. The entire trek to the waterfall should take you an hour or so.

From the waterfall, turn around and retrace your steps along the River Trail until you come to a fork and the **Sendero Tosi (Tosi Trail).** Follow this shortcut, which leads through varied terrain, back to the reserve entrance.

Once you've got the River Trail and waterfall under your belt, I recommend a slightly more strenuous hike to a lookout atop the Continental Divide. The **Sendero Bosque Nuboso (Cloud Forest Trail)** ★ heads east from the reserve entrance. As its name implies, the trail leads through thic[...] Keep your eyes op[...] bird and mammal [...] cans, trogans, hone[...] howler monkeys. S[...] of massive strangle[...] trail. These trees start as parasitic vines and eventually engulf their host tree. After 1.9km (1.2 miles), you will reach the Continental Divide. Despite the sound of this, there's only a modest elevation gain of some 65m (213 ft.).

A couple of lookout points on the Divide are through clearings in the forest, but the best is **La Ventana (The Window)** ★, just beyond the end of this trail and reached via a short spur trail. Here you'll find a broad, elevated wooden deck with panoramic views. Be forewarned: It's often misty and quite windy up here.

On the way back, take the 2km (1.2-mile) **Sendero Camino (Road Trail).** As its name implies, much of this trail was once used as a rough all-terrain road. Since it is wide and open in many places, this trail is particularly good for bird-watching. About halfway along, you'll want to take a brief detour to a **suspended bridge** ★. Some 100m (330-ft.) long, this midforest bridge gives you a bird's-eye view of the forest canopy. The entire loop should take around 3 hours.

(www.reservacuricancha.com; ✆ **2645-6915**) is an excellent alternative, especially for folks looking to avoid some of the crowds at the area's namesake attraction. The reserve covers some 86 hectares (240 acres), of which almost half is primary cloud forest. The trails here are rich in flora and fauna, and quetzals are frequently spotted. The reserve is open daily from 7am to 3pm and again from 5:30 to 7:30pm. Entrance is $14 per person, and a 3- to 4-hour guided hike is an additional $15 per person. Children 6 and under are free.

CANOPY & CANYONING TOURS

Selvatura Park ★★ (www.selvatura.com; ✆ **2645-5929**), located close to the Santa Elena Cloud Forest Reserve, is the best one-stop shop for various adventures and attractions in the area. In addition to an extensive canopy tour,

bles connecting 15 platforms, it has a network of trails and sus-
bridges, along with a huge butterfly garden, hummingbird garden,
e exhibit, and wonderful insect display and museum. Prices vary depend-
g on how much you want to see and do. Individually, the canopy tour costs
$45; the walkways and bridges, $30; the snake and reptile exhibit, the butterfly garden, and the insect museum, $15 each. Combination packages are
available, although it can be confusing picking the right one. For $132, you
get the run of the entire joint, including the tours, lunch, and round-trip transportation from your Monteverde hotel. It's open daily from 7am to 4:30pm.

Another popular option is offered by the folks at **Sky Adventures** ★★
(www.skyadventures.travel; © **2479-4100**), which is part of a large complex
of aerial adventures and hiking trails. This is one of the more extensive canopy
tours in the country, and begins with a cable car ride (or **Sky Tram**) up into
the cloud forest, where a zip-line canopy tour commences, featuring 10 zip-
line cables. The longest of these is some 770m (2,525 ft.) long, high above the
forest floor. There are no rappel descents here, and you brake using the pulley
system for friction. Nearby, the **Sky Walk** ★★ operation is a network of forest paths and suspension bridges that provide visitors with a view previously
reserved for birds and monkeys. The bridges reach 39m (128 ft.) above the
ground at their highest point. This attraction is located about 3.5km (2¼
miles) outside the town of Santa Elena, on the road to the Santa Elena Cloud
Forest Reserve. The Sky Walk is open daily from 7am to 4pm; admission is
$35, which includes a knowledgeable guide. For $89 per person, you can do
the Sky Trek canopy tour and Sky Tram, and then walk the trails and bridges
of the Sky Walk. Reservations are recommended; round-trip transportation
from Santa Elena is $7.50 per person.

Finally, if you want to add a bit more excitement to your adventure, and
definitely more water, try the **Finca Modelo Canyoning Tour** ★★ (www.
familiabrenestours.com; © **2645-5581**). This tour involves a mix of hiking
and then rappelling down the face of a series of forest waterfalls. The tallest
of these waterfalls is around 39m (130 ft.). You will get wet on this tour. The
cost is $70.

Anybody in average physical condition can do any of the adventure tours in
Monteverde, but they're not for the fainthearted or those with a fear of being
in high places. Also, beware of touts on the streets of Monteverde, who make
a commission and frequently try to steer tourists to the operator paying the
highest percentage.

HORSEBACK RIDING

Monteverde has excellent terrain for horseback riding. **Horse Trek Monteverde** ★ (www.costaricahorsebackridingvacations.com; © **866/811-0522** in
U.S. and Canada, or 2645-5874 in Costa Rica) and **Sabine's Smiling Horses** ★
(www.smilinghorses.com; © **2645-6894**) are the most established operators,
offering guided rides for around $20 to $30 per hour. Horseback/boat trips
link Monteverde/Santa Elena with La Fortuna.

More Attractions in Monteverde

Butterflies abound here, and the long-established **Monteverde Butterfly Garden** ★ (www.monteverdebutterflygarden.com; ℂ **2645-5512**) displays many of Costa Rica's most beautiful species. Besides the hundreds of preserved and mounted butterflies, there's a garden and greenhouse where you can watch live butterflies. The garden is open daily from 8:30am to 4pm; admission, including a guided tour, is $15 for adults, $10 for students, and $5 for kids ages 4 to 6. If you can, visit between 9 and 11am, when the butterflies tend to be most active.

If your taste runs toward the slithery, check out the informative displays at the **Monteverde Serpentarium** ★ (ℂ **2645-5238**), on the road to the reserve. It's open daily from 9am to 8pm and charges $13 for admission.

Monteverde Theme Park ★ (www.ranariomonteverde.com; ℂ **2645-6320**), a couple of hundred meters north of the Monteverde Lodge, is another good bet. The entrance fee ($13.50 for adults and $12 for students) gets you a 45-minute guided tour, and your ticket is good for 1 week, allowing for multiple visits. A variety of amphibians populate a series of glass terrariums. These folks also have a butterfly garden and on-site canopy tour. It's open daily from 9am to 8:30pm. I especially recommend that you stop by at least once after dark, when the tree frogs are active.

The **Bat Jungle** ★★★ (www.batjungle.com; ℂ **2645-7701**) provides an in-depth look into the life and habits of these odd flying mammals. A visit here includes several different types of exhibits, from skeletal remains to a large enclosure where you can see various live species in action—the enclosure and room are kept dark, and the bats' biological clocks have been tricked into thinking that it's night. The Bat Jungle is open daily from 9am to 7:30pm. The tour lasts around 45 minutes; the last tour starts at 6:45pm. Admission is $13 for adults and $11 for students. Children 5 and under are free.

If you've had your fill of birds, snakes, bugs, butterflies, and bats, you might want to stop at the **Orchid Garden** ★★ (www.monteverdeorchidgarden.net; ℂ **2645-5308**), in Santa Elena next to Morpho's Restaurant (see p. 184). This botanical garden boasts more than 425 species of orchids. The tour is fascinating, especially given the fact that you need (and are given) a magnifying glass to see some of the flowers in bloom. Admission is $10 for adults, $7 for students, and $5 for kids 6 to 12. It's open daily from 8am to 5pm.

AGRICULTURAL & CULINARY TOURISM

Don Juan Coffee Tour ★★ (www.donjuancoffeetour.com; ℂ **2645-7100**) is a local, family-farm operation, which leads a 2-hour tour on the sprawling farm. Coffee is the primary crop and focus of the tour, although these folks also have a range of crops, including macadamia; a *trapiche,* or sugar cane mill; and a small boutique-chocolate production area. As a bonus, you get a snack and coffee tasting, and you may even get to meet the farm's namesake septuagenarian, Don Juan. The tour costs $35 for adults and $15 for children 6 to 12, including transportation.

El Trapiche Tour ★★ (www.eltrapichetour.com; ✆ **2645-7780** or 2645-7650) is another family-run tour, which gives you insight into the traditional means of harvesting and processing sugar cane, as well as the general life on a farm that includes bananas, macadamia, and citrus groves. Back at the farmhouse, you get to see how the raw materials are turned into cane liquor, raw sugar, and local sweets. The 2-hour tour includes a ride in an ox-drawn cart, and a visit to the family's coffee farm and roasting facility. Depending on the season, you may even get to pick a bushel of raw coffee beans. Tours run daily at 10am and 3pm, and cost $32 for adults and $12 for children 6 to 12, and include transportation.

Finally, if you want a detailed explanation of the processes involved in growing, harvesting, processing, and producing chocolate, be sure to stop by Café Caburé (p. 184) for its **Chocolate Tour.** You'll take some chocolate beans right through the roasting, grinding, and tempering processes in the 45-minute tour. The tour is offered most days at 1:30pm, and by appointment. The cost is $10.

SHOPPING

The **Monteverde Cloud Forest Biological Reserve** has a well-stocked gift shop just off the entrance. Another good option is **CASEM COOP** ★ (http://casemcoop.blogspot.com; ✆ **2645-5190**), on the right side of the main road, just across from Stella's Bakery. This crafts cooperative sells embroidered clothing, T-shirts, posters, Boruca weavings, locally grown and roasted coffee, and many other items to remind you of your visit. CASEM COOP is open daily from 7am to 5pm.

Over the years, Monteverde has developed a nice little community of artists. Around town, you'll see paintings by local artists such as Paul Smith and Meg Wallace, whose works are displayed at Hotel Fonda Vela and Stella's Bakery, respectively. Also check out **Casa de Arte** ★★ (www.monteverdearthouse.com; ✆ **2645-5275**), which has a mix of Arts and Crafts in many media.

ENTERTAINMENT & NIGHTLIFE

Perhaps the most popular after-dark activities in Monteverde are night hikes in one of the reserves. However, if you want a taste of the local party scene, head to **Bar Amigos** (www.baramigos.com; ✆ **2645-5071**), a large and often loud sports bar in the heart of Santa Elena. I prefer **La Taberna** ★ (✆ **8839-5569**), on the edge of Santa Elena town, below the Serpentarium. With a more contemporary club vibe, this place attracts a mix of locals and tourists, cranks its music loud, often gets people dancing, and occasionally has live bands.

THE CENTRAL PACIFIC COAST

After Guanacaste, the beaches of Costa Rica's central Pacific coast are the country's most popular. Options here range from the surfer and snowbird hangout of Jacó, to the ecotourist mecca of Manuel Antonio and beyond, where you'll find remote undeveloped beaches, jungle-clad hillsides, and rainforest waterfalls. With a newish modern highway connecting San José to the coast, and improvements along the Costanera Sur highway heading south, this region is now even easier to visit.

Jacó and Playa Herradura are the closest major beach destinations to San José. They have historically been the first choice for young surfers and city-dwelling Costa Ricans. Just north of Playa Herradura sits **Carara National Park ★★**, one of the few places in Costa Rica where you can see the disappearing dry forest join the damp, humid forests that extend south down the coast. It's also a great place to see scarlet macaws in the wild.

Just a little farther south, Manuel Antonio is one of the country's foremost ecotourist destinations. It has a host of lodgings and an easily accessible national park that combines the exuberant lushness of a lowland tropical rainforest with several gorgeous beaches. **Manuel Antonio National Park ★★** is home to all four of Costa Rica's monkey species, and a wealth of other easily viewed flora and fauna.

If you're looking to get away from it all, **Dominical** and the **beaches south of Dominical ★** should be your top destinations on this coast. The beach town of Dominical is still a small village, flanked by even more remote and undeveloped beaches, including those found inside **Ballena Marine National Park ★★**.

PLAYA HERRADURA & PLAYA DE JACÓ

Jacó: 117km (73 miles) W of San José; 75km (47 miles) S of Puntarenas; Playa Herradura: 108km (67 miles) W of San José; 9km (6 miles) NW of Playa de Jacó

Playa Herradura is the first major beach you'll hit as you head south along the Southern Coastal Highway. **Playa Herradura** is a long

Los Sueños Marriott Ocean & Golf Resort.

stretch of brown sand that is home to the massive **Los Sueños Marriott Ocean & Golf Resort ★★** (www.marriott.com; ✆ **888/236-2427** in the U.S. and Canada, or 2630-9000 in Costa Rica) and its attached marina. North of Herradura, you'll find a few other small beaches and resorts, including the elegant boutique hotel **Villa Caletas ★★★** (p. 196).

Playa de Jacó is a long stretch of beach strung with a dense hodgepodge of hotels in all price categories, souvenir shops, seafood restaurants, pizza joints, and rowdy bars. The number-one attraction here is the surf, and this is definitely a surfer-dominated beach town. Surfers love the consistent beach break; however, the beach itself is not particularly appealing, consisting of dark-gray sand with lots of little rocks (it's often pretty rough for swimming). Still, given its proximity to San José, Jacó is almost always packed with a mix of foreign and Tico vacationers. Beyond the surf, Jacó is known for its nightlife. A range of raging bars here offer everything from live music to chill lounge environments to beachfront sports bars with pool and *foosball* (table football) tables.

Essentials

GETTING THERE & DEPARTING   By Car: Head west out of San José on the San José–Caldera Highway (CR27). Just past the tollbooth at Pavón, the road connects with the Costanera Sur (CR34), or Southern Coastal Highway. The exit is marked for Jacó and CR34. From here, it's a straight, flat shot down the coast to Playa Herradura. The trip should take about an hour.

By Bus: Transportes Jacó express buses (www.transportesjacoruta655. com; ✆ **2290-2922**) leave San José daily every 2 hours between 7am and 7pm from the Coca-Cola bus terminal at Calle 16 between avenidas 1 and 3. The trip takes between 2½ and 3 hours; the fare is C2,445. On weekends and holidays, extra buses are sometimes added, so it's worth calling to check. No

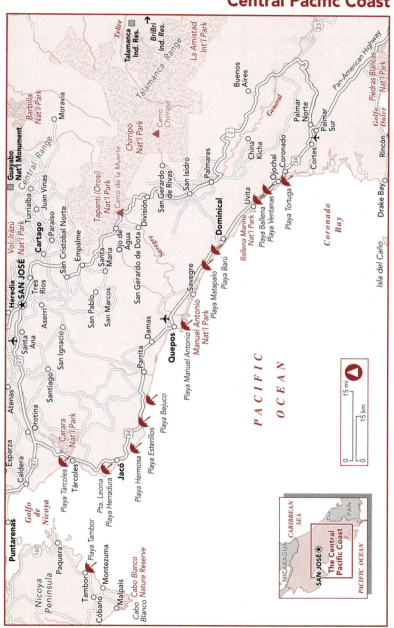

Croc Spotting

The Costanera Highway passes over the Tárcoles River just outside the entrance to **Carara National Park,** about 23km (14 miles) south of Orotina. This is a popular spot to pull over and spot gargantuan crocodiles, some of which reach 3.7 to 4.6m (12–15 ft.) in length. Usually anywhere from 10 to 20 are easily visible, either swimming in the water or sunning on the banks. But be careful. First, you'll have to brave walking on a narrow sidewalk along the side of the bridge with cars speeding by. And second, car break-ins are common here, including in the seemingly safe restaurant parking lots at the north end of the bridge. Although a police post has somewhat reduced the risk, don't leave your car or valuables unguarded for long. Better yet, leave someone at the car and take turns watching the crocs.

direct buses run all the way into Playa Herradura. All buses to Jacó will drop off passengers at the entrance to Playa Herradura, which is about 1km (½ mile) or so from the beach.

The Jacó bus station is at the north end of town, at a small mall across from the Jacó Fiesta Hotel. Buses for San José leave daily roughly every 2 hours between 5am and 5pm. Buses returning to San José from Quepos pass periodically and pick up passengers on the highway. Because schedules can change, it's best to ask at your hotel about current departure times.

Gray Line (www.graylinecostarica.com; ✆ **800/719-3105** in the U.S. and Canada, or 2220-2126 in Costa Rica) and **Interbus** (www.interbusonline. com; ✆ **4100-0888**) both offer two buses daily (one in the morning, one in the afternoon) leaving San José for Jacó and Playa Herradura. Call or check the websites for times. The fare is around $40. Both companies will pick you up at most San José–area hotels. Both also have connections to most major tourist destinations in the country.

Buses from San José to **Quepos** and Manuel Antonio also pass by Jacó. (They let passengers off on the highway about 1km/½ mile from town.) However, during the busy months, some of these buses will refuse passengers getting off in Jacó or will accept them only if they pay the full fare to Quepos or Manuel Antonio.

CITY LAYOUT Playa Herradura is a short distance off the Southern Coastal Highway. Just before you hit the beach, you'll see the entrance to the Los Sueños resort complex and marina on your right. There's no real town in Herradura. One dirt road runs parallel to the beach, with a few restaurants and a makeshift line of parking spots.

Playa de Jacó is also located a short distance off the Southern Coastal Highway. One main road runs parallel to the beach, with a host of arteries heading toward the water; you'll find most of the town's hotels and restaurants off these roads.

GETTING AROUND Almost everything is within walking distance in Jacó, but you can call **Asotaxi** (✆ **2643-2020** or 2643-1919) for a cab.

Bikes and scooters are for rent from a variety of shops and streetside stands along the main street. Bicycle rental should run around $10 to $15 per day, and a scooter should cost between $40 and $70 per day.

For longer excursions, you can rent a car from **Budget** (⌀ 2643-2665), **Economy** (⌀ 2643-1719), **National** (⌀ 2643-3224), or **Zuma** (⌀ 2643-1528).

FAST FACTS Playa Herradura has no real town. At the main intersection with the Southern Coastal Highway, you'll find a modern strip mall, with a large Automercado supermarket, and some restaurants, shops, and a couple of ATMs. A handful of banks have branches along the main road in Jacó. The **health center** (⌀ 2643-3667) and **post office** (⌀ 2643-2175) are at the Municipal Center at the south end of town. However, the best-equipped medical center is the **ProSalud** (⌀ 2643-5059), located 4 blocks inland from Pop's ice-cream shop. You'll find a half-dozen or so pharmacies, and a similar number of Internet cafes, all along the town's main drag.

There's a gas station on the main highway, between Playa Herradura and Jacó, and another station, **El Arroyo,** on the highway on the southern edge of Jacó. Both are open 24 hours.

Where to Stay

EXPENSIVE

In addition to the places mentioned below, early 2015 saw the opening of **Croc's Casino & Resort** (www.crocscasinoresort.com; ⌀ **800/809-5506** in the U.S. and Canada, or 4001-5398 in Costa Rica), a massive high-rise resort on the southern end of Jacó, with 150 hotel rooms, 3 restaurants, a large modern casino, and condominium and fractional ownership units.

In addition to the Marriott resort, the Los Sueños complex has scores of condominium units for rent. All come with kitchens, access to swimming pools, and rights to golf here. These are excellent options for families who want to do some cooking, and for longer stays. If you want to rent a condo here, contact **Stay In Costa Rica** (www.stayincostarica.com; ⌀ **866/439-5922** in the U.S. and Canada, or 2637-2661 in Costa Rica).

Club del Mar Condominiums & Resort ★★★
My favorite hotel in Playa Jacó, it's located at the far southern end of the beach, so it feels removed from the crowds and craziness that can sometimes plague Jacó. Most of the accommodations here are one- and two-bedroom condominiums with green tile floors, large living and dining rooms, and fully equipped kitchens, although there are some more typical hotel rooms and a lavish penthouse. The best units are closest to the waves (fab views). The beach here is somewhat protected by the rocky headlands, making it a top spot for swimming and beginning surf lessons; there's also a midsize pool with a volleyball net that often attracts a casual pick-up game. This place caters to, and is great for, families.

Playa de Jacó. www.clubdelmarcostarica.com. ⌀ **866/978-5669** in the U.S. and Canada, or 2643-3194 in Costa Rica. 27 units. $167 double; $236–$335 condo; $395 penthouse. **Amenities:** Restaurant; bar; outdoor pool; spa; room service; babysitting; free Wi-Fi.

Villa Caletas ★★★ This opulent, cliff-top collection of private villas and blocks of rooms is honeymoon heaven. Rooms are quite large and feature refined neoclassical decor. Most provide impressive views of the ocean over the forested hillside below. The separate Zephyr Palace is similar in luxury, but the rooms here each feature a unique design theme, ranging from the Egyptian suite to the Imperial suite, with several other distinct cultures represented. And while the service and attention are top-notch throughout, the Zephyr Palace also provides personal concierge services. The Greek-inspired amphitheater at Villa Caletas is a popular spot for catching a sunset.

Btw. Punta Leona and Playa Herradura. www.hotelvillacaletas.com. © **2630-3000.** 54 units. $195–$226 double; $268 villa; $352–$657 suite; $347–$1,586 Zephyr Palace suites. Extra person $42 at Villa Caletas; $85 at Zephyr Palace. **Amenities:** 3 restaurants; 2 bars; 4 midsize outdoor pools; spa; Jacuzzi; concierge; free Wi-Fi.

MODERATE

In addition to the places listed below, the oceanfront **Apartotel Girasol ★★** (www.girasol.com; © **800/923-2779** in the U.S. and Canada, or 2643-1591 in Costa Rica), with 16 fully equipped one-bedroom apartments, is a good option, especially for longer stays, while **Canciones del Mar ★** (www.canciones delmar.com; © **888/260-1523** in the U.S. and Canada, or 2643-3273 in Costa Rica) and **Hotel Catalina ★** (www.hotelcatalinacr.com; © **2643-1237**) are two other good beachfront choices.

Hotel Nine ★ An intimate and well-run little boutique hotel on a quiet stretch of beach toward the southern end of Jacó, it features clean and contemporary rooms in a range of sizes and prices. A small multitiered pool with a swim-up bar, waterfall, and Jacuzzi is at the center of the complex and ocean views can be had from the narrow shared veranda that fronts most rooms.

Playa de Jacó, Puntarenas. www.hotelnine.com. © **800/477-2486** in U.S. and Canada, or 2643-5335 in Costa Rica. 14 units. $118–$143 double; $273–$398 suite. Rates include breakfast. Children 5 and under not allowed. **Amenities:** Restaurant; bar; outdoor pool; Jacuzzi; free watersports equipment rentals; room service; free Wi-Fi.

INEXPENSIVE

There are quite a few budget hotels around town, so if you're looking to stay on the cheap, simply walk the strip and see who's got the best room at the best price.

Hotel Mar de Luz ★★ This family-friendly hotel is located about a half-block inland from the main street and feels like an oasis amidst the bustle of Jacó. Owner Victor Keulen runs a tight ship, and provides excellent value. Rooms are kept very clean. Some feature striking masonry walls of smooth river stones. All have at least a microwave and minifridge, and others have full kitchens. The hotel has several pools, including one for kids, a children's playground, and a small garden area, with a couple of grills for guests' use. The hotel's sister property, **Hotel Playa Bejuco,** is about 20 minutes down the road in remote Playa Bejuco.

Playa de Jacó. www.mardeluz.com. © **2643-3000.** 29 units. $100 double; $100 bungalow; $135 family room. Rates include breakfast. **Amenities:** Restaurant; Jacuzzi; 3 outdoor pools; free Wi-Fi.

Hotel Perico Azul ★★ Located a couple blocks inland from the water, on the south end of Jacó, this hotel is a favorite of surfers and backpackers. Clean, well-kept rooms surround a central courtyard with a popular, albeit small, plunge pool. Rooms are adorned with local paintings and Indonesian wooden geckos, and many feature a wall or two painted sea blue or lavender. A couple of rooms have their own kitchenettes, but there's also a communal kitchen for all guests. The best room is the second-floor one-bedroom studio, with its own private veranda. Owners Mike and Celine are very hands-on and also run a surf school, Tortuga Surf.

Playa de Jacó, Puntarenas. www.hotelpericoazuljaco.com. ✆ **2643-1341.** 6 units. $60–$70 double. Rates include taxes. **Amenities:** Pool; free Wi-Fi.

Where to Eat

Playa de Jacó has a variety of restaurants, many catering to surfers and budget travelers. **El Barco de Mariscos** (✆ **2643-2831**) and **El Recreo** (✆ **2643-1172**) both serve standard but high-quality Tico beach fare: seafood, sandwiches, chicken, and steak. Sushi lovers should head to **Tsunami Sushi** (✆ **2643-3678**), inside the El Galeón strip mall. For a coffee break and freshly baked pastries and breads, try **Café del M@r** (✆ **2643-1250**) or **Pachi's Pan** (✆ **2643-6068**).

At the Los Sueños marina, you'll find **El Galeón,** an upscale fusion restaurant; **Bambu,** a sushi bar and Pan-Asian restaurant; **La Linterna,** a fancy Italian restaurant; and **Hook Up,** an excellent American-style grill and restaurant. You can make reservations at any of the marina restaurants by calling ✆ **2630-4444.**

EXPENSIVE

Lemon Zest ★★ SEAFOOD/FUSION Chef/owner Richard Lemon left a teaching gig at Le Cordon Bleu and moved to Jacó, and the local culinary scene is better for it. His second-floor restaurant serves up excellent and creative contemporary cuisine showing a range of world influences. The Korean barbecue skewers come with homemade banana ketchup, while the local jumbo shrimp are battered, coated in coconut and plantain, and then fried crisp. I find the acoustics of the main dining room a bit deafening at times, and much prefer the few wooden tables on the outdoor balcony overlooking Jaco's main drag.

Downtown Jacó. www.lemonzestjaco.com. ✆ **2643-2591.** Reservations recommended in high season. Main courses $11–$29. Daily 5–10pm; closed Mon in off season. Closed mid-Sept through Oct.

MODERATE

El Pelícano ★★ SEAFOOD/COSTA RICAN This is the best local restaurant in Playa Herradura and an excellent beachfront spot. Heavy iron tables and chairs are spread around several rooms and makeshift shade structures. You can also get steak and chicken dishes, but I recommend the seafood that's caught and brought in daily. Most meals include the small salad bar.

On the beach in Playa Herradura. www.elpelicanorestaurante.com. ✆ **2637-8910.** Reservations recommended in high season. Main courses C6,500–C38,000. Daily noon–10pm.

Graffiti Resto Café & Wine Bar ★★★ FUSION   It's a little hard to find this place wedged in the far back corner of a nondescript strip mall near the center of town, but it's worth the search. The interior is decorated with graffiti art, and each night you'll find a short selection of specials drafted up on a chalkboard, based on the chef's whims and what's fresh. I almost always order one of the specials, but the regular menu is also excellent and features Graffiti's signature cacao- and coffee-crusted tenderloin and Asian-spiced seared tuna. There is also a small sushi bar, and—as the name suggests—a good wine list. Occasionally, live music is on the menu.

Centro Comercial Pacific Center, downtown Jacó. www.graffiticr.com. ℂ **2643-1708.** Reservations recommended in high season. Main courses C5,000–C18,500. Mon–Sat 5–10pm.

INEXPENSIVE

Caliche's Wishbone ★ SEAFOOD/MEXICAN   The brainchild and baby of a local surfing legend, Caliche, this local landmark serves up hearty, fresh fare, the menu running the gamut from pizzas, burritos, and stuffed potatoes to fresh, seared tuna in a soy-wasabi sauce (my fave). Surf videos play on TVs in the main dining room, but I prefer the tables closest to the busy sidewalk, on the covered veranda.

On the main road in Jacó. ℂ **2643-3406.** Main courses C3,500–C13,000. Thurs–Tues noon–10pm.

Taco Bar ★ MEXICAN/INTERNATIONAL   Taco Bar is so popular that it opened branches in San José, and it's looking to expand elsewhere. An open-air joint, it features two long, heavy wooden bars with seating on wooden "swings" supported by heavy ropes. There are also more traditional tables and picnic tables. But your choices don't end there. The menu has a wide range of tacos, burritos, and pizzas that you can have with any of several freshly caught fish served in any number of sauces. Other possible fillings include shrimp, calamari, grilled chicken, and steak. After choosing the main plate, head to the well-stocked and inventive salad bar. This place is also open for breakfast.

½ block inland from Pop's, central Jacó. www.tacobar.info. ℂ **2643-0222.** Main courses C3,675–C7,000. Mon 11–10pm; Tues–Sun 7am–10pm.

Exploring Jacó & Playa Herradura

In addition to the tours and activities mentioned below, Manuel Antonio is only about an hour south of Jacó, making it an easy day trip. Most local operators offer a variety of tour options in **Manuel Antonio,** including trips to the national park and the Damas Island estuary.

ATV TOURS   Several operations take folks out on ATV tours through the surrounding countryside. Tours range in length from 2 to 6 hours and cost $70 to $175 per person. Contact **Adventure Tours Costa Rica** (www.adventure tourscostarica.com; ℂ **2643-5720**).

BEACHES   **Playa Herradura** is a calm and protected beach, although the dark sand is rocky in places and not very attractive. The calmest section of beach is toward the north end, where you'll find the Los Sueños Marriott Ocean & Golf Resort. When the swell is big, the center section of beach here can be a good place to bodysurf, boogie board, or try some beginning surf moves.

Punta Leona, just a few kilometers north of Playa Herradura, is a cross between a hotel, a resort, and a private country club, and has some of the nicer beaches in the area. Although the place has effectively restricted access to its beaches, this is technically illegal in Costa Rica, and you have the right to enjoy both playas **Manta** ★ and **Blanca** ★, two nice, white-sand beaches inside the complex. The public access beach road is south of the main Punta Leona entrance and not very well marked.

Jacó's beach has a reputation for dangerous riptides (as does most of Costa Rica's Pacific coast). Even strong swimmers have been known to drown in the powerful rips. In general, the far southern end of the beach is the calmest and safest place to swim.

In addition, you may want to visit other nearby beaches, like **Playa Hermosa, Playa Esterillos,** and **Playa Bejuco.** These beaches are easily reached by car, moped, or even bicycle—if you've got a lot of energy. All are south of Jacó and signposted.

CANOPY TOURS   The easiest way to get up into the canopy here is on the **Rainforest Aerial Tram Pacific** ★ (www.rfat.com; ✆ 866/759-8726 in the U.S. and Canada, or 2257-5961 in Costa Rica). A sister project to the original Rainforest Aerial Tram Atlantic (p. 288), this attraction features modified ski-lift type gondolas that take you through and above the transitional forests bordering Carara National Park. The $60 entrance fee ($30 for kids 11 and under) includes the guided 40-minute tram ride and a guided 45-minute hike on a network of trails. Also on-site: a zip-line canopy tour, botanical gardens, and serpentarium. The Aerial Tram is a few kilometers inland from an exit just north of the first entrance into Jacó.

Quite a few zip-line and harness-style canopy tours are in this area. **Vista Los Sueños Canopy Tour** ★ (www.canopyvistalossuenos.com; ✆ 321/220-9631 in the U.S. and Canada, or 2637-6020 in Costa Rica) is set in the hills above Playa Herradura. The tour features 12 zip-lines, some excellent views, and boasts the longest cable in the area (almost ½-mile in length). The cost is $60 per person, and round-trip transportation can be added. Horseback-riding tours to a nearby waterfall are also available.

CROCODILE TOURS   Nearly all the boat tour operators in the area bring along freshly killed chickens to attract the crocs—a practice I cannot endorse. That's why I suggest going with the more responsible tour operator, **Eco Jungle Cruises** ★ (www.ecojunglecruisescom; ✆ 2582-0181). These folks don't believe in feeding the crocs or altering their behaviors. There are still plenty (hundreds, in fact) of crocodiles to be seen along the stretch of river and mangrove they run, and plenty of top-notch photo opportunities. The cost of their 2-hour tour is $72 for adults and $36 for children ages 4 to 10 (free for children 3 and under). Transportation from Jacó, Playa Herradura, Manuel Antonio, or San José is available.

GOLF The excellent **La Iguana,** an 18-hole golf course at the Los Sueños Marriott Ocean & Golf Resort (www.golflaiguana.com; ℂ **2630-9028**), is open to nonguests. Greens fees are $150. Club and shoe rentals are available.

HORSEBACK RIDING Horseback-riding tours give you a chance to get away from all the development in Jacó and see a bit of nature. The best operator in the area, with the best horses, is **Discovery Horseback** (www.horse ridecostarica.com; ℂ **8838-7550**), down in Playa Hermosa. It's $75 per person for a 2½-hour tour. The various tours include beach riding to trails through the rainforest with stops at a jungle waterfall.

KAYAKING **Kayak Jacó** (www.kayakjaco.com; ℂ **2643-1233**) offers tours in single and tandem sea kayaks, as well as eight-person outrigger canoes. Along the way, you'll be able to admire the beautiful coastline, and—when conditions permit—take a snorkel break. Kayak fishing tours and sailing trips aboard 25-foot trimarans are also available. Most run around 4 hours and include transportation to and from the put-in, as well as fresh fruit and soft drinks during the trip. The tours cost between $55 and $140 per person, depending on the particular trip and group size.

SPORTFISHING, SCUBA DIVING & SEABORNE FUN A number of dependable operators base themselves at Los Sueños Marriott Ocean & Golf Resort and its adjacent 250-slip marina. I recommend **Maverick Sportfishing Yachts** (www.maverickyachtscostarica.com; ℂ **800/405-8206** in the U.S. or 8712-9683 in Costa Rica) and **Costa Rica Dreams** (www.costaricadreams. com; ℂ **337/205-0665** in the U.S. or 2637-8942 in Costa Rica). A half-day fishing trip for four people costs around $800 to $1,500, and a full day costs between $1,000 and $2,000.

SURFING The same waves that often make Playa de Jacó dangerous for swimmers make it one of the most popular beaches in the country with surfers. Nearby **Playa Hermosa, Playa Tulin,** and **Playa Escondida** are also excellent surfing beaches. Those who want to challenge the waves can rent surfboards and boogie boards, for around $3 an hour or $10 to $20 per day, from any one of the numerous surf shops along the main road. If you want to learn how to surf, try the **Del Mar Surf Camp ★★** (www.delmarsurfcamp. com; ℂ **855/833-5627** in the U.S. or 2643-3197 in Costa Rica) or **Jacó Surf School** (www.jacosurfschool.com; ℂ **8829-4697**).

Carara National Park ★★

A little more than 17km (10 miles) north of Playa Herradura is **Carara National Park** (ℂ **2637-1054** for visitor center), a world-renowned nesting ground for **scarlet macaws.** It has a few kilometers of trails open to visitors. The **Sendero Acceso Universal (Universal Access Trail),** which heads out from the national park office, is broad, flat, and wheelchair-accessible (hence the trail name). The first half of this 1km (.7-mile) stretch leads into the forest and features various informative plaques, in both English and Spanish, pointing out prominent flora. About 10 or 15 minutes into your hike, you'll see that the trail splits, forming a loop (you can go in either direction). The entire loop trail should take you about an hour. The macaws migrate daily, spending their days in the park and their nights among the coastal mangroves. It's best to view them in the early morning when they arrive, or around sunset when they head back to the coast for the evening, but a good guide can usually find them for you during the day. Whether or not you see them, you should be able to hear their loud squawks. Among the other wildlife that you might see here are caimans, coatimundis, armadillos, pacas, peccaries, and, of course, hundreds of species of birds.

Be sure to bring along insect repellent or, better yet, wear long sleeves and pants made of light cotton. The reserve is open daily from 7am to 4pm. Admission is $10 per person at the gate.

Most hotel desks and tour agencies in the area can arrange for a guided hike to Carara National Park, and you can usually hire one at the entrance for around $15 per person. Although you can certainly hike the gentle and well-marked trails of Carara independently, if you take a tour you'll learn a lot more about your surroundings.

Entertainment & Nightlife

Playa de Jacó is the central Pacific's party town, with tons of bars and several discos. For a casual atmosphere, head to either **Los Amigos** or **Tabacón ★** on the main street, near the center of town. Tabacón has popular pool and *foosball* (table football) tables, and often has live music. **Morada Haze** (which is Spanglish for Purple Haze) and **Le Loft ★**, both on the main street and near the center of town, attract a more sophisticated and chic clubbing crowd.

Other popular bars in town include **Monkey Bar,** with DJs and a large dance floor, and **Jacó Taco,** a two-story affair with regular live bands, which is open 24 hours every day of the year. Both of the aforementioned bars are along the main strip through town. *Note:* You will see prostitutes around town, though it's not necessarily a sign that a bar is bad.

Sports freaks can catch the latest games at **Clarita's Beach Bar & Grill, Hotel Copacabana** (both are right on the beach toward the north end of town), or **Hotel Poseidon** (on a side street near the center of town). The first two serve up good reasonably priced burritos, burgers, and bar food, while the latter offers much the same in its upstairs sports bar, as well as some items from its Pan Asian-Fusion restaurant downstairs.

If you're into casino games, head to the **Casino Amapola** (℡ 2643-2255) at the Hotel Amapola. The latter is a modest casino situated toward the southern end of the main road through Jacó (Av. Pastor Díaz), about a block beyond where it takes a sharp turn inland toward the Costanera Sur.

Heading South from Playa de Jacó: Playas Hermosa, Esterillos & Bejuco

South of Jacó, Costa Rica's coastline is a long, almost entirely straight stretch of largely undeveloped beach backed by thick forests and low-lying rice and African palm plantations.

Playa Hermosa ★, 10km (6¼ miles) southeast of Jacó, is the first beach you'll hit as you head down the Southern Coastal Highway. This is primarily a surfers' beach, but it is still a lovely spot to spend some beach time. In fact, even though the surf conditions here can be rather rough, and the beach is made of dark volcanic sand, I find Playa Hermosa and the beaches south of it much more attractive than Jacó. Be careful on Playa Hermosa, as the fine, dark sand can get extremely hot in the tropical sun. Aside from a small grouping of hotels and restaurants, most of Playa Hermosa is protected, as **olive ridley sea turtles** lay eggs here from July to December. During turtle nesting season, all of the hotel tour desks and local tour agencies can help you arrange a nighttime turtle nesting tour, for around $40 to $50 per person.

Playa Hermosa is the only beach in this section located right along the Southern Coastal Highway; all of the rest are a kilometer or so set in from the road and reached by a series of dirt access roads. If you exit the highway in Playa Hermosa, you can follow a dirt-and-sand access road that runs parallel to the shore along several miles of deserted, protected beach, as Playa Hermosa eventually becomes **Playa Tulin,** near the Tulin River mouth. This is another popular surf spot, but be careful—crocodiles live in the Tulin River.

As you continue down the coastal highway from Playa Hermosa, you'll hit Esterillos. **Playa Esterillos,** 22km (14 miles) south of Jacó, is long and wide and almost always nearly deserted. Playa Esterillos is so long, in fact, that it has three separate entrances and sections, Esterillos Oeste, Centro, and Este— West, Center, and East, in that order as you head away from Jacó.

If you keep heading south (really southeast), you next come to **Playa Bejuco,** another long, wide, nearly deserted stretch of sand. Playa Bejuco, which features a very narrow strip of land fronting the beach, with mangroves and swampland behind, has very little development.

Note: While beautiful, isolated, and expansive, the waters of Hermosa, Esterillos, and Bejuco can be dangerous for swimming. Caution is highly advised here.

MANUEL ANTONIO NATIONAL PARK ★★

140km (87 miles) SW of San José; 69km (43 miles) S of Playa de Jacó

Manuel Antonio was Costa Rica's first major ecotourist destination and remains one of its most popular. The views from the hills overlooking Manuel Antonio are spectacular, the beaches (especially those inside the national park) are idyllic, and its rainforests are crawling with howler, white-faced, and squirrel monkeys, among other forms of exotic wildlife. The downside is that you'll have to share it with more fellow travelers than you would at other rainforest destinations around the country. Moreover, booming tourism and development have begun to destroy what makes this place so special. What was once a smattering of small hotels tucked into the forested hillside has become a long string of lodgings along the 7km (4⅓ miles) of road between

Manuel Antonio & Quepos

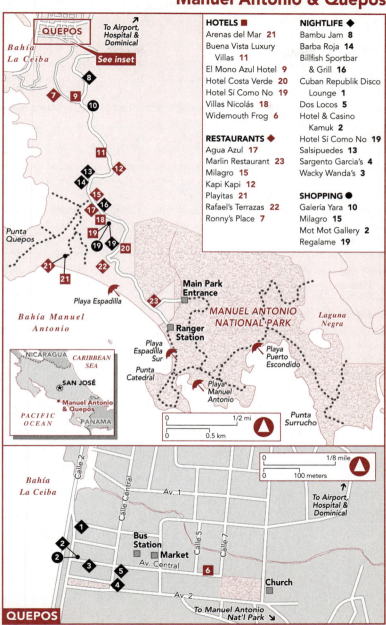

HOTELS ■
Arenas del Mar **21**
Buena Vista Luxury
 Villas **11**
El Mono Azul Hotel **9**
Hotel Costa Verde **20**
Hotel Sí Como No **19**
Villas Nicolás **18**
Widemouth Frog **6**

RESTAURANTS ◆
Agua Azul **17**
Marlin Restaurant **23**
Milagro **15**
Kapi Kapi **12**
Playitas **21**
Rafael's Terrazas **22**
Ronny's Place **7**

NIGHTLIFE ◆
Bambu Jam **8**
Barba Roja **14**
Billfish Sportbar
 & Grill **16**
Cuban Republik Disco
 Lounge **1**
Dos Locos **5**
Hotel & Casino
 Kamuk **2**
Hotel Sí Como No **19**
Salsipuedes **13**
Sargento Garcia's **4**
Wacky Wanda's **3**

SHOPPING ●
Galería Yara **10**
Milagro **15**
Mot Mot Gallery **2**
Regalame **19**

QUEPOS

To Airport,
Hospital &
Dominical

*Bahía
La Ceiba*

See inset

*Punta
Quepos*

Playa Espadilla

*Bahía Manuel
Antonio*

Main Park
Entrance

Ranger
Station

*Playa
Espadilla
Sur*

*Punta
Catedral*

**MANUEL ANTONIO
NATIONAL PARK**

*Laguna
Negra*

*Playa
Puerto
Escondido*

*Playa
Manuel
Antonio*

*Punta
Surrucho*

NICARAGUA
**CARIBBEAN
SEA**
SAN JOSÉ
● Manuel Antonio
& Quepos
*PACIFIC
OCEAN*
PANAMA

0   1/2 mi
0   0.5 km

0   1/8 mile
0   100 meters

*Bahía
La Ceiba*

Calle 2

Calle Central

Av. 1

Bus
Station

Market

Calle 5

Calle 7

Av. Central

To Airport,
Hospital &
Dominical

Church

Av. 2

QUEPOS

To Manuel Antonio
Nat'l Park ↘

Quepos and the national park entrance. Hotel roofs now regularly break the tree line, and there seems to be no control over zoning or construction. A jumble of snack shacks, souvenir stands, and makeshift parking lots choke the beach road just outside the park, making the entrance road look more like a shanty than a national park.

Still, this remains a beautiful destination, with a wide range of attractions and activities. Gazing down on the blue Pacific from high on the hillsides of Manuel Antonio, it's almost impossible to hold back a gasp of delight. Offshore, rocky islands dot the vast expanse of blue, and in the foreground, the rich, deep green rainforest sweeps down to the water.

One of the most popular national parks in the country, Manuel Antonio is also one of the smallest, covering fewer than 680 hectares (1,680 acres). Its several small, nearly perfect beaches are connected by trails that meander through the rainforest. The mountains surrounding the beaches quickly rise as you head inland from the water; however, the park was created to preserve not its beautiful beaches, but its forests, home to endangered squirrel monkeys, three-toed sloths, purple-and-orange crabs, and hundreds of other species of birds, mammals, and plants. Once, this entire stretch of coast was a rainforest teeming with wildlife, but now only this small rocky outcrop of forest remains.

Those views that are so bewitching also have their own set of drawbacks. If you want a great view, you aren't going to be staying on the beach—in fact, you probably won't be able to walk to the beach. This means that you'll be driving back and forth, taking taxis, or riding the public bus. Also, keep in mind that it's hot and humid here, and it rains a lot. However, the rain is what keeps Manuel Antonio lush and green, and this wouldn't be the tropics if things were otherwise.

If you're traveling on a rock-bottom budget or are mainly interested in sportfishing, you might end up staying in the nearby town of **Quepos,** which was once a quiet banana port and now features an assortment of restaurants, souvenir and crafts shops, and lively bars; the land to the north was used by Chiquita to grow its bananas. Disease wiped out most of the banana plantations, and now the land is planted primarily with African oil-palm trees. To reach Quepos by road, you pass through miles of these **oil-palm plantations;** see "Profitable Palms" (below) for info.

Essentials

GETTING THERE & DEPARTING By Plane: Both **Nature Air** (www.natureair.com; ⓒ **800/235-9272** in the U.S. and Canada, or 2299-6000 in Costa Rica) and **Sansa** (www.flysansa.com; ⓒ **877/767-2672** in the U.S. and Canada, or 2290-4100 in Costa Rica) offer several daily direct flights to the **Quepos airport** (no phone; airport code: XQP). The flight is 30 minutes long; the fare is $60 to $90 each way.

Both **Sansa** (ⓒ **2777-1912** in Quepos) and **Nature Air** (ⓒ **2777-2548** in Quepos) provide minivan airport-transfer service coordinated with their arriving and departing flights. The service costs around $8 per person each way,

Manuel Antonio National Park.

depending on where your hotel is located. Speak to your airline's agent when you arrive to confirm your return flight and coordinate a pickup at your hotel for that day, if necessary. Taxis meet incoming flights as well. Expect to be charged between $10 and $20 per car for up to four people, depending on the distance to your hotel.

By Car: From San José, take the San José–Caldera Highway (CR27) west to Orotina. Just past the toll-booth at Pavón, this road connects with the Costanera Sur (CR34), or Southern Coastal Highway. The exit is marked for Jacó and CR34. From here, it's a straight and flat shot down the coast to Quepos and Manuel Antonio.

If you're coming from Guanacaste or any point north, take the Interameri-can Highway to the Puntarenas turnoff and follow signs to the San José–Caldera Highway (CR27). Take this east toward Orotina, where it connects with the Costanera Sur (CR34). It's about a 4½-hour drive from Liberia to Quepos and Manuel Antonio.

By Bus: Tracopa buses (www.tracopacr.com; ✆ **2221-4214**) to Manuel Antonio leave San José regularly throughout the day between 6am and 7:30pm from Calle 5 between avenidas 18 and 20. Trip duration is around 3 hours; the fare is C4,675. These buses go all the way to the park entrance and will drop you off at any hotels along the way.

For your return trip, the **Quepos bus station** (✆ **2777-0263**) is next to the market, located 3 blocks east of the water and 2 blocks north of the road to Manuel Antonio. Buses depart for San José daily between 4am and 5pm.

Gray Line (www.graylinecostarica.com; ✆ **800/719-3105** in the U.S. and Canada, or 2220-2126 in Costa Rica) and **Interbus** (www.interbusonline.com; ✆ **4100-0888**) both have two buses daily leaving San José for Quepos and Manuel Antonio, one in the morning and one in the afternoon. The fare is

---

Travel Tips

If you plan carefully, you can avoid many of the problems that detract from Man-uel Antonio's appeal. Steer clear of the peak months (Dec–Mar), and you can miss most of the crowds. If you must come during the peak period, try to avoid weekends, when the beach is packed with families and young Ticos from San José. Plan to arrive early in the morning, and then leave when the crowds begin to show up at midday. In the afternoon, you can lounge by your pool or on your patio.

Profitable Palms

On any drive to or from Quepos and Manuel Antonio, you will pass through miles and miles of African palm plantations. Native to West Africa, *Elaeis guineensis* was planted along this stretch in the 1940s by United Fruit, in response to a blight that was attacking its banana crops. The palms took hold and soon proved quite profitable, being blessed with copious bunches of plum-size nuts that are rich in oil. This oil is extracted and processed in plantations that dot the road between Jacó and Quepos. The smoke and distinct smell of this processing is easily noticed. The processed oil is eventually shipped overseas and used in a wide range of products, including soaps, cosmetics, lubricants, and food products.

These plantations are a major source of employment in the area—note the small, orderly "company towns" built for workers—but their presence is controversial. The palm trees aren't native, and the farming practices are thought by some to threaten Costa Rica's biodiversity.

around $50. Both companies will pick you up at most San José–area hotels. Both also have connections to most major tourist destinations in the country.

Many of the buses for Quepos stop to unload and pick up passengers in **Playa de Jacó.** If you're in Jacó heading toward Manuel Antonio, you can try your luck at one of the covered bus stops out on the Interamerican Highway.

In the busy winter months, tickets sell out well in advance, especially on weekends; if you can, purchase your ticket several days in advance. However, you must buy your Quepos-bound tickets in San José and your San José return tickets in Quepos. If you're staying in Manuel Antonio, you can buy your return ticket for a direct bus in advance in Quepos, and then wait along the road to be picked up. There's no particular bus stop; just make sure you are out to flag down the bus and give it time to stop—you don't want to be standing in a blind spot when the bus comes flying around a tight corner.

GETTING AROUND   A **taxi** between Quepos and Manuel Antonio (or any hotel along the road toward the park) costs between C4,000 and C5,000, depending upon the distance. At night or if the taxi must leave the main road (for hotels such as La Mariposa, Parador, Makanda, and Arenas del Mar), the charge is a little higher. If you need to call a taxi, dial ℂ **2777-1207** or 2777-0425. Taxis are supposed to use meters, although this isn't always the case. If your taxi doesn't have a meter, or the driver won't use it, try to negotiate in advance. Ask your hotel desk what a specific ride should cost, and use that as your guide.

The **bus** between Quepos and Manuel Antonio (ℂ **2777-0318**) takes 15 minutes each way and runs roughly every half-hour from 5:30am to 9:30pm daily. The buses, which leave from the main bus terminal in Quepos, near the market, go all the way to the national park entrance before turning around and returning. You can flag down these buses from any point on the side of the road. The fare is C250.

You can also rent a car from **Adobe** (ℂ **2777-4242**), **National** (ℂ **2777-3344**), **Economy** (ℂ **2777-5353**), or **Hertz** (ℂ **2777-3365**) for around $53 to $150 a day. All have offices in downtown Quepos or Manuel Antonio, but with advance notice, someone will meet you at the airport with your car for no extra charge.

If you rent a car, never leave anything of value in it unless you intend to stay within sight of the car at all times. Car break-ins are common here. A couple of parking lots just outside the park entrance cost around $3 for the entire day. You should definitely keep your car in one of these while exploring the park or soaking up sun on the beach. And although these lots do offer a modicum of protection and safety, you still should not leave anything of value exposed in the car. The trunk is probably safe, though.

CITY LAYOUT   Quepos is a small port city at the mouth of the Boca Vieja Estuary. If you're heading to Manuel Antonio, or any hotel on the way to the park, after crossing the bridge into town, take the lower road (to the left of the high road). In 4 blocks, turn left, and you'll be on the road to Manuel Antonio. This road winds through town a bit before starting over the hill to all the hotels and the national park.

FAST FACTS   The telephone number of the **Quepos Hospital** is ✆ **2777-0922.** In the event of an emergency, you can also call the **Cruz Roja** (Red Cross; ✆ **2777-0116**). For the **local police,** call ✆ **2777-1511.**

Several major Costa Rican banks have branches and ATMs in downtown Quepos, and a couple of ATMs have sprung up along the road to the national park. An ample array of **Internet cafes** can be found around Quepos and along the road to Manuel Antonio, and many hotels have them as well.

There are several pharmacies in Quepos, including one at the hospital and another close to the park entrance. A half-dozen or so launderettes and laundry services are in town.

Where to Stay
EXPENSIVE
Buena Vista Luxury Villas ★★ (www.buenavistaluxuryvillas.net; ✆ **866/569-6241** in the U.S. and Canada, or 2777-0580 in Costa Rica) is the current incarnation of the former Tulemar Resort. It features a wide range of private villas and bungalows in a gated community; each unit has access to Buena Vista's own secluded and protected bit of beach.

If you're coming for an extended stay with the family or a large group, consider **Escape Villas** ★★★ (www.escapevillas.com; ✆ **888/771-2976** in the U.S., or 2203-4401 in Costa Rica) or **Manuel Antonio Rentals** ★★ (www.manuelantoniovacationrentals.com; ✆ **985/247-4558** in the U.S., or 8913-9415 in Costa Rica). Both outfits rent a broad selection of large and luxurious private villas and homes, with all the amenities and some of the best views in Manuel Antonio.

Arenas del Mar ★★★   This beachfront resort is in a league of its own in Manuel Antonio, with handsome rooms, fabulous views, great dining, and direct access to not one, but two, beaches. All of the rooms are large and feature antique-style tile floors and sleek, minimalist decor. Most come with a private outdoor Jacuzzi tub on a private balcony. There are two main centers of operation here—one near the highest point of the property, the other down by one of the beaches—and each has its own pool, restaurant, and bar. This property is a leader in sustainable tourism and conservation.

Manuel Antonio. www.arenasdelmar.com. *C* **2777-2777.** 38 units. $350–$470 double; $590–$780 suite. Additional person $70. Rates include full breakfast and free local and international calls. **Amenities:** 2 restaurants; 2 bars; 2 outdoor pools; spa; concierge; room service; babysitting; free Wi-Fi.

Hotel Si Como No ★★

This boutique resort occupies a privileged position on a high ridge about midway between Quepos and the Manuel Antonio National Park. Upon arrival, you'll be drawn to the jutting triangular lookout point just off the lobby. It's all thick rainforest below, with beautiful views out to the Pacific Ocean from most of the rooms, almost all of which feature private balconies. Monkey sightings are quite common here. There are two restaurants, two pools (one is for adults only, the other has a fun waterslide for the kids), and an air-conditioned theater with nightly movie showings. Hotel Si Como No is an early leader in sustainable tourism in Costa Rica and was awarded "5 Leaves" in the CST Sustainable Tourism program.

Manuel Antonio. www.sicomono.com. *C* **888/742-6667** in the U.S. or 2777-0777 in Costa Rica. 57 units. $275–$350 double; $400–$450 suite. Rates include full breakfast. Extra person $30. Children 5 and under stay free in parent's room. **Amenities:** 2 restaurants; 2 bars; 2 outdoor pools, spa; Jacuzzi; concierge; babysitting; free Wi-Fi.

MODERATE

Hotel Costa Verde ★

This sprawling complex features everything from rustic rooms and cottages to a converted 727 airplane that serves as a two-bedroom suite, with the cockpit and nose appearing to be flying out of the forest. Most of the rooms, however, are in two tall buildings (one for families, one adults only), featuring large balconies with superb rainforest and ocean views. The studio and studio-plus rooms all have kitchenettes. Not all of the rooms have air-conditioning or televisions, so check before making your final choice. The complex is located on a steep hillside leading down to the beach, so the return trip from the sands and to some of the rooms can be strenuous. Breakfast is served at the main hotel complex; three additional restaurant locations are across the street.

Manuel Antonio. www.costaverde.com. *C* **866/854-7958** in the U.S. and Canada, or 2777-0584 in Costa Rica. 70 units. $125–$200 double; $210–$350 bungalows; $500–$727 Fuselage suite. **Amenities:** 4 restaurants; 4 bars; 3 outdoor pools; free Wi-Fi.

Villas Nicolás ★★

Located right next to Hotel Si Como No (see above), this collection of spacious condo units provides the very same classic Manuel Antonio views, but at near bargain prices. Virtually all of the rooms here come with large, rainforest- and ocean-facing balconies. Every balcony comes equipped with a siesta-inducing rope hammock. Some units have full kitchens, and many can be combined to accommodate families or groups. There's a lovely pool set amidst lush gardens, and the service here is friendly and personal.

Manuel Antonio. www.villasnicolas.com. *C* **2777-0481.** 19 units. $125–$160 double; $180–$230 suite; $305–$340 villas. Weekly, monthly, and off-season (May–Nov) rates available. Rates include full breakfast. **Amenities:** Restaurant; bar; small outdoor pool; free Wi-Fi.

INEXPENSIVE

Budget hotels are hard to come by in and around Quepos and Manuel Antonio. Your best bet is the **Widemouth Frog** ★ (www.widemouthfrog.org; © **2777-2798**), a hostel right in downtown Quepos, which offers everything from bunk-bed dorm rooms with shared bathrooms to cozy double rooms with a private bathroom. It even has its own swimming pool.

El Mono Azul Hotel ★   Also known as The Blue Monkey, this little hotel has a hostel-like feel and social vibe, with slightly more upscale accommodations. Rooms are on both sides of the main road that runs from Quepos to the national park entrance, and vary quite a bit in size and amenities. The decor in some of the rooms feels a bit dated. The several pool areas are quite nice, with lush overgrown gardens and plenty of shade. These folks were instrumental in founding Kids Saving the Rainforests, a nonprofit conservation and art program, and part of their proceeds goes to support the project. The little restaurant here is a hub of activity and great place to meet fellow travelers.

Manuel Antonio. www.monoazul.com. © **2777-1548.** 20 units. $65–$95 double. **Amenities:** Restaurant; bar; lounge; 2 outdoor pools; free Wi-Fi.

Where to Eat

Scores of dining options are available around Manuel Antonio and Quepos, and almost every hotel has some sort of restaurant. For the cheapest meals around, try a simple *soda* in Quepos, or head to one of the open-air joints on the beach road before the national park entrance. Here, the standard Tico menu prevails, with prices in the C3,000 to C5,000 range. Of these, **Marlin Restaurant** ★ (© **2777-1134**), right in front of Playa Espadilla, is your best bet. **Mi Lugar,** or **"Ronny's Place"** ★ (www.ronnysplace.com; © **2777-5120**), on the outskirts of Quepos, is another good option.

For lunch, try the beachfront **Playitas** ★★ at Arenas del Mar (see above); in addition to its great location and secure parking, you get pool privileges for the price of an excellent meal.

EXPENSIVE

Kapi Kapi ★★★ FUSION/NUEVO LATINO   If you're looking for a quiet, romantic, and elegant meal, Kapi Kapi is hard to beat. The menu and decor both show a strong Asian influence, although both incorporate as much in the way of local produce and products as possible. The local fresh shrimp is skewered on long spikes of sugar cane, grilled, and then bathed in a glaze of rum, tamarind, and coconut; the mahimahi is crusted in crushed macadamia nuts, and served with a sweet plum-chili sauce and a side of Jasmine rice. The wine list is wide-ranging.

On the road btw. Quepos and Manuel Antonio. www.restaurantekapikapi.com. © **2777-5049.** Reservations recommended. Main courses C8,500–C14,500. Daily 4–10pm.

MODERATE

Agua Azul ★★ INTERNATIONAL   Sitting high above the rainforest with panoramic views over rainforest trees to the Pacific Ocean below, this open-air restaurant has one of the best settings in town. There's little in the way of decor, as there are virtually no walls here, just open space on three sides under a corrugated zinc roof. This is a prime viewing place for sunsets, and the tables closest to the thin steel railing fill up early and fast. Agua Azul serves bar food standards, but often with a creative twist, like its signature Tuna Margarita, which consists of seared tuna served over a cucumber salad with a lime vinaigrette, all served in a salt-rimmed margarita glass. You can also get burgers, burritos, nachos, chicken fingers, and a few more substantial plates, like whole snapper in a tamarind sauce, and the chef's nightly pasta special.

Manuel Antonio, near Villas del Parque. www.cafeaguaazul.com. *C* **2777-5280.** Main courses C4,500–C10,500. Mon–Tues and Wed–Sun 11am–10pm.

Milagro ★★★ NUEVO LATINO/FUSION An institution in Manuel Antonio, Milagro is the nerve center of a bustling little local empire that has grown out of their Café Milagro coffee-roasting business. As you'd expect, this spot is an excellent coffeehouse with the full range of barista-brewed concoctions. They also serve breakfast, lunch, and dinner. For lunch, I like their take on a traditional Cuban sandwich, replacing the pork with fresh, local mahimahi. The dinner menu features fusion-inspired Latin fare with everything from jerk chicken to shrimp in a coconut-rum sauce. They have creative, contemporary cocktails, as well as a good list of South American wines. There's often live music at night, and the bar is a great casual hangout. One of the best little gift shops in town has locally sourced Arts and Crafts, as well as fresh roasted beans and assorted coffee paraphernalia.

On the road btw. Quepos and Manuel Antonio. www.cafemilagro.com. *C* **2777-2272.** Reservations recommended. Main courses C6,300–C13,000. Daily 7am–10pm.

Rafael's Terrazas ★ SEAFOOD/COSTA RICAN   This simple open-air restaurant has a stunning location, clinging to a steep hillside with a perfect view of the Pacific Ocean over zinc roofs and a small patch of thick rainforest. The hillside is so steep that the dining rooms are terraced (hence the name) and spread over three floors connected by steep steps. The menu features a host of Tico classics and is heavy on fresh seafood. You can get some excellent ceviche as a starter, and a *casado* (full meal) of fish, chicken, or beef for a main course. There are also some more worldly options, including seared tuna with a ginger,

---

Yo Quiero Hablar Español

Academia de Español D'Amore (www.academiadamore.com; *C* **877/434-7290** in the U.S. and Canada, or 2777-0233 in Costa Rica) runs language-immersion programs out of a former hotel on the road to Manuel Antonio. A 2-week conversational Spanish course, including a homestay and two meals daily, costs $1,100. Or try the **Costa Rica Spanish Institute** (**COSI;** www.cosi.co.cr; *C* **2234-1001** or 2777-0021), which charges $1,180 for a similar 2-week program with a homestay.

soy, and wasabi sauce. Meat lovers should try the bacon-wrapped tenderloin in a fresh mushroom sauce.

On the road btw. Quepos and Manuel Antonio. ✆ **2777-6310.** Reservations recommended. Main courses C5,300–C15,000. Tues–Sun 11am–11pm.

Exploring the National Park

Manuel Antonio is a small park with three major trails. Most visitors come primarily to lie on a beach and check out the white-faced monkeys, which sometimes seem as common as tourists. A guide is not essential here, but unless you're experienced in rainforest hiking, you'll see and learn a lot more with one. A 2- or 3-hour guided hike should cost between $25 and $50 per person, plus the entrance fee. Almost any of the hotels in town can help you set up a tour of the park. If you decide to explore the park on your own, see the trail map on the inside front cover of this book.

ENTRY POINT, FEES & REGULATIONS   The park (✆ **2777-5185**) is open Tuesday through Sunday from 7am to 4pm year-round. In 2015, the park was open every day of the week during the high season, but it's not clear if that will continue. The entrance fee is $16 per person. The **main park entrance** is located almost a mile inland, at the end of the road that leads off perpendicular to Playa Espadilla just beyond Marlin Restaurant.

There is another ranger station and exit point at the end of the road from Quepos. This ranger station is located across a small river that's little more than ankle-deep at low tide, but that can be knee- or even waist-deep at high tide. It's even reputed to be home to a crocodile or two. For years, there has been talk of building a bridge over this stream; in the meantime, access to or from the park via this point is prohibited.

Tickets are sold and entry allowed only at the inland entrance. This requires about 20 to 30 minutes of hiking along a sometimes muddy access road before you get to the beach and principal park trails. *Note:* The parks service allows only 800 visitors to enter each day, which could mean that you stand the chance of not getting in if arriving at a peak period during the high season. Personally, I like arriving early, as the wildlife tends to be more active and the tropical heat hasn't kicked into full gear. Camping is not allowed.

I recommend entering the park with a guide. You'll see much more and learn a lot. You can always stay on inside the park after your guided tour is over. Most hotels can set you up with a reputable guide; if not, contact **Manuel Antonio Expeditions** (http://manuelantonioexpeditions.blogspot.com; ✆ **8365-1057**), run by Juan Brenes, who does a wonderful job. Be careful of touts dressed as guides stopping you on the street and doing a hard sell. Avoid these types of "guides."

THE BEACHES   **Playa Espadilla Sur** (as opposed to Playa Espadilla, which is just outside the park) is the first beach within the actual park boundaries. It's usually the least crowded. However, if there's any surf, this is also the roughest beach in the park. If you want to explore further, you can walk along this soft-sand beach or follow a trail through the rainforest parallel to the beach. **Playa Manuel Antonio,** which is the most popular beach inside the park, is a short, deep crescent of white sand backed by lush rainforest. The water here is sometimes clear enough to offer good snorkeling along the rocks at either end, and it's usually fairly calm. At low tide, Playa Manuel Antonio shows a unique relic: a circular stone turtle trap left by its pre-Columbian residents. From Playa Manuel Antonio, another slightly longer trail leads to **Puerto Escondido,** where a blowhole sends up plumes of spray at high tide.

THE HIKING TRAILS From either Playa Espadilla Sur or Playa Manuel Antonio, you can take a circular loop trail (1.4km/.9 mile) around a high promontory bluff. The highest point on this hike, which takes about 25 to 30 minutes round-trip, is **Punta Catedral ★★**, where the view is spectacular. The trail is a little steep in places, but anybody in average shape can do it. I have done it in sturdy sandals, but you might want to wear good hiking shoes. This is a good place to spot monkeys, although you're more likely to see a white-faced monkey than a rare squirrel monkey. Another good place to see monkeys is the **trail inland** from Playa Manuel Antonio. This is a linear trail and mostly uphill, but it's not too taxing. It's great to spend hours exploring the steamy jungle and then take a refreshing dip in the ocean.

Finally, a trail connects Puerto Escondido (see above) and **Punta Surrucho,** which has some sea caves. Be careful when hiking beyond Puerto Escondido: What seems like easy beach hiking at low tide becomes treacherous to impassable at high tide. Don't get trapped.

Hitting the Water

BEACHES OUTSIDE THE PARK **Playa Espadilla,** the gray-sand beach just outside the park boundary, can be a bit rough for casual swimming, but with no entrance fee, it's the most popular beach with locals and visiting Ticos. Shops by the water rent boogie boards, beach chairs, and umbrellas. (These are not available inside the park.) This beach is actually a great spot to learn how to surf. Several open-air shops along the beachfront road rent surfboards and boogie boards for $5 to $10 per hour, and around $20 to $30 per day. If you want a lesson, I recommend the **Blue Horizon Surf School** (www.bluehorizonsurfschool.com; ☎ **8994-1424**), which provides excellent attention for individuals, small groups, and families.

BOATING, KAYAKING, RAFTING & SPORTFISHING TOURS **Iguana Tours** (www.iguanatours.com; ☎ **2777-2052**), the most established tour operator in the area, offers river rafting, sea kayaking, mangrove tours, and guided

A Damas Island boat tour.

hikes. Both Iguana and **Amigos del Río** (www.amigosdelrio.net; ☏ **877/393-8332** in the U.S. or 2777-0082 in Costa Rica), have full-day rafting trips for around $85 to $110. Large multiperson rafts are used during the rainy season, and single-person "duckies" are broken out when the water levels drop. Half-day rafting adventures and sea-kayaking trips are available for around $65 to $90. Depending on rainfall and demand, they will run either the Naranjo River or the Savegre River. I very much prefer the **Savegre River** ★★ for its stunning scenery.

Another of my favorite tours in the area is the mangrove tour of the **Damas Island estuary.** These trips generally include lunch, a stop on Damas Island, and roughly 3 to 4 hours of cruising the waterways. You'll see loads of wildlife. The cost is usually around $60 to $80. **Manuel Antonio Expeditions** (manuelantonioexpeditions.blogspot.com; ☏ **8365-1057**) is my choice operator.

Among the other boating options around Quepos/Manuel Antonio are excursions in search of dolphins and sunset cruises. **Iguana Tours** (see above) and **Planet Dolphin** ★ (www.planetdolphin.com; ☏ **800/943-9161** in the U.S. or 2777-1647 in Costa Rica) offer these tours for around $75 per person, depending on the size of the group and the length of the cruise. Most tours include a snorkel break and, if you're lucky, dolphin sightings.

Quepos is one of Costa Rica's sportfishing centers, and sailfish, marlin, and tuna are all common in these waters. Over the years, freshwater and brackish water fishing in the mangroves and estuaries has also become popular. If you're into sportfishing, try **Blue Fin Sportfishing** (www.bluefinsportfishing.com; ☏ **2777-0000**) or **Luna Tours Sport Fishing** (www.lunatours.net; ☏ **2777-0725**). A full day of fishing should cost between $600 and $2,100, depending on size of the boat, distance traveled, tackle provided, and amenities. Stop by the marina and shop around to get the best price.

More Activities in the Area

ATV   If you want to try riding a four-wheel ATV (all-terrain vehicle), check in with the folks at **Midworld** ★★ (www.midworldcostarica.com; ☏ **2777-7181**), who offer a range of tours through forests and farmlands at their adventure center on the outskirts of Quepos and Manuel Antonio.

BUTTERFLY GARDEN   **Manuel Antonio Nature Park** ★★ (www.manuelantonionaturepark.com; ☏ **2777-0850**) is just across from (and run by) Hotel Si Como No (p. 208). A lovely bi-level **butterfly garden** ★ is the centerpiece attraction here, but there is also a private reserve and a small network of well-groomed trails through the forest. A 1-hour guided tour of the butterfly garden costs $15 per person. This is also a good place to do a night tour ($39).

CANOPY ADVENTURES   The most adventurous local canopy tour is **Midworld** ★★ (www.midworldcostarica.com; ✆ 2777-7181). Its main zip-line tour features 10 cables, including the longest cables in the area. However, there is also a "Superman" cable, which is very long, very fast, and ridden in a prone position. Though it may seem scary, it's also a lot of fun and provides a unique and unforgettable bird's-eye perspective on the world below. This company also gives a ropes course. Its ATV tours through the surrounding rainforest stop at a waterfall pool for a dip. **Canopy Safari** ★ (www.canopy safari.com; ✆ **888/765-8475** in the U.S. and Canada, or 2777-0100 in Costa Rica), is another good option, featuring 18 treetop platforms connected by a series of cables and suspension bridges, a Tarzan-type swing, and two rappels. The on-site butterfly garden and serpentarium are a bonus. A canopy tour should run $55 to $85 per person, and up to $130 for a combo package that includes various adventures and lunch.

HORSEBACK RIDING   While you can still sometimes find locals renting horses on the beaches outside the national park, I discourage this, as there are just too many crowds, the beach is too short, and the horse droppings are problematic. Better yet, head back into the hills and forests. Both **Finca Valmy** (www.toemmers.com; ✆ **2779-1118**) and **Brisas del Nara** (www.horsebacktour.com; ✆ **2779-1235**) offer horseback rides that pass through primary and secondary forest and feature a swimming stop or two at a jungle waterfall. Full-day tours, including breakfast and lunch, cost between $70 and $80 per person. Finca Valmy also offers an overnight tour for serious riders, with lodgings in rustic cabins in the Santa María de Dota Mountains.

ONE-STOP ADVENTURE HOT SPOT   The **ADR Adventure Park** ★★ (www.adradventurepark.com; ✆ **877/393-8332** in the U.S. and Canada, or 2777-0082 in Costa Rica) is an excellent one-stop spot for adventure travelers and thrill seekers. Billing itself as a 10-in-1 adventure tour, the 7-hour, full-day tour here includes a zip-line canopy ride, waterfall rappels, a high plunge into a jungle river pool, horseback riding, and much more. The cost is $130, and includes transportation and lunch.

SPICE UP YOUR LIFE   Located 16km (10 miles) outside of Quepos, **Villa Vanilla** ★★ (www.rainforestspices.com; ✆ **2779-1155** or 8839-2721) offers an informative and tasty tour of its open-air botanical gardens and spice farm. An on-site commercial vanilla operation is the centerpiece of the show, but you'll also learn about a host of other tropical spices and assorted flora. You'll even sample some sweet and savory treats and drinks made with the on-site bounty. The half-day guided tour runs daily at 9am and 1pm, and costs $50, which includes round-trip transportation from any area hotel. Be sure to stock up at their small shop, which sells pure vanilla, cinnamon, and locally grown pepper.

Especially for Kids

TAKE A TOUR ON THE TICO SIDE ★ For a good taste of local Tico rural culture, mixed in with some fabulous scenery and adventure, sign up for the **Santa Juana Mountain Tour & Canopy Safari** ★★ (www.sicomono.com; © **888/742-6667** in the U.S. and Canada, or 2777-0777 in Costa Rica). This full-day tour starts off with a visit to the Canopy Safari (p. 214) and then takes you to a local farming village in the mountains outside of Quepos. Depending upon your needs and interests, once you arrive in the village, you can tour the surrounding coffee and citrus farms, go for a horseback ride, hike the trails, swim in rainforest pools, fish for tilapia, and see how sugar cane is processed. A typical Tico lunch is included. Rates are $129 to $155 per person, depending on the size of your group, and $89 for children 11 and under.

Shopping

If you're looking for souvenirs, you'll find plenty of beach towels, beachwear, and handmade jewelry in a variety of small shops in Quepos and at impromptu stalls down near the national park. The best of these is **Mot Mot Gallery** (© **2777-3559**), located downtown in the first floor of the Hotel Kamuk.

My favorite gift shop is the one found inside **Milagro** ★★ (see p. 210), which features a host of excellent, locally sourced craft items, as well as amazing freshly roasted coffee.

For higher-end gifts, check out Hotel Si Como No's **Regalame** (www.regalameart.com) gift shop, which has a wide variety of craft works, clothing, and original paintings and prints, or **Galería Yara** (© **2777-4846**), a contemporary, tropical art gallery in the Plaza Yara shopping center.

Nightlife & Entertainment

The bars at the **Barba Roja** restaurant, about midway along the road between Quepos and Manuel Antonio, and the **Hotel Si Como No** (p. 208) are good places to hang out and meet people in the evenings. To shoot some pool, I head to the **Billfish Sportbar & Grill** ★ at the Byblos Resort (on the main road btw. Quepos and the park entrance). For tapas and local *bocas* (appetizers), try **Salsipuedes** (roughly midway along the road btw. Quepos and the National Park entrance). **Bambu Jam** ★ (along the road btw. Quepos and the park entrance) and **Dos Locos** (in the heart of downtown) are your best bets for live music. In downtown Quepos, **Sargento Garcia's** and **Wacky Wanda's** are popular hangouts. For real late-night action, the hottest club in town is the **Cuban Republik Disco Lounge,** in the heart of downtown Quepos.

The **Hotel & Casino Kamuk** in Quepos and the **Byblos Resort** both have small casinos and will even foot your cab bill if you try your luck. If you want to see a flick, check what's playing at **Hotel Si Como No's** (p. 208) little theater, although you have to eat at the restaurant or spend a minimum at the bar to earn admission.

A Day Trip South of Manuel Antonio ★★

With a stunning setting and miles of nearly deserted beaches backed by rainforest-covered mountains, the coastline south of Manuel Antonio is an excellent place to find uncrowded stretches of sand, spectacular views, and remote jungle.

Leaving Manuel Antonio, the well-paved Costanera Sur highway (CR34) runs by mile after mile of oil-palm plantations, until just before the tiny village of Dominical, where the mountains again meet the sea. From Dominical south, the coastline is dotted with tide pools, tiny coves, and cliffside vistas. Dominical is the largest village in the area, with an enviable location on the banks of Río Barú, right where it widens considerably before emptying into the ocean. The banks of the river and throughout the surrounding forests provide good birding. Along the coast and rivers, you're likely to see numerous shore and seabirds, including herons, egrets, and kingfishers, while the forests are home to colorful and lively tanagers, toucans, and trogons. Dominical is also one of the prime surf destinations in Costa Rica, with both right and left beach breaks. When the swell is big, the wave here is a powerful and hollow tube.

EXPLORING DOMINICAL & BALLENA MARINE NATIONAL PARK

This area is best explored with a rental car, although it can be done by local bus. A short distance south of Dominical, you will come to **Dominicalito,** a small beach and cove that can be a decent place to swim, but continue on a bit. You'll soon hit **Playa Hermosa,** a long stretch of desolate beach with fine sand. The beach is unprotected and can be rough, but it's a nicer place to sunbathe and swim than Dominical.

At the village of Uvita, 16km (10 miles) south of Dominical, you'll reach the northern end of the **Ballena Marine National Park ★★**, which protects a coral reef that stretches from Uvita south to Playa Piñuela and includes the little Isla Ballena, just offshore. To get to **Playa Uvita** (which is inside the park), turn in at the village of Bahía and continue until you hit the ocean. Here the beach is actually well protected and good for swimming. At low tide, an exposed sandbar allows you to walk about and explore another tiny island. This park is named for the whales that are sometimes sighted close to shore in the winter months. If you ever fly over this area, you'll also notice that this little island and the spit of land formed at low tide compose the perfect outline of a whale's tail. An office at the entrance here regulates the park's use and even runs a small turtle-hatching shelter and program. Entrance to the national park is $10 per person. Camping is allowed here for $2 per person per day, including access to a public restroom and shower.

Outdoor & Other Activities in the Area

In addition to the activities mentioned below, other adventure activities in Dominical include kayak tours of the mangroves, river floats in inner tubes, and day tours to Caño Island and Corcovado National Park. To arrange any of these activities, check in with **Dominical Adventures** (www.dominicalsurf adventures.com; © **2787-0431**), or the folks at the **Hotel Roca Verde** (www. rocaverde.net; © **2787-0036**).

DIVING   If you want to take a snorkel or scuba-diving trip out to the rocky sites off Ballena Marine National Park or all the way out to Isla del Caño, call **Mystic Dive Center** (www.mysticdive.com; © **2786-5217**), which has its main office in a small roadside strip mall down toward Playa Tortuga and Ojochal. These folks are open only from December 1 through April 15, and prices for Ballena Marine National Park are $80 for snorkeling and $100 for a two-tank dive; prices for Isla del Caño are $130 for snorkeling and $170 for a two-tank dive.

HIKING & HORSEBACK RIDING   Several local farms offer horseback tours through forests and orchards, and some of these farms provide overnight accommodations. **Hacienda Barú** ★ (www.haciendabaru.com; © **2787-0003**) takes several different hikes and tours, including a walk through mangroves and along the riverbank (for some good bird-watching), a rainforest hike through 80 hectares (198 acres) of virgin jungle, an all-day trek from beach to mangrove to jungle that includes a visit to Indian petroglyphs, an overnight camping trip, and a combination horseback-and-hiking tour. The operation, which is dedicated to conservation and reforestation, even has tree-climbing tours and a small canopy platform 30m (98 ft.) above the ground, as well as one of the more common zip-line canopy tours. Prices range from $25 for the mangrove hike to $125 for overnight in the jungle. In addition to its ecotourism and adventure-tourism activities, Hacienda Barú has a range of rooms and cabins, some with full kitchens, two bedrooms, and a living room (prices range from $80–$90 for a double, including breakfast). Hacienda Barú is about 1.5km (1 mile) north of Dominical on the road from Manuel Antonio.

WATERFALLS   The jungles just outside of Dominical are home to two spectacular waterfalls. The most popular and impressive is the **Santo Cristo** or **Nauyaca Waterfalls** ★★, a two-tiered beauty with an excellent swimming

A Special Snake & Reptile Showcase

In my opinion, **Parque Reptilandia** ★★ (www.crreptiles.com; © **2787-0343**) is the best snake and reptile attraction in Costa Rica. With more than 70 well-designed and spacious terrariums and enclosed areas, the collection includes a wide range of snakes, frogs, turtles, lizards, crocodiles, and caimans. Some of my favorite residents here are the brilliant eyelash pit viper and sleek golden vine snake. Both native and imported species are on display, including the only Komodo dragon in Central America. For those looking to spice up their visit, Fridays are feeding days. It's open daily from 9am to 4:30pm; admission is $12 adults, and $6 for children 14 and under. The park is a few miles outside Dominical on the road to San Isidro.

hole. Most of the hotels in town can arrange for the horseback ride up here, or you can contact **Don Lulo** (www.cataratasnauyaca.com; ✆ **2787-0541**) directly. A full-day tour, with both breakfast and lunch, should cost around $70–$90 per person, including transportation to and from Dominical. The tour is a mix of hiking, horseback riding, and hanging out at the falls. It is also possible to reach these falls by horseback from an entrance near the small village of Tinamaste. (You will see signs on the road.) Similar tours (at similar prices) are offered to the **Diamante Waterfalls,** which are a three-tiered set of falls with a 360m (1,180-ft.) drop, but not quite as spacious and inviting a pool as the one at Santo Cristo.

THE SOUTHERN ZONE

C osta Rica's southern zone is an area of jaw-dropping beauty, with vast expanses of virgin lowland rainforest, loads of wildlife, tons of adventure opportunities, and few cities, towns, or settlements. Lushly forested mountains tumble into the sea, streams still run clear and clean, scarlet macaws squawk raucously in the treetops, and dolphins and humpback whales frolic just offshore and inside the Golfo Dulce. The Osa Peninsula is the most popular attraction in this region and one of the premier ecotourism destinations in the world. It's home to **Corcovado National Park ★★★**, the largest single expanse of lowland tropical rainforest in Central America, and its sister, **Piedras Blancas National Park ★★**. Scattered around the edges of these national parks and along the shores of the Golfo Dulce are some of the country's finest nature lodges.

But this beauty doesn't come easy. It's a long way from San José, and many of the most fascinating spots can be reached only by small plane or boat—although hiking and four-wheeling will get you into some memorable surroundings as well. Tourism is still underdeveloped here, with no large resorts in this neck of the woods. Moreover, the heat and humidity are more than some people can stand. Put some forethought into planning a vacation down here, and book your rooms and transportation in advance.

DRAKE BAY ★★

145km (90 miles) S of San José; 32km (20 miles) SW of Palmar

While Drake Bay remains one of the more isolated spots in Costa Rica, the small town located at the mouth of the **Río Agujitas** has boomed a bit over the years. Most of that is due to the year-round operation of the small airstrip here, and the sometimes passable condition of the rough dirt road connecting Drake Bay to the coastal highway—just a decade or so ago, there was no road and the nearest regularly functioning airstrip was in Palmar Sur. That said, the village of Drake Bay is still tiny, and the lodges listed here

Dolphin-watching tour in Drake Bay.

remain quiet and remote getaways catering to naturalists, anglers, scuba divers, and assorted vacationers.

The bay is named after Sir Francis Drake, who is believed to have anchored here in 1579. Emptying into a broad bay, the tiny Río Agujitas acts as a protected harbor for small boats and is a lovely place to canoe or swim. Many of the local lodges dock their boats and many **dolphin- and whale-watching tours** leave from here. Stretching south from Drake Bay are miles of deserted beaches and dense primary tropical rainforests. Adventurous explorers will find tide pools, spring-fed rivers, waterfalls, forest trails, and some of the best bird-watching in all of Costa Rica. If a paradise such as this appeals to you, Drake Bay makes a good base for exploring the peninsula.

South of Drake Bay are the wilds of the **Osa Peninsula,** including **Corcovado National Park.** Corcovado National Park covers about half of the peninsula and contains the largest single expanse of virgin lowland rainforest in Central America. For this reason, Corcovado is well known among researchers studying rainforest ecology. If you come here, you'll learn firsthand why they call them rainforests: Some parts of the peninsula receive more than 635cm (250 in.) of rain per year.

Drake Bay hosts a collection of mostly high-end hotels, very

Helping Out

If you want to help local efforts in protecting the fragile rainforests and wild areas of the Osa Peninsula, contact the **Corcovado Foundation** (www.corcovado foundation.org; ⌀ **2297-3013**) or **Osa Conservation** (www.osaconservation. org; ⌀ **2735-5756**).

Both groups have volunteer programs ranging from trail maintenance to environmental and English-language education to sea-turtle-nesting protection.

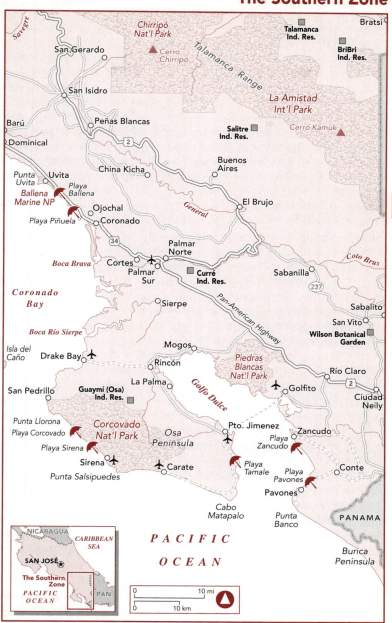

Savegre

Chirripó
Nat'l Park

Talamanca
Ind. Res.

Bratsi

BriBri
Ind. Res.

San Gerardo

Cerro
Chirripó

Talamanca Range

La Amistad
Int'l Park

San Isidro

Cerro Kamuk

Barú

Peñas Blancas

Salitre
Ind. Res.

Dominical

Buenos
Aires

Punta
Uvita

Uvita

China Kicha

El Brujo

Ballena
Marine NP

Playa
Ballena

General

Playa Piñuela

Ojochal

Coronado

Palmar
Norte

Boca Brava

Cortes

Palmar
Sur

Curré
Ind. Res.

Sabanilla

Coto Brus

Coronado
Bay

Sierpe

Pan-American Highway

Sabalito

San Vito

Boca Río Sierpe

Wilson Botanical
Garden

Isla del
Caño

Drake Bay

Mogos

Rincón

Piedras
Blancas
Nat'l Park

Río Claro

San Pedrillo

La Palma

Golfo Dulce

Golfito

Ciudad
Neily

Guaymí (Osa)
Ind. Res.

Punta Llorona

Playa Corcovado

Corcovado
Nat'l Park

Osa
Peninsula

Pto. Jimenez

Zancudo

Playa Sirena

Playa
Zancudo

Sirena

Carate

Playa
Tamale

Conte

Punta Salsipuedes

Playa
Pavones

Pavones

Cabo
Matapalo

Punta
Banco

PANAMA

PACIFIC

OCEAN

Burica
Peninsula

NICARAGUA

CARIBBEAN
SEA

SAN JOSÉ

The Southern
Zone

PAN.

PACIFIC
OCEAN

0   10 mi

0   10 km

isolated and mostly accessible only by boat. Travelers using these hotels can enjoy great day hikes and guided tours into Corcovado National Park, but **Puerto Jiménez** (p. 227) is the best base if you want to spend a lot of time hiking in and camping inside the park or exploring the area independently. (It has budget hotels, the parks office, and "taxi/bus" service to Carate and Los Patos, from which visitors can hike into the various stations.) From the Drake Bay side, you're much more dependent on a boat ride/organized tour from one of the lodges to explore the park.

Essentials

Because Drake Bay is so remote, I recommend that you have a room reservation and transportation arrangements (usually arranged with your hotel) before you arrive. Most of the lodges listed here are scattered along several kilometers of coastline, and it is not easy to go from one to another looking for a room.

Tip: A flashlight and rainwear are always useful to have on hand in Costa Rica; they're absolutely essential in Drake Bay.

GETTING THERE   By Plane: Most people fly directly into the little airstrip at Drake Bay, although some tourists still fly to Palmar Sur (see below). All lodges will either arrange transportation for you or include it in their packages. Both **Nature Air** (www.natureair.com; ℰ **800/235-9272** in the U.S. and Canada, or 2299-6000 in Costa Rica) and **Sansa** (www.flysansa.com; ℰ **877/767-2672** in the U.S. and Canada, or 2290-4100 in Costa Rica) have daily direct flights to Drake Bay from the San José area. The flight duration is 40 minutes, although this flight often includes brief stops in Quepos, Golfito, or Puerto Jiménez. Fares range from $120 to $210 one-way. Flights also depart San José daily for Palmar Sur; that fare runs from $100 to $140 each way.

If your travels take you to Drake Bay via Palmar Sur, you must then take a 15-minute bus or taxi ride to the small town of **Sierpe.** This route runs through several **African palm plantations** and quickly past some important archaeological sites. In Sierpe, you board a small boat for a 40km (25-mile) ride to Drake Bay; see "By Taxi & Boat from Sierpe," below. The first half of this trip snakes through a maze of mangrove canals and rivers before heading out to sea for the final leg to the bay. *Warning:* Entering and exiting the Sierpe River mouth is often treacherous; I've had several very white-knuckle moments here.

By Bus: Tracopa buses (www.tracopacr.com; ℰ **2221-4214** or 2258-8939) leave San José daily for the southern zone throughout the day, between 5am and 6:30pm from Calle 9 and Avenida 18. Almost all stop in Palmar Norte, but make sure to ask. The ride takes around 6 hours; fares range from C7,590 to C7,970.

Once in Palmar Norte, ask when the next bus goes out to Sierpe. If it doesn't leave for a while (buses aren't frequent), consider taking a taxi (see below).

By Taxi & Boat from Sierpe: When you arrive at either the Palmar Norte bus station or the Palmar Sur airstrip, you'll most likely first need to take a taxi to the village of Sierpe. The fare should be around $20. If you're booked into one of the main lodges, chances are your transportation is included. Even if you're not booked into one of the lodges, a host of taxi and minibus drivers offer the trip. When you get to Sierpe, head to the dock and try to find space on a boat. This should run you another $20 to $40. If you don't arrive early enough, you might have to hire an entire boat, which usually costs $100 to $150 for a boat that can carry up to six passengers. Make sure that you feel confident about the boat and skipper, and, if possible, try to find a spot on a boat from one of the established lodges in Drake Bay.

By Car: I don't recommend driving to Drake Bay. But if you insist, take the San José–Caldera Highway (CR27) to the first exit past the Pozón toll-booth, where you will pick up the Southern Highway, or Costanera Sur (CR34). Take this south through Jacó, Quepos, and Dominical to Palmar Norte, where you'll meet up with the Interamerican Highway (CR2). Take this south to the turnoff for La Palma, Rincón, and Puerto Jiménez (at the town of Chacarita; it's clearly marked). Then at Rincón, turn onto the rough road leading into Drake Bay. This road fords some 10 rivers and is usually not passable during the rainy season. Moreover, it only reaches into the small heart of the village of Drake Bay, though almost all of the hotels I list below are farther out along the peninsula, where only boats reach. The only hotels that you can actually drive up to are very basic cabins in town. Alternatively, you can securely park your car in Sierpe, and take one of the boat taxis (see above) to Drake Bay.

DEPARTING If you're not flying directly out of Drake Bay, have your lodge arrange a boat trip back to Sierpe for you. Be sure that the lodge also arranges for a taxi to meet you in Sierpe for the trip to Palmar Sur or Palmar Norte. (If you're on a budget, you can ask around to see whether a late-morning public bus is still running from Sierpe to Palmar Norte.) In the two Palmars, you can make onward plane and bus connections. At the Palmar Norte bus terminal, almost any bus heading north will take you to San José, and almost any bus heading south will take you to Golfito.

Where to Stay & Eat

Given the remote location and logistics of reaching Drake Bay, as well as the individual isolation of each hotel, nearly all the hotels listed below deal almost exclusively in package trips that include transportation, meals, tours, and taxes. I list the most common packages, although all the lodges will work with you to accommodate longer or shorter stays. Nightly room rates are listed only where they're available and practical, generally at the more moderately priced hotels.

EXPENSIVE

La Paloma Lodge ★★★   This has long been one of my favorite nature lodges in Costa Rica, and for good reason. The views are to die for, the setting is sublime, and the wildlife-viewing and adventure opportunities are as good as it gets. The best rooms are the large private ranchos, but even the slightly more humble standard rooms are big, lush, and inviting. Food and service are top-notch. The lodge takes conservation and sustainable development seriously, and is actively involved in protecting the region. A small pool is set on the edge of a jungle-clad hillside, with great views of the ocean and Caño Island in the distance, and Cocolito Beach is a short hike on a winding trail through the rainforest.

Drake Bay. www.lapalomalodge.com. ✆ **2293-7502.** 11 units. $990–$1,245 per person for 4 days/3 nights with 2 tours; $1,235–$1,575 per person for 5 days/4 nights with 2 tours. Rates based on double occupancy and include all meals, park fees, and indicated tours. Rates slightly lower in off season. Closed Sept 15–Nov 1. **Amenities:** Restaurant; bar; outdoor pool; free canoe/kayak rentals; free Wi-Fi.

MODERATE

In addition to the spot listed below, you might check out **Finca Maresia ★** (www.fincamaresia.com; ✆ **2775-0279**), a pretty boutique property located between Drake Bay and the national park.

Drake Bay Wilderness Resort ★★   This is one of the first and best located of the lodges in Drake Bay. The resort sits on a large chunk of land with the Río Agujitas on one side and the area's namesake Drake Bay on the other. Most rooms have beautiful bay views from a front porch equipped with a couple of locally made wooden sitting chairs. Inside you'll find concrete walls with hand-painted murals of local wildlife and fauna. A couple of budget rooms have shared bathroom and shower facilities, while a more plush honeymoon suite is good for those looking to splurge. The owner Marlene's chocolate-chip cookies are regionally renowned.

Drake Bay. www.drakebay.com. ✆ **2725-1715.** 20 units. $865 per person for 4 days/3 nights with 2 tours, including all meals and taxes. **Amenities:** Restaurant; bar; saltwater pool; free canoe/kayak rentals; free Wi-Fi.

INEXPENSIVE

Hotel Jinetes de Osa ★   Set just off the water at the far southern end of the footpath that runs along the shoreline of Drake Bay, this has long been the best true budget pick in the area. The superior rooms here are located higher up on the property and come with wonderful views of the bay. The standard rooms are more hostel-like, and some can feel a little dark, and few have any bay or rainforest views to speak of. These folks specialize in dive trips and offer full-service PADI certification courses.

Drake Bay. www.jinetesdeosa.com. ✆ **866/553-7073** in the U.S. and Canada, or 2231-5806 in Costa Rica. 9 units. $96–$160 double. Rates include breakfast. **Amenities:** Restaurant; bar; free Wi-Fi.

THOSE MYSTERIOUS stone spheres

Although Costa Rica lacks the great cities, giant temples, and bas-relief carvings of the Maya, Aztec, and Olmec civilizations of northern Mesoamerica, its pre-Columbian residents did leave a unique and mysterious legacy. Over a period of several centuries, hundreds of painstakingly carved and carefully positioned granite spheres were left by the peoples who lived throughout the Diquís Delta, which flanks the Terraba River in southern Costa Rica. The orbs, which range from grapefruit size to more than 2m (6½ ft.) in diameter, can weigh up to 15 tons, and many reach near-spherical perfection.

Archaeologists believe that the spheres were created during two defined cultural periods. The first, called the Aguas Buenas period, dates from around A.D. 100 to 500. Few spheres survive from this time. The second phase, during which spheres were created in apparently greater numbers, is called the Chiriquí period and lasted from approximately A.D. 800 to 1500. The "balls" believed to have been carved during this time frame are widely dispersed along the entire length of the lower section of the Terraba River. To date, only one known quarry for the spheres has been discovered, in the mountains above the Diquís Delta, which points to a difficult and lengthy transportation process.

Some archaeologists believe that the spheres were hand-carved in a very time-consuming process, using stone tools, perhaps aided by some sort of firing process. Another theory holds that granite blocks were placed at the bases of powerful waterfalls, and the hydraulic beating of the water eventually turned and carved the rock into these near-perfect spheres. And more than a few proponents have credited extraterrestrial intervention for the creation of the stone balls.

Most of the stone balls have been found at the archaeological remains of defined settlements and are associated with either central plazas or known burial sites. Their size and placement have been interpreted to have both social and celestial importance, although their exact significance remains a mystery. Unfortunately, many of the stone balls have been plundered and are currently used as lawn ornaments in the fancier neighborhoods of San José. Some have even been shipped out of the country. The **Museo Nacional de Costa Rica** (p. 82) has a nice collection, including one massive sphere in its center courtyard. It's a never-fail photo op. You can also see the stone balls near the small **airports in Palmar Sur** and **Drake Bay,** and on **Isla del Caño** (which is 19km/12 miles off the Pacific coast near Drake Bay).

However, the best place to see the stone spheres is the **Finca 6 Archeological Museum ★★** (ⓒ 2100-6000), located between Palmar Sur and Sierpe. It is estimated that nearly 10% of all stone spheres produced in Costa Rica can be found on the 10 or so acres that comprise Finca 6. A small museum building provides background and displays of some smaller spheres and other artifacts. From here, trails lead out to several excavations of archaeological finds where a range of large stone spheres, stellae, and other relics are displayed in their natural and original positioning. Finca 6 is located 6km south of Palmar Sur, and is open daily from 8am–4pm. Admission is $6. This unique archaeological site is easily visited by anyone arriving or departing Drake Bay via Sierpe.

Exploring Drake Bay

Beaches, forests, wildlife, and solitude are the main attractions of Drake Bay. Although Corcovado National Park (see "Puerto Jiménez: Gateway to Corcovado National Park," below) is the area's star attraction, plenty of other attractions are in and around Drake Bay. The Osa Peninsula is home more than 140 species of mammals, some 400 species of birds, and 130 species of amphibians and reptiles. You aren't likely to see anywhere near all of these animals, but you can expect to see quite a few, including several types of monkeys, coatimundis, scarlet macaws, parrots, and hummingbirds. Other park inhabitants include jaguars, tapirs, sloths, and crocodiles. If you're lucky, you might even see one of the region's namesake *osas* (giant anteaters).

All lodges in the area have their own in-house tour operations and offer a host of half- and full-day tours and activities, including hikes in Corcovado National Park, trips to Caño Island, horseback rides, and sportfishing. In some cases, tours are included in your room rate or package; in others, they must be bought a la carte. Other options include mountain biking and sea kayaking. Most of these tours run between $60 and $120, depending on the activity, with scuba diving ($100–$140 for a two-tank dive) and sportfishing ($900–$1,800) costing a bit more.

CANOPY TOUR   If you want to try a zip-line canopy adventure, the **Drake Bay Canopy Tour** (www.canopytourdrakebay.com; ✆ **8314-5454**) has six cable runs, several "Tarzan swings," and a hanging bridge, all set in lush forests just outside of Drake Bay. The 2-hour tour costs $35.

ISLA DEL CAÑO   One of the most popular excursions from Drake Bay is a trip out to **Isla del Caño** and the **Caño Island Biological Reserve ★★** for a bit of exploring, snorkeling, or scuba diving. The island is about 19km (12 miles) offshore from Drake Bay and was once home to a pre-Columbian culture about which little is known. A trip to the island might include a visit to an ancient cemetery, where you'll see some of the stone spheres believed to have been carved by this area's ancient inhabitants (see "Those Mysterious Stone Spheres," above). Few animals or birds live on the island, but the coral reefs just offshore teem with life. This is one of Costa Rica's prime **scuba spots ★★**. Visibility is often quite good, and the beach has easily accessible snorkeling. All of the lodges listed above offer trips to Isla del Caño. As of 2014, the Costa Rican National Park service has been severely restricting access to the island, and visiting groups are no longer allowed to picnic on the island. Typically, tours arrive in the morning, conduct their snorkel and scuba excursions, and then head back to the mainland for a picnic lunch and some beach time.

NIGHT TOUR   One of the most interesting tour options in Drake Bay is a 2-hour **night tour ★★★** (www.thenighttour.com; ✆ **8701-7356;** $35 per person) offered by Tracie Stice, who is affectionately known as the "Bug Lady," and her partner Gianfranco Gómez. Equipped with flashlights, participants get a bug's-eye view of the forest at night. You might see reflections of some larger forest dwellers, but most of the tour is a fascinating exploration of the nocturnal insect and arachnid world, with the occasional discovery of some frogs, toads, or snakes. Consider yourself lucky if she finds the burrow of a trap-door spider or large tarantula. Any hotel in Drake Bay can book the tour for you. However, the travel distance makes it impossible for those staying at hotels outside of walking distance of the town.

WHALE-WATCHING   Drake Bay is one of the best places to go **whale-watching** in Costa Rica; humpback whales are most commonly spotted in the area between late July and March. There are currently no dedicated whale-watching operators in the area, but all the hotels listed above can arrange whale-watching, as well as dolphin-spotting, trips. Two resident marine biologists, **Shawn Larkin** (www.costacetacea.com) and **Roy Sancho,** are often hired by the better hotels, but depending on demand and availability, the hotels may send you out with one of their own guides and/or captains. These folks also offer deep-water free-diving and snorkel tours, which provide the chance to swim in close proximity to the large pelagic fish, mammals, and reptiles found in the area.

PUERTO JIMÉNEZ: GATEWAY TO CORCOVADO NATIONAL PARK

35km (22 miles) W of Golfito by water (90km/56 miles by road); 85km (53 miles) S of Palmar Norte

Don't let its small size and languid pace fool you. **Puerto Jiménez ★** is a bustling little burg, where rough jungle gold-panners mix with wealthy ecotourists, budget backpackers, serious surfers, and a smattering of celebrities seeking a dose of anonymity and escape. Located on the southeastern tip of the Osa Peninsula, the town itself is just a couple of streets wide in any direction, with a handful of general stores, some inexpensive *sodas* (diners), and several bars.

Corcovado National Park ★★★ has its headquarters here, and this town makes an excellent base for exploring this vast wilderness area. This is also a prime surf spot. **Cabo Matapalo** (the southern tip of the Osa Peninsula) is home to several very dependable right point breaks. When it's working, the waves at Pan Dulce and Backwash actually connect, and can provide rides almost as long and tiring as those to be had in more famous Pavones.

Essentials

GETTING THERE & DEPARTING   **By Plane:** Both **Nature Air** (www.natureair.com; ✆ **800/235-9272** in the U.S. and Canada, or 2299-6000 in Costa Rica) and **Sansa** (www.flysansa.com; ✆ **877/767-2672** in the U.S. and Canada, or 2290-4100 in Costa Rica) have daily direct flights to Puerto Jiménez from San José. The flight duration is around 55 minutes, although this

The legendary left at Pavones.

flight often includes brief stops in Quepos, Golfito, or Drake Bay. Fares range from $104 to $150 one-way.

Note that due to the remoteness of this area and the unpredictable flux of traffic, both Sansa and Nature Air frequently improvise on scheduling. Sometimes this means an unscheduled stop in Quepos, Drake Bay, or Golfito, either on the way to or from San José, which can add some time to your flight. Less frequently, it might mean a change in departure time, so it's always best to confirm.

Taxis are generally waiting to meet incoming flights. A ride into downtown Puerto Jiménez should cost around C1,500. If you're staying at a hotel outside of downtown, it's best to have them arrange for a taxi to meet you. Depending on how far out on the peninsula you're staying, it could cost up to $80 for a rugged four-wheel-drive vehicle that can carry up to four people.

By Car: Take the San José–Caldera Highway (CR27) to the first exit past the Pozón tollbooth, where you will pick up the Southern Highway, or Costanera Sur (CR34). Take this south through Jacó, Quepos, and Dominical to Palmar Norte, where you'll meet up with the Interamerican Highway (CR2). Take this south to the turnoff for La Palma, Rincón, and Puerto Jiménez.

By Bus: Transportes Blanco-Lobo express buses (© **2257-4121** in San José, or 2771-4744 in Puerto Jiménez) leave San José daily at 8am and noon from Calle 12, between avenidas 7 and 9. The trip takes 7 to 8 hours; the fare is C7,500. Buses depart Puerto Jiménez for San José daily at 5am and 9am.

By Boat: Several speedboats work as boat taxis between Puerto Jiménez and Golfito. The fare is C3,000, and the ride takes a little under 30 minutes. These boats leave five or six times throughout the day, or whenever they fill up, beginning at around 5am and finishing up about 5pm. Ask around town, or at the docks for current schedules.

CITY LAYOUT   Puerto Jiménez is a dirt-lane town on the southern coast of the Osa Peninsula. The public dock is over a bridge past the north end of the soccer field; the bus stop is 2 blocks east of the center of town.

GETTING AROUND   Four-wheel-drive taxis are actually fairly plentiful in Puerto Jiménez. You can usually find them cruising or parked along the main street in town. Alternatively, have your hotel or restaurant call one for you. You can even rent a car down here from **Solid Car Rental** (www.solid carrental.com; ☏ **2735-5777**).

Where to Stay in Puerto Jiménez
INEXPENSIVE
In addition to the hotel listed below, **Cabinas Marcelina** (☏ **2735-5007**) is a clean, dependable budget lodging right in the heart of town.

Cabinas Jiménez ★★   You really can't do better right in town than this waterfront hotel. A perennial budget favorite, its large, wood-and-bamboo rancho has a commanding view of the Puerto Jiménez harbor. Down on the harbor shore, the hotel keeps some kayaks that are free for guest use, and they also maintain a fleet of bikes for you to cruise around town, also complimentary.

Downtown, 50m (165 ft.) north of the soccer field, Puerto Jiménez, Puntarenas. www. cabinasjimenez.com. ☏ **2735-5090.** 15 units. $65–$130 double. **Amenities:** Outdoor pool; free Wi-Fi.

Where to Eat in Puerto Jiménez
In addition to Il Giardino mentioned below, you can get good pizzas and pastas at **Pizza Mail.it** (☏ **2735-5483**), next to the post office.

Il Giardino ★★ ITALIAN/INTERNATIONAL/SEAFOOD   For years, this has been the best restaurant in Puerto Jiménez, and now they've got a waterfront location that matches their fine cooking. The pastas and ravioli are all homemade and delicious, and the seafood is freshly caught and perfectly prepared. Although it's an odd combination, these folks also frequently do sushi nights, and are even open for breakfast. Everything is made fresh to order, so the kitchen can be a bit slow at times.

On the beachfront, just down from the public pier, Puerto Jiménez. www.ilgiardino italianrestaurant.com. ☏ **2735-5129.** Main courses C5,000–C14,000. No credit cards. Daily 7am–10pm.

Soda Carolina ★ COSTA RICAN   This simple Costa Rican restaurant is the social and tourist hub of Puerto Jiménez. Bright rainforest scenes and

Puerto Jiménez: Gateway to Corcovado National Park

animals are painted on the interior walls, while the open-air front walls open up to the city's main street. You can get filling *casados* (plates of the day), fresh grilled fish, and a number of other typical local dishes.

On the main street. ℂ **2735-5185.** Main courses C3,300–C9,800. Daily 6am–10pm.

Where to Stay in Playa Plantanares
EXPENSIVE

Iguana Lodge ★★   Located on the outskirts of Puerto Jiménez, this beachfront mini-resort is backed by tall rainforest trees and fronts a calm section of beach where the Golfo Dulce and Pacific Ocean meet. You'll find rooms in a wide range of prices here. I prefer the second-floor units of the two-story casitas, although the club rooms are a good value. There's a large, open-air, wood-floor studio, and yoga is a big attraction. Often there are yoga classes or a visiting group conducting a retreat. The gardens are lush, and gentle Plantanares Beach is just steps away.

Playa Plantanares. www.iguanalodge.com. ℂ **800/259-9123** in the U.S. and Canada, or 8848-0752 in Costa Rica. 19 units. $180 double club room; $440 casita double; $650 3-bedroom beach house. Rates for club room include breakfast. Rates for casita include breakfast and dinner; villa rates do not include meals. All rates include taxes. **Amenities:** 2 restaurants; bar; outdoor pool; spa; Jacuzzi; watersports equipment rental; free Wi-Fi.

Where to Stay & Eat Around the Osa Peninsula

As with most of the lodges in Drake Bay, the accommodations listed in this section include three meals a day in their rates and do a large share of their bookings in package trips. Per-night rates are listed, but the price categories have been adjusted to take into account the fact that all meals are included. Ask about package rates if you plan to take several tours and stay a while: They could save you money.

In addition to the lodges listed below, several other options range from small B&Bs to fully equipped home rentals. Surfers, in particular, might want to inquire into one of the several rental houses located close to the beach at Matapalo. Contact **Jiménez Hotels** (www.jimenezhotels.com; ℂ **8632-8150**), which handles a host of rentals.

Finally, Carate has several lodges. In addition to those listed below, look into **Finca Exótica Eco-Lodge** ★ (www.fincaexotica.com; ℂ **4070-0054**), a delightful oceanview lodge, and **La Leona Eco-Lodge** ★ (www.laleonaeco-lodge.com; ℂ **2735-5705**), a tent-camp on the outskirts of the national park.

This is a very isolated area, with just one rough dirt road connecting all the lodges, nature reserves, and parks. Almost all visitors here take all meals at their hotel or lodge. If you want to venture away for some good fresh food and simple home cooking, head to Martina's **Buena Esperanza** (no phone), on the main road.

EXPENSIVE

The following lodges are some of the best ecolodges Costa Rica has to offer, and most are pretty pricey. However, keep in mind that despite paying top dollar, the rooms have no TVs, no telephones, and no air-conditioning, and the town has no discos, very limited shopping, and no paved roads. Consequently, there are also no crowds and very few modern distractions.

Bosque del Cabo Rainforest Lodge ★★★   There are many reasons this place is popular, but primarily it's all about the wildlife, views, attention to detail, great food and service, and rich primary rainforest all around. The best rooms are the private cabins overlooking the forest and Pacific Ocean below. Families might want to grab one of the fully equipped houses, while those on a bit more of a budget can opt for a garden room. There's great hiking right from the lodge grounds, as well as a bird- and wildlife-viewing platform high up in a tall Manu tree. These folks have a huge private reserve and have earned "4 Leaves" in the CST Sustainable Tourism program.

Osa Peninsula. www.bosquedelcabo.com. ✆ **2735-5206** or 8389-2846. 17 units. $215–$325 per person. Rates include 3 meals daily and taxes. $30 per person, round-trip transportation from Puerto Jiménez Airport. **Amenities:** Restaurant; bar; outdoor pool; surfboard rentals; free Wi-Fi.

El Remanso ★★   This delightful collection of rooms, private cabins, and duplexes is set in a region of thick rainforest, just up the road from Bosque del Cabo. The large main lodge and restaurant area is a tropical fantasy surrounded by towering rainforest trees and entirely open, with a soaring thatch roof and large open deck areas both under the roof and extending beyond. Rooms are widely spread around the sprawling gardens and grounds, and a few have ocean views. Families or groups will want to look at Casa Osa, which sleeps up to eight. For a real treat, be sure to have breakfast atop the tree platform at least once here. This place uses only renewable energy, and has earned "5 Leaves" in the CST Sustainable Tourism program.

Osa Peninsula. www.elremanso.com. ✆ **2735-5569** or 8814-5775. 14 units. $170–$380 per person. Rates include 3 meals daily and all taxes. **Amenities:** Restaurant; bar; outdoor pool; free Wi-Fi.

Lapa Ríos ★★   This trailblazing lodge was one of the first to put ecotourism in the Osa Peninsula on the map. The rooms are all very large, with open screen walls, high-peaked thatch roofs, and large private decks overlooking the rainforest and Pacific Ocean in the distance. The rooms are housed in a series of duplex units stretching in a straight line down the edge of a mountain ridge. If you get one of the lower units, be prepared for a bit of a hike to and from the main lodge, restaurant, and pool area. Lapa Ríos sits on a 400-hectare (988-acre) private rainforest reserve, with a well-maintained trail system and abundance of flora and fauna.

Osa Peninsula. www.laparios.com. ✆ **2735-5130.** 16 units. $430 double. Rates include 3 meals daily, 9 guided tours per stay, and round-trip transportation to Puerto Jiménez.

Discounts for children 11 and under. **Amenities:** Restaurant; bar; outdoor pool; spa; free Wi-Fi.

Exploring Puerto Jiménez

While Puerto Jiménez has typically been a staging ground for adventures much farther out toward Carate and the park, quite a few activities and tours can be undertaken closer to town.

If you're looking to spend some time on the beach, head just east of town for a long, pretty stretch of sand called **Playa Plantanares.** The waves are generally fairly gentle, and quite a few hotels have begun to pop up here. If you head farther out on the peninsula, you'll come to the beaches of **Pan Dulce, Backwash,** and **Matapalo,** all major surf spots with consistently well-formed right point breaks. When the waves aren't too big, these are excellent places to learn how to surf.

You'll find a couple of Internet cafes in town; the best of these is **Cafe Net El Sol** (www.soldeosa.com; ✆ **8632-8150**), which is a great place to book tours and get information, and is also a Wi-Fi hot spot.

Osa Aventura (www.osaaventura.com; ✆ **2735-5758** or 8372-6135) and **Osa Corcovado Tour & Travel** (www.soldeosa.com; ✆ **8632-8150**) are local tour companies that offer a host of guided tours and wildlife-watching expeditions around the Osa Peninsula and into Corcovado National Park. Rates run between $80 and $300 per person, depending upon group size and the tour.

AN APTLY NAMED ADVENTURE TOUR For a real adventure, check in with **Psycho Tours ★★★** (www.psychotours.com; ✆ **8353-8619**). These folks, who also call themselves Everyday Adventures, run a variety of tours, but their signature combo trip features a free climb (with a safety rope attached) on the roots and trunks of a 60m-tall (200-ft.) strangler fig up to a natural platform at around 18m (60 ft.), where you take a leap of faith into space and are belayed down by your guide. This is preceded by an informative hike through primary rainforest, often wading through a small river, and followed by a couple of rappels down jungle waterfalls, the highest of which is around 30m (100 ft.). You can do either one of the above adventures separately, but I recommend the 5- to 6-hour combo tour, which costs $120.

CHOCOLATE TOUR Finca Kobo ★ (www.fincakobo.com; ✆ **8398-7604**), which is located near La Palma, 17km (11 miles) northwest of Puerto Jiménez, offers an informative tour through its organic cacao plantation. You'll see all of the various stages involved in the process of growing cacao and transforming these precious beans into chocolate. At the end of the tour, samples involve dipping local fruit into fresh chocolate fondue. The tour costs $32; children 8 and under are half-price.

SPORTFISHING If you're interested in **bill-fishing** or **deep-sea fishing,** you'll probably want to stay at or fish with **Crocodile Bay Resort** (www.crocodilebay.com; ✆ **800/733-1115** in the U.S. and Canada, or 2735-7990 in

Costa Rica). This upscale fishing lodge is close to the Puerto Jiménez airstrip. Alternatively, you can contact **Southern Costa Rica Sportfishing** (www. costaricasportsman.com; © **2735-5298**). Rates can run between $900 and $2,200 for a full day, or between $700 and $1,500 for a half-day, varying by boat, tackle, number of anglers, and fishing grounds.

SURF & SUP LESSONS   If you want to learn to surf, contact **Pollo's Surf School ★** (www.pollosurfschool.com; © **8366-6559**), near some excellent learning waves on Pan Dulce Beach. Pollo's is also the place to go to try your hand at stand-up paddling (SUP). A 2-hour lesson runs $55 per person.

Exploring Corcovado National Park ★★★

Exploring Corcovado National Park is not something to be undertaken lightly, but neither is it the prohibitive expedition that some people make it out to be. Within a couple of hours of Puerto Jiménez (by 4WD vehicle) are several entrances to the park; the park has no roads, however, so once you reach any of the entrances, you'll have to start hiking. The heat and humidity are often quite extreme, and frequent rainstorms can make trails fairly muddy. If you choose the alternative—hiking on the beach—you'll have to plan your hiking around the tides, when often there is no beach at all and some rivers are impassable.

Corcovado National Park is amazingly rich in biodiversity. It is one of the only places in Costa Rica that is home to all four of the country's monkey species—howler, white-faced, squirrel, and spider. Its large size makes it an

ideal habitat for wildcat species, including the endangered jaguar, as well as other large mammals, like the Baird's tapir. Apart from the jaguar, other cat species found here include the ocelot, margay, jaguarundi, and puma. More than 390 species of birds have been recorded inside the park. Scarlet macaws are commonly sighted here. Other common bird species include any number of antbirds, manakins, toucans, tanagers, hummingbirds, and puffbirds. Once thought to be extinct in Costa Rica, the harpy eagle has been spotted here as well. Most rivers in Corcovado are home to crocodiles; moreover, at high tide, they are frequented by bull sharks. For this reason, river crossings must be coordinated with low tides.

Scarlet macaws in Corcovado.

Corcovado National Park

Because of its size and remoteness, Corcovado National Park is best explored over several days; it is possible, however, to enter and hike a bit of it on day trips. The best way to do this is to book a tour with your lodge on the Osa Peninsula, from a tour company in Puerto Jiménez, or through a lodge in Drake Bay (see "Where to Stay & Eat," above).

GETTING THERE & ENTRY POINTS The park has four primary entrances, which are really just ranger stations reached by rough dirt roads. When you've reached them, you'll have to strap on a backpack and hike. Perhaps the most common entry point from Puerto Jiménez is **La Leona ranger station,** accessible by car, bus, or taxi.

If you choose to drive, take the dirt road from Puerto Jiménez to Carate (Carate is at the end of the road). From Carate, it's a 3km (2-mile) hike to La Leona. To travel there by "public transportation," pick up one of the collective buses (actually, a 4WD pickup truck with a tarpaulin cover and slat seats in

> ### Trail Distances in Corcovado National Park
>
> It's 14km (8.7 miles) from La Leona to Sirena. From Sirena to San Pedrillo, it's 23km (14 miles) along the beach. From San Pedrillo, it's 20km (13 miles) to Drake Bay. It's 19km (12 miles) between Sirena and Los Patos.

the back) that leaves Puerto Jiménez for Carate daily at 6am and 1:30pm, returning at 8am and 4pm. Remember, these "buses" are very informal and change their schedules regularly to meet demand or avoid bad weather, so always ask in town. The one-way fare is around $9. A small fleet of these pickups leaves just south of the bus terminal, and will stop to pick up anyone who flags them down along the way. Your other option is to hire a taxi to suit your schedule, which will charge between $60 and $100 (depending on road conditions) to or from Carate.

En route to Carate, you will pass several campgrounds and small lodges as you approach the park. If you are unable to get a spot at one of the campsites in the park, you can stay at one of these and hike the park during the day.

You can also travel to **El Tigre,** about 14km (8¾ miles) by dirt road from Puerto Jiménez, site of another ranger station. But note that trails from El Tigre go only a short distance into the park.

The third entrance is in **Los Patos,** which is reached from the town of La Palma, northwest of Puerto Jiménez. From here, a 19km (12-mile) trail runs through the center of the park to **Sirena,** a ranger station and research facility (see "Beach Treks & Rainforest Hikes," below). Sirena has a landing strip used by charter flights.

The northern entrance to the park is **San Pedrillo,** which you can reach by hiking from Sirena or by taking a boat from Drake Bay or Sierpe. It's 14km (8¾ miles) from Drake Bay.

If you're not into hiking in the heat, you can charter a plane in Puerto Jiménez to take you to Carate or Sirena. A five-passenger plane costs $200 to $450, one-way, depending on your destination. Contact **Alfa Romeo Air Charters** (www.alfaromeoair.com; ✆ **2735-5353** or 2735-5112) for details.

FEES & REGULATIONS   Park admission is $15 per person, per day. Only the Sirena station is equipped with dormitory-style lodgings and a simple *soda;* the others have basic campsites and toilet facilities. All must be reserved in advance by contacting the **ACOSA** (Area de Conservacion de Osa) in Puerto Jiménez (pncorcovado@gmail.com; ✆ **2735-5036**). However, they are notoriously poor at answering e-mails and attending to reservations. Its offices are adjacent to the airstrip. Only a limited number of people are allowed to camp at each ranger station, so make your reservations well in advance. Your best bet is probably to contact **Osa Aventura** (www.osaaventura.com; ✆ **2735-5758** or 8372-6135) or **Osa Corcovado Tour & Travel** (www.soldeosa.com; ✆ **8632-8150**), who will make the reservations and arrangements for you, for a fee.

BEACH TREKS & RAINFOREST HIKES The park has quite a few good hiking trails. Two of the better-known ones are the beach routes, starting at either La Leona or San Pedrillo ranger stations. Between any two ranger stations, the hiking is arduous and takes all or most of a day, so it's best to rest for a day or so between hikes, if possible. Remember, this is quite a wild area. Never hike alone, and be especially careful about crossing or swimming in any isolated rivers or river mouths. Most rivers in Corcovado are home to crocodiles; moreover, at high tide, some are frequented by bull sharks. For this reason, river crossings must be coordinated with low tides. During the wet months (July–Nov), parts of the park may be closed. One of the longest and most popular hikes, between San Pedrillo and La Sirena, can be undertaken only during the dry season.

Sirena is a fascinating destination. As a research facility and ranger station, it's frequented primarily by scientists studying the rainforest. The network of trails here can easily keep you busy for several days. Just north of the station lies the mouth of the Río Sirena. Most days at high tide, bull sharks swarm and feed in this river mouth. Large crocodiles also inhabit these waters, so swimming is seriously discouraged. Still, it's quite a spectacle. The **Claro Trail** will bring you to the mouth of the Río Claro. A bit smaller, this river also houses a healthy crocodile population, although allegedly fewer bull sharks. However, if you follow the Claro trail upstream a bit, you can find several safe and appropriate swimming spots.

WHERE TO STAY & EAT IN THE PARK: CAMPSITES, CABINS & CANTINAS Reservations are essential at the various ranger stations if you plan to eat or sleep inside the park (see "Fees & Regulations," above). **Sirena** has a modern research facility with dormitory-style accommodations for 28 people, as well as a campground, *soda*, and landing strip for charter flights. Camping is available at **La Leona, Los Patos,** and **San Pedrillo** ranger stations. Every ranger station has potable water, but it's advisable to pack in your own; whatever you do, don't drink stream water. Campsites in the park are $4 per person, per night. A dorm bed at the Sirena station will run you $11—you must bring your own sheets, and a mosquito net is highly recommended.

Meals here are $11 for breakfast, $15 for lunch, and $20 for dinner. Everything must be reserved in advance.

Shopping

Jagua Arts & Craft Store ★★ (☎ 2735-5267) is near the airstrip, and is definitely worth a visit. Owner Karen Herrera has found excellent local and regional Arts and Craft works, including some fine jewelry and blown glass. *Tip:* Many folks head to this store while waiting for their departing flight out of Puerto Jiménez. Make sure to give yourself enough time, as the store has a somewhat extensive collection.

Along the Shores of the Golfo Dulce

Playa Nicuesa Rainforest Lodge ★★★   This is one of the more remote ecolodges in the southern zone, accessible only by boat, a 30-minute ride from Golfito deep inside the Golfo Dulce. The lodge and its various rooms and private cabins are rich in varnished local hardwoods. Try to get one close to the water or set apart in the thick rainforest. The wildlife and nature viewing here is fabulous, and a good place to find the endemic Golfo Dulce frog. Playa Nicuesa offers fabulous hikes through primary forest on its own 66-hectare (163-acre) private reserve adjoining the much larger Piedras Blancas National Park. Great kayaking and snorkel tours are also provided on the Golfo Dulce, where dolphins are common and whale sharks are occasionally spotted. Guests enjoy unlimited free use of kayaks, snorkeling gear, and fishing equipment. Finally, the lodge has a yoga deck, some lovely lounge areas facing the gulf, and a small stream.

Golfo Dulce. www.nicuesalodge.com. ☎ **866/504-8116** in the U.S., or 2258-8250 in Costa Rica. 9 units. $225–$460 per person per day, double occupancy. $125 children 6–12. Rates include all meals, taxes, and transfers to Golfito or Puerto Jiménez. Required 3-night minimum stay; 4-night minimum stay required during peak season. Closed Oct 1–Nov 15. **Amenities:** Restaurant; bar; free watersports equipment rentals.

THE CARIBBEAN COAST

Costa Rica's Caribbean coast is a world apart from the rest of the country. The pace is slower, the food is spicier, the tropical heat is more palpable, and the rhythmic lilt of patois and reggae music fills the air. This remains one of Costa Rica's least discovered and explored regions. More than half of the coastline here is still inaccessible except by boat or small plane. This inaccessibility has helped preserve large tracts of virgin lowland rainforest, which are now set aside as **Tortuguero National Park ★★** and **Barra del Colorado National Wildlife Refuge ★**. These two parks, on the coast's northern reaches, are among Costa Rica's most popular destinations for adventurers and ecotravelers. Of particular interest are the sea turtles that nest here. Farther south, **Cahuita National Park ★★** is another popular national park, located just off its namesake beach village. It was set up to preserve 200 hectares (494 acres) of coral reef, but its palm tree–lined white-sand beaches and gentle trails are stunning.

So remote was the Caribbean coast from Costa Rica's population centers in the Central Valley that it developed a culture all its own. The original inhabitants of the area included people of the Bribri, Cabécar, and Kéköldi tribes, and these groups maintain their cultures on indigenous reserves in the Talamanca Mountains. Until the 1870s, this area had few non-indigenous people. But when American businessman Minor Cooper Keith built the railroad to San José and began planting bananas, he brought in black laborers from Jamaica and other Caribbean islands to lay the track and work the plantations. These workers and their descendants established communities up and down the coast. Today, dreadlocked Rastafarians, reggae music, Creole cooking, and the English-based patois of this Afro-Caribbean culture give this region a quasi-Jamaican flavor, a striking contrast to the Spanish-derived Costa Rican culture.

The Caribbean coast has only one major city, **Limón,** a major commercial port and popular cruise ship port. The city itself is of

0   15 mi
0   15 km

NICARAGUA

SAN JOSÉ ★

The Caribbean Coast

PACIFIC OCEAN

Boca del Río Colorado
Barra del Colorado

Barra del Colorado Wildlife Refuge

NICARAGUA

Boca del Río Tortuguero
Tortuguero

Tortuguero Nat'l Park

Tortuguero

Tortuguero Canal

Cariari

Parismina

Reventazón

Guacimo

Carmen

Pacuare

Guapiles

CARIBBEAN SEA

Boca del Río Pacuare

Vol. Turrialba Nat'l Park
Siquirres

Matina

▲ Volcán Turrialba

32

Guayabo Nat'l Monument

Barbilla Nat'l Park

Playa Bonita

Moín
Limón

Vol. Irazú Nat'l Park

Central Range

Westfalia

Juan Vinas

Turrialba

Moravia

Chirripó Atlántico

36

Tapantí (Orosí) Nat'l Park

Playa Cahuita

Cahuita

Cahuita Nat'l Park

Playa Cocles Punta Uva

Ojo de Agua

Cerro de la Muerte

Telire

Puerto Viejo

Uatsi

Hitoy-Cerere Biological Res.

Manzanillo

Chirripó Nat'l Park

Talamanca Range

Talamanca Ind. Res.

Bratsi

Gandoca-Manzanillo NWR

2

▲ Cerro Chirripó

BriBri Ind. Res.

Sixaola

San Gerardo

La Amistad Int'l Park

PANAMA

Buenos Aires

Bahia
Ballena Marine Nat'l Park

The Caribbean coast has a unique weather pattern. Whereas you'll almost never get even a drop of rain in Guanacaste during Costa Rica's typical dry season (mid-Nov to Apr), on the Caribbean coast it can rain, at least a bit, almost any day of the year. However, the months of September and October, when torrential rains pound the rest of the country, most of the time are oddly two of the drier and more dependably sunny months along the Caribbean coast.

little interest to most visitors, who quickly head south to the coast's fab beaches, or north to the jungle canals of Tortuguero.

Over the years, the Caribbean coast has garnered a reputation as being a dangerous, drug-infested zone, rife with crime and danger. This is somewhat deserved because of several high-profile crimes in the area; petty theft is a major problem. And it's generally not safe to walk dark deserted beaches or streets here at night. Still, overall this reputation is exaggerated. The same crime and drug problems found here exist in San José and most of the more popular beach destinations on the Pacific coast. Use common sense and take normal precautions, and you should have no problems.

TORTUGUERO ★★

250km (155 miles) NE of San José; 79km (49 miles) N of Limón

Tortuguero is a tiny fishing village connected to the rest of mainland Costa Rica by a series of rivers and canals. This aquatic highway is lined with a mix of farmland and dense tropical rainforest that is home to howler and spider monkeys, three-toed sloths, toucans, and great green macaws. A trip through the canals surrounding Tortuguero is a lot like cruising the Amazon basin—on a much smaller scale.

"Tortuguero" comes from the Spanish name for the giant sea turtles (*tortugas*) that nest on the beaches of this region every year from early March to mid-October (prime season is July–Oct, and peak months are Aug–Sept). The chance to see this nesting attracts many people to this remote region, but just as many come to explore the intricate network of jungle canals that serve as the region's main transportation arteries.

Very important: More than 500cm (200 in.) of rain falls here annually, so you can expect a downpour at any time of the year. Most of the lodges will provide you with rain gear (including ponchos and rubber boots), but it can't hurt to carry your own.

Independent travel is not the norm here, although it's possible. Most travelers rely on their lodge for boat transportation through the canals and into town. At most of the lodges around Tortuguero, almost everything (bus rides to and from, boat trips through the canals, and even family-style meals) is done in groups.

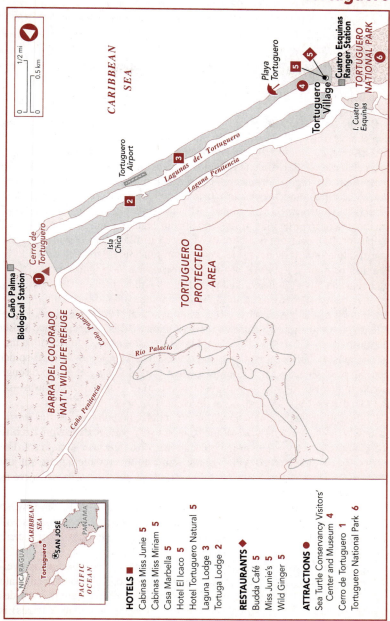

CARIBBEAN SEA

Cerro de Tortuguero

Tortuguero Airport

Lagunas del Tortuguero

Laguna Penitencia

Isla Chica

Playa Tortuguero

Cuatro Esquinas Ranger Station

Tortuguero Village

TORTUGUERO NATIONAL PARK

I. Cuatro Esquinas

TORTUGUERO PROTECTED AREA

Caño Palma Biological Station

BARRA DEL COLORADO NAT'L WILDLIFE REFUGE

Caño Palacio

Caño Penitencia

Río Palacio

1/2 mi
0.5 km

NICARAGUA
CARIBBEAN SEA
SAN JOSÉ
PANAMA
Tortuguero
PACIFIC OCEAN

HOTELS ■
Cabinas Miss Junie **5**
Cabinas Miss Miriam **5**
Casa Marbella **5**
Hotel El Icaco **5**
Hotel Tortuguero Natural **5**
Laguna Lodge **3**
Tortuga Lodge **2**

RESTAURANTS ◆
Budda Café **5**
Miss Junie's **5**
Wild Ginger **5**

ATTRACTIONS ●
Sea Turtle Conservancy Visitors'
  Center and Museum **4**
Cerro de Tortuguero **1**
Tortuguero National Park **6**

Essentials

GETTING THERE & DEPARTING   By Plane: Nature Air (www.natureair.com; 📞 **800/235-9272** in the U.S. and Canada, or 2299-6000 in Costa Rica) departs for the **Tortuguero** airstrip from Juan Santamaría International Airport in San José. Additional flights are sometimes added during high season. In addition, many local lodges operate charter flights as part of their package trips. Nature Air also offers a morning direct flight from the Tortuguero airstrip to La Fortuna/Arenal departing at 7:05am. Frequency of this flight varies seasonally.

Be sure to arrange with your hotel to pick you up at the airstrip. Otherwise you'll have to plead with one of the other hotel's boat captains to give you a lift, which they will usually do, either for free or for a few dollars.

By Car: It's not possible to drive to Tortuguero.

By Boat: Flying to Tortuguero is convenient if you don't have much time, but a boat trip through the canals and rivers of this region is often the highlight of a visit. However, be forewarned: Although this trip can be stunning and exciting, it can also be long, tiring, and uncomfortable. You'll first have to ride by bus or minivan from San José to Moín, Caño Blanco, or one of the other embarkation points; then it's 2 to 3 hours on a boat, usually with hard wooden benches or plastic seats. All of the more expensive lodges listed offer their own bus and boat transportation packages, which include the boat ride through the canals. However, if you're coming here on the cheap and plan to stay at one of the less expensive lodges or at a budget *cabina* in Tortuguero, you will have to arrange your own transportation. In this case, you have a few options.

The most popular, economical, and dependable way get to Tortuguero by bus and boat is via the small farming town of Cariari. To take this route, begin by catching the 9am or 10:30am direct bus to Cariari from the **Gran Terminal del Caribe,** on Calle Central, north of Avenida 13 (📞 **2222-0610**). The fare is C1,715. This bus will actually drop you off at the main bus terminal in Cariari, from which you'll have to walk 4 blocks east to a separate bus station, known locally as *la estación vieja,* or the old station. Look for a booth marked COOPETRACA or CLIC CLIC. At these booths, you can buy your bus ticket for La Pavona. The bus fare is around C1,300. Buses to La Pavona leave at 6am, 11am, and 3pm.

A boat or two will be waiting to meet the bus at the dock at the edge of the river at around 2:30pm (and again at 4pm). Check out the boats heading to Tortuguero, pick the one that looks most comfortable and safe, and then pay on board. The boat fare to Tortuguero is not regulated, and the price sometimes varies for foreigners. It can be as low as C1,600 each way, which is what locals pay. However, the boat captains often try to gouge tourists. Stand firm; you should not have to pay more than C3,000. You can buy your ticket for the boat at the cashier of the very prominent (and only) restaurant at La Pavona.

Return boats leave Tortuguero for La Pavona every morning at 6am and 11:30am, and 3pm, making return bus connections to Cariari.

Warning: Be careful if you decide to take this route. I've received reports of unscrupulous operators providing misinformation to tourists. Folks from a company called **Bananera** have offices at the Gran Terminal del Caribe and in Cariari, offering to sell you "packaged transportation" to Tortuguero. However, all they are doing is charging you extra to buy the individual tickets described above. Be especially careful if the folks selling you boat transportation aggressively steer you to a specific hotel, claim that your first choice is full, or insist that you must buy a package with them that includes the transportation, lodging, and guide services. If you have doubts or want to check on the current state of this route, check out the site **www.tortuguerovillage.com,** which has detailed directions about how to get to Tortuguero by a variety of routes.

VILLAGE LAYOUT   Tortuguero is one of the most remote locations in Costa Rica. With no roads into this area and no cars in the village, all transportation is by boat or foot. Most of the lodges are spread out over several kilometers to the north of Tortuguero Village on either side of the main canal; the small airstrip is at the north end of the beachside spit of land. At the far northern end of the main canal, you'll see the **Cerro de Tortuguero (Turtle Hill),** which, at some 120m (390 ft.), towers over the area. The hike to the top of this hill is a popular half-day tour and offers some good views of the Tortuguero canal and village, as well as the Caribbean Sea.

Tortuguero Village is a small collection of houses connected by footpaths. The village is spread out on a thin spit of land, bordered on one side by the Caribbean Sea and on the other by the main canal. At most points, it's less than 300m (984 ft.) wide.

If you stay at a hotel on the ocean side of the canal, you'll be able to walk in and explore the village at your leisure; if you're across the canal, you'll be dependent on the lodge's boat transportation. However, some of the lodges across the canal have their own network of jungle trails that might appeal to naturalists.

FAST FACTS   Tortuguero has no banks, ATMs, or currency-exchange houses, so be sure to bring sufficient cash in colones to cover any expenses. The local hotels and shops generally charge a commission to exchange dollars.

Where to Stay

Although the room rates below may appear high, keep in mind that they usually include round-trip transportation from San José (which amounts to approximately $100 per person), plus all meals, taxes, and usually some tours. When broken down into nightly room rates, most of the lodges are really charging only between $60 and $150 for a double room. *Note:* When I list package rates below, I have always listed the least expensive travel option, which is a bus and boat combination both in and out. All of the lodges also offer packages with the option of either one-way or round-trip air flights.

EXPENSIVE

Tortuga Lodge ★★★   This is the top hotel in Tortuguero: The accommodations, service, guides, and food are all a notch above the rest. You can get lunch cooked by a private chef and served on a table with a linen tablecloth on the beach, or a pre-turtle tour private beach barbecue. That said, the rooms do not have air-conditioning or televisions—this is still a remote ecolodge, after all. The large, canal-front deck is built on several levels stepping up from the water and merging with the large, main dining room and bar. The lodge has a small stone-lined pool that appears to blend into the canal just in front of it. There is also an extensive network of trails leading into thick rainforests. Costa Rica Expeditions, a leader in sustainable ecotourism in Costa Rica, owns and runs this property.

Tortuguero. www.tortugalodge.com. ℰ **2257-0766** for reservations in San José, or 2709-8136 at the lodge. 27 units. Starting at $588 per person for 3 days/2 nights. Rates are double occupancy, and include round-trip transportation from San José, 3 meals daily, and some tours. **Amenities:** Restaurant; bar; outdoor pool; free Wi-Fi.

MODERATE

Laguna Lodge ★★   This well-run lodge sits on the ocean side of the main canal, about a 20- to 30-minute walk north of Tortuguero Village. Rooms are housed in a series of one-story buildings—most of them raised off the ground, with wood walls and floors and rustic furnishings. All enjoy a shared veranda overlooking the gardens or pool area. There are, in fact, two separate pools, as well as open-air butterfly and frog gardens on-site, and the beach is just a couple hundred yards away. Creative mosaic tile works can be found embedded in walkways and on walls, and the main lobby and reception area is topped with a giant seashell. Meals are served buffet-style in a large, covered, open-air dining room overlooking Tortuguero's main canal.

Tortuguero. www.lagunatortuguero.com. ℰ **888/259-5615** in the U.S. and Canada, or 2272-4943 in Costa Rica. 100 units. $235 per person for 2 days/1 night; $298 per person for 3 days/2 nights. Rates are double occupancy and include round-trip transportation from San José, tours, taxes, and 3 meals daily. Children 5–11 pay half-price. Children 4 and under free. **Amenities:** Restaurant; 2 bars; 2 outdoor pools; free Wi-Fi.

INEXPENSIVE

Several basic *cabinas* in the village of Tortuguero offer budget lodgings for between $25 and $55 per person. **Cabinas Miss Junie** (ℰ **2709-8102**) and **Cabinas Miss Miriam** (ℰ **2709-8002**) are the traditional favorites, although in my opinion, the best of the batch are the **Hotel El Icaco** (www.hotelelicaco. com; ℰ **2709-8044**) and **Hotel Tortuguero Natural** (www.hoteltortuguero natural.com; ℰ **2767-0466**).

Casa Marbella ★   My pick for budgeteers and independent travelers, Casa Marbella is co-owned by Daryl Loth, one of the most respected local guides around. A simple B&B, it occupies a converted home right on the canal in the heart of the village. All rooms are spartan, but well kept. The best rooms have views of the water, and, of these, the second-floor superior is the best in class. There's a small covered canal-front patio where breakfast is served, and it's also a nice spot to relax, read, or bird-watch. Daryl either conducts or helps arrange a wide variety of tours and activities in the area.

Tortuguero, Limón. http://casamarbella.tripod.com. © **2709-8011** or 8833-0827. 11 units. $40–$45 double; $55–$65 superior. Rates include breakfast. No credit cards. **Amenities:** Free Wi-Fi.

Where to Eat

The town has a couple of simple *sodas* (diners); the best of these is **Miss Junie's** (© **2709-8102**).

Budda Café ★ INTERNATIONAL
This is the most popular independent restaurant in Tortuguero—an important distinction, because a vast majority of visitors stay at lodges where all their meals are included. Tables and chairs are spread around several open-air spaces, and the best seats are those on a deck jutting out over the water. Chinese lanterns provide lighting and you can hear the sound of water lapping against pilings below your feet. Pizzas, pastas, stuffed crepes, and a range of main dishes are offered. Start things off with some fresh ceviche, and save room for the excellent desserts.

On the main canal, next to the ICE building, Tortuguero Village. www.buddacafe.com. © **2709-8084.** Main courses C4,500–C13,000. Daily noon–9pm.

Wild Ginger ★ INTERNATIONAL
Located on the ocean side of the village, this small spot has boldly sought to make a mark on the local dining scene. Their culinary philosophy could be defined as "California meets Costa Rica." The menu features everything from seasonal lobster and mango ceviche to beef tenderloin in a coffee rub. I especially like the ginger-marinated chicken with a passion fruit sauce. Vegetarians and vegans will find plenty to choose from. For dessert, be sure to try their molten chocolate-espresso cake. A large dining room set on a simple, polished concrete floor opens out through huge doors onto a front patio with more chairs.

On the ocean-side path, north end of Tortuguero Village. www.wildgingercr.com. © **2709-8240.** Main courses C6.000–C13,000. Daily 12:30–3pm and 6–9pm.

Exploring Tortuguero National Park ★★

According to existing records, sea turtles have frequented Tortuguero National Park since at least 1592, largely due to its extreme isolation. Over the years, turtles were captured and their eggs were harvested by local settlers; by the 1950s, this practice became so widespread that turtles faced extinction. Regulations controlling this mini-industry were passed in 1963, and in 1970 Tortuguero National Park was established.

Today, four different species nest here: the green turtle, the hawksbill, the loggerhead, and the giant leatherback. The park's beaches are excellent places

Turtles in Tortuguero National Park.

to watch sea turtles nest, especially at night. As appealingly long and deserted as the beaches are, however, they're not good for swimming. The surf is usually rough, and the river mouths attract sharks that feed on the turtle hatchlings and many fish that live here.

Green turtles are the most common turtle found in Tortuguero, so you're more likely to see one of them than any other species if you visit during the prime nesting season from **July to mid-October** (Aug–Sept are peak months). **Loggerheads** are very rare, so don't be disappointed if you don't see one. The **giant leatherback** is perhaps the most spectacular sea turtle to watch laying eggs. The largest of all turtle species, the leatherback can grow to 2m (6½ ft.) long and weigh well over 1,000 pounds. It nests from late February to June, mainly in the southern part of the park.

You can explore the park's rainforest, either by foot or by boat, and look for some of the incredible varieties of wildlife that live here: **jaguars, anteaters, howler monkeys, collared** and **white-lipped peccaries,** some **350 species of birds,** and countless **butterflies,** among others. Some of the more colorful and common bird species you might see in this area include the rufescent and tiger herons, keel-billed toucan, northern jacana, red lored parrot, and ringed kingfisher. Boat tours are far and away the most popular way to visit this park, although there is one frequently very muddy trail that starts at the park entrance and runs for about 2km (1.25 miles) through the coastal rainforest and along the beach.

ENTRY POINT, FEES & REGULATIONS   The Tortuguero National Park entrance is at the south end of Tortuguero Village. The ranger station is inside a landlocked old patrol boat, and a small, informative open-air kiosk explains a bit about the park and its environs. Admission to the park is $15. However, most people visit Tortuguero as part of a package tour. Be sure to confirm whether the park entrance is included in the price. Moreover, only certain canals and trails leaving from the park station are actually within the park. Many hotels and private guides take their tours to a series of canals that border the park and are very similar in terms of flora and fauna, but don't require a park entrance. When the turtles are nesting, arrange a night tour in advance with either your hotel or one of the private guides working in town. These guided tours generally run between $10 and $20.

ORGANIZED TOURS   Most visitors come to Tortuguero on an organized tour. All of the lodges listed above, with the exception of the most inexpensive accommodations in Tortuguero Village, offer package tours that include various hikes and river tours; this is generally the best way to visit the area.

In addition, several San José–based tour companies offer budget 2-day/1-night excursions to Tortuguero, including transportation, all meals, and limited tours around the region. Prices for these trips range between $150 and $300 per person, and—depending on the price—guests are lodged either in one of the basic hotels in Tortuguero Village or one of the nicer lodges listed above. Reputable companies offering these excursions include **Exploradores Outdoors** ★ (www.exploradoresoutdoors.com; © **646/205-0828** in the U.S. and Canada, or 2222-6262 in Costa Rica), **Jungle Tom Safaris** (www.jungle tomsafaris.com; © **2221-7878**), and **Iguana Verde Tours** (www.iguanaverde tours.com; © **2231-6803**). Some operators offer 1-day trips on which tourists spend almost all their time coming and going, but that do allow for a quick tour of the canals and lunch in Tortuguero. They generally run between $100 and $120 per person. However, if you really want to experience Tortuguero, I recommend staying for at least 2 nights.

Alternatively, you could go with **Fran and Modesto Watson** ★ (www. tortuguerocanals.com; © **2226-0986**), who are pioneering guides in this region and operate their own boat. The couple offers a range of overnight and multiday packages to Tortuguero, with lodging options at most of the major lodges here.

BOAT CANAL TOURS   Aside from watching turtles nest, the thing to do in Tortuguero is tour the canals by boat, keeping your eye out for tropical birds and native wildlife. Most lodges can arrange a canal tour for you, but you can also arrange a tour through one of the operators in Tortuguero Village. I recommend **Daryl Loth** (http://casamarbella.tripod.com; ☎ **8833-0827**), who runs the Casa Marbella (see above) in the center of the village. I also recommend **Ernesto Castillo** (☎ **8343-9565**). Most guides charge $15 to $25 per person for a tour of the canals. If you travel through the park, you'll also have to pay the park entrance fee of $15 per person.

Exploring Tortuguero Village

The most popular attraction in town is the small **Sea Turtle Conservancy Visitors' Center and Museum ★** (www.conserveturtles.org; ☎ **2709-8091**). The museum has information and exhibits on a whole range of native flora and fauna, but its primary focus is on the life and natural history of the sea turtles. Most visits to the museum include a short informative video on the turtles. All the proceeds from the small gift shop go toward conservation and turtle protection. The museum is open daily from 10am to noon and 2 to 5pm. Admission is $2, but more generous donations are encouraged.

In the village, you can also rent dugout canoes, known in Costa Rica as *cayucos* or *pangas*. Be careful before renting and taking off in one of these;

A Tortuguero National Park boat tour.

they tend to be heavy, slow, and hard to maneuver, and you might be getting more than you bargained for.

You'll find a handful of souvenir shops spread around the center of the village. The **Paraíso Tropical Gift Shop** has the largest selection of gifts and souvenirs. But I prefer the **Jungle Shop,** which has a higher-end selection of wares and donates 10% of its profits to local schools.

CAHUITA ★, PUERTO VIEJO ★★ & THE BEACHES OF COSTA RICA'S SOUTHERN CARIBBEAN COAST ★★★

Cahuita: 200km (124 miles) E of San José; 42km (26 miles) S of Limón; 13km (8 miles) N of Puerto Viejo

A single two-lane highway heads south from the somewhat seedy port town of Limón. Along this stretch, you'll find some of Costa Rica's best beaches and a couple of quaint Caribbean towns that are both fun and unique. The towns and villages here trace their roots to Afro-Caribbean fishermen and laborers who settled in this region in the mid-1800s, and today the population is still primarily English-speaking blacks whose culture and language set them apart from other Costa Ricans.

Cahuita is a tiny town and the first beach destination heading south out of Limón. The few dirt and gravel streets here are host to a languid parade of pedestrian traffic, parted occasionally by a bicycle, car, or bus. People come to Cahuita for the miles of pristine beaches that stretch both north and south from town. The southern beaches, the forest behind them, and the coral reef offshore (one of just a handful in Costa Rica) are all part of **Cahuita National Park ★★**. Silt and pesticides washing down from nearby banana plantations have taken a heavy toll on the coral reefs, so don't expect the snorkeling to be world-class. But on a calm day, it can be pretty good, and the beaches are idyllic every day.

Puerto Viejo is the Caribbean coast's top destination. Even though Puerto Viejo is farther down the road from Cahuita, it's much, much more popular, with a livelier vibe and many more hotels and restaurants to choose from. Much of this is due to the scores of surfers who come to ride the town's famous and fearsome Salsa Brava wave, and only a slightly mellower beach break farther south at Playa Cocles. Nonsurfers can enjoy other excellent swimming beaches, plenty of active adventure options, nearby rainforest trails, and a collection of great local and international restaurants.

As you continue south on the coastal road from Puerto Viejo, you'll come to several of Costa Rica's best beaches. Soft white sands are fronted by the Caribbean Sea and backed by thick rainforest. **Playa Cocles** is a popular surf spot, with a powerful and dependable beach break. South of here, the isolated

Playa Chiquita is characterized by small pocket coves and calm pools formed by dead coral reefs raised slightly above sea level by the 1991 earthquake. Beyond this lies **Punta Uva,** a long curving swath of beach punctuated by its namesake point (*punta*), a rainforest-clad mound of land that looks vaguely like a bunch of grapes from the distance. The tiny village of Manzanillo is literally the end of the road. The shoreline heading south from Manzanillo, located inside the **Gandoca–Manzanillo Wildlife Refuge,** is especially beautiful, with a series of pocket coves and small beaches, with small islands and rocky outcroppings offshore. This park stretches all the way to the Panamanian border.

Essentials

GETTING THERE & DEPARTING   By Car: The Guápiles Highway (CR32) heads north out of San José on Calle 3 before turning east and passing close to Barva Volcano and through the rainforests of Braulio Carrillo National Park, en route to Limón. The drive takes about 2½ hours and is spectacularly beautiful in parts, especially when it's not raining or misty.

As you enter Limón, about 5 blocks from the busiest section of downtown, watch for a marked intersection, with signs pointing toward Cahuita and Puerto Viejo on your right, just before the railroad tracks. Take this road (CR36) south to Cahuita, passing the airstrip and the beach on your left as you leave Limón. Alternatively, there's a turnoff with signs for Sixaola and La Bomba several miles before Limón. This winding shortcut skirts the city and hits the coastal road (CR36) several miles south of town.

To reach Puerto Viejo, continue south from Cahuita on CR36 for another 16km (10 miles). Watch for a prominent and well-marked fork in the highway. The right-hand leg continues on to Bribri, Sixaola, and the Panamanian border. The left-hand leg (it actually appears to be a straight shot) takes you into Puerto Viejo on 5km (3 miles) of sporadically paved road.

A single two-lane road runs south out of Puerto Viejo and ends in Manzanillo. A few dirt roads lead off this paved but rutted road, both toward the beach and into the mountains.

By Bus: Mepe express buses (www.mepecr.com; ⓒ **2257-8129**) to Cahuita and Puerto Viejo leave San José daily at 6 and 10am, noon, and 2 and 4pm from the Caribbean bus terminal (Gran Terminal del Caribe) on Calle Central, Avenida 13. The trip's duration is 4 to 5 hours; the fare is C4,650 to Cahuita and C5,810 to Puerto Viejo. During peak periods, extra buses are sometimes added. Always ask if the bus is continuing on to **Manzanillo** (especially helpful if you're staying in a hotel south of town). If not, local buses to **Punta Uva** and **Manzanillo** leave Puerto Viejo about a half-dozen times throughout the day.

Interbus (www.interbusonline.com; ⓒ **2283-5573**) has a daily shuttle from San José to the Caribbean coast beaches. The fare is $50.

GETTING AROUND   Both Cahuita and Puerto Viejo are tiny villages and you'll have no problem navigating each. You can rent scooters and bicycles from a handful of roadside stands in either town.

Taxis are also fairly easy to come by. In Cahuita, for a taxi, call **Alejandro** (© **8875-3209**) or **Dino** (© **2755-0012**). In Puerto Viejo, you can try calling **Taxi PV** (© **2750-0439**).

LAYOUT   Cahuita has only about eight dirt streets. The highway runs parallel to the coast, with three main access roads running perpendicular. The northernmost of these access roads bypasses town and brings you to the northern end of Playa Negra. It's marked with signs for the Magellan Inn and other hotels up on this end. The second road in brings you to the southern end of Playa Negra, a half-mile closer to town. The third road is the principal entrance into town. The village's main street in town, which parallels the highway, dead-ends at the national park entrance (a footbridge over a small stream).

Buses drop off their passengers at a bus terminal at the back of a small strip mall on the main entrance road into town. If you come in on the bus and are staying at a lodge on Playa Negra, there will be cabs waiting. Alternatively, you can head out walking north on the street that runs between Coco's Bar and the small park. This road curves to the left and continues a mile or so out to Playa Negra.

As you reach Puerto Viejo, the road in from the highway runs parallel to Playa Negra, or Black Sand Beach (not to be confused with Playa Negra in Cahuita), for about 200m (650 ft.) before entering the town of Puerto Viejo, which has all of about 10 streets, some of them actually paved. The sea is on your left and forested hills on your right as you come into town.

As you drive south from town, the first beach you will hit is **Playa Cocles ★**, which is 2km (1¼ miles) from Puerto Viejo. A little farther, you'll find **Playa Chiquita ★**, which is 5km (3 miles) from Puerto Viejo, followed by **Punta Uva ★★** at 8.4km (5¼ miles) away, and **Manzanillo ★★**, some 13km (8 miles) away.

FAST FACTS   You'll find a couple of banks and ATMs, as well as pharmacies and Internet cafes in the heart of both Puerto Viejo and Cahuita.

Where to Stay in Cahuita

In addition to the places listed below, **El Encanto B&B** (www.elencanto cahuita.com; © **2755-0113**) is a lovely, well-run little B&B on the outskirts of the village. **Coral Hill Bungalows ★** (www.coralhillbungalows.com; © **2755-0479**) has three individual bungalows and a separate two-story house, in a lush garden setting, about a block or so inland from the beach at Playa Negra.

INEXPENSIVE

Magellan Inn ★   Terry Newton is the caring, second-generation owner/manager of this quaint and cozy bed-and-breakfast. Rooms are plain, and most are on the small size, but the lush gardens, ample covered veranda complete with a Persian rug, attentive service, and lovely pool built into the local coral make this a wonderful choice. Only about half of the rooms have air-conditioning, and it's definitely worth this small upgrade. Televisions with satellite reception are an additional upgrade. The hotel is located a few hundred yards north and inland from Playa Negra, so it helps to have a rental car when staying here.

At the far end of Playa Negra (about 2km/1¼ miles north of Cahuita), Cahuita. www.magellaninn.com. © **2755-0035** or 8858-1140. 6 units. $65–$75 double; $130 deluxe. Rates include full breakfast. **Amenities:** Bar; lounge; outdoor pool; free Wi-Fi.

Playa Negra Guesthouse ★★★ The best beachfront hotel in Cahuita (it's just across a dirt and sand lane from the waves), the Playa Negra Guesthouse has vibrant gardens; beautiful, well-kept rooms; and individual plantation-style cottages. A couple of these cottages come with full kitchens and are good for families or those planning an extended stay. No meals are served, but several restaurants are within easy walking distance. The center of Cahuita is a mile away.

On Playa Negra (about 1.5km/1 mile north of town), Cahuita. www.playanegra.cr. © **2755-0127.** 6 units. $75–$85 double room; $95 cottage; $160 2-bedroom cottage. **Amenities:** Outdoor pool; free Wi-Fi.

Where to Stay in Puerto Viejo

In addition to the places below, **Mother Dear Cottages ★★** (www.motherdearcr.com) offers two fully equipped, raised-stilt cottages right on the beach, in Playa Negra.

MODERATE

Banana Azul Guest House ★★ This boutique, adults-only hotel is located on the far northern end of Playa Negra, and sits just steps from the sand. A vast stretch of undeveloped beach stretches north from here all the way to Cahuita National Park. The rooms and suites are heavy on varnished wood and creative mosaic-tile accents; suites feature more space and usually a tub or Jacuzzi. Their Azul Beach Club is a big hit, offering up chaise lounges, reclined seating, shade trees, and umbrellas, as well as waiter service. The owners and staff are especially helpful, with a full-service tour desk and bicycles for rent.

Playa Negra Puerto Viejo, Limón. www.bananaazul.com. © **877/284-5116** in the U.S. and Canada, or 2750-2035 in Costa Rica. 14 units. $104–$165 double; $164–$207 suite or apt. Rates include full breakfast. Children 16 and under not allowed. **Amenities:** Restaurant; bar; outdoor pool; Jacuzzi; bike rentals; free Wi-Fi.

INEXPENSIVE

True budgeteers will find an abundance of basic hotels in downtown Puerto Viejo in addition to what's listed below. Of these, **Hotel Pura Vida** (www.hotel-puravida.com; © **2750-0002**) is a good pick in the heart of town, while

Rocking J's ★ (www.rockingjs.com; ✆ **2750-0665**) is a backpacker's fave on the southern outskirts of town.

Casa Verde Lodge ★★   You can't beat Casa Verde right in Puerto Viejo. It has grown from a simple, hostel-like option in the heart of the village to a beautiful mini-resort, with spa services, a massage hut, and a lovely, landscaped pool area. You can still choose everything from their shared-bathroom Heliconia and Bromelia units, to the larger individual cabins and rooms with private bathrooms. The gardens are lush and overflowing and the rooms and grounds are immaculately maintained. The owners, a charming Swiss-Tico couple, are committed to local environmental and educational causes.

Puerto Viejo, Limón. www.cabinascasaverde.com. ✆ **2750-0015.** 17 units, 9 with private bathroom. $60–$68 double with shared bathroom; $84 double with private bathroom. Rates include taxes. Discounts for cash payments. **Amenities:** Outdoor pool; free Wi-Fi.

Where to Stay South of Puerto Viejo

Rent a car if you plan to stay at one of these hotels; public transportation is sporadic and taxis aren't always available. If you arrive by bus, however, a rented bicycle or scooter might be all you need to get around.

EXPENSIVE

Tree House Lodge ★★★   These unique houses are easily the best accommodations to be had on the Caribbean coast. Although somewhat rustic and mostly wide-open, their artistic touches and distinctive architectural features make each unit memorable. The namesake Tree House is built on high stilts and reached via a suspension bridge, while the three-bedroom Beach Suite features a massive, domed bathroom lit by fanciful portholes and skylights of multicolored glass. Each of the four units has a full kitchen, but only two have air-conditioning. These folks also run an iguana conservation project (see below) and have been awarded "4 Leaves" in the CST Sustainable Tourism program.

Punta Uva, Puerto Viejo, Limón. www.costaricatreehouse.com. ✆ **2750-0706.** 4 units. $177–$345 double. Rates include taxes. No credit cards. **Amenities:** Free Wi-Fi.

MODERATE

Cariblue Bungalows ★★   This is a well-run, small resort with extensive grounds, overflowing gardens, cozy rooms, and two restaurants. You'll find a range of room options, from budget rooms with no air-conditioning to deluxe rooms, individual bungalows, and large suites. I favor the Superior Bungalows, which are individual wooden cabins raised off the ground a bit, and featuring a nice private balcony. The pool here is the largest in the region, with ample broad shallow areas for lazy lounging. Cariblue Bungalows is located directly in front of Playa Cocles, about 1.6km (1 mile) south of Puerto Viejo.

Playa Cocles, Puerto Viejo, Limón. www.cariblue.com. ✆ **2750-0035.** 29 units. $113–$147 double; $170–$249 suite. Rates include breakfast buffet. Rates slightly lower in off season. **Amenities:** 2 restaurants; bar/lounge; two outdoor pools; Jacuzzi; bike rentals; free Wi-Fi.

INEXPENSIVE

La Costa de Papito ★   Just a short way down the road from Cariblue (see above), this hotel is the loving work of New York transplant Eddie Ryan. The individual and duplex wooden bungalows feature artistically tiled bathrooms and cool, shady verandas. Most of the furnishings here are handmade from local lumber, often using whole tree limbs or trunks, or massive planks. There's no pool here, but the beach is just across the street. The hotel's **Qué Rico Papito** restaurant is excellent, and sometimes features live music.

Playa Cocles, Puerto Viejo, Limón. www.lacostadepapito.com. ✆ **2750-0704.** 13 units. $50–$103 double. Rates include breakfast. **Amenities:** Restaurant; bar; spa; watersports equipment rentals; bike rentals; free Wi-Fi.

Where to Eat

Coconut meat and milk figure into a lot of the regional cuisine here. Most nights, local women cook up pots of local specialties and sell them from the front porches of the two discos or from streetside stands; a full meal will cost you around $2 to $5.

IN CAHUITA

In addition to the places listed below, **El Girasol** (✆ 2755-1164) is a small, elegant, family-run joint serving up good Italian food, located on the main road into town. Another popular option for pizza and Italian food is **Pizzeria Cahuita** (✆ 2755-0179), located between the police station and Restaurant Edith, facing the ocean.

La French Riviera ★★ PIZZA/SANDWICHES/CREPES   This laid-back open-air bistro is owned and run by a friendly French couple. The crepes are light and authentic. They serve up a serious croque-monsieur, and I also really enjoy the burgers served on home-baked sesame seed buns with crisp, twice-fried potatoes. There's a small shop just off the open kitchen where you can stock up on cold-pressed coconut oil and other locally produced goods.

On the main road into town, across from the bus station. ✆ **2755-0050.** Main courses C3,000–C6,000; sandwiches C2,000–C3,000; pizzas C3,000–3,8000. No credit cards. Daily 10am–9pm.

Restaurant Edith ★ CREOLE/COSTA RICAN   Miss Edith Brown is a local legend and has been serving up traditional meals for decades out of this humble open-air restaurant. Today, she's helped by her daughters and other family members. I recommend the spicy *rondon* soup, which can come with fish or chicken, although everything on the menu is tasty. These folks even have a range of vegetarian and vegan dishes. Be forewarned, however, that service can be very slow at times. Ask about cooking classes.

By the police station, Cahuita. ✆ **2755-0248.** Main courses C3,000–C18,000. No credit cards. Tues–Sun 7:30am–10pm.

Sobre Las Olas ★★★ SEAFOOD/ITALIAN   This small oceanfront restaurant has the finest setting in the region, and one of the best settings of any restaurant in Costa Rica. The sea is just steps away, and there's a stunning view down the coastline. The Italian owners specialize in preparing the freshest local seafood in a variety of ways, touching on their home-country heritage and Caribbean seasonings in equal measure. After eating, you can move just slightly and commandeer one of the hammocks strung between the trees.

> ### That Run-Down Feeling
>
> *Rondon* soup is a spicy coconut milk–based soup or stew made with anything the cook can "run down"—it usually includes local tubers (potato, sweet potato, or yuca), other vegetables (carrots or corn), and often some seafood. Be sure to try this authentic taste of the Caribbean.

Just north of town on the road to Playa Negra. ℂ **2755-0109.** Main courses C5,000–C10,500. Wed–Mon noon–10pm.

IN PUERTO VIEJO & SOUTH OF PUERTO VIEJO

To really sample the local cuisine, you need to look up a few local women. Ask around for **Miss Dolly, Miss Sam, Miss Isma,** and **Miss Irma,** who all dish out sit-down meals in their modest little *sodas.* In addition to locally seasoned fish and chicken served with rice and beans, these joints are usually a great place to find *pan bon* (a local sweet, dark bread), ginger cakes, *patys* (meat-filled turnovers), and *rondon* (see "That Run-Down Feeling," above).

In addition to the restaurants listed below, **Cabinas Selvin** (ℂ **2750-0664**) at Punta Uva is an excellent option for local cuisine and fresh seafood, while **Pita Bonita** (ℂ **2756-8173**) serves up wonderful Middle Eastern cuisine at an open-air spot between Playa Chiquita and Punta Uva. The intimate **El Refugio Grill** ★★ (ℂ **2759-9007**) is an Argentine-owned restaurant that offers grilled steaks, sausages, and seafood in a romantic rainforest setting.

Finally, near the end of the line, where the road first hits the beach at Manzanillo, **Cool & Calm Café** (ℂ **2750-3151**) is winning faithful fans with its local cuisine and friendly atmosphere.

EXPENSIVE

La Pecora Nera ★★★ ITALIAN   Whenever I'm asked to name my favorite restaurant in Costa Rica, I always answer, "La Pecora Nera." Yes, it's that good. Chef/owner Ilario Gionnoni is a master and a marvel of perpetual motion. He is constantly innovating, raises his own chickens and pigs, and grows as much of his fresh fruit, vegetables, and herbs as he can. There's a long and varied menu, but I always just ask Ilario what he recommends that day. The large, multilevel, open-air dining room is dimly lit and romantic, with heavy wooden tables spread widely for privacy. It sits under a massive thatched roof that seems to jut off in every direction.

50m (164 ft.) inland from a well-marked turnoff on the main road south just beyond the soccer field in Cocles. ℂ **2750-0490.** Reservations recommended. Main courses C6,000–C17,500. Tues–Sun 5:30–10pm.

MODERATE

Jungle Love Café ★★ INTERNATIONAL An intimate, family-run restaurant, Jungle Love serves up primo wood-oven pizzas, creative pasta dishes, healthy salads, and a mix of nightly specials. The owner's signature dish is a family pasta recipe with carrots, leeks, and a spicy brandy-cream sauce, served here with fresh shrimp. The Tokyo Tuna adds a local twist to the traditional, Asian-style seared tuna by adding fresh tamarind juice to the marinade. Save room for the desserts, which are whipped up daily. This place fills up fast, and reservations are definitely recommended.

Playa Chiquita. www.junglelovecafe.com. ℂ **2750-0162.** Main courses C5,500–C8,000. Tues–Sun 5–9:30pm.

Stashu's Con-Fusion ★★★ INTERNATIONAL Stashu is a local legend, and his cooking and restaurant have been a Puerto Viejo mainstay for years, serving up a mix of world fusion cuisine. The menu features fresh fish, seafood, and vegetarian entrees in spicy curries or with Thai- or Mexican-tinged sauces. One of the more popular recurring blackboard specials is a macadamia-crusted fish filet with a white-wine-and-white-chocolate sauce. A large open-air space under an exposed zinc roof, Stashu's is filled with a mix of creative artwork and sculptures. At night, the mood is romantic, with lighting provided by a series of painted paper lanterns.

On the main road just south of downtown, about 1 block beyond Stanford's. ℂ **2750-0530.** Main courses C4,000–C18,000. Thurs–Tues 5–10pm.

INEXPENSIVE

Bread & Chocolate ★★ BREAKFAST/AMERICAN This is a top spot for breakfast, lunch, coffee break—or chocolate fix. You can get a range of typical breakfast plates, as well as sandwiches, salads, and various baked goods. As the restaurant's name might suggest, the bread (biscuits, bagels, and such) is baked fresh. And the chocolate is served up as a drink, in a range of truffles, and in several fabulous brownie flavors, including my favorite, the mint-chocolate brownie. The open-air dining room is small, with just a handful of wooden tables and chairs, and it fills up fast. It's not uncommon to have to wait a little on weekends and during high season.

½ block south of Café Viejo, downtown Puerto Viejo. ℂ **2750-0723.** Main courses C3,200–C4,500. No credit cards. Tues–Sat 6:30am–6:30pm; Sun 6:30am–2:30pm.

Exploring Costa Rica's Southern Caribbean Coast

CAHUITA NATIONAL PARK ★★

This little gem of a national park sits at the southern edge of Cahuita town. Although the pristine white-sand beach, with its picture-perfect line of coconut palms and lush coastal forest backing it, is the main draw, the park was actually created to preserve the 240-hectare (595-acre) **coral reef** that lies just

The beach in Cahuita National Park.

offshore. The reef contains 35 species of coral and provides a haven for hundreds of brightly colored tropical fish. You can walk on the beach itself or follow the trail that runs through the forest just behind the beach to check out the reef. The trail behind the beach is great for bird-watching, and if you're lucky, you might see some monkeys or a sloth. This trail stretches a little more than 9km (5.6 miles) to the southern end of the park at **Puerto Vargas** (© **2755-0302**), where you'll find a beautiful white-sand beach. The best section of reef is off the point at Punta Cahuita, and you can snorkel here. If you don't dawdle, the 3.8km (2.35-mile) hike to Punta Cahuita should take a little over an hour each way—but I'd allow plenty of extra time to marvel at the flora and fauna and to take a dip or two in the sea. Bring plenty of mosquito repellent!

Although you can snorkel from the shore at Punta Cahuita, it's best to have a boat take you out to the nicest coral heads just offshore. A 3-hour **snorkel trip** costs between $25 and $35 per person, with equipment. You can arrange one with any of the local tour companies listed below. *Note:* These trips are best taken when the seas are calm—for safety's sake, visibility, and comfort.

ENTRY POINTS, FEES & REGULATIONS   The **in-town park entrance** is just over a footbridge at the end of the village's main street. It has restroom facilities, changing rooms, and storage lockers. This is the best place to enter if you just want to spend the day on the beach and maybe take a little hike in the bordering forest.

> ### Damaged & Endangered
>
> While patches of living, vibrant reef survive off Costa Rica's Caribbean coast, much of it has been killed off, or is severely threatened by over-fishing, pollution, rain, and mud runoff during the rainy season. Much of the damage can be traced to the massive banana plantations that line this coastline, which have had a direct role in increasing the amount of muddy runoff and have dumped tons of plastic and pesticides into the fragile, inshore reef systems.

The alternate park entrance is at the southern end of the park in **Puerto Vargas.** This is where you should come if you don't feel up to hiking a couple of hours to reach the good snorkeling spots. The road to Puerto Vargas is approximately 5km (3 miles) south of Cahuita on the left.

Officially, **admission** is $5 per person per day, but this is collected only at the Puerto Vargas entrance. You can enter the park from the town of Cahuita for free or with a voluntary contribution. The park is open from dawn to dusk for day visitors.

EXPLORING CAHUITA OUTSIDE THE PARK

Outside the park, the best place for swimming is **Playa Negra.** The stretch right in front of the Playa Negra Guesthouse (p. 252) is my favorite spot. The waves here are often good for bodysurfing, boogie boarding, or surfing. If you want to rent a board or try a surf lesson, check in with Rennie at **Willie's Tours** (see below).

Cahuita has plenty of options for organized adventure trips or tours. I recommend **Cahuita Tours** (www.cahuitatours.com; ✆ **2755-0101**) or **Willie's Tours** (www.williestourscostarica.com; ✆ **2755-1024** or 8917-6982). Both are located along Cahuita's main road and offer a choice of tours ranging from snorkel outings, to rainforest hikes, to visits to nearby indigenous reserves, as well as multiday trips to Tortuguero and to Bocas del Toro, Panama.

Exploring Puerto Viejo & the Beaches South
THE BEACHES & SURF

Surfing was originally the main draw here, but increasing numbers of folks are coming for the miles of beautiful and uncrowded **beaches ★★★**, acres of lush rainforest, and laid-back atmosphere. If you aren't a surfer, the same activities that prevail in any quiet beach town are the norm here—sunbathe, go for a walk on the beach, read a book, or take a nap. If you have more energy, there's a host of tours and hiking options, or you can rent a bicycle or a horse.

Just offshore from the tiny village park is a shallow reef where powerful, storm-generated waves sometimes reach 6m (20 ft.). **Salsa Brava ★★★**, as it's known, is the prime surf break on the Caribbean coast. Even when the waves are small, this spot is recommended only for very experienced surfers because of the danger of the reef. Other popular beach breaks are south of town on Playa Cocles. Several operators and makeshift roadside stands offer bicycles, scooters, boogie boards, surfboards, and snorkel gear for rent. Shop around to compare prices and the quality of the equipment before settling on any particular one.

For swimming and sunbathing, locals like to hang out on the small patches of sand in front of the **Lazy Mon @ Stanford's** and **Johnny's Place** (see below for both). Small, protected tide pools are in front of each of these bars for cooling off. The Lazy Mon has several hammocks, and this is where you're likely to stumble upon a pickup beach volleyball or soccer match.

If you want a more open patch of sand and sea, you can head north out of the village to **Playa Negra,** along the road into town, or, better yet, to the beaches south of town, which are some of the most picturesque beaches in the country. For all intents and purposes, this string of beaches is an extension of Puerto Viejo, and all of the tours, activities, and attractions mentioned above can be enjoyed by those staying here.

Leaving the village, the first beach you'll come to is **Playa Cocles ★★**, also known as Beach Break. This long, white-sand beach is popular with surfers. As you head south, the coastline is broken up by coral outcroppings and tide pools in an area generally called **Playa Chiquita ★★**. Beyond Playa Chiquita lies **Punta Uva ★★★**, or "Grape Point." Characterized by a large, rainforest-covered bit of land jutting out into the sea, the beach just north of Punta Uva is a lovely, gently curving stretch of white sand that is mostly protected and, hence, excellent for swimming. At the end of the line, you'll reach **Manzanillo ★★★**, the last beach before the Gandoca-Manzanillo Wildlife Refuge (see below). Manzanillo is a long, straight stretch of white sand backed by coconut palms and protected by a coral reef that makes this a top spot for swimming and snorkeling. There's a cute, tiny village here as well.

GANDOCA–MANZANILLO WILDLIFE REFUGE ★★

The Gandoca–Manzanillo Wildlife Refuge encompasses the small village of Manzanillo and extends all the way to the Panamanian border. Manatees, crocodiles, and more than 350 species of birds live within the boundaries of the reserve. The reserve also includes the coral reef offshore—when the seas are calm, this is the best **snorkeling** and **diving** spot on this entire coast. Four species of **sea turtles** nest on one 9km (5½-mile) stretch of beach within the reserve between March and July. Three species of dolphins also inhabit and frolic in the waters just off Manzanillo, home to the Atlantic spotted, bottle-nose, and rare tucuxi dolphins. This latter species favors the brackish estuary waters, but has actually been observed mating with local bottlenose dolphins. Many local operators offer boat trips out to spot them.

If you want to explore the refuge, you can easily find the single, well-maintained trail by walking along the beach just south of town until you have to wade across a small river. On the other side, you'll pick up the trailhead. Otherwise, you can ask around the village for local guides, contact either **Abel Bustamante** (www.manzanillo-caribe.com; ✆ **2759-9043**) or **Omar Cook** (www.costa-rica-manzanillo.com; ✆ **2759-9143**).

CULTURAL & ADVENTURE TOURS   The **Asociación Talamanqueña de Ecoturismo y Conservación ★★** (ATEC; Talamancan Association of Ecotourism and Conservation; www.ateccr.org; ✆ **2750-0398**) is a local organization concerned with preserving the environment and cultural heritage of this area and promoting ecologically sound development. (If you plan to stay in Puerto Viejo for an extended period of time and would like to contribute to the community, ask about volunteering.) In addition to functioning as the local information center, Internet cafe, and traveler's hub, ATEC runs a little shop that sells T-shirts, maps, posters, and books.

ATEC also offers quite a few tours, including **half-day walks** that focus on nature and either the local Afro-Caribbean culture or the indigenous Bribri culture. These walks pass through farms and forests, and along the way you'll learn about local history, customs, medicinal plants, and Indian mythology, and have an opportunity to see sloths, monkeys, iguanas, keel-billed toucans, and other wildlife. A range of different walks lead through the nearby **Bribri Indians' Kéköldi Reserve,** as well as more strenuous hikes through the primary rainforest. **Bird walks** and **night walks** will help you spot more of the area wildlife; there are even overnight treks. The local guides have a wealth of information and make a hike through the forest a truly educational experience. ATEC can arrange snorkeling trips to the nearby coral reefs, as well as snorkeling and fishing trips in dugout canoes, and everything from surf lessons to dance classes. ATEC can also help you arrange overnight and multiday **camping trips** into the Talamanca Mountains and through neighboring indigenous reserves, as well as trips to Tortuguero and even a 7- to 10-day transcontinental trek to the Pacific coast. Half-day tours (and night walks) are $25 to $60, and full-day tours run between $75 and $120. Some tours require minimum groups of three or four people and several days' advance notice. The ATEC office is open Monday through Saturday from 8am to 8pm and Sunday from 11am to 7 pm.

Local tour operators **Exploradores Outdoors** ★★ (www.exploradoresoutdoors.com; ✆ **2750-2020**), **Gecko Trail Adventures** ★★ (www.geckotrail.com; ✆ **2756-8412**), and **Terraventuras** ★ (www.terraventuras.com; ✆ **2750-0750**) all offer a host of half- and full-day adventure tours into the jungle or sea for $40 and $280 per person. One especially popular tour is Terraventuras' zip-line canopy tour, which features 22 treetop platforms, a large harnessed swing, and a rappel.

HORSEBACK RIDING   Located between Punta Uva and Manzanillo, the folks at **Caribe Horse Riding Club** ★★(www.caribehorse.com; ✆ **8705-4250**) run one of the better and more interesting horseback-riding operations in the country. They offer a range of rides, from short 90-minute beach jaunts to full-day excursions into the mountains and nearby reserves. My favorite is the Hippo Camp Tour, which features a human and equine wade in the warm waters of the Caribbean Sea. Rates range from $50 to $160 per person, depending upon the tour chosen.

(ORGANIC) PEAS & LOVE   Inside the Gandoca–Manzanillo Wildlife Refuge is the **Punta Mona Center For Sustainable Living & Education** ★ (www.puntamona.org). With organic permaculture gardens and a distinctly alternative vibe, this place is open for day visits, overnight stays, yoga training, and work-exchange and educational programs.

SCUBA DIVING   Scuba divers can check in with **Reef Runners Dive Shop** (www.reefrunnerdivers.com; ✆ **2750-0480**). These folks frequent a variety of dive sites between Punta Uva and Manzanillo, and if you're lucky the seas will be calm and the visibility good—although throughout most of the year, it can be a bit rough and murky here. Reef Runners has an office in downtown Puerto Viejo. Rates run from $80 to $110 for a two-tank boat dive.

SWEET STUFF Another great educational tour is the 2-hour **Caribeans Chocolate Tour** ★★ (www.caribeanschocolate.com; ✆ **8836-8930**) through a working organic cacao plantation and chocolate production facility. The tour shows you the whole process of growing, harvesting, and processing cacao and, of course, there's a tasting at the end. The tour runs Monday at 10am, Tuesday and Thursday at 10am and 2pm, and Friday and Saturday at 2pm. It costs $30 per person. When you get around to the tasting, organic wine pairings are also available.

ESPECIALLY FOR KIDS

Several wildlife rescue centers and animal preservation centers operate in the area. The **Jaguar Refuge Center** ★★ (www.jaguarrescue.com; ✆ **2750-0710**) is the most extensive of the batch. This small center is located in Playa Chiquita and features a broad assortment of local fauna, including monkeys, sloths, snakes, caimans, turtles, birds, and more. These folks do great educational and rehabilitative work. I have mixed feelings about the human-monkey interactions, but most guests are quite thrilled with the opportunity to enter an enclosure and have direct contact. Note that, despite the name, this place has never housed a jaguar. Guided tours are offered Monday through Saturday at 9:30 and 11:30am. The cost is $18 per person, free for children 9 and under. Private tours can be arranged with advance notice.

Bird-watchers and sloth lovers should head 9km (5½ miles) north of Cahuita to the **Sloth Sanctuary of Costa Rica** ★★ (www.slothsanctuary.com; ✆ **2750-0775**). Its signature tour includes an informative visit to the sloth rehabilitation project and learning center, as well as the opportunity to hike some of the trails at your leisure. More than 330 species of birds have been spotted here. You'll get an up-close look at a range of rescued wild sloths, both adults and babies, as well as several bred in captivity. Open Tuesday through Sunday, tours leave every hour beginning at 8am, with the last tour of the day leaving at 2pm. The price of the standard tour is $30 per person, $15 for children 5 to 11. It's best to make reservations in advance.

Also down in Playa Chiquita, at the Tree House Lodge (see above), is the **Green Iguana Conservation Tour** (www.iguanaverde.com; ✆ **2750-0706**). This educational tour focuses on the life cycle, habits, and current situation of this endangered reptile. The tour features a walk around a massive natural enclosure, as well as a video presentation. The cost is $15. Regular tours are offered Tuesday and Thursday at 10am. Additional tours may be arranged by appointment.

Shopping

Cahuita and Puerto Viejo attract a lot of local and international bohemians, who seem to survive solely on the sale of handmade jewelry, painted ceramic trinkets (mainly pipes and cigarette-lighter holders), and imported Indonesian textiles. You'll sometimes find a score or so of them at makeshift stands set up by Puerto Viejo's *parquecito* (little park), which comprises a few wooden benches in front of the sea between Soda Tamara and the Lazy Mon.

In addition to the makeshift outdoor stands, a host of well-stocked gift and crafts shops are spread around town. **Luluberlu ★** (*ℂ* **2750-0394**), located inland across from Cabinas Guaraná, features locally produced craftwork, including shell mobiles and mirrors with mosaic-inlaid frames, as well as imports from Thailand and India.

Tip: My favorite purchase here is locally produced chocolate, which is made by several local outfits, and can be found for sale at many gift shops and restaurants around town.

Nightlife & Entertainment

Cahuita is a rather quiet little town. **Coco's Bar ★**, a classic Caribbean watering hole at the main crossroads in town, has traditionally been the place to spend your nights (or days, for that matter) if you like cold beer and very loud reggae and soca music. Toward the park entrance, the **National Park Restaurant** has a popular bar, with loud music and dancing on most nights during the high season and on weekends during the off season. Out toward Playa Negra, the **Reggae Bar ★** has a convivial vibe, blasting thumping tropical tunes most nights.

Puerto Viejo is much more happening. For a large party scene and dancing, **Johnny's Place ★★** (*ℂ* **2750-2000**), near the Rural Guard station, is the place to be. The action spills out from the small dance floor and onto the beach most nights, where you'll find candlelit tables set near the water's edge. Another popular waterfront spot is the **Lazy Mon @ Stanford's ★** (www.thelazymon.com; *ℂ* **2750-2116**), with a bit more of a sports bar vibe to it. It's got a pool table, dartboard, and Xbox. The bar can get rocking at night, with regular live bands or DJs. Old-timers like me, who still remember reggae nights at the long-lost Bambu Bar, are finding solace Wednesday, Friday, and Sunday nights at the oceanfront **Salsa Brava ★★** (*ℂ* **2750-0241**).

Right in the center of town, it's hard to miss **Hot Rocks** (*ℂ* **8708-3183**), with its massive stage, loud tunes, packed bar, and pool and foosball tables. Another option is the **Mango Sunset Bar ★★** (no phone), near the water, beside the bus station, with either live music or a DJ most nights. For a more sophisticated ambience, try the oceanfront **Koki Beach ★** (www.kokibeach.com; *ℂ* **2250-0902**).

An Isolated Ecolodge in the Talamanca Mountains

Selva Bananito Lodge ★★   This remote ecolodge is set high on the slopes of rainforest-covered mountains. Selva Bananito provides many of the same types of experiences as those offered at ecolodges down on the Osa Peninsula, while it combines well with stops in Tortuguero and Caribbean beach towns. The simple, yet spacious, wood cabins have solar hot-water showers and large wraparound verandas or balconies. All have stunning views of the surrounding forests. There's great hiking and horseback riding, as well as tree-climbing, waterfall rappelling, and zip-line tours, all on-site. Meals are served family-style in the large open-air main lodge building. The owners are dedicated conservationists; the property was awarded "5 Leaves" in the CST Sustainable Tourism program. You'll need a four-wheel drive vehicle to reach the lodge itself, although most leave their rental cars in Bananito and let the lodge drive them the final bit. You can also arrange to be picked up in San José.

Bananito. www.selvabananito.com. ✆ **2253-8118.** 11 units. $128–$144 double. Rates include 3 meals daily, 1 tour daily, and all taxes. **Amenities:** Restaurant; free Wi-Fi.

PLANNING YOUR TRIP

Costa Rica is no longer the next new thing. Neither is it old hat. As Costa Rica has matured as a tourist destination, things have gotten easier and easier for international travelers. That said, most travelers—even experienced travelers and repeat visitors—will want to do some serious planning. This chapter provides a variety of planning tools, including information on how to get there, how to get around, and a "Fast Facts" section for on-the-ground resources and handy info.

GETTING THERE
By Plane

It takes between 3 and 7 hours to fly to Costa Rica from most U.S. cities, the origin of most direct and connecting flights. Most international flights still land in San José's **Juan Santamaría International Airport** (http://fly2sanjose.com; ✆ **2437-2626** for 24-hr. airport information; airport code SJO). However, more and more direct international flights are touching down in Liberia's **Daniel Oduber International Airport** (✆ **2668-1010;** airport code LIR).

Liberia is the gateway to the beaches of the Guanacaste region and the Nicoya Peninsula. A direct flight here eliminates the need for a separate commuter flight in a small aircraft, or roughly 5 hours in a car or bus. If you're planning to spend all, or most, of your vacation time in this region, you'll want to fly in and out of Liberia. However, San José is a much more convenient gateway if you're planning to head to Manuel Antonio, the Central Pacific coast, the Caribbean coast, or the southern zone.

Numerous airlines fly into Costa Rica. Be warned that the smaller Latin American carriers tend to make several stops (sometimes unscheduled) en route to San José, thus increasing flying time.

From North America, **Air Canada, Alaska Airlines, American Airlines, Delta, Frontier, Grupo Taca, JetBlue, Southwest Airlines, Spirit Air,** and **United** all have regular direct flights to Costa Rica.

From Europe, **Iberia** is the only airline with regular routes to San José, some direct and others with one connection. Alternatively, you can fly to any major U.S. hub city and make connections to one of the airlines mentioned above.

By Bus

Bus service runs regularly from Panama City, Panama, and Managua, Nicaragua. If at all possible, it's worth the splurge for a deluxe or express bus. In terms of travel time and convenience, it's always better to get a direct bus rather than one that stops along the way—and you've got a better chance of getting a working restroom in a direct/express or deluxe bus. Some even show movies.

Several bus lines with regular daily departures connect the major capital cities of Central America. Call **King Quality** (© **2258-8834**), **Transnica** (www.transnica.com; © **2223-4242**), or **Tica Bus Company** (www.tica-

A Costa Rican oxcart.

bus.com; © **2296-9788**) for further information. All of these lines service Costa Rica directly from Managua, with connections to the other principal cities of Central America. Tica Bus also has service between Costa Rica and Panama. None of them will reserve a seat by telephone, and schedules change frequently according to season and demand, so buy your ticket in advance— several days in advance, if you plan to travel on weekends or holidays. From Managua, it's 11 hours and 450km (280 miles) to San José, and the one-way fare is around $30 to $50. From Panama City, it's a 20-hour, 900km (560-mile) trip. The one-way fare is around $40 to $60.

Whenever you're traveling by bus through Central America, try to keep a watchful eye on your belongings, especially at rest and border stops, whether they're in an overhead bin or stored below decks in a luggage compartment.

GETTING AROUND

By Plane

Flying is one of the best ways to get around Costa Rica. Because the country is quite small, flights are short and not too expensive. Sansa and Nature Air

THE BEST websites ABOUT COSTA RICA

- **The Tico Times** (www.ticotimes.net): The English-language *Tico Times* makes it easy for English speakers to see what's happening in Costa Rica. Now entirely online, it offers a range of local and regional news, and travel reviews, as well as an extensive classified section. There's also a link to current currency-exchange rates.

- **Latin American Network Information Center** (http://lanic.utexas.edu/la/ca/cr): This site houses a vast collection of information about Costa Rica, and is hands-down the best one-stop shop for browsing, with helpful links to a diverse range of tourism and general information sites.

- **The U.S. Embassy in Costa Rica** (http://costarica.usembassy.gov): The official site of the U.S. Embassy in Costa Rica has a good base of information and regular updates of concern to U.S. citizens abroad, and about Costa Rica in general.

- **CostaRicaLiving E-Board** (http://costaricaliving.proboards.com): This is an information clearinghouse site put together by the folks at Costa Rica Living newsgroup. The site is chock-full of useful information, suggestions, reviews, and tips. If you want more information, feel free to join the newsgroup. The active newsgroup deals with a wide range of issues, and its membership includes many long-time residents and bona fide experts.

are the country's domestic airlines. In the high season (late Nov to late Apr), be sure to book reservations well in advance.

Sansa (www.flysansa.com; © **877/767-2672** in the U.S. and Canada, or 2290-4100 in Costa Rica) operates from a private terminal at San José's **Juan Santamaría International Airport** (see above).

Nature Air (www.natureair.com; © **800/235-9272** in the U.S. and Canada, or 2299-6000 in Costa Rica) operates from the main terminal at the **Juan Santamaría International Airport** in San José (see above).

By Car

Renting a car in Costa Rica is no idle proposition. The roads are riddled with potholes, most rural intersections are unmarked, and, for some reason, sitting behind the wheel of a car seems to turn peaceful Ticos into homicidal maniacs. But unless you want to see the country from the window of a bus or pay exorbitant amounts for private transfers, renting a car might be your best option for independent exploring.

Be forewarned, however: Although rental cars no longer bear special license plates, they are still readily identifiable to thieves and are frequently targeted. (Nothing is ever safe in a car in Costa Rica, although parking in guarded parking lots helps.) Transit police also seem to target tourists; never pay money directly to a police officer who stops you for any traffic violation.

Before driving off with a rental car, be sure that you inspect the exterior and point out to the rental-company representative every tiny scratch, dent, tear, or any other damage. It's a common practice with many Costa Rican car-rental companies to claim that you owe payment for minor dings and dents that the company finds when you return the car. Also, if you get into an accident, be sure that the rental company doesn't try to bill you for a higher amount than the deductible on your rental contract.

These caveats aren't meant to scare you off from driving in Costa Rica. Tens of thousands of tourists rent cars here every year, and the large majority of them encounter no problems. Just keep your wits about you and guard against car theft, and you'll do fine. Also, keep in mind that four-wheel-drives are particularly useful in the rainy season (May to mid-Nov) and for navigating the poorly paved roads year-round.

Among the major international agencies operating in Costa Rica are **Alamo, Avis, Budget, Hertz, National, Payless,** and **Thrifty.**

GASOLINE (PETROL) Gasoline is sold as "regular" and "super." Both are unleaded; super is just higher octane. Diesel is available at almost every gas station, as well. Most rental cars run on super, but always ask your rental agent what type of gas your car takes. When going off to remote places, try to leave with a full tank of gas because gas stations can be hard to find. If you need to gas up in a small town, you can sometimes get gasoline from enterprising families who sell it by the liter from their houses. Look for hand-lettered signs that say GASOLINA. At press time, a liter of super cost C536, or roughly $1.02 per liter, and $3.86 per gallon.

ROAD CONDITIONS The awful road conditions throughout Costa Rica are legendary, and deservedly so. Despite constant promises to fix the problem and sporadic repair attempts, the hot sun, hard rain, and rampant corruption outpace any progress made toward improving the condition of roads. Even paved roads are often badly potholed, so stay alert. Conditions get especially tricky during the rainy season, when heavy rains and runoff can destroy a stretch of pavement in the blink of an eye.

Route numbers are somewhat sporadically and arbitrarily used. You'll also find frequent signs listing the number of kilometers to various towns or cities. Still, your best bets for on-road directions are billboards and advertisements for hotels. It's always a good idea to know the names of a few hotels at your destination, just in case your specific hotel hasn't put up any billboards or signs.

Most car-rental agencies now offer the opportunity to rent out GPS units along with your car rental. Rates run between $8 and $15 per day. If you have your own GPS unit, several maps to Costa Rica are available. While you still can't simply enter a street address, most commercial GPS maps of Costa Rica feature hundreds of prominent points of interest (POI), and you should be able to plug in a POI close to your destination.

RENTER'S INSURANCE   Third Party Waiver, or Supplemental Liability Insurance (SLI) is mandatory in Costa Rica, regardless of your home policy or credit card coverage. Supplemental collision and damage insurance is optional. Even if you hold **your own car-insurance policy** at home, coverage doesn't always extend abroad. Be sure to find out whether you'll be covered in Costa Rica, whether your policy extends to all persons who will be driving the rental car, how much liability is covered in case an outside party is injured in an accident, and whether the type of vehicle you are renting is included under your contract.

DRIVING RULES   A current foreign driver's license is valid for the first 3 months you are in Costa Rica. Seat belts are required for the driver and front-seat passengers. Motorcyclists must wear helmets. Highway police use radar, so keep to the speed limit (usually 60–90kmph/35–55 mph) if you don't want to be pulled over. Speeding tickets can be charged to your credit card for up to a year after you leave the country if they are not paid before departure.

To reduce congestion and fuel consumption, a rotating ban on rush-hour traffic takes place in the central core of San José Monday through Friday from 7 to 8:30am and from 4 to 5:30pm. The ban affects cars with licenses ending in the digits 1 or 2 on Monday; 3 or 4 on Tuesday; 5 or 6 on Wednesday; 7 or 8 on Thursday; and 9 or 0 on Friday. If you are caught driving a car with the banned license plate during these hours on a specified day, you will be ticketed.

BREAKDOWNS   Be warned that emergency services, both vehicular and medical, are extremely limited outside San José, and their availability is directly related to the remoteness of your location at the time of breakdown. You'll find service stations spread over the entire length of the Interamerican Highway, and most of these have tow trucks and mechanics. The major towns of Puntarenas, Liberia, Quepos, San Isidro, Palmar, and Golfito all have hospitals, and most other moderately sized cities and tourist destinations have some sort of clinic or health-services provider.

If you're involved in an accident, contact **National Insurance Institute (INS)** at ☎ **800/800-8000.** You should probably also call the **Transit Police** (☎ **2222-9330**); if they have a unit close by, they'll send one. An official transit police report will greatly facilitate any insurance claim. If you can't get help from any of these, try to get written statements from any witnesses. Finally, you can also call ☎ **911,** and they should be able to redirect your call to the appropriate agency.

If the police do show up, you've got a 50-50 chance of finding them helpful or downright antagonistic. Many officers are unsympathetic to the problems of what they perceive to be rich tourists driving around in fancy cars with lots of expensive toys and trinkets. Success and happy endings run about equal with horror stories.

If you don't speak Spanish, expect added difficulty in any emergency or stressful situation. Don't expect that rural (or urban) police officers, hospital personnel, service-station personnel, or mechanics will speak English.

Finally, although not endemic, there have been reports of folks being robbed by seemingly friendly Ticos who stop to give assistance. To add insult to injury, there have even been reports of organized gangs who puncture tires of rental cars at rest stops or busy intersections, only to follow them, offer assistance, and make off with belongings and valuables. If you find yourself with a flat tire, try to ride it to the nearest gas station. If that's not possible, try to pull over into a well-lit public spot. Keep the doors of the car locked and an eye on your belongings while changing the tire.

By Bus

This is by far the most economical way to get around Costa Rica. Buses are inexpensive and relatively well maintained, and they go nearly everywhere. There are two types. **Local buses,** the cheapest and slowest, stop frequently and are generally a bit dilapidated. **Express buses** run between San José and most beach towns and major cities; these tend to be newer units and more comfortable, although very few are so new or modern as to have restroom facilities, and they sometimes operate only on weekends and holidays.

Two companies run regular, fixed-schedule departures in passenger vans and small buses to most of the major tourist destinations in the country. **Gray Line** (www.graylinecostarica.com; ℂ **800/719-3105** in the U.S. and Canada, or 2220-2126 in Costa Rica) has about 10 departures leaving San José each morning and heading or connecting to Jacó, Manuel Antonio, Liberia, Playa Hermosa, La Fortuna, Tamarindo, and playas Conchal and Flamingo. There are return trips to San José every day from these destinations and a variety of interconnecting routes. A similar service, **Interbus** (www.interbusonline. com; ℂ **4100-0888**) has a similar route map and connections. Fares run between $50 and $95, depending on the destination. Gray Line offers an unlimited weekly pass for all of its shuttle routes for $198.

Beware: Both of these companies offer pickup and drop-off at a wide range of hotels. This means that if you are the first picked up or last dropped off, you might have to sit through a long period of subsequent stops before finally hitting the road or reaching your destination. Moreover, I've heard some disheartening stories about both bus lines concerning missed or severely delayed connections and rude drivers. For details on how to get to various destinations from San José, see the "Getting There" sections in the preceding chapters.

By Taxi

Taxis are readily available in San José and most popular tourist towns and destinations. In San José, your best bet is usually just to hail one on the street.

Somewhere between late 2015 and early 2016, San Jose will have a new centralized bus terminal for all bus traffic to and from Guanacaste. The **Terminal Central 7-10** (www.terminal7-10.com) will be a four-story affair with scores of bays for the arriving and departing buses, as well as a food court and a centralized counter area for purchasing tickets. As this book goes to press, the list of bus lines that will move to this new terminal hasn't been announced, but it is likely to include many of those listed in the various "Getting There/By Bus" sections in chapter 6. The terminal will be located at Avenida 7 and Calle 10 in Barrio Mexico. However, your best bet will probably be to tell your taxi driver *"diagonal al antiguo Cine Libano"* ("diagonal to the old Cine Libano").

However, during rush hour and rainstorms, and in more remote destinations, it is probably best to call a cab. Throughout the book, I list numbers for local taxi companies in the "Getting Around" sections. If no number is listed, ask at your hotel, or, if you're out and about, at the nearest restaurant or shop; someone will be more than happy to call you a cab.

All city taxis, and even some rural cabs, have meters (called *marías*), although drivers sometimes refuse to use them, particularly with foreigners. If this is the case, be sure to negotiate the price upfront. Always try to get drivers to use the meter first (say, *"ponga la maría, por favor"*). The official rate at press time is C640 per kilometer (½ mile). If you have a rough idea of how far it is to your destination, you can estimate how much it should cost from these figures, or you can ask at your hotel how much a specific ride should cost. After 10pm, taxis are legally allowed to add a 20% surcharge. Some of the meters are programmed to include the extra charge automatically, but be careful: Some drivers will use the evening setting during the daytime (or at night) to charge an extra 20% on top of the higher meter setting.

STAYING HEALTHY

Staying healthy on a trip to Costa Rica is mainly a matter of being a little cautious about what you eat and drink, and using common sense. Know your physical limits and don't overexert yourself in the ocean, on hikes, or during athletic activities. As you climb above 3,000m (10,000 ft.), you may feel the effects of altitude sickness. Be sure to drink plenty of water and not overexert yourself. Limit your exposure to the tropical sun, especially during the first few days of your trip and, thereafter, from 11am to 2pm. Use sunscreen with a high protection factor, and apply it liberally. Remember that kids need more protection than adults. I recommend buying and drinking bottled water or soft drinks, but the water in San José and in most of the country's heavily visited spots is safe to drink.

General Availability of Healthcare

In general, Costa Rica has a high level of medical care and services for a developing nation. The better private hospitals and doctors in San José are very good. In fact, given the relatively budget nature of care and treatment, a sizable number of Americans come to Costa Rica each year for elective surgery and other care.

Pharmacies are widely available and generally well stocked. In most cases, you will not need a doctor's script to fill or refill a prescription.

I list **additional emergency numbers** in the various destination chapters, as well as in "Fast Facts: Costa Rica," below.

If You Get Sick

Your hotel front desk should be your best source of information and assistance if you get sick while in Costa Rica. In addition, your local consulate in Costa Rica can provide a list of area doctors who speak English. I list the best hospitals in San José in "Fast Facts: San José" in chapter 5; these have the most modern facilities in the country. Most state-run hospitals and walk-in clinics around the country have emergency rooms that can treat most conditions, although I highly recommend the private hospitals in San José if your condition is not life-threatening and can wait for treatment until you reach one of them.

Regional Health Concerns

TROPICAL ILLNESSES   Your chance of contracting any serious tropical disease in Costa Rica is slim, especially if you stick to the beaches or traditional spots for visitors. However, malaria, dengue fever, and leptospirosis all exist in Costa Rica, so it's a good idea to know what they are.

Malaria is found in the lowlands on both coasts and in the northern zone. Although it's rarely found in urban areas, it's still a problem in remote wooded regions and along the Caribbean coast. Malaria prophylaxes are available, but several have side effects, and others are of questionable effectiveness. Consult your doctor regarding what is currently considered the best preventive treatment for malaria. Be sure to ask whether a recommended drug will cause you to be hypersensitive to the sun; it would be a shame to come down here for the beaches and then have to hide under an umbrella the whole time. Because malaria-carrying mosquitoes usually come out at night, you should do as much as possible to avoid being bitten after dark. If you are in a malaria-prone area, wear long pants and long sleeves, use insect repellent, and either sleep under a mosquito net or burn mosquito coils (similar to incense, but with a pesticide).

Of greater concern is **dengue fever,** which has had periodic outbreaks in Latin America since the mid-1990s. Dengue fever is similar to malaria and is spread by an aggressive daytime mosquito. This mosquito seems to be most common in lowland urban areas, and Puntarenas, Liberia, and Limón have been the worst-hit cities in Costa Rica. Dengue is also known as "bone-break fever" because it is usually accompanied by severe body aches. The first infection with dengue fever will make you very sick but should cause no serious damage. However, a second infection with a different strain of the dengue virus can lead to internal hemorrhaging and could be life threatening.

Many people are convinced that taking B-complex vitamins daily will help prevent mosquitoes from biting them. I don't think the American Medical Association has endorsed this idea yet, but I've run across it in enough places to think that there might be something to it.

If you develop a high fever accompanied by severe body aches, nausea, diarrhea, or vomiting during or shortly after a visit to Costa Rica, consult a physician as soon as possible.

DIETARY RED FLAGS Even though the tap water in San José and most popular destinations in Costa Rica is generally safe, and even if you're careful to buy bottled water, order *frescos en leche* (fruit shakes made with milk rather than water), and drink your soft drink without ice cubes, you still might encounter some intestinal difficulties. Most of this is just due to tender stomachs coming into contact with slightly more aggressive Latin American intestinal flora. *Never* drink water from any stream, waterfall, or body of water. In extreme cases of diarrhea or intestinal discomfort, it's worth taking a stool sample to a lab for analysis. The results will usually pinpoint the amoebic or parasitic culprit, which can then be readily treated with available over-the-counter medicines.

Except in the most established and hygienic of restaurants, it's also advisable to avoid ceviche, a raw seafood salad, especially if it has any shellfish in it. It could be home to any number of bacterial critters.

BUGS, BITES & OTHER WILDLIFE CONCERNS Although Costa Rica has Africanized bees (the notorious "killer bees" of fact and fable) and several species of venomous snakes, your chances of being bitten are minimal, especially if you refrain from sticking your hands into hives or under rocks in the forest. If you know that you're allergic to bee stings, consult your doctor before traveling.

At the beaches, you'll probably be bitten by *pirujas* (sand fleas). These nearly invisible insects leave an irritating welt. Try not to scratch because this can lead to open sores and infections. *Pirujas* are most active at sunrise and sunset, so you might want to cover up or avoid the beaches at these times.

Snake sightings, much less snakebites, are very rare. Moreover, the majority of snakes in Costa Rica are nonpoisonous. If you do encounter a snake, stay calm, don't make any sudden movements, and do not try to handle it. Avoid sticking your hands under rocks, fallen branches, and fallen trees.

Scorpions, black widow spiders, tarantulas, bullet ants, and biting insects of many types can all be found in Costa Rica. In general, they are not nearly the danger or nuisance most visitors fear. Watch where you stick your hands. In addition, you might want to shake out your clothes and shoes before putting them on to avoid any unpleasant and painful surprises.

TROPICAL SUN Limit your exposure to the sun, especially during the first few days of your trip and, thereafter, from 11am to 2pm. Use a sunscreen with a high protection factor, and apply it liberally. Remember that children need more protection than adults.

RIPTIDES Many of Costa Rica's beaches have riptides. A riptide occurs when water that has been dumped on the shore by strong waves forms a channel back out to open water. These channels have strong currents that can drag swimmers out to sea. If you get caught in a riptide, you can't escape the current by swimming toward shore; it's like trying to swim upstream in a river. To break free of the current, swim parallel to shore and use the energy of the waves to help you get back to the beach.

[Fast FACTS] COSTA RICA

Area Codes There are no area codes in Costa Rica. All phone numbers are eight-digit numbers.

Business Hours Banks are usually open Monday through Friday from 9am to 4pm, although many have begun to offer extended hours. Post offices are generally open Monday through Friday from 8am to 5:30pm, and Saturday from 7:30am to noon. (In small towns, post offices often close on Sat.) Stores are generally open Monday through Saturday from 9am to 6pm (many close for 1 hr. at lunch), but stores in modern malls generally stay open until 8 or 9pm and don't close for lunch. Most bars are open until 1 or 2am, although some go later.

Cellphones See "Mobile Phones," later in this section.

Crime See "Safety," later in this section.

Customs Visitors to Costa Rica are permitted to bring in all manner of items for personal use, including cameras, video cameras and accessories, tape recorders, personal computers, and music players. Customs officials in Costa Rica seldom check tourists' luggage.

Doctors Your hotel front desk will be your best source of information on what to do if you get sick and where to go for treatment. Most have the number of a trusted doctor on hand. In addition, your local consulate in Costa Rica can provide a list of area doctors who speak English. Also see "Staying Healthy," earlier in this chapter.

Drinking Laws Alcoholic beverages are sold every day of the week throughout the year, with the exception of the 2 days before Easter and the 2 days before and after a

presidential election. The legal drinking age is 18, although it's only sporadically enforced. Liquor— everything from beer to hard spirits—is sold in specific liquor stores, as well as at most supermarkets and even convenience stores.

Driving Rules See "Getting Around," earlier in this chapter.

Electricity The standard in Costa Rica is the same as in the United States and Canada: 110 volts AC (60 cycles). However, three-pronged outlets can be scarce, so it's helpful to bring along an adapter. Wherever you go, bring a **connection kit,** plus phone adapters, a spare phone cord, and a spare Ethernet network cable—or find out whether your hotel supplies them to guests.

Embassies & Consulates The following are located in San José: **United**

States Embassy, Calle 98 and Avenida Central, Pavas (© **2519-2000;** http:// costarica.usembassy.gov); **Canadian Embassy,** Oficentro Ejecutivo La Sabana, Edificio 5 (© **2242-4400;** www.costarica.gc.ca); and **British Embassy,** Edificio Colón, 11th Floor, Paseo Colón between calles 38 and 40 (© **2258-2025;** www.gov.uk/government/ world/costa-rica). San José does not have an Australian, Irish, or New Zealand embassy.

Emergencies In case of any emergency, dial © **911** (which should have an English-speaking operator); for an ambulance, call © **1028;** and to report a fire, call © **1118.** If 911 doesn't work, you can contact the police at © **2222-1365** or 2221-5337, and hopefully they can find someone who speaks English.

Family Travel Hotels in Costa Rica often give discounts for children and allow them to stay for free in a parent's room. Still, discounts for children and the cutoff ages vary according to the hotel; in general, don't assume that your kids can stay in your room for free.

Some hotels, villas, and *cabinas* come equipped with kitchenettes or full kitchen facilities. These can be a real money-saver for those traveling with children, and I list many of these accommodations in the destination chapters in this book.

Hotels offering regular, dependable babysitting service are few and far between. If you will need babysitting, make sure that your hotel offers it, and be sure to ask whether the babysitters are bilingual. In many cases, they are not. This is usually not a problem with infants and toddlers, but it can cause problems with older children.

Gasoline See "Getting Around: By Car," earlier in this chapter.

Insurance For information on traveler's insurance, trip-cancellation insurance, and medical insurance while traveling, visit www.frommers.com/planning.

Internet & Wi-Fi Cybercafes can be found all over Costa Rica, especially in the more popular tourist destinations. Moreover, an ever-increasing number of hotels, restaurants, cafes, and retailers around Costa Rica are offering high-speed Wi-Fi access, either free or for a small fee.

Language Spanish is the official language of Costa Rica. However, in most tourist areas, you'll be surprised by how well Costa Ricans speak English. See chapter 13 for some key Spanish terms and phrases.

Legal Aid If you need legal help, your best bet is to first contact your local embassy or consulate. See "Embassies & Consulates," above, for contact details.

LGBT Travelers Costa Rica is a Catholic, conservative, macho country where public displays of same-sex affection are rare and considered somewhat shocking. Public figures, politicians, and religious leaders periodically denounce homosexuality. However, gay and lesbian tourism to Costa Rica is quite robust, and gay and lesbian travelers are generally treated with respect and should not experience any harassment.

The following website is the most comprehensive and updated guide and resource for the LGBT community that I've found: www.costaricagaymap.com.

If you speak Spanish, you'll want to connect with the **Comunidad Arco Iris (CARI;** www.caricr.com), which serves as a meeting place and information clearinghouse for the entire LGBT community.

Mail At press time, it cost C365 to mail a letter to the United States and C435 to Europe. You can get stamps at post offices and at some gift shops in large hotels. Given the Costa Rican postal service's track record, I recommend paying an extra C550 to have anything of any value certified. Better yet, use an international courier service or wait until you get home to post it. **DHL,** on Paseo Colón between calles 30 and 32 (© **2209-6000;** www.dhl.com); **EMS Courier,** with desks at most post offices nationwide (☎ **2223-9766;** www.correos.go.cr); **FedEx,** which is based in Heredia but will arrange pickup anywhere in the metropolitan area (☎ **2239-0576;** www. fedex.com); and **United Parcel Service,** in Pavas (☎ **2290-2828;** www.ups. com), all operate in Costa Rica.

If you're sending mail to Costa Rica, it generally takes between 10 and 14 days to reach San José, although it can take as much as a month to get to the more remote corners of the country. Plan ahead. Also note that many hotels and ecolodges have mailing addresses in the United States. Always use these addresses when writing from North America or Europe. Never send cash, checks, or valuables through the Costa Rican mail system.

Medical Requirements

No shots or inoculations are required to enter Costa Rica. The exception to this is for those who have recently been traveling in a country or region known to have yellow fever. In this case, proof of a yellow fever vaccination is required. Also see "Staying Healthy," earlier in this chapter.

Mobile Phones

Costa Rica uses **GSM** (Global System for Mobile Communications) networks. If your cellphone is on a GSM system, and you have a world-capable multiband phone, you should be able to make and receive calls in Costa Rica. Just call your wireless operator and ask for "international roaming" to be activated on your account. Per-minute charges can be high, though—up to $5 in Costa Rica, depending on your plan.

There are three main cellphone companies in Costa Rica, and a couple of smaller outfits. The main providers are the government-run ICE/Kolbi and the international giants Claro and Movistar. All offer a range of prepaid and traditional phone plans. Pricing and coverage are competitive, and I don't recommend one over the other.

You can purchase a **prepaid SIM card for an unlocked GSM phone** at the airport and at shops all around the country. A prepaid SIM card costs around $2 to $4. Cards usually come loaded with some minutes, and you can buy additional minutes separately either online or at

cellphone stores and ICE offices around the country.

If you don't have your own unlocked GSM phone, you might consider buying one here. Shops around the country offer basic, functional phones with a local line, for prices beginning at around $35.

In addition, most of the major car-rental agencies offer cellphone rentals. Rates run around $5 to $7 per day or $25 to $50 per week for the rental, with charges of 50¢ to $1.50 per minute for local calls and $1 to $3 per minute for international calls.

Money & Costs

The unit of currency in Costa Rica is the **colón.** In this book, prices are listed in the currency you are most likely to see quoted. Hence, nearly all hotel prices and most tour and transportation prices are listed in dollars, since the hotels, airlines, tour agencies, and transport companies quote their prices in dollars. Many restaurants do, as well. Still, a good many restaurants, as well as taxis and other local goods and services, are advertised and quoted in *colones.* In those cases, prices listed are in *colones* (C).

THE VALUE OF THE COLÓN VS. OTHER POPULAR CURRENCIES

Colones	Aus$	Can$	Euro (€)	NZ$	UK £	US$
530	A$1.28	C1.10	€.90	NZ$1.32	65p	$1.00

WHAT THINGS COST IN COSTA RICA	US$	COSTA RICAN COLONES
Taxi from the airport to downtown San José	25.00–40.00	C13,250–C21,200
Double room, moderate	120.00	C63,600
Double room, inexpensive	70.00	C37,100
Three-course dinner for one without wine, moderate	20.00–30.00	C10,600–C15,900
Bottle of beer	1.50–3.00	C795–C1,590
Cup of coffee	1.00–1.50	C530–C795
1 gallon/1 liter of premium gas	3.86 per gallon; 1.02 per liter	2,029 per gallon; 536 per liter
Admission to most museums	2.00–5.00	C1,060–C2,650
Admission to most national parks	15.00	C7,950

The *colón* is divided into 100 **céntimos.** You'll find gold-hued 5-, 10-, 25-, 50-, 100-, and 500-colón coins.

Paper notes come in denominations of 1,000, 2,000, 5,000, 10,000, and 20,000 *colones.* You might hear people refer to a *rojo* or *tucán,* which are slang terms for the 1,000- and 5,000-*colón* bills, respectively. The 100-*colón* denominations are called *tejas,* so *cinco tejas* is 500 *colones.* I've yet to encounter a slang equivalent for the 2,000, 10,000, and 20,000 bills.

Forged bills are not entirely uncommon. When receiving change in *colones,* it's a good idea to check the larger-denomination bills, which should have protective bands or hidden images that appear when held up to the light.

You can change money at all banks in Costa Rica. Since banks handle money exchanges, Costa Rica has

very few exchange houses. One major exception to this is the **Global Exchange** (www.globalexchange.co.cr; ☎ **2431-0686**) offices at the international airports. However, be forewarned they exchange at more than 10% below the official exchange rate. Airport taxis accept U.S. dollars, so there isn't necessarily any great need to exchange money the moment you arrive.

Hotels will often exchange money and cash traveler's checks, as well; there usually isn't much of a line, but they might shave a few *colones* off the exchange rate.

If you plan on carrying around dollars to pay for goods and services, be aware that most Costa Rican businesses, be they restaurants, convenience stores, or gas stations, will give a very unfavorable exchange rate.

Your best bet for getting *colones* is usually by direct

withdrawal from your home account via a bank card or debit card, although check in advance whether you will be assessed any fees or charges by your home bank. In general, ATMs in Costa Rica still don't add on service fees. Paying with a credit card will also get you the going bank exchange rate. But again, try to get a credit card with no foreign transaction fees.

Be very careful about exchanging money on the street; it's extremely risky. In addition to forged bills and short counts, street money-changers frequently work in teams that can leave you holding neither *colones* nor dollars. Also be very careful when leaving a bank. Criminals often target foreigners who have just withdrawn or exchanged cash.

The currency conversions provided in "The Value of the Colón vs. Other Popular Currencies" (see above) were correct at press time.

However, rates fluctuate, so before departing, consult a currency exchange website such as **www.oanda.com/currency/converter** to check up-to-the-minute rates.

MasterCard and **Visa** are the most widely accepted credit cards in Costa Rica, followed by American Express. Most hotels and restaurants accept all of these, especially in tourist destination areas. Discover and Diners Club are far less commonly accepted.

Beware of hidden credit card fees while traveling. Check with your credit or debit card issuer to see what fees, if any, will be charged for overseas transactions. Recent reform legislation in the U.S., for example, has curbed some exploitative lending practices. But many banks have responded by increasing fees in other areas, including fees for customers who use credit and debit cards while out of the country—even if those charges were made in U.S. dollars. Fees can amount to 3% or more of the purchase price. Check with your bank before departing to avoid any surprise charges on your statement.

Costa Rica has a modern and widespread network of ATMs. You should find ATMs in all but the most remote tourist destinations and isolated nature lodges. In response to several "express kidnappings" in San José, in which folks were taken at gunpoint to an ATM to clean out their bank accounts, both Banco Nacional and Banco de Costa Rica stopped ATM service between the hours of 10pm and 5am. Other networks still dispense money 24 hours a day.

It's probably a good idea to change your PIN to a four-digit PIN. While many ATMs in Costa Rica will accept five- and six-digit PINs, some will accept only four-digit PINs.

For help with currency conversions, tip calculations, and more, download Frommer's convenient Travel Tools app for your mobile device. Go to www.frommers.com/go/mobile and tap on the "Travel Tools" icon.

Newspapers & Magazines Costa Rica has a half-dozen or so Spanish-language dailies, and you can get several major U.S. newspapers at some hotel gift shops and a few of the bookstores in San José. If you read Spanish, *La Nación* is the paper you'll want. Its "Viva" and "Tiempo Libre" sections list what's going on in the world of music, theater, dance, and more.

Packing Everyone should be sure to pack the essentials: sunscreen, insect repellent, camera, bathing suit, a wide-brimmed hat, all prescription medications, and so forth. You'll want good hiking shoes and/or beach footwear, depending on your itinerary. I also like to have a waterproof headlamp or flashlight and refillable water bottle.

Lightweight, long-sleeved shirts and long pants are good protection from both the sun and insects. Surfers use "rash guards," quick-drying Lycra or polyester shirts, which provide great protection from the sun while swimming.

If you're heading only to Guanacaste between December and March, you won't need anything for the rain. Otherwise, I recommend an umbrella, some rainwear, or both. Most high-end hotels provide umbrellas. If you plan to do any wildlife-viewing, it's a good idea to bring your own binoculars, as well as a field guide.

Passports Citizens of the United States, Canada, Great Britain, and most European nations may visit Costa Rica for a maximum of 90 days. No visa is necessary, but you must have a valid passport. You should carry a photocopy with you at all times while you're in Costa Rica and leave your passport locked in your hotel room. Citizens of Australia, Ireland, and New Zealand can enter the country without a visa and stay for 30 days, although once in the country, visitors can apply for an extension.

It is advised to always have at least one or two consecutive blank pages in your passport to allow space for visas and stamps that need to appear together. It is also important to note when your passport expires. Many countries require your passport to have at least 6 months left before its expiration in order to allow you into the destination.

See "Embassies & Consulates," above, for whom to contact if you lose your passport while traveling. For other information, contact the following agencies:

Australia   Australian Passport Information Service (© **131-232**; www. passports.gov.au).

Canada   Passport Office, Dept. of Foreign Affairs and International Trade, Ottawa, ON K1A 0G3 (© **800/567-6868**; www.ppt.gc.ca).

Ireland   Passport Office, Setanta Centre, Molesworth Street, Dublin 2 (© **01/671-1633**; www.foreignaffairs. gov.ie).

New Zealand   Passports Office, Dept. of Internal Affairs, 109 Featherston St., Wellington, 6140 (© **0800/225-050** or 04/463-9360; www.passports.govt.nz).

United Kingdom   Visit your nearest passport office, major post office, or travel agency, or contact the Identity and Passport Service (IPS), 89 Elston Square, London, SW1V 1PN (© **0300/222-0000**; www.ips.gov.uk).

United States   To find your regional passport office, check the U.S. State Department website (travel. state.gov/passport) or call the National Passport Information Center (© **877/487-2778**) for automated information.

Petrol   See "Getting Around: By Car," earlier in this chapter.

Police   In most cases, dial © **911** for the police, and you should be able to get someone on the line who speaks English. Other numbers for the **Judicial Police** are © **2222-1365** and 2221-5337. The numbers for the **Traffic Police (Policía de Tránsito)** are © **800/8726-7486** toll-free nationwide, or 2222-9245.

Safety   Although most of Costa Rica is safe, petty crime and robberies committed against tourists are endemic. San José, in particular, is known for its pickpockets, so never carry a wallet in your back pocket. A woman should keep a tight grip on her purse (keep it tucked under your arm). Thieves also target gold chains, cameras and video cameras, prominent jewelry, and nice sunglasses. Be sure not to leave valuables unsecured in your hotel room, or unattended—even for a moment—on the beach. Given the high rate of stolen passports in Costa Rica, mostly as collateral damage in a typical pickpocketing or room robbery, it is recommended that, whenever possible, you leave your passport in a hotel safe and travel with a photocopy of the pertinent pages. Don't park a car on the street in Costa Rica, especially in San José; plenty of public parking lots are open around the city.

Rental cars generally stick out and are easily spotted by thieves. Don't leave anything of value in a car parked on the street, not even for a moment. Be wary of solicitous strangers who stop to help you change a tire or take you to a service station. Although most are truly good Samaritans, there have been reports of thieves preying on roadside breakdowns. See "Getting Around: By Car," above, for more info.

Inter-city buses are also frequent targets of stealthy thieves. Try not to check your bags into the hold of a bus if they will fit in the rack above your seat. If it can't be avoided, keep your eye on what leaves the hold. If you put your bags in an overhead rack, be sure you can see the bags at all times. Try not to fall asleep.

Single women should use common sense and take precaution, especially after dark. I don't recommend that single women walk alone anywhere at night, especially on seemingly deserted beaches or dark, uncrowded streets.

Senior Travelers   Be sure to mention that you're a senior when you make your travel reservations. Although it's not common policy in Costa Rica to offer senior discounts, don't be shy about asking for one anyway. You never know. Always carry some kind of identification, such as a driver's license, that shows your date of birth, especially if you've kept your youthful glow.

Many reliable agencies and organizations target the 50-plus market. **Road Scholar,** formerly known as Elderhostel (www.road-scholar.org; ℰ 800/454-5768 in the U.S. and Canada), arranges Costa Rica study programs for those age 55 and older, as well as intergenerational trips good for families. **ElderTreks** (www.eldertreks.com; ℰ 800/741-7956 in the U.S. and Canada, or 0808-234-1714 in the U.K.) offers small-group tours to Costa Rica, restricted to travelers 50 and older.

Smoking Many Costa Ricans smoke, but in March 2012, Costa Rica's legislature passed a strict anti-smoking law. Under this law, smoking is prohibited in all public spaces, including restaurants, bars, offices, and such outdoor areas as public parks and bus stops. The law also raises taxes on cigarettes and places restrictions and controls on advertising.

By law, all hotel rooms should be no-smoking. However, many midrange hotels and budget options are pretty laissez-faire when it comes to smoking.

Student Travelers Although you won't find any discounts at the national parks, most museums and other attractions around Costa Rica do offer discounts for students. It always pays to ask.

Taxes The national 13% value-added tax (often written as IVA in Costa Rica) is added to all goods and services. This includes hotel and restaurant bills. Restaurants also add on a 10% service charge, for a total of 23% more on your bill.

The airport departure tax is $29, and must be purchased prior to check-in. By the time this book goes to print, this tax should automatically be included in the airline ticket price at time of purchase. If not, you will be able to pay it at check-in.

Telephones Costa Rica has an excellent and widespread phone system. A phone call within the country costs around C10 per minute. Pay phones are relatively scarce. If you do find one, it might take a calling card or 5-, 10-, or 20-*colón* coins. Calling cards are much more practical. You can purchase calling cards in a host of gift shops and pharmacies. However, there are several competing calling-card companies, and certain cards work only with certain phones. **CHIP** calling cards work with a computer chip and just slide into specific phones, although these phones aren't widely available. Better bets are the **197** and **199** calling cards, which are sold in varying denominations. These have a scratch-off PIN and can be used from any phone in the country. Generally, the 197 cards are sold in smaller denominations and are used for local calling, while the 199 cards are deemed international and are easier to find in larger denominations. Either card can be used to make any call, however, provided that the card can cover the costs. Another perk of the 199 cards is the fact that you can get the instructions in English. For local calls, it is often easiest to call from your hotel, although you may be charged around C150 to C300 per call.

You might also see about getting yourself a local mobile phone; for information on this, see "Mobile Phones" above.

To call Costa Rica from abroad:

1. Dial the international access code: 011 from the U.S. and Canada; 00 from the U.K., Ireland, or New Zealand; or 0011 from Australia.
2. Dial the country code 506.
3. Dial the eight-digit number.

To make international calls: First dial 00 and then the country code (U.S. or Canada 1, U.K. 44, Ireland 353, Australia 61, New Zealand 64). Next dial the area code and number. For example, if you want to call the British Embassy in Washington, D.C., you would dial 00-1-202-588-7800.

For directory assistance: Dial 1113 if you're looking for a number inside Costa Rica, and dial 1024 for numbers to all other countries.

For operator assistance: If you need operator assistance in making a call, dial 1116 if you're trying to make an international call, and 0 if you want to call a number in Costa Rica.

Toll-free numbers: Numbers beginning with 0800 or 800 within Costa Rica are toll-free, but calling an 800 number in the U.S. from Costa Rica is not toll-free. In fact, it costs the same as an overseas call.

Time   Costa Rica is on Central Standard Time (same as Chicago and St. Louis), 6 hours behind Greenwich Mean Time. Costa Rica does not use daylight saving time, so the time difference is an additional hour from early March through early November.

Tipping   Tipping is not necessary in restaurants, where a 10% service charge is always added to your bill (along with a 13% tax). If service was particularly good, you can leave a little at your own discretion, but it's not mandatory. Porters and bellhops get around C500 to C1,000 per bag. You don't need to tip a taxi driver unless the service has been superior; a tip is not usually expected.

Toilets   These are known as *sanitarios, servicios sanitarios,* or *baños.* They are marked DAMAS (women) and HOMBRES or CABALLEROS (men). Public restrooms are hard to come by. You will almost never find a public restroom in a city park or downtown area. Public restrooms are usually at most national-park entrances, and much less frequently inside the national park. In towns and cities, it gets much

trickier. One must count on the generosity of some hotel or restaurant. The same goes for most beaches. However, most restaurants, and, to a lesser degree, hotels, will let you use their facilities, especially if you buy a soft drink or something else. Bus and gas stations often have restrooms, but many of these are pretty grim. In some restrooms around the country, especially more remote and natural areas, it's common practice not to flush any foreign matter, aside from your business, down the toilet. This includes toilet paper, sanitary napkins, cigarette butts, and so forth. You will usually find a little sign advising you of this practice in the restroom.

Travelers with Disabilities   Although Costa Rica does have a law mandating Equality of Opportunities for People with Disabilities, and some facilities have been adapted, in general, there are relatively few buildings or public buses accessible for travelers with disabilities in the country. In San José, sidewalks are particularly crowded and uneven, and they are non-existent in most of the rest of the country. Few hotels offer wheelchair-accessible accommodations. In short, it can be difficult for a person with disabilities to get around San José and Costa Rica.

Many travel agencies offer customized tours and itineraries for travelers with disabilities. Among them

are **Eco Adventure International** (www.eaiadventure.com; ☎ **888/710-9453** in the U.S. and Canada); **Flying Wheels Travel** (www.flyingwheelstravel.com; ☎ **507/451-5005**); and **Accessible Journeys** (www.disabilitytravel.com; ☎ **800/846-4537** or 610/521-0339).

VAT   See "Taxes," earlier in this section.

Visitor Information   In the United States or Canada, you can get basic information on Costa Rica by contacting the **Costa Rican Tourist Board (ICT,** or Instituto Costarricense de Turismo; www.visitcostarica.com; ☎ **866/267-8274** in the U.S. and Canada, or 2299-5827 in Costa Rica). Travelers from the United Kingdom, Australia, and New Zealand will have to rely primarily on this website, or call direct to Costa Rica, because the ICT does not have toll-free access in these countries.

In addition to this official site, you'll be able to find a wealth of Web-based information on Costa Rica with a few clicks of your mouse. In fact, you'll be better off surfing, as the ICT site is rather limited and clunky. See "The Best Websites About Costa Rica," on p. 266, for some helpful suggestions about where to begin your online search.

You can pick up a map at the Chamber of Tourism's information desk at the airport when you arrive (although the destination maps that come with this book are sufficient for most purposes). Perhaps the best map to have is the water-proof country map of Costa Rica put out by **Toucan Maps** (www.mapcr.com), which can be ordered directly from their website or any major online book-seller, such as Amazon.com.

Water Although the water in San José is gener-ally safe to drink, water quality varies outside the city. Because many travelers have tender digestive tracts, I recommend playing it safe and sticking to bottled drinks as much as possible. Also avoid ice.

Wi-Fi See "Internet & Wi-Fi," earlier in this section.

Women Travelers For lack of better phrasing, Costa Rica is a typically "macho" Latin American nation. Single women can expect catcalls, hisses, whis-tles, and car horns, espe-cially in San José. In most cases, while annoying, this is harmless and intended by Tico men as a compliment. Nonetheless, women should be careful walking alone at night throughout the coun-try. Also, see "Safety," ear-lier in this section.

SPECIAL-INTEREST TRIPS & TOURS

12

A ctive and adventure travelers will have their hands full and hearts pumping in Costa Rica. While it's possible to stay clean and dry, most visitors want to spend at least some time getting their hair wet, their feet muddy, and their adrenaline flowing. From scuba diving with white tip sharks and manta rays off Isla de Caño to kiteboarding over the white caps on Lake Arenal, opportunities abound. And Costa Rica is not just for thrill seekers. You can search the treetops in a cloud forest for the sight of a toucan or quetzal, or spend some time with a local family learning the language, or sign up for a volunteer program.

This chapter lays out your options, from tour operators who run multi-activity package tours that often include stays at ecolodges, to the best places in Costa Rica to pursue active endeavors (with listings of tour operators, guides, and outfitters that specialize in each). I also list some educational and volunteer travel options for those of you who desire to actively contribute to the country's social welfare, or assist Costa Rica in the maintenance and preservation of its natural wonders.

ORGANIZED ADVENTURE TRIPS

Because many travelers have limited time and resources, organized ecotourism or adventure-travel packages, arranged by tour operators in either Costa Rica or the United States, are a popular way of combining several activities. Bird-watching, horseback riding, rafting, and hiking can be teamed with, say, visits to Monteverde Cloud Forest Biological Reserve and Manuel Antonio National Park.

Traveling with a group has several advantages over traveling independently: Your accommodations and transportation are arranged, and most (if not all) meals are included in the package cost. If your tour operator has a reasonable amount of experience and a decent track record, you should proceed to each of your destinations quickly without snags and long delays. You'll also have the opportunity to meet like-minded souls who are interested in nature and active sports. Of course, you'll pay more for the convenience of having all your arrangements handled in advance.

In the best cases, group size is kept small (10–20 people), and tours are escorted by knowledgeable guides who are either naturalists or biologists. Be sure to ask about difficulty levels when you're choosing a tour. Most companies offer "soft adventure" packages for those in moderately good, but not phenomenal, shape; others focus on more hard-core activities geared toward only seasoned athletes or adventure travelers.

Surfing in Tamarindo.

Costa Rican Tour Agencies

Because many U.S.-based companies subcontract portions of their tours to established Costa Rican companies, some travelers like to cut out the middleman and set up their tours directly with these companies. That means that these packages are often less expensive than those offered by U.S. companies, but it doesn't mean they are cheap. You're still paying for the convenience of having your arrangements handled for you. Still, these local operators tend to be a fair share less expensive than their international counterparts, with 10-day tours generally costing in the neighborhood of $1,900 to $4,500 per person, not including airfare to Costa Rica.

ACTUAR ★★ (www.actuarcostarica.com; ✆ 866/393-5889 in the U.S., or 2290-7514 in Costa Rica) is a great option for budget travelers and anyone looking to get a taste of real, rural Costa Rica. These folks bring together a network of small rural lodges and tour operators. In many cases, accommodations are quite rustic. Bunk beds and thin foam mattresses are common. However, all the hotels, lodges, and tour operators are small-scale and local. In many cases, they are family operations.

Costa Rica Expeditions ★★ (www.costaricaexpeditions.com; ✆ 877/312-0787 in the U.S., or 2257-0766 in Costa Rica) offers everything from 10-day tours covering the entire country to 3-day/2-night and 2-day/1-night tours of Monteverde Cloud Forest Biological Reserve and Tortuguero National Park, where they run their own lodges. It also offers 1- to 2-day white-water rafting trips and other excursions. All tours and excursions include transportation, meals, and lodging. Its tours are some of the most expensive in the country, but it is arguably the most meticulous outfitter, with excellent customer service.

Horizontes Nature Tours ★ (www.horizontes.com; ✆ **888/786-8748** in the U.S. and Canada, or 2222-2022 in Costa Rica) is not a specifically adventure-oriented operator, but it offers a wide range of individual, group, and package tours, including those geared toward active and adventure travelers, as well families and even honeymooners. The company hires responsible and knowledgeable guides, and is a local leader in sustainable tourism practices.

International Tour Operators

These agencies and operators specialize in well-organized and coordinated tours. Many travelers prefer to have everything arranged and confirmed before arriving in Costa Rica, and this is a good idea for first-timers and during the high season. *Be warned:* Most of these operators are not cheap, with 10-day tours generally costing in the neighborhood of $3,000 to $5,000 per person, not including airfare to Costa Rica.

U.S.-BASED TOUR OPERATORS

Nature Expeditions International ★ (www.naturexp.com; ✆ **800/869-0639**) specializes in educational and "low-intensity adventure" trips tailored to independent travelers and small groups. These folks have a steady stream of programmed departures or can customize a trip to your needs.

Overseas Adventure Travel ★★ (www.oattravel.com; ✆ **800/955-1925**) provides natural history and "soft-adventure" itineraries with optional add-on excursions. Tours are limited to 16 people and are guided by naturalists. All accommodations are in small hotels, lodges, or tent camps, and they offer up very good bang for your buck.

Tauck ★★ (www.tauck.com; ✆ **800/788-7885**) is a soft-adventure company catering to higher-end travelers. It offers various Costa Rica trips, including a family tour and a Costa Rica–Panama Canal package.

In addition to these companies, many environmental organizations, including the **Sierra Club** (www.sierraclub.org; ✆ **415/977-5522**) and the **Smithsonian Institute** (www.smithsonianjourneys.org; ✆ **855/330-1542**), regularly take organized trips to Costa Rica.

U.K.–BASED TOUR OPERATORS

Journey Latin America ★ (www.journeylatinamerica.co.uk; ℂ **020/3432-9325** in the U.K.) is a large British operator specializing in Latin American travel. It offers a range of escorted tours around Latin America, including a few that touch down in Costa Rica. It also designs custom itineraries, and often has excellent deals on airfare.

ACTIVITIES A TO Z

Each listing in this section describes the best places to practice a particular sport or activity and lists tour operators and outfitters. If you want to focus on only one active sport during your Costa Rica stay, these companies are your best bets for quality equipment and knowledgeable service.

Adventure activities and tourism, by their very nature, carry certain risks and dangers. Over the years, there have been several deaths and dozens of minor injuries in activities ranging from mountain biking to white-water rafting to canopy tours. Here, I try to list only the most reputable and safest of companies. However, if you ever have any doubt as to the safety of the guide, equipment, or activity, it's better to be safe than sorry. Moreover, know your limits and abilities, and don't try to exceed them.

See "The Best Costa Rica Adventures" in chapter 2 for additional tour ideas.

Biking

Costa Rica has several significant regional and international touring races each year, but as a general rule the major roads are dangerous and inhospitable for cyclists. Roads are narrow and without a shoulder, and most drivers show little care or consideration for those on two wheels. The options are much more appealing for mountain bikers and off-track riders. If you plan to do a lot of biking and are very attached to your rig, bring your own. However, several companies in San José and elsewhere rent bikes, and the quality of the equipment is improving all the time. I list rental shops in each of the regional chapters.

Ruta de los Conquistadores

Each year, Costa Rica hosts what many consider to be the most challenging and grueling mountain-bike race on the planet. La Ruta de los Conquistadores (Route of the Conquerors; www.adventurerace.com) retraces the path of the 16th-century Spanish conquistadores from the Pacific Coast to the Caribbean Sea—all in 4 days. The race usually takes place in mid-November, and draws hundreds of competitors from around the world.

The area around **Lake Arenal** and **Arenal Volcano** wins my vote as the best place for mountain biking in Costa Rica. The scenery's great, with primary forests, waterfalls, and plenty of trails. The trails range from relatively flat, rural dirt roads around the lake, to steeper single-track trails up into the hills and forests. And the hot springs at nearby Tabacón Grand Spa Thermal Resort are a perfect place for those with aching muscles to unwind at the end of the day. See chapter 7 for full details.

TOUR OPERATORS & OUTFITTERS

Bike Arenal ★ (www.bikearenal.com; ✆ **866/465-4114** in the U.S. and Canada, or 2479-7150 in Costa Rica) is based in La Fortuna and specializes in 1-day and multiday trips around the Arenal area.

    Coast to Coast Adventures ★ (www.ctocadventures.com; ✆ **2280-8054**) has mountain-biking itineraries among its many tour options.

Bird-Watching

With more than 850 species of resident and migrant birds identified throughout the country, Costa Rica abounds with great bird-watching sites.

    Some of the best parks and preserves for serious birders are **Monteverde Cloud Forest Biological Reserve** (for resplendent quetzals and hummingbirds); **Corcovado National Park** (for scarlet macaws); **Caño Negro Wildlife Refuge** (for wading birds, including jabiru storks); **Wilson Botanical Gardens** and **Las Cruces Biological Station,** near San Vito (the thousands of flowering plants here are bird magnets); **Guayabo, Negritos,** and **Pájaros Islands biological reserves** in the Gulf of Nicoya (for magnificent frigate birds and brown boobies); **Palo Verde National Park** (for ibises, jacanas, storks, and roseate spoonbills); **Tortuguero National Park** (for great green macaws); and **Rincón de la Vieja National Park** (for parakeets and curassows). Rafting trips down the Corobicí and Bebedero rivers near Liberia, boat trips to or at Tortuguero National Park, and hikes in any cloud forest also provide good bird-watching opportunities.

COSTA RICAN TOUR AGENCIES

Costa Rica Expeditions ★★ (www.costaricaexpeditions.com; ✆ **877/312-0787** in the U.S., or 2257-0766 in Costa Rica) and **Costa Rica Sun Tours** ★ (www.crsuntours.com; ✆ **866/271-6263** in the U.S. and Canada, or 2296-7757 in Costa Rica) are well-established companies with very competent and experienced guides who take a variety of tours to some of the better birding spots in Costa Rica.

INTERNATIONAL TOUR OPERATORS

Costa Rican Bird Route ★★ (www.costaricanbirdroute.com; ✆ **608/698-3448** in the U.S. and Canada) is a bird-watching and conservation effort that has created several bird-watching specific itineraries, which are offered as guided tours or self-guided adventures.

PLANNING A COSTA RICAN wedding

Marriage may be an adventure, but getting married in Costa Rica is simple and straightforward. In most cases, all you need are current passports. You'll have to provide some basic information, including a copy of each passport, your dates of birth, your occupations, your current addresses, and the names and addresses of your parents. Two witnesses are required to be present at the ceremony. If you're traveling alone, your hotel or wedding consultant will provide the required witnesses.

Things are slightly more complicated if one or both partners were previously married. In such a case, the previously married partner must provide an official copy of the divorce decree.

Most travelers who get married in Costa Rica do so in a civil ceremony officiated by a local lawyer. After the ceremony, the lawyer records the marriage with Costa Rica's National Registry, which issues an official marriage certificate. This process generally takes between 4 and 6 weeks. Most lawyers or wedding coordinators then have the document translated and certified by the Costa

Rican Foreign Ministry and at the embassy or consulate of your home country within Costa Rica before mailing it to you. From here, it's a matter of bringing this document to your local civil or religious authorities, if necessary.

Because Costa Rica is more than 90% Roman Catholic, arranging for a church wedding is usually easy in all but the most isolated and remote locations. To a lesser extent, a variety of denominational Christian churches and priests are often available to perform or host the ceremony. If you're Jewish, Muslim, Buddhist, or a follower of some other religion, bringing your own officiant is a good idea.

Tip: Officially, the lawyer must read all or parts of the Costa Rican civil code on marriage during your ceremony. This is a rather uninspired and somewhat dated legal code that, at some weddings, can take as much as 20 minutes to slog through. Most lawyers and wedding coordinators are quite flexible and can work with you to design a ceremony and text that fits your needs and desires. Insist on this.

Victor Emanuel Nature Tours ★★ (www.ventbird.com; ✆ **800/328-8368**) is a well-respected, long-standing, small-group tour operator specializing in bird-watching trips.

WINGS ★ (www.wingsbirds.com; ✆ **866/547-9868**) is a specialty bird-watching travel operator with more than 30 years of field experience. Group size is usually between 6 and 14 people.

Camping

Heavy rains, difficult access, and limited facilities make camping a challenge in Costa Rica. Nevertheless, a backpack and tent will get you far from the crowds and into some of the most pristine and undeveloped nooks and crannies of the country. Camping is forbidden in some national parks, so read the descriptions for each park carefully before you pack a tent.

If you'd like to participate in an organized camping trip, contact **Coast to Coast Adventures** ★ (www.ctocadventures.com; ℂ **2280-8054**) or **Serendipity Adventures** ★ (www.serendipityadventures.com; ℂ **888/226-5050** in the U.S. and Canada, or 2556-2222 in Costa Rica).

In my opinion, the best places to pop up a tent on the beach are in **Santa Rosa National Park** and **Ballena Marine National Park.** The best camping treks are, without a doubt, a hike through **Corcovado National Park.**

Canopy Tours

Canopy tours are all the rage in Costa Rica, largely because they are such an exciting and unique way to experience tropical rainforests. It's estimated that some two-thirds of a typical rainforest's species live in the canopy (the uppermost, branching layer of the forest). From the relative luxury of Rainforest Aerial Tram's high-tech funicular to the rope-and-climbing-gear rigs of zipline operations, a trip into the canopy will give you a bird's-eye view of a Neotropical forest.

Most canopy tours involve strapping yourself into a climbing harness and climbing up to a platform some 30m (100 ft.) above the forest floor. From here, the tours consist of a series of treetop platforms connected by steel cables. Once up on the first platform, you click your harness into a pulley and glide across the cable to the next (slightly lower) platform. On some, you use your hand (protected by a thick leather glove) as a brake, on others the braking is done for you. When you reach the last platform, you rappel or climb down to the ground.

Although this can be a lot of fun, do be careful because these tours are popping up all over the place and there is precious little regulation of the activity. Some of the tours are set up by fly-by-night operators (I don't list any of those). Be especially sure that you feel comfortable and confident with the safety standards, guides, and equipment before embarking. Before you sign on to any tour, ask whether you have to hoist yourself to the top under your own steam or whether you'll be transported, and then make your decision accordingly. Most canopy tours run between $45 and $75 per person.

There are now canopy-tour operations in or close to nearly every major tourist destination in the country. See the individual destination chapters for specific recommendations on canopy tours around the country.

Canyoning Tours

Canyoning tours are even more adventurous than canopy tours. Hardly standardized, most involve hiking down along a mountain stream, river, and/or canyon, with periodic breaks to rappel down the face of a waterfall or swim in a jungle pool. The best canyoning operations in Costa Rica are offered by **Hacienda Guachipelín** ★★ (p. 122), in Rincón de la Vieja; **Pure Trek Canyoning** ★★ (p. 169) and **Desafío Expeditions** ★★ (p. 169), both in La

Fortuna; **Finca Modelo Canyoning Tour** ★★ (p. 188), in Monteverde; and **Psycho Tours** ★★★ (p. 232), which operates outside of Puerto Jiménez. The latter is arguably my favorite adventure tour in the country.

Diving & Snorkeling

Many islands, reefs, caves, and rocks lie off the coast of Costa Rica, providing excellent spots for underwater exploration. Visibility varies with season and location. Generally, heavy rainfall tends to swell the rivers and muddy the waters, even well offshore. Rates run from $70 to $150 per person for a two-tank dive, including equipment, and $35 to $75 per person for snorkelers. Most of the dedicated dive operators listed throughout this book also offer certification classes.

Banana plantations and their runoff have destroyed most of the Caribbean reefs, although **Isla Uvita,** just off the coast of Limón, and **Manzanillo,** near the Panamanian border, still have good diving. Most divers choose Pacific dive spots such as **Isla del Caño, Bat Island,** and the **Catalina Islands,** where you're likely to spot manta rays, moray eels, white-tipped sharks, and plenty of smaller fish and coral species. But the ultimate in Costa Rican dive experiences is 7 to 10 days on a chartered boat, diving off the coast of **Isla del Coco.**

Snorkeling is not incredibly common or rewarding in Costa Rica. The rain, runoff, and wave conditions that drive scuba divers well offshore tend to make coastal and shallow-water conditions less than optimal. If the weather is calm and the water is clear, you might just get lucky. Ask at your hotel or check the beach listings in this book to find snorkeling options and operators up and down Costa Rica's coasts. The best snorkeling experience to be had here is on the reefs off **Manzanillo Beach** in the southern Caribbean coast, particularly in the calm months of September and October.

DIVING OUTFITTERS & OPERATORS

In addition to the company listed below, check the listings at specific beach and port destinations in the regional chapters.

Undersea Hunter ★★ (www.underseahunter.com; ✆ **800/203-2120** in the U.S., or 2228-6613 in Costa Rica) runs the *Undersea Hunter* and its sister ship, the *Sea Hunter,* two pioneers of the live-aboard diving excursions to Isla del Coco.

Fishing

Anglers in Costa Rican waters have landed over 100 world-record catches, including blue marlin, Pacific sailfish, dolphin, wahoo, yellowfin tuna, guapote, and snook. Whether you want to head offshore looking for a big sail, wrestle a tarpon near a Caribbean river mouth, or choose a quiet spot on Arenal Lake to cast for guapote, you'll find it here. You can raise a marlin anywhere along the Pacific coast, while feisty snook can be found in mangrove estuaries along both coasts.

Many of the Pacific port and beach towns—**Quepos, Puntarenas, Playa del Coco, Tamarindo, Flamingo, Golfito, Drake Bay, Zancudo**—support large charter fleets and have hotels that cater to anglers; see earlier chapters for recommended boats, captains, and lodges. Fishing trips usually range between $400 and $2,500 per day (depending on boat size) for the boat, captain, tackle, drinks, and lunch, so the cost per person depends on the size of the group.

Costa Rican law requires all fishermen to purchase a license. The cost is $30, and the license is good for 1 year from the date of purchase, and covers both saltwater and freshwater fishing. All boats, captains, and fishing lodges listed here and throughout the book will help you with the technicalities of buying your license.

In addition to the specialized fishing lodges listed below, I list various charter boats, captains, and tour operators for fishing excursions in the destination chapters throughout the book.

Águila de Osa Inn ★★ (www.aguiladeosa.com; © **866/924-8452** in the U.S. and Canada, 2296-2190 in San José, or 8840-2929 at the lodge) is a fabulous ecolodge on the shores of Drake Bay with a top-notch fishing operation. This is a great choice for those looking to ply the Pacific Ocean in search of big-game marlin, sailfish, roosterfish, dorado, tuna, and more.

Silver King Lodge ★ (www.silverkinglodge.net; © **877/335-0755** in the U.S.) is a dedicated fishing lodge in the Barra del Colorado (mouth of the Colorado River) region. Come here to land some very large tarpon, as well as snook and other game fish.

Zancudo Lodge ★★ (www.thezancudolodge.com; © **800/854-8791** in the U.S. and Canada, or 2776-0008 in Costa Rica) is a beautiful boutique lodge located on the tip of remote Playa Zancudo. The food, service, and fishing here are excellent.

Golfing

Costa Rica is not one of the world's great golfing destinations. Currently, seven regulation 18-hole courses are open to the public and visitors. These courses offer some stunning scenery, and almost no crowds. However, be prepared—strong seasonal winds make playing most of the Guanacaste courses very challenging from December through March.

The most spectacular course in Costa Rica is at **Four Seasons Resort** ★★★ (p. 105), but it is open only to hotel guests. Play 18 holes for $250 and 9 holes or Twilight Adult Golf (after 12:30pm) for $185.

Another very lovely option open exclusively to hotel guests here and in the surrounding area is the **Reserva Conchal course** ★★ at the **Westin Playa**

Conchal Resort & Spa (p. 115) in Guanacaste. Greens fees are $150 and include use of a cart.

Hacienda Pinilla ★★ (www.haciendapinilla.com/golf; ✆ **2681-4500**) is an 18-hole, links-style course located south of Tamarindo. This might just be the most challenging course in the country, and the facilities, though limited, are top-notch. Currently, the course is open to golfers staying at hotels around the area, with advance reservations. Greens fees run around $200 for 18 holes, including a cart; add another $35 to rent clubs.

Another major resort course is at the **Los Sueños Marriott Ocean & Golf Resort** ★★★ (p. 192) in Playa Herradura. Greens fees, including a cart, run around $150 for the general public, and guests pay slightly less.

Currently, the best option for golfers staying in and around San José is **Parque Valle del Sol** ★ (www.vallesol.com; ✆ **2282-9222,** ext. 3), an 18-hole course in the western suburb of Santa Ana. Greens fees are $99.

Golfers who want the most up-to-date information, or those who are interested in a package deal that includes play on a variety of courses, should contact **Costa Rica Golf Adventures** ★ (www.golfcr.com; ✆ **888/536-8510** in the U.S. and Canada) or **Tee Times Costa Rica** (www.teetimescostarica. com; ✆ **866/448-3182** in the U.S. and Canada).

Horseback Riding

Costa Rica's rural roots are evident in the continued use of horses for real work and transportation throughout the country. Visitors will find that horses are easily available for riding, whether you want to take a sunset trot along the beach, ride through the cloud forest, or take a multiday trek through the northern zone.

Most travelers simply saddle up for a couple of hours, but those looking for a more specifically equestrian-based visit should check in with the following folks; rates run between $15 to $30 per hour, depending upon group size and the length of the ride. Also, check the destination chapters in this book for additional recommendations.

Cabalgata Don Tobías ★ (www.cabalgatadontobias.com; ✆ **2479-1212**) runs my favorite horseback tour in the Arenal area, with very well-trained and well-mannered horses.

Some of my favorite rides include those through the farms and forests around Monteverde and on the flanks of the Arenal Volcano.

Motorcycling

Visiting bikers can either cruise the highways or try some off-road biking around Costa Rica. All the caveats about driving conditions and driving customs in Costa Rica apply equally for bikers. If you want to rent a plush street bike for cruising around the country, **Costa Rica Motocycle Tours & Rentals** (www.costaricamotorcycletours.com; ✆ **888/803-3344** in the U.S., or

2280-6705 in Costa Rica) conducts guided bike tours and rents well-equipped late-model BMWs by the day or the week. To rent a bike, you will need a Costa Rican motorcycle license or foreign equivalent. Note that a rental company will want you to demonstrate sufficient experience and proficiency before letting you take off on their bike.

Paragliding & Ballooning

Paragliding is taking off (pardon the pun) in the cliff areas around Caldera, just south of Puntarenas, as well as other spots around the Central Pacific coast. If you're looking to paraglide, check in with the folks at **Grampa Ninja B&B** (www.paraglidecostarica.com; © **908/545-3242** in the U.S., or 2200-4824 in Costa Rica). These folks cater to paragliders and offer lessons or tandem flights. Lessons run around $120 per day, including equipment, while a 30- to 45-minute tandem flight with an experienced pilot will run you around $85.

Serendipity Adventures ★ (www.serendipityadventures.com; © **888/226-5050** in the U.S. and Canada, or 2556-2222 in Costa Rica) will take you up, up, and away in a hot-air balloon near Arenal Volcano. A basic flight costs around $345 per passenger, with a two-person minimum, and a five-person or 800-pound maximum.

Spas & Yoga Retreats

Overall, prices for spa treatments in Costa Rica are generally less expensive than those in the United States or Europe, although some of the fancier options, like the Four Seasons or Tabacón Grand Spa Thermal Resort, rival the services, facilities, and prices found anywhere else on the planet.

o **Florblanca Resort** ★★★ in Santa Teresa has some of the most beautiful boutique spa facilities that I have ever seen. Two large treatment rooms are set over a flowing water feature (p. 155).

o **Four Seasons Resort** ★★★ on the Papagayo Peninsula has ample and luxurious facilities and treatment options, as well as scheduled classes in yoga, Pilates, and other disciplines (p. 105).

o **Pranamar Villas & Yoga Retreat** ★★★ in Santa Teresa is a new, upscale, beachfront resort, with a beautiful, open-air yoga space. A range of daily classes are offered, and a steady stream of visiting teachers and groups use the spot for longer retreats and seminars (p. 156).

o **Tabacón Grand Spa Thermal Resort** ★★★ in Tabacón is a top-notch spa with spectacular hot springs, lush gardens, and a volcano view. A complete range of spa services and treatments is available at reasonable prices (p. 163).

Surfing

Significant sections of the movie *Endless Summer II*, the sequel to the all-time surf classic, were filmed in Costa Rica. Point and beach breaks that work year-round are located all along Costa Rica's immense coastline. **Playas Hermosa, Jacó,** and **Dominical,** on the central Pacific coast, and **Tamarindo** and **Guiones,** in Guanacaste, are mini surf meccas. **Salsa Brava** in Puerto Viejo is a steep and fast wave that peels off both right and left over shallow coral. It has a habit of breaking boards, but the daredevils keep coming back for more. Beginners and folks looking to learn should stick to the mellower sections of **Jacó** and **Tamarindo**—surf lessons are offered at both beaches. Crowds are starting to gather at the more popular breaks, but you can still stumble onto secret spots on the **Osa** and **Nicoya peninsulas** and along the northern **Guanacaste** coast. Costa Rica's signature wave is still found at **Playa Pavones,** which is reputed to have one of the longest lefts in the world. The cognoscenti, however, also swear by places such as **Playa Grande, Playa Negra, Matapalo, Malpaís,** and **Witch's Rock.** An avid surfer's best bet is to rent a dependable four-wheel-drive vehicle with a rack and take a surfin' safari around Guanacaste.

If you're looking for an organized surf vacation, contact **Tico Travel** (www.ticotravel.com; ℂ **800/493-8426** in the U.S. and Canada, or 2257-7118 in Costa Rica), or check out **www.crsurf.com.** For swell reports, general surf information, live wave-cams, and great links pages, point your browser to **www.surfline.com.** Although killer sets are possible at any particular spot at any time of the year, depending upon swell direction, local winds, and distant storms, in broad terms, the northern coast of Guanacaste works best from December to April; the central and southern Pacific coasts work best from April to November; and the Caribbean coast's short big-wave season is December through March. Surf lessons, usually private or in a small group, will run you anywhere from $20 to $40 per hour, including the board.

White-Water Rafting & Kayaking

Whether you're a first-time rafter or a world-class kayaker, Costa Rica's got some white water suited to your abilities. Rivers rise and fall with the rainfall, but you can get wet and wild here even in the dry season. Full-day rafting trips run between $75 and $110 per person.

The best white-water rafting ride is still the scenic **Pacuare River;** although there has been talk about damming it to build a hydroelectric plant, the project has thankfully failed to materialize. If you're just experimenting with river rafting, stick to Class II and III rivers, such as **Reventazón, Sarapiquí, Peñas Blancas,** and **Savegre.** If you already know which end of the paddle goes in the water, you'll have plenty of Class IV and V sections to run.

Aventuras Naturales ★★ (www.adventurecostarica.com; ✆ **888/680-9031** in the U.S., or 2225-3939 in Costa Rica) is a major rafting operator that runs daily trips on the most popular rivers in Costa Rica. Its **Pacuare Jungle Lodge ★★★** is very plush, and a great place to spend the night on one of its 2-day rafting trips.

Exploradores Outdoors ★ (www.exploradoresoutdoors.com; ✆ **646/205-0828** in the U.S. and Canada, or 2222-6262 in Costa Rica) is another excellent company run by a longtime and well-respected river guide. They run the Pacuare, Reventazón, and Sarapiquí rivers, and even combine a 1-day river trip with onward transportation to or from the Caribbean coast, or the Arenal Volcano area, for no extra cost.

Ríos Tropicales ★★ (www.riostropicales.com; ✆ **866/722-8273** in the U.S. and Canada, or 2233-6455 in Costa Rica) is one of the major operators in Costa Rica, with tours on most of the country's popular rivers. Accommodations options include a very comfortable lodge on the banks of the Pacuare River for the 2-day trips.

Windsurfing & Kiteboarding

Windsurfing is not very popular on the high seas here, where winds are fickle and rental options are limited, even at beach hotels. However, **Lake Arenal** is considered one of the top spots in the world for high-wind boardsailing. During the winter months, many of the regulars from Washington's Columbia River Gorge take up residence around the nearby town of Tilarán. Small boards, water starts, and fancy gibes are the norm. The best time for windsurfing on Lake Arenal is between December and March. The same winds that buffet Lake Arenal make their way down to **Bahía Salinas** (also known as Bolaños Bay), near La Cruz, Guanacaste, where you can get in some good windsurfing. Both spots also have operations offering lessons and equipment rentals in the high-action sport of kiteboarding. Board rentals run around $55 to $85 per day, while lessons can cost $50 to $100 for a half-day private lesson. See "Along the Shores of Lake Arenal," in chapter 7, for details.

MEDICAL & DENTAL TOURISM

Costa Rica is an increasingly popular destination for dental and medical tourists. Facilities and care are excellent, and prices are quite low compared to the United States and other private care options in the developed world. Travelers are coming for everything from a simple dental checkup and cleaning to elective cosmetic surgery or a triple heart bypass operation. In virtually every case, visitors can save money on the overall cost of care and get a Costa Rican vacation thrown into the bargain. In some cases, the savings are quite substantial.

The country's two top hospitals boast modern facilities and equipment, as well as excellent corps of doctors and nurses, many of whom speak English.

Clínica Bíblica, Avenida 14 between calles Central and 1 (www.clinica biblica.com; ☏ **2522-1000**), is conveniently close to downtown, while the **Hospital CIMA** (www.hospitalcima.com; ☏ **2208-1000**) is located in Escazú on the Próspero Fernández Highway, which connects San José and the western suburb of Santa Ana. The latter has the most modern facilities in the country. An annex of the Hospital CIMA has even opened in the outskirts of Liberia, close to the beaches of Guanacaste.

The website and book *Patients Beyond Borders* (www.patientsbeyond borders.com) are another excellent resource for reputable doctors and clinics in Costa Rica and around the globe.

The United States embassy in Costa Rica maintains a fairly comprehensive list of recommended doctors, dentists, and other specialists at **http://costa rica.usembassy.gov/medical.html.**

STUDY & VOLUNTEER PROGRAMS

Language Immersion

As more people travel to Costa Rica with the intention of learning Spanish, the number of options for Spanish immersion vacations increases. You can find courses of varying lengths and degrees of intensiveness, and many that include cultural activities and day excursions. Many of these schools have reciprocal relationships with U.S. universities, so, in some cases, you can even arrange for college credit. Most Spanish schools can arrange for homestays with a middle-class Tico family for a total-immersion experience. Classes are often small, or even one-on-one, and can last anywhere from 2 to 8 hours a day. Listed below are some of the larger and more established Spanish-language schools, with approximate costs. Most are in San José, but schools are also in Monteverde, Manuel Antonio, Playa Flamingo, Malpaís, Playa Nosara, and Tamarindo. A 1-week class with 4 hours of class per day, including a homestay, tends to cost between $350 and $500. (I'd certainly rather spend 2 weeks or a month in one of these spots than in San José.) Contact the schools for the most current price information.

Adventure Education Center (AEC) Spanish Institute ★ (www.adventure spanishschool.com; ☏ **800/237-2730** in the U.S. and Canada, or 2787-0023 in Costa Rica) has branches in Dominical and Turrialba, and specializes in combining language learning with adventure activities.

Centro Panamericano de Idiomas (CPI) ★ (www.cpi-edu.com; ☏ **877/ 373-3116** in the U.S., or 2265-6306 in Costa Rica) has three campuses: one in the quiet suburban town of Heredia, another in Monteverde, and one at the beach in Playa Flamingo.

Costa Rican Language Academy ★ in San José (www.spanishandmore. com; ℂ **866/230-6361** in the U.S., or 2280-1685 in Costa Rica) has intensive programs with classes held Monday to Thursday to give students a chance for longer weekend excursions. The academy also integrates Latin dance and Costa Rican cooking classes into the program.

Wayra Instituto de Español (www.spanish-wayra.co.cr; ℂ **2653-0359**) is a long-standing, well-run operation located in the beach town of Tamarindo.

Alternative Educational Travel

Adventures Under the Sun ★★ (www.adventuresunderthesun.com; ℂ **866/897-5578** in the U.S. and Canada, or 2289-0404 in Costa Rica) is a Costa Rican–based outfit specializing in adventure and volunteer-focused teen travel. Its strong suit is organizing custom group itineraries, but it also runs periodic "summer day camps" and set itineraries.

Outward Bound Costa Rica ★★ (www.crrobs.org; ℂ **800/676-2018** in the U.S., or 2278-6062 in Costa Rica) is the local branch of this well-respected, international, adventure-based, outdoor-education organization. Courses range from 2 weeks to a full semester, and they include surfing, kayaking, tree climbing, and learning Spanish.

The **Monteverde Institute** ★ (www.mvinstitute.org; ℂ **2645-5053**) offers study programs in Monteverde and also has a volunteer center that helps in placement and training of volunteers.

The **Organization for Tropical Studies** ★★ (www.threepaths.co.cr; ℂ **919/684-5774** in the U.S., or 2524-0607 in Costa Rica) represents several Costa Rican and U.S. universities. This organization's mission is to promote research, education, and the wise use of natural resources in the tropics. Research facilities include La Selva Biological Station near Braulio Carrillo National Park and Palo Verde, and the Wilson Botanical Gardens near San Vito. Housing is provided at one of the research facilities. The wide variety of programs range from full-semester undergraduate programs to specific graduate courses (of varying duration) to tourist programs. (These are generally sponsored/run by established operators such as Costa Rica Expeditions or Road Scholar [formerly Elderhostel].) Programs range in duration from 3 to 10 days, and costs vary greatly. Entrance requirements and competition for some of these courses can be demanding.

Sustainable Volunteer Projects

Below are some institutions and organizations that are working on ecology and sustainable development projects in Costa Rica.

Asociación de Voluntarios para el Servicio en Áreas Protegidas de Costa Rica (ASVO) ★ (www.asvocr.org; ℂ **2258-4430**) organizes volunteers to work in Costa Rican national parks. A 2-week minimum commitment is required, as is the ability to adapt to basic conditions and to converse in basic

Spanish. Housing is provided at a rustic ranger station; a $245 weekly fee covers lodging, logistics, and food, which is standard Tico fare.

Sea Turtle Conservancy (www.conserveturtles.org; © **800/678-7853** in the U.S. and Canada, or 2278-6058 in Costa Rica) is a nonprofit organization dedicated to sea-turtle research, protection, and advocacy. Its main operation in Costa Rica is headquartered in Tortuguero, where volunteers can aid in various scientific studies, as well as conduct nightly patrols of the beach during nesting seasons to prevent poaching.

Vida (www.vida.org; © **2221-8367**) is a local nongovernmental organization working on sustainable development and conservation issues; it can often place volunteers.

SPANISH TERMS & PHRASES

13

Costa Rican Spanish is neither the easiest nor the most difficult dialect to understand. Ticos speak at a relatively relaxed speed and enunciate clearly, without dropping too many final consonants. The "y" and "ll" sounds are subtly, almost inaudibly, pronounced. Perhaps the most defining idiosyncrasy of Costa Rican Spanish is the way Ticos overemphasize, and almost chew, their "r"s.

BASIC WORDS & PHRASES

English	Spanish	Pronunciation
Hello	Buenos días	*Bweh-nohss dee-ahss*
How are you?	¿Cómo está usted?	*Koh-moh ehss-tah oo-stehd*
Very well	Muy bien	*Mwee byehn*
Thank you	Gracias	*Grah-syahss*
Goodbye	Adiós	*Ad-dyohss*
Please	Por favor	*Pohr fah-vohr*
Yes	Sí	*See*
No	No	*Noh*
Excuse me (to get by someone)	Perdóneme	*Pehr-doh-neh-meh*
Excuse me (to begin a question)	Discúlpeme	*Dees-kool-peh-meh*
Give me	Deme	*Deh-meh*
Where is . . . ?	¿Dónde está . . . ?	*Dohn-deh ehss-tah*
the station	la estación	*la ehss-tah-syohn*
the bus stop	la parada	*la pah-rah-dah*
a hotel	un hotel	*oon oh-tehl*
a restaurant	un restaurante	*oon res-tow-rahn-teh*
the toilet	el servicio	*el ser-vee-syoh*
To the right	A la derecha	*Ah lah deh-reh-chah*
To the left	A la izquierda	*Ah lah ees-kyehr-dah*
Straight ahead	Adelante	*Ah-deh-lahn-teh*
I would like . . .	Quiero . . .	*Kyeh-roh*
to eat	comer	*ko-mehr*
a room	una habitación	*oo-nah ah-bee-tah-syohn*
How much is it?	¿Cuánto?	*Kwahn-toh*
When?	¿Cuándo?	*Kwan-doh*

English	Spanish	Pronunciation
What?	¿Qué?	**Keh**
Yesterday	Ayer	**Ah-*yehr***
Today	Hoy	**Oy**
Tomorrow	Mañana	**Mah-*nyah*-nah**
Breakfast	Desayuno	**Deh-sah-*yoo*-noh**
Lunch	Almuerzo	**Ahl-*mwehr*-soh**
Dinner	Cena	***Seh*-nah**
Do you speak English?	¿Habla usted inglés?	***Ah*-blah oo-*stehd* een-*glehss***
I don't understand Spanish very well.	No entiendo muy bien el español.	**Noh ehn-*tyehn*-do mwee byehn el ehss-pah-*nyohl***

NUMBERS

English	Spanish	Pronunciation
zero	cero	***seh*-roh**
one	uno	***oo*-noh**
two	dos	**dohss**
three	tres	**trehss**
four	cuatro	***kwah*-troh**
five	cinco	***seen*-koh**
six	seis	**sayss**
seven	siete	***syeh*-teh**
eight	ocho	***oh*-choh**
nine	nueve	***nweh*-beh**
ten	diez	**dyehss**
eleven	once	***ohn*-seh**
twelve	doce	***doh*-seh**
thirteen	trece	***treh*-seh**
fourteen	catorce	**kah-*tohr*-seh**
fifteen	quince	***keen*-seh**
sixteen	dieciséis	**dyeh-see-*sayss***
seventeen	diecisiete	**dyeh-see-*syeh*-teh**
eighteen	dieciocho	**dyeh-*syoh*-choh**
nineteen	diecinueve	**dyeh-see-*nweh*-beh**
twenty	veinte	***bayn*-teh**
thirty	treinta	***trayn*-tah**
forty	cuarenta	**kwah-*rehn*-tah**
fifty	cincuenta	**seen-*kwehn*-tah**
sixty	sesenta	**seh-*sehn*-tah**
seventy	setenta	**seh-*tehn*-tah**
eighty	ochenta	**oh-*chehn*-tah**
ninety	noventa	**noh-*behn*-tah**
one hundred	cien	**syehn**
one thousand	mil	**meel**

DAYS OF THE WEEK

English	Spanish	Pronunciation
Monday	lunes	*loo*-nehss
Tuesday	martes	*mahr*-tehss
Wednesday	miércoles	*myehr*-koh-lehss
Thursday	jueves	*wheh*-behss
Friday	viernes	*byehr*-nehss
Saturday	sábado	*sah*-bah-doh
Sunday	domingo	doh-*meen*-goh

SOME TYPICAL TICO WORDS & PHRASES

Birra   Slang for beer.

Boca   Literally means "mouth," but also a term to describe a small appetizer served alongside a drink at many bars.

Bomba   Translates literally as "pump," but is used in Costa Rica for "gas station."

Brete   Work, or job.

Buena nota   To be good, or have a good vibe.

Casado   Literally means "married," but is the local term for a popular restaurant offering that features a main dish and various side dishes.

Chapa   Derogatory way to call someone stupid or clumsy.

Chepe   Slang term for the capital city, San José.

Choza   Slang for house or home. Also called "chante."

Chunche   Knickknack; thing, as in "whatchamacallit."

Con mucho gusto   With pleasure.

De hoy en ocho   In 1 week's time.

Diay   An untranslatable but common linguistic punctuation, often used to begin a sentence.

Estar de chicha   To be angry.

Fría   Literally "cold," but used to mean a cold beer ("una fría, por favor").

Fut   Short for "fútbol," or soccer.

Goma   Hangover.

Harina   Literally "flour," but used to mean money.

La sele   Short for "la selección," the Costa Rican national soccer team.

Limpio   Literally means "clean," but is the local term for being broke, or having no money.

Macha or **machita**   A blonde woman.

Mae   Translates like "man;" used by many Costa Ricans, particularly teenagers, as frequent verbal punctuation.

Maje   A lot like "mae," above, but with a slightly derogatory connotation.

Mala nota   Bad vibe, or bad situation.

Mala pata   Bad luck.

Mejenga   An informal, or pickup, soccer game.

Pachanga or **pelón**   Both terms are used to signify a big party or gathering.

Ponga la maría, **por favor**   This is how you ask taxi drivers to turn on the meter.

Pulpería   The Costa Rican version of the "corner store" or small market.

Pura paja   Pure nonsense or BS.

Pura vida   Literally, "pure life"; translates as "everything's great."

Qué torta   What a mess; what a screw-up.

Si Dios quiere   God willing; you'll hear Ticos say this all the time.

Soda   A casual diner-style restaurant serving cheap Tico meals.

Tico   Costa Rican.

Tiquicia   Costa Rica.

Tuanis   Similar in usage and meaning to "pura vida," above.

Una teja   100 colones.

Un rojo   1,000 colones.

Un tucán   5,000 colones.

¡Upe!   Common shout to find out if anyone is home; used frequently since doorbells are so scarce.

Zarpe   Last drink of the night, or "one more for the road."

MENU TERMS

FISH

Almejas   Clams

Atún   Tuna

Bacalao   Cod

Calamares   Squid

Camarones   Shrimp

Cangrejo   Crab

Ceviche   Marinated seafood salad

Dorado   Dolphin or mahimahi

Langosta   Lobster

Lenguado   Sole

Mejillones   Mussels

Ostras   Oysters

Pargo   Snapper

Pulpo   Octopus

Trucha   Trout

MEATS

Albóndigas   Meatballs

Bistec   Beefsteak

Cerdo   Pork

Chicharrones   Fried pork rinds

Chorizo   Sausage

Chuleta   Literally chop, usually pork chop

Cordero   Lamb

Costillas   Ribs

Delmonico   Rib-eye

Jamón Ham
Lengua Tongue
Lomito Tenderloin
Lomo Sirloin
Pato Duck
Pavo Turkey
Pollo Chicken
Salchichas Hot dogs, but sometimes refers to any sausage

VEGETABLES

Aceitunas Olives
Alcachofa Artichoke
Berenjena Eggplant
Cebolla Onion
Elote Corn on the cob
Ensalada Salad
Espinacas Spinach
Frijoles Beans
Lechuga Lettuce
Maíz Corn
Palmito Heart of palm
Papa Potato
Pepino Cucumber
Tomate Tomato
Yuca Yucca, cassava, or manioc
Zanahoria Carrot

FRUITS

Aguacate Avocado
Banano Banana
Carambola Star fruit
Cereza Cherry
Ciruela Plum
Durazno Peach
Frambuesa Raspberry
Fresa Strawberry
Granadilla Sweet passion fruit
Limón Lemon or lime
Mango Mango
Manzana Apple
Maracuyá Tart passion fruit
Melón Melon
Mora Blackberry
Naranja Orange
Papaya Papaya
Piña Pineapple
Plátano Plantain

Sandía   Watermelon
Toronja   Grapefruit

BASICS
Aceite   Oil
Ajo   Garlic
Arreglado   Small meat sandwich
Azúcar   Sugar
Casado   Plate of the day
Gallo   Corn tortilla topped with meat or chicken
Gallo pinto   Rice and beans
Hielo   Ice
Mantequilla   Butter
Miel   Honey
Mostaza   Mustard
Natilla   Sour cream
Olla de carne   Meat and vegetable soup
Pan   Bread
Patacones   Fried plantain chips
Picadillo   Chopped vegetable side dish
Pimienta   Pepper
Queso   Cheese
Sal   Salt
Tamal   Filled cornmeal pastry
Tortilla   Flat corn pancake

DRINKS
Agua purificada   Purified water
Agua con gas   Sparkling water
Agua sin gas   Plain water
Bebida   Drink
Café   Coffee
Café con leche   Coffee with milk
Cerveza   Beer
Chocolate caliente   Hot chocolate
Jugo   Juice
Leche   Milk
Natural   Fruit juice
Natural con leche   Milkshake
Refresco   Soft drink
Ron   Rum
Té   Tea
Trago   Alcoholic drink

OTHER RESTAURANT TERMS
Al grill   Grilled
Al horno   Oven-baked
Al vapor   Steamed

Asado   Roasted
Caliente   Hot
Cambio or **vuelto**   Change
Cocido   Cooked
Comida   Food
Congelado   Frozen
Crudo   Raw
El baño   Toilet
Frío   Cold
Frito   Fried
Grande   Big or large
La cuenta   The check
Medio   Medium
Medio rojo   Medium rare
Muy cocido   Well-done
Pequeño   Small
Poco cocido or **rojo**   Rare
Tres cuartos   Medium-well-done

OTHER USEFUL TERMS

HOTEL TERMS

Aire acondicionado   Air-conditioning
Almohada   Pillow
Baño   Bathroom
Baño privado   Private bathroom
Caja de seguridad   Safe
Calefacción   Heating
Cama   Bed
Cobija   Blanket
Colchón   Mattress
Cuarto or **Habitación**   Room
Escritorio   Desk
Habitación simple/sencilla   Single room
Habitación doble   Double room
Habitación triple   Triple room
Llave   Key
Mosquitero   Mosquito net
Sábanas   Sheets
Seguro de puerta   Door lock
Silla   Chair
Telecable   Cable TV
Ventilador   Fan

TRAVEL TERMS

Aduana   Customs
Aeropuerto   Airport

Avenida Avenue
Avión Airplane
Aviso Warning
Bus Bus
Cajero ATM, also called *cajero automático*
Calle Street
Cheques viajeros Traveler's checks
Correo Mail, or post office
Cuadra City block
Dinero or **plata** Money
Embajada Embassy
Embarque Boarding
Entrada Entrance
Equipaje Luggage
Este East
Frontera Border
Lancha or **bote** Boat
Norte North
Occidente West
Oeste West
Oriente East
Pasaporte Passport
Puerta de salida or **puerta de embarque** Boarding gate
Salida Exit
Sur South
Tarjeta de embarque Boarding pass
Vuelo Flight

EMERGENCY TERMS

¡Auxilio! Help!
Ambulancia Ambulance
Bomberos Fire brigade
Clínica Clinic or hospital
Doctor or **médico** Doctor
Emergencia Emergency
Enfermo/enferma Sick
Enfermera Nurse
Farmacia Pharmacy
Fuego or **incendio** Fire
Hospital Hospital
Ladrón Thief
Peligroso Dangerous
Policía Police
¡Váyase! Go away!

Index

Accommodations

Photo Credits